PASTORALISM AND DEVELOPMENT IN AFRICA

Once again, the Horn of Africa has been in the headlines. And once again the news has been bad: drought, famine, conflict, hunger, suffering and death. The finger of blame has been pointed in numerous directions: at the changing climate, at environmental degradation, at overpopulation, at geopolitics and conflict, at aid agency failures, and more. But it is not all disaster and catastrophe. Many successful development efforts at 'the margins' often remain hidden, informal, sometimes illegal; and rarely in line with standard development prescriptions. If we shift our gaze from the capital cities to the regional centres and their hinterlands, then a very different perspective emerges. These are the places where pastoralists live. They have for centuries struggled with drought, conflict and famine. They are resourceful, entrepreneurial and innovative peoples. Yet they have been ignored and marginalized by the states that control their territory and the development agencies that are supposed to help them. This book argues that, while we should not ignore the profound difficulties of creating secure livelihoods in the Greater Horn of Africa, there is much to be learned from development successes, large and small.

This book will be of great interest to students and scholars with an interest in development studies and human geography, with a particular emphasis on Africa. It will also appeal to development policy-makers and practitioners.

Andy Catley is a Research Director at the Feinstein International Center, Tufts University. He has worked on regional and international policy issues related to livestock development and pastoralism in the Horn of Africa for many years, and established the Center's Africa Regional Office in Addis Ababa in 2005.

Jeremy Lind is currently a Research Fellow at the Institute of Development Studies, where he convenes a research theme on pastoralism for the Future Agricultures Consortium.

Ian Scoones is a Professorial Fellow at the Institute of Development Studies, and co-director of the ESRC STEPS Centre (www.steps-centre.org) and joint coordinator of the Future Agricultures Consortium (www.future-agricultures.org).

Pathways to Sustainability Series

This book series addresses core challenges around linking science and technology and environmental sustainability with poverty reduction and social justice. It is based on the work of the Social, Technological and Environmental Pathways to Sustainability (STEPS) Centre, a major investment of the UK Economic and Social Research Council (ESRC). The STEPS Centre brings together researchers at the Institute of Development Studies (IDS) and SPRU (Science and Technology Policy Research) at the University of Sussex with a set of partner institutions in Africa, Asia and Latin America.

Series Editors:
Melissa Leach, Ian Scoones and Andy Stirling
STEPS Centre at the University of Sussex

Editorial Advisory Board:
Steve Bass, Wiebe E. Bijker, Victor Galaz, Wenzel Geissler, Katherine Homewood, Sheila Jasanoff, Colin McInnes, Suman Sahai, Andrew Scott

Titles in this series include:

Dynamic sustainabilities
Technology, environment, social justice
Melissa Leach, Ian Scoones and Andy Stirling

Avian influenza
Science, policy and politics
Edited by Ian Scoones

Rice biofortification
Lessons for global science and development
Sally Brooks

Epidemics
Science, governance and social justice
Edited by Sarah Dry and Melissa Leach

Contested agronomy
Agricultural research in a changing world
James Sumberg and John Thompson

Pastoralism and development in Africa
Dynamic change at the margins
Edited by Andy Catley, Jeremy Lind and Ian Scoones

'In 2010 the African Union released the first continent-wide policy framework to support pastoralism and pastoralist areas in Africa. The policy draws on a central argument of this new book, being that innovative and dynamic changes are occurring in pastoralist areas in response to increasing livestock marketing opportunities, domestically, regionally and internationally, and these changes are providing substantial but often hidden economic benefits. At the same time, the book also shows very clearly how we also need to accelerate support to alternative livelihood options in addition to supporting pastoralism and livestock production.'

– Abebe Haile Gabriel, Director, Department of Rural Economy and Agriculture, African Union Commission

'There is a rich array of case studies in this book, which capture the vitality and innovation of pastoral societies. They are a welcome antidote to the negativity that infects far too much of the discourse on pastoralism. Each chapter also illuminates the forces that are driving change in pastoral areas and the impact of change on rich and poor, women and men. In such a fluid environment, policy-makers and practitioners need to start 'seeing like pastoralists' if they are to find the right way forward. This book will help us do so.'

– Mohamed Elmi, Minister of State for Development of Northern Kenya and other Arid Lands, Kenya

'This book is essential reading for anyone concerned with the future of pastoralism in Africa. In Ethiopia, pastoralism is a vital economic sector and essential for the country's development. This book will provide important guidance for both policymakers and development practitioners.'

– Ahmed Shide, State Minister, Ministry of Finance and Economic Development, Ethiopia

'This book is exceptionally deep in the analysis of the conditions of pastoralists and provides far-sighted and comprehensive options for improving their livelihoods within the context of country-specific reality and regional and global challenges. Understanding the resilience of pastoralists in the face of growing complex challenges moves us away from a focus on traditional coping strategies to innovative efforts which provide more robust and sustainable solutions for the livelihoods of pastoralists.'

– Luka Biong Deng, formerly National Minister for Cabinet Affairs of Sudan

'This is a candid and thought provoking scrutiny of some of the diverse, complex and often emotive issues around pastoral development and investment. The book is an important and timely resource as African countries embark on securing the future of pastoralists as espoused by the recently approved AU Policy Framework for Pastoralism in Africa.'

– Simplice Nouala, African Union Inter-African Bureau for Animal Resources (AU-IBAR)

'This book is a fascinating, timely collection of case studies by researchers, activists and policymakers (many of whom are African pastoralists themselves) that document the creativity of pastoralists in seeking economically secure, politically stable and environmentally sustainable livelihoods – and the many challenges they face.? By analyzing what pastoralists are actually doing (rather than dictating what they should be doing), the book will be of tremendous value to anyone with an interest in the future of pastoralists and pastoralism in the Greater Horn of Africa.'

– Dorothy Hodgson, Rutgers, State University of New Jersey, USA

'This book drives home the tremendous scale and pace of change in northeast African pastoralism. Grounded in authoritative knowledge of general context as well as incisive analysis of social and historical particularities, the book spans resources and production, commercialisation and markets, land and conflict, established and emerging alternative livelihoods. The book brings alive the way this seemingly remote and notoriously volatile region, with its rapid and violent shifts in socio-political and biophysical environments, connects at all levels with national and international arenas, policies and economic flows. It traces the multiple and divergent directions of pastoralist enterprise, the risks run and opportunities seized, the striking innovations developed alongside robust, tried and tested strategies being maintained, and the successful diversification for some as against spiralling impoverishment for others. The book conveys the vigour, dynamism and adaptability of these arid and semi arid land populations, and their ability to embrace and exploit change, in a context of policies that too often constrain rather than enable.'

– Katherine Homewood, University College London, UK

'This timely and highly relevant publication challenges the prevailing view that there is no future for pastoralism in the Horn of Africa. It further advances the debate and deepens our understanding of pastoralism and its dynamics in the drylands of Africa, providing a nuanced and differentiated analysis of its potential and limitations in the face of new opportunities and challenges. Its detailed case studies and fresh empirical evidence offer clear insights into a range of potential pathways for the development of these complex and uncertain environments.'

– Ced Hesse, International Institute for Environment and Development, UK

'This important book helps narrow the prevailing knowledge gap on pastoralism and pastoral development.'

– Tezera Getahun, Executive Director, Pastoralist Forum Ethiopia

'This book, about one of the most diverse pastoral regions of the world, brings together many cutting-edge studies on the sustainability of pastoral development. The book provides cause for optimism as well as pause for thought, since pastoralism is evidently thriving in drylands that are also home to some of the world's worst poverty. The book illustrates how sustainable pastoralist development depends on development partners doing what pastoralists have always done: managing complexity.'

– Jonathan Davies, Global Drylands Initiative, IUCN, the International Union for Conservation of Nature

PASTORALISM AND DEVELOPMENT IN AFRICA

Dynamic change at the margins

Edited by Andy Catley,
Jeremy Lind and Ian Scoones

Routledge
Taylor & Francis Group

LONDON AND NEW YORK

from Routledge

First edition published 2013
by Routledge
2 Park Square, Milton Park, Abingdon, Oxon OX14 4RN

Simultaneously published in the USA and Canada
by Routledge
711 Third Avenue, New York, NY 10017

Routledge is an imprint of the Taylor & Francis Group, an informa business

British Library Cataloguing in Publication Data
A catalogue record for this book is available from the British Library

Library of Congress Cataloging-in-Publication Data
Pastoralism and development in Africa : dynamic change at the margins / edited by Ian Scoones, Andy Catley and Jeremy Lind. — 1st ed.
  p. cm.
Includes bibliographical references.
1. Herders—Horn of Africa—Economic conditions. 2. Herders—Africa,
Eastern—Economic conditions. 3. Pastoral systems—Horn of Africa. 4. Pastoral systems—Africa, Eastern. 5. Horn of Africa—Economic conditions. 6. Africa, Eastern—Economic conditions. 7. Economic development—Horn of Africa.
8. Economic development—Africa, Eastern. I. Scoones, Ian. II. Catley, Andy.
III. Lind, Jeremy.
GN650.P39 2013
333.74'150963--dc23
2012003309

ISBN13: 978-0-415-54071-1 (hbk)
ISBN13: 978-0-415-54072-8 (pbk)
ISBN13: 978-0-203-10597-9 (ebk)

Typeset in Bembo by
Keystroke, Station Road, Codsall, Wolverhampton

CONTENTS

FIGURES

TABLES

CONTRIBUTORS

Abdi Abdullahi has an M.A. from the Institute of Development Studies at the University of Sussex. He has more than 30 years of experience working as a development practitioner serving in different capacities in various international and national NGOs concerned with pastoral issues in Ethiopia and the Horn of Africa. He is currently leading an Ethiopian NGO, Pastoral Concern.

Yacob Aklilu is a senior researcher at the Feinstein International Center, Tufts University. He is a livelihoods specialist with in-depth knowledge of humanitarian and development programming and policies in Africa. An agricultural economist, he has more than 25 years' experience of policy analysis and reform at national and regional levels. He has specialist knowledge of livestock marketing at domestic, regional and international levels and was the instigator of the Pastoral Livestock Marketing Groups approach in Ethiopia and Kenya.

Mustafa Babiker has worked with the Development Studies and Research Institute (DSRI), University of Khartoum since 1988. He holds a Ph.D. in sociology and social anthropology. Currently he is seconded to Sultan Qaboos University in Oman. His main research interests are in the field of natural resource management and conflict in pastoral areas.

Roy Behnke was trained in Islamic studies and social anthropology at the Universities of Chicago and California, and undertakes research on extensive livestock production and rangeland management in semi-arid Africa and Central Asia. He is a Fellow of Imperial College London and a researcher for the Odessa Centre Ltd. Currently he is conducting research on pastoral land use in Turkmenistan and attempting to quantify the economic contribution of livestock to national economies in East Africa.

Solomon Bekure is an economist with more than 40 years of extensive experience in academia (Haile Selassie I University, 1963–65 and 1970–72), government (Ethiopian Ministry of Agriculture, 1974–76), national and international research (ILRI, 1976–1998) and development and finance institutions (the World Bank, 1988–2002 and the Agricultural and Industrial Development Bank of Ethiopia, 1972–74). Throughout he has had a focus on agricultural policy, rural development, livestock production, marketing, finance, natural resources and land tenure and land-use systems. He has led multidisciplinary teams in formulating, reviewing, monitoring, and evaluating the policies, performance and status of the agriculture sector of many African countries. He has worked in Botswana, Cameroon, Ethiopia, Ghana, Guinea, Kenya, Lesotho, Nigeria, Tanzania, Zambia and Zimbabwe. He graduated from Oklahoma State University, U.S.A. with a Ph.D. (1970) and M.Sc. (1967) and Haile Selassie I University (1963).

Andy Catley is a research director at the Feinstein International Center, Tufts University. He established the Center's Africa Regional Office in Addis Ababa, Ethiopia in 2005, and has worked on development and humanitarian issues in pastoralist areas of the Horn of Africa since 1992.

Jan de Leeuw is a team leader at ILRI in Nairobi, leading research on vulnerability in pastoral systems. He holds a Ph.D. in ecology. He has worked in higher education and research in environmental science in a wide variety of environments around the world. At ILRI, he works on ways to reduce pastoral vulnerability, including early warning systems and more appropriate drought relief strategies, and options for livelihood diversification through payment for environmental services. Current activities include mapping and valuation of ecosystem services in drylands, assessment of the potential for carbon sequestration in African dryland ecosystems and economic analysis of benefits derived from income from wildlife based tourism in conservancies in Kenya.

Stephen Devereux has been a fellow at the Institute of Development Studies since 1996. He is a food security and social protection specialist whose research has been conducted mainly in rural areas of Sub-Saharan Africa. His work with pastoralists includes a survey (as team leader) of livelihoods and vulnerability in the Somali Region, Ethiopia, and an evaluation (as a team member) of the Hunger Safety Net Programme in arid and semi-arid districts of northern Kenya.

Abdirahman Eid has a Masters degree in agricultural economics from Haramaya University. He has five years of experience working in Somali Regional Research Institution, Somali Regional Agriculture Bureau where he once served as deputy head. He is currently a lecturer at Jigjiga University.

Polly Ericksen is a senior scientist at ILRI in Nairobi, Kenya. Her specific areas of research are adapting food systems to enhance both food security and key ecosystem services; options for lessening the vulnerability of pastoral livelihoods to climate and other shocks; strategies for adaptation to climate change in agricultural systems; and using participatory scenarios for planning under uncertainty. She holds a B.A. in history, an M.Sc. in Economics and a Ph.D. in Soil Science. She has worked extensively in Latin America, Africa and South Asia with both research and development organizations.

Elliot Fratkin is a professor of Anthropology at Smith College in Northampton, Massachusetts, a member of the graduate faculty of the University of Massachusetts-Amherst, and editor of the *African Studies Review*. He has studied nomadic pastoralists in East Africa since the 1970s, particularly Ariaal (mixed Samburu/Rendille) of northern Kenya. In 2003 Fratkin was a US Fulbright Scholar at the University of Asmara in Eritrea and in 2011–12 at Hawassa University in Ethiopia.

John G. Galaty pursued his graduate studies in Anthropology at the University of Chicago and in Paris. He is now a professor in the Department of Anthropology, an associate member of the McGill School of the Environment, president of the McGill Association of University Teachers, and director of the Centre for Society, Technology and Development. He serves as a member of the Scientific Advisory Board of the Max Planck Institute for Social Anthropology, is scientific advisor to the International Foundation for Science, and is an editorial board member for *Nomadic Peoples*. He has been president of the Canadian Association of African Studies, an FAO expert and social analyst, and an international elections monitor (in Kenya and Tanzania) for Rights and Democracy. He has worked closely with pastoral communities in Kenya and Tanzania as a researcher, an international advisor to the IDRC Arid Lands and Resource Management Network (ALARM), and director of McGill's ongoing Pastoral Property and Poverty Project.

Paul Goldsmith completed a Ph.D. in anthropology and tropical agriculture from the University of Florida. After graduating in 1993, he returned to Africa where he has continued to undertake research, teach on a periodic basis, publish in the local press and scholarly publications, and work actively with civil society initiatives. His main areas of interest are pastoralism, environmental management, conflict analysis and minority rights. He recently completed a study of the Mombasa Republic Council, a secessionist movement on Kenya's coast and is currently involved in several projects on the coast and an advocacy campaign for indigenous land rights and the ecological and cultural conservation of the Lamu archipelago.

Mario Herrero is a senior agro-ecological systems analyst with more than 15 years experience working on livestock, livelihoods and the environment interactions in Africa, Latin America and Asia. He leads ILRI's Sustainable Livestock Futures Group and he also coordinates ILRI's work on climate change. He works in the areas of livestock and global change, climate change (impacts, adaptation and mitigation), development of scenarios of livestock and livelihoods futures, multi-scale integrated assessment, sustainable development pathways for livestock systems, ex-ante impact assessment of livestock interventions and investment opportunities, and others. He has contributed to numerous international assessments and international task forces. He has published widely in his areas of expertise and is currently on the editorial board of *Agricultural Systems*, and a guest editor for the *Proceedings of the National Academy of Sciences* journal (PNAS) in the area of livestock, sustainability science and global change.

Carol Kerven trained in social anthropology and is the director of the Odessa Centre, Ltd, is a fellow of Imperial College London, and senior editor of the journal *Pastoralism: research, policy and practice*. She has published extensively on pastoralism in both Africa and Asia. She is currently investigating rangeland tenure in Kazakhstan and continuing a long-term interest in the production and marketing of fine fibres from pastoral livestock.

Saverio Krätli works as an independent researcher and scientific advisor specializing in the interface between pastoral producers, science and development. His main fieldwork experience is amongst the WoDaaBe (central Niger), Turkana (Kenya) and Karamojong (Uganda). He is editor of *Nomadic Peoples*.

John Letai has over 16 years' experience in the Horn and East Africa drylands working with pastoralists and other marginalized groups living in these areas. He has a wealth of knowledge in working with communities on natural resource man- agement, insecurity or conflicts and other development issues. He is a strong advocate of pastoral land tenure reform and has been involved in land policy formulation, as well as policy advocacy and implementation. He has worked with different actors including governments, local and national NGOs, international organizations among them International Committee of the Red Cross, Resource Conflict Institute (RECONCILE), IIED and Oxfam GB.

Jeremy Lind is a development geographer with over 10 years' research and advisory experience on livelihoods, conflict and the delivery of aid in pastoral areas of the Horn of Africa. He is currently a research fellow at the Institute of Development Studies (IDS), where he jointly convenes a research theme on Pastoralism for the Future Agricultures Consortium. An area of his work relating to pastoralism concerns the linkages between resources and conflict. He (co)edited *Scarcity and surfeit: the ecology of Africa's conflicts* (2002).

Peter D. Little is an economic and development anthropologist who received his graduate training in anthropology from Indiana University. Currently he is a professor of Anthropology and Director of Emory University's new Development Studies Program. Prior to moving to Emory he most recently was chair and professor of Anthropology, University of Kentucky (1994–2007). During the past 27 years, his research has addressed the anthropology of development and globalization, political economy of agrarian change, pastoralism, environmental politics and change, informal economies and statelessness, and food insecurity in several African countries. Most of his field studies have been conducted in Africa, with a primary emphasis on eastern Africa (Kenya, Somalia, and Ethiopia).

John Livingstone studied economics at the University of Warwick and Queen Mary College (London). After brief stints as a researcher at UEA (Norwich) and the Institute for European–Latin American relations (Madrid) in the 1990s, he has worked as a consultant for several international development agencies and as regional policy officer for PENHA (the Pastoral and Environmental Network in the Horn of Africa), a non-profit organization focused on pastoralism.

Hussein Abdullahi Mahmoud holds a Ph.D. in anthropology from the University of Kentucky and is a senior lecturer in the Department of Social Sciences, Pwani University College, Kilifi, a constituent college of Kenyatta University, Kenya. His current research projects include an association with the Future Agricultures Consortium as a researcher and co-convener of the Pastoralism Theme. He is also Co-PI on the Climate Induced Vulnerability and Pastoralist Livestock Marketing Chains in the Horn of Africa project with Peter Little at Emory University. He was lead researcher on CARE/FAO/DFID project on Sustainable Pastoralism in Sool and Sanaag Regions of Northern Somalia and on the Informal Cross-Border Livestock Trade on the Kenya/Somalia Borderlands project of the FAO Subregional Office for Eastern Africa, Addis Ababa, Ethiopia.

Seid Mohammed has an M.Sc. in Tropical Ecology and Management of Natural Resources from the University of Life Sciences, Norway. He has five years of experience teaching pastoral related subjects such as range ecology and management in both in Mekelle and Jigjiga Universities, Ethiopia. Currently he is serving as Academic and Research Vice President of Jigjiga University.

John Morton has a B.A. in social anthropology from the University of Cambridge and a Ph.D. from the University of Hull. He has worked at the Natural Resources Institute, University of Greenwich since 1993, most recently as a professor of Development Anthropology, and head of the Livelihoods and Institutions Department. His work focuses on social, institutional and policy aspects of livestock and pastoralist development, as well as on climate change impacts on pastoralists and on the rural poor in general. He has field experience in numerous African countries (especially in the Horn of Africa), South Asia and Mongolia.

Abebe Mulatu is a property rights lawyer working with the Ethiopia – Strengthening Land Administration Program, a USAID assisted project implemented by Tetra Tech ARD, providing technical and financial assistance to the regional states of Afar and Somali among others. He was a Land Tenure and Land Dispute specialist (2005–08) in a preceding project. He has worked as Head of the Property

Laws Reform Department in the Ethiopian Justice and Legal System Reform Institute, a government think tank between 1999 and 2005. He was also a part-time lecturer in law at the Addis Ababa University, Law Faculty and the Ethiopian Civil Service College, Law Faculty (1998–2008). He has consulted for various organizations on policy and regulatory frameworks regarding land tenure and natural resource administration and management. He holds an LL.M. degree from Temple University School of Law, Philadelphia (1996) and an LL.B. degree from the Law Faculty of Addis Ababa University (1986).

An Notenbaert is a land use planner with 15 years of research and development experience in Belgium and Africa. Currently she is working as a Spatial Analyst working in the 'Sustainable Livestock Futures' programme at ILRI. In this capacity she provides spatial analysis for a wide range of studies across the institute, thereby interacting with and supporting a multi-disciplinary research team of economists, systems analysts, natural resource managers, epidemiologists, etc. Her work focuses on methodologies for strategic analysis on the poverty–environment nexus with a special interest in climate change issues.

Abdirizak Arale Nunow was born in Garissa District, among the Somali pastoralists of north-eastern Kenya. He holds a Ph.D. degree in Environmental Science from the University of Amsterdam, the Netherlands, and his dissertation studied the market participation of the pastoralists with a view to improving their food security situation. He also holds an M.Phil. degree in Environmental Planning and Management (Moi University, 1994) and a B.A. in Economics and Business Studies (Kenyatta University, 1990). He has over 17 years' experience in development issues in arid and semi-arid areas in Eastern Africa and his main interests include commercialization of the pastoral economy and pastoral livelihood systems in the drylands. He currently teaches in the School of Environmental Studies of Moi University, Kenya, besides undertaking diverse consultancy work in land use systems in the drylands and pastoralist studies in the Horn of Africa. He is currently involved in research on pastoralist marketing and wealth differentiation of pastoral households in commercialization of the pastoral economy.

Gufu Oba is a professor at the Department of International Environment and Development Studies (Noragric) at the Norwegian University of Life Sciences. He is currently on a sabbatical at Emory University, Atlanta. He has since 1981 carried out research on rangelands and pastoralists across Africa, with extended field experience in eastern Africa and the Horn, as well as Northern Namibia. He has combined his long-term research working with pastoralists and his personal knowledge from that background to develop new ways of understanding pastoralism and grazing lands. He has published articles in more than 25 different scientific journals.

Everse Ruhindi graduated from Makerere University and did postgraduate studies in Women's Law and Business Administration. From the late 1990s, she has worked in community development, with the Uganda Gender Resource Centre (UGRC) and the Pastoral and Environmental Network in Horn of Africa (PENHA). She has conducted action-oriented studies on a range of development issues, with a focus on gender and women in pastoralist communities.

Mohammed Said is a research scientist working with ILRI and joined the institute in 2003. His background is in ecological monitoring, specialising in aerial counts, remote sensing, land use and land cover mapping, community mapping, spatial analysis and modeling. His interest is in analysing information and linking knowledge to various uses by community, researchers and decision makers in resource management. He holds a Ph.D. in Ecology from Wageningen University and ITC in the Netherlands.

Stephen Sandford was born in Ethiopia and first travelled through the pastoral areas of northern Kenya and southern Ethiopia 70 years ago. From 1966 until 1968 he researched the economics of irrigation in East Africa. Between 1970 and 1975 he was a member of an Ethiopian government team that prepared ambitious projects for pastoral development. The work included the construction and operation of a pilot spate irrigation scheme for Afar pastoralists. From 1975 to 1982 he established and ran the Overseas Development Institute (ODI) Pastoral Development Network, which for 20 years thereafter led the international exchange of information on pastoral development. In 1983 he published an influential book on pastoral development, *Management of pastoral development in the third world*. He subsequently worked for the CGIAR's International Livestock Centre for Africa and for the British NGO, FARM Africa. Since 2000 he has become increasingly convinced (and noisy, under the slogan 'Too many people, too few livestock') that the conventional approaches to pastoral development, through improved animal health and better managed rangelands, need to be matched by much greater efforts to assist pastoralists to develop alternative livelihoods not dependent on animal production based on rangelands. Recently he has been involved in planning an Ethiopian NGO's project, which includes irrigation, to assist pastoralists and adjacent farmers in Afar Region.

Ian Scoones is a professorial fellow at the Institute of Development Studies, co-director of the ESRC STEPS Centre (www.steps-centre.org) and joint coordinator of the Future Agricultures Consortium (www.future-agricultures.org). He originally trained as an ecologist but has since worked on the institutional and policy issues surrounding agricultural and environmental change in Africa. He has worked on livestock development issues in Africa for many years and was (co-) editor of *Range ecology at disequilibrium* (1993) and *Living with uncertainty: new directions in pastoral development in Africa* (1995).

David Siele is a holder of a M.Ed. degree from Leeds University. Earlier he acquired a B.Ed. from the University of Nairobi in Kenya. He served as a high school teacher of physics and chemistry before moving to Kenya's Ministry of

Education where he held several offices, including that of provincial director of Education. Eventually he rose to the position of director of Higher Education at the national office. Later he moved to the Ministry of Northern Kenya and Other Arid Lands as a director in charge of human capital development. The ministry is mandated with looking at alternative ways of reaching children from pastoralist communities, hence the move to give them education through distance learning.

Jeremy Swift was formerly a fellow at the Institute of Development Studies at the University of Sussex. He works on research and policy processes in nomadic pastoral societies in Africa, the Middle East and Central Asia. His main interests include natural resource management, conflict, education and famine.

Boku Tache was born into a pastoralist family in southern Ethiopia, trained in sociology and social anthropology at Addis Ababa University, and received his Ph.D. in Development Studies from the Norwegian University of Life Sciences. He has worked for international organizations on pastoral development in Ethiopia, including pastoral community health, social forestry, shared management of common property resources, empowerment of customary institutions and participatory resource mapping. His main areas of his research interest include social development and poverty reduction, sustainable pastoral livelihoods, resource tenure issues, culture and conservation, community-based natural resource management and climate change and development, on which he has published articles and book chapters. He is currently working as an independent consultant based in Addis Ababa.

Philip Thornton is leader of the Integration for Decision Making research theme of the CGIAR Research Programme on Climate Change, Agriculture and Food Security (CCAFS) at the International Livestock Research Institute (ILRI) in Nairobi, Kenya. He is also an honorary research fellow in the Institute of Atmospheric and Environmental Sciences at the University of Edinburgh. He holds a Ph.D. in Farm Management from the University of Canterbury, New Zealand. He has worked for over 25 years in Latin America, Europe, North America and Africa in agricultural research for development. He has published widely on systems modelling and impact assessment, with a current focus on the effects of global change on agriculture in developing countries.

Karen Tibbo has 14 years of food security and livelihoods experience in Africa. She was the Nairobi-based coordinator of the impact evaluation of the Hunger Safety Net Programme in northern Kenya. Previously she was the regional social protection adviser for CARE, based in Johannesburg, and an Oxfam food security adviser for Southern Africa and Kenya. She also has worked with DFID and FAO.

ACKNOWLEDGEMENTS

This book has emerged out of a highly productive collaboration between the pastoralism theme of the Future Agricultures Consortium (FAC) (www.future-agricultures.org) and the Pastoralist Livelihood Initiative (PLI) at the Feinstein Center, Tufts University in Addis Ababa (http://fic.tufts.edu). The contributions to this book were originally presented at an international conference on 'The future of pastoralism in Africa' held in Addis Ababa in March 2011 (http://www.future-agricultures.org/pastoralism.html). The 'end piece', Chapter 21, was written by Peter Little in response to the near-final manuscript.

We gratefully acknowledge support from the UK Department for International Development (to FAC), the United States Agency for International Development in Ethiopia (under the PLI) and CORDAID (for support to African conference participants). We would like to thank Leah Plati, Oliver Burch and Shona McCulloch at IDS and Fasil Yemane and Yemisrach Weldearegai at Tufts University in Addis Ababa for making the conference a huge success, as well as the facilities and communications team at the campus of the International Livestock Research Institute where the conference was held. David Hughes and Liz Adams did a great job providing communications support, and a conference website where the original papers, plus videos, blogs and more are available. The conference was attended by over 100 scholars, pastoralist representatives and officials from inter-governmental agencies, governments and donors. We would like to thank all conference participants for their many contributions to the conference, which have greatly enriched the insights shared in this book.

Ced Hesse and Dorothy Hodgson shared critical feedback on the book outline, and Katherine Homewood also commented on the full manuscript. The STEPS Centre 'Pathways to Sustainability' series editors also provided useful guidance. Indeed, many of the themes discussed at the conference and elaborated in this book are central to the concerns of the STEPS Centre (www.steps-centre.org), as uncovering alternative pathways for development and towards sustainability often does happen 'at the margins' and outside the mainstream.

Naomi Vernon and Manus McGrogan provided invaluable copy-editing assistance. Marion Clarke worked efficiently at short notice with Alison Davies, a map-maker, to produce several of the maps in the book. Acknowledgements linked to individual chapter contributions are contained in the endnotes at the close of each chapter.

ABBREVIATIONS

ABET	Alternative Basic Education for Turkana
ACDI-VOCA	Agricultural Cooperative Development International/Volunteers in Overseas Cooperative Assistance
ADC	Agricultural Development Corporation
AFCON	Advanced Frigate Consortium of the US Army
ALRMP	Arid Lands Resource Management Project
ASAL	arid and semi-arid lands
ASARECA	Association for Strengthening Agricultural Research in Eastern and Central Africa
AU	African Union
CCAFS	Challenge Programme on Climate Change, Agriculture and Food Security
CCPP	Contagious caprine pleuropneumonia
CEWARN	Conflict Early Warning and Response Mechanism
CMIP3	Coupled Model Intercomparison Project Phase Three
COMESA	Common Market for Eastern and Southern Africa
CSR	Corporate Social Responsibility
DCM	Drought Cycle Management
DFID	Department for International Development (UK)
DRSRS	Department of Resource Surveys and Remote Sensing
EAC	East Africa Community
EB	Ethiopian Birr
EDRI	Ethiopian Development Research Institute
EMOPs	Emergency Operations
ENSO	El Niño Southern Oscillation
EPRDF	Ethiopian People Revolutionary Democratic Front
EWS	Early Warning System

FAC	Future Agricultures Consortium
FAO	Food and Agriculture Organization of the United Nations
FAOSTAT	Food and Agriculture Organization Statistical Database
FCAR, now FQRSC	Québec Fonds pour la Formation de Chercheurs et l'Aide à la Recherche
FDRE	Federal Democratic Republic of Ethiopia
GCA	Game Controlled Area
GCMs	General Circulation Models
GSU	General Services Unit
HHS	High Heights Services
HSNP	Hunger Safety Net Programme
HVA	Handels Vereniging Amsterdam
IBLI	Index-Based Livestock Insurance
ICRC	International Committee of the Red Cross
ICU	Islamic Courts Union
IDS	Institute of Development Studies
IGAD	Intergovernmental Authority on Development
IIED	International Institute for Environment and Development
IK	Industri Kapital
ILRI	International Livestock Research Institute
INSEAD	Institut Européen d'Administration des Affaires
IPCC	Intergovernmental Panel on Climate Change
ITCZ	inter-tropical convergence zone
IUCN	International Union for Conservation of Nature
KBC	Kenya Broadcasting Corporation
KCPE	Kenya Certificate of Primary Education
KIE	Kenya Institute of Education
KIPOC	Korongoro Integrated People Oriented to Conservation
KNEC	Kenya National Examinations Council
LAPSSET	Lamu Port South Sudan and Ethiopia Transport Corridor
LGP	Length of the Growing Period
LIU	Livelihoods Information Unit
MAADE	Middle Awash Agricultural Development Enterprise
MDNKOAL	Ministry for Development of Northern Kenya and Other Arid Lands
MGNREGA	Mahatma Gandhi National Rural Employment Guarantee Act
MIS	Management Information Systems
MMD	The Multi-Model Data Set
MOESTK	Ministry of Education, Science and Technology
MPIDO	Mainyoito Pastoral Development Organization
MRC	Mombasa Republican Council
NACONEK	National Commission on Nomadic Education in Kenya
NAO	North Atlantic Oscillation
NDVI	Normalized Difference Vegetation Index

NPV	Net Present Value
OBC	Ortello Business Corporation
OECD	Organization for Economic Co-operation and Development
PARIMA	Pastoral Risk Management Programme
PCMDI	Program for Climate Model Diagnosis and Intercomparison
PMAC	Provisional Military Administration Council (Derg)
PRRO	Protracted Relief and Recovery Operation
PSNP	Productive Safety Net Programme
REC	Regional Economic Community
SCUS	Save the Children US
SCUK	Save the Children UK
SNNPR	Southern Nations Nationalities and Peoples' Regional State
SOS	Stamp Out Sleeping Sickness Campaign, Uganda
SRES	*Special Report on Emissions Scenarios*
TARDA	Tana Athi River Development Authority
TLU	Tropical Livestock Unit/Total Livestock Unit
TNRF	Tanzania Natural Resource Forum
TSC	Teachers Service Commission
UCRT	Ujamaa Community Resource Team
UNDP	United Nations Development Programme
UNEP	United Nations Environment Programme
UNESCO	United Nations Educational, Scientific and Cultural Organization
UNFPA	United Nations Population Fund
UNHCR	United Nations High Commissioner for Refugees
UNICEF	United Nations Children's Fund
UNOCHA	United Nations Office for the Coordination of Humanitarian Affairs
USAID	The United States Agency for International Development
WCED	World Commission on Environment and Development
WCRP	World Climate Research Programme
WFP	World Food Programme
WMA	Wildlife Management Area
WMO	World Meteorological Organization

1
DEVELOPMENT AT THE MARGINS

Pastoralism in the Horn of Africa

Andy Catley, Jeremy Lind and Ian Scoones

Introduction

Once again, the Horn of Africa has been in the headlines. Once again the news has been bad: drought, famine, conflict, hunger, suffering and death. And once again, development and humanitarian aid experts have said we need to rethink. The famine of 2011–12 in southern Somalia and the humanitarian crisis in neighbouring areas of Kenya and Ethiopia have undoubtedly caused immense human suffering. The finger of blame has been pointed in numerous directions: to the changing climate, to environmental degradation, to overpopulation, to political interference, to geo-politics and conflict, to aid agency failures, and more. Of course this is not the first – or likely the last – time that the Horn of Africa has featured so prominently in global debates. But sadly the lessons are rarely learned and business-as-usual quickly returns.

This book argues that, while we should not ignore the profound difficulties of creating secure livelihoods for the majority of people in the Horn of Africa, there is much to be learned from development successes, large and small, in these areas. And that building from these is essential if future disasters are to be avoided. It offers a more positive, yet also nuanced, assessment than the doom and gloom view of powerless, suffering famine victims that is depicted by 24-hour news channels. It argues that development pathways at 'the margins' are imagined and constructed in new ways; ones that do not get recognized, appreciated or adopted easily by the mainstream. Such pathways often remain hidden, under the radar, informal, some-times illegal, sometimes in contradiction to the priorities and interests of national political elites in the region, and rarely in line with standard, mainstream prescrip-tions. But if we shift our gaze from London, Washington, Rome or Geneva, not to the capital cities of Nairobi, Addis Ababa, Khartoum or Kampala, but to the regional centres of Jijiga, Hargeisa, Garissa, Gode, Isiolo or Moyale, and their hinterlands, then a very different set of development pathways emerge. These are the places where pastoralists – people who gain a substantial portion of their livelihood from livestock – live. They have for centuries struggled with drought, conflict and famine. They are resourceful, entrepreneurial and innovative peoples by necessity. This book addresses some of the recurrent misunderstandings about pastoral livelihoods, highlighting the particular features of pastoral resource and land management strategies, commercialization and marketing options, as well as wider livelihood dilemmas in the drylands.[1]

A view of 'development at the margins' is one that highlights innovation and entrepreneurialism, not just coping or adaptation, as well as cooperation and net-working across social and ecological borders, not just conflict and armed violence. It emphasizes diverse scenarios for responding to changing economic, ecological and political drivers, with multiple pathways envisaged for the future development of pastoral areas. It highlights the importance of the political and cultural contexts of such areas as central to addressing development challenges, and moves us beyond an 'aid' or 'project'-driven intervention focus to a more systemic understanding of the complex, often uncertain, and always dynamic challenges and opportunities.

This book, focusing on pastoral societies across the Greater Horn of Africa (in this book a broadly defined region[2]), is not simply a story of marginal peoples living in marginal places, struggling in the face of exceptional hardships, remoteness and outside of the development mainstream. The challenges and opportunities of development at the margins have a far wider resonance in rethinking development more generally. The creative projects and innovative repertoires of those living in the margins offer many important lessons (Tsing, 1993). For, even in the places more connected to the mainstream – the 'high potential' farming areas and the com-paratively fecund highland areas of north-eastern Africa, which are usually contrasted with the dryland 'margins' – we can observe many of the same challenges. The uncertainties of highly liberalized financial systems, heightened vulnerability provoked by climate change, variability of non-equilibrium ecologies, inequalities generated by an engagement with global markets and trade, ambivalent relationships between citizens and a retreating central state, threats posed by cross-border conflict and unconventional warfare and scarcities unleashed by competition over limited resources are evident in many places, not just at the so-called margins.

Just as with other 'crises' provoked by similar drivers, but in different contexts, decision-makers are perplexed as to how to respond. The system is broken, they say, but what do we do? In pastoral areas, many organizations – governments, NGOs, donors and research groups – lack long-term strategies based on solid evidence and insight into the multiple potential pathways for development. This book offers a guide to more suitable responses. While our focus is on the particular challenges of pastoral areas in the Horn of Africa, many of the emergent lessons are, as we discuss below, of more general importance for recasting development as a more effective response to current contexts characterized by uncertainty and complexity.

Contexts, complexities and commonalities

The Greater Horn of Africa region is a highly dynamic political-economic region (Figure 1.1), with different countries having very different political histories, cultural and religious affiliations, geopolitical positioning and development pathways. The colonial period split traditional socio-economic and spatial units with new state borders, and so reconfigured dramatically social and economic systems (Clapham, 1996). Pastoralists often found themselves both on the physical edges of new states, and in a situation where traditional movements to gain access to grazing, water or markets were prohibited due to their nature of cutting across both borders within new colonial states, as well as across newly established international boundaries. This period marked the beginnings of pastoral geographical and political marginalization in many countries (Lewis, 1983; Abbink, 1997; Schlee, 2003). In addition, colonial policies further isolated pastoralists from development, with, for example, an emphasis on agrarian highland areas and livestock development strategies in the lowlands based on ranching (Sandford, 1983; Baxter, 1991). African administrations in the post-colonial era often adopted or re-enforced the colonial policies, and these old attitudes and understandings are still very evident today, some 50 years or more after independence. Even in Ethiopia, which was never colonized, misunderstandings at a policy level about pastoralism, economics and mobility are strikingly similar today to those in Kenya or Uganda. Whereas in 1965, Jomo Kenyatta's economic blueprint formalized the inequitable allocation of resources to agricultural areas, Ethiopia's relatively recent policies describe pastoral areas as 'backward' and within the last five years, government resettlement schemes indicate that pastoralists should be displaced from riverine areas to make way for more commercially orientated investors (Lavers, 2012). The other defining aspects of pastoralist areas of the Horn have been violent conflict and drought, and the related humanitarian crises and famines. Natural and human causal factors combine in a deadly mix, as in the Afar region of Ethiopia (Markakis, 2003; Unruh, 2005), Darfur in Sudan (de Waal, 1989; Johnson, 2003; Young et al., 2005, 2009), the Uganda-Kenya border (Mkutu, 2007; Lind, 2012) or in southern Somalia today.

While such generalizations of geographical and political marginalization, misguided policy, and conflict and crisis apply to much of the Horn of Africa region, there are marked differences in the specific ways these trends have played out in different places. Each local set of conflict and livelihoods issues has a long and complex history, a history that is often poorly understood by policy-makers and development planners. Compare, for example, the myriad of contextual factors, varying over time, that contributed to local conflict between the Somali Issa and Oromo in eastern Ethiopia from the 1960s (Shide, 2005), conflict and livelihood collapse in Karamoja in Uganda (Stites et al., 2007) or the violent drivers of famine in Bahr el Ghazal in South Sudan in the 1990s and early 2000s (Deng, 2002). Variations occur between and within countries, and across time. There is no simple cause–effect story for how crises emerge.

Further layers of complexity are evident in many pastoral areas because local conflict, trade and livelihood issues are so often linked to national, regional and

FIGURE 1.1 The Greater Horn of Africa.

international political and economic trends. Where, for example, does one draw a boundary around the causes of conflict currently seen in South Sudan or Somalia? Are the challenges facing pastoralism in South Sudan merely due to local conflict drivers, or are there important north–south factors or, in some areas, cross-border links to conflicts in northern Kenya and Uganda, and south-west Ethiopia? And if so much of the conflict in South Sudan centres on the control of oil reserves in Upper Nile, where do foreign interests become critical (Coalition for International Justice 2006)? In Somalia, a long history of conflict is really a regional and international history. The regional elements include tensions with Ethiopia dating back to the Ogaden war in the 1970s and before, and reflected more recently by Ethiopian army incursions into southern Somalia in 2006. But would these events have happened without Soviet and US interests in the Horn during the Cold War, or more recent post-9/11 US foreign policy, framed around counter-terrorism objectives, or tense Ethiopia-Eritrea relations and Ethiopia's reliance on the Djibouti port?

In order to understand both past and future pathways of change, in-depth, longitudinal analysis of complex, interacting factors is required. There is no shortage of high-quality research on the Horn of Africa. Consider the long-term research efforts around livelihoods, conflict and crisis in Darfur (de Waal, 1989; Young *et al.*, 2005, 2009), the dynamics of the cross-border livestock trade from southern Somalia (Little and Mahmoud, 2005), conflict analyses in Afar, Ethiopia (Markakis, 2003), the emergence of stable government in Somaliland (Bradbury, 2008), and the changes observed in Maasai (Galaty, this book), Turkana (Little and Leslie, 1999; McCabe, 2004) and Rendille (Fratkin, 1991) areas of Kenya, or the Somali region of Ethiopia (Devereux, 2006). Across the drylands of Africa, there is better understanding of the dynamics of non-equilibrium environments (Ellis and Swift, 1988; Behnke *et al.*, 1993; Vetter, 2005), and how pastoralists both live with and off uncertainty (Scoones, 1995a; Little *et al.*, 2001; Lybbert *et al.*, 2004; Umar and Baulch, 2007; Krätli and Schareika, 2010). Yet whether local or regional, the analysis is becoming even more complex, with long-term trends combining with unpredictable events and shifting narratives. Today the high-profile concerns are, among others, climate change, counter-terrorism, food prices and global financial crises. One might also ask how the profound political events in the Arab world will affect conflict, oil and stability in the Horn. Or will the emergence of the 'world's newest pseudostate', being the US-backed buffer state of Azania/Jubaland in southern Somalia (Thurston, 2011), help to support pastoralism, peace and trade, or create new barriers? Furthermore, how will China's increasing involvement in aid in Africa affect pastoralists, and to what extent might China's domestic policies affect African thinking, as Goldsmith asks in this book? Against these storylines, the more mundane, but possibly more important trends quietly continue: population growth, commercialization and its impacts, and urbanization and out-migration.

Given the regional dimensions of livelihoods for so many pastoralists in the Horn, harmonized regional policies and support to the African organizations mandated to lead these processes are especially important. Yet, as in Europe, there are many challenges in bringing together governments with contrasting histories and political ideologies, and very different levels of legitimacy and stability. In terms of economies and trade, different states are pulled in different directions – towards the Middle East and North Africa, towards the highland core of East Africa or towards Central Africa, depending on market, political and cultural ties. As a category therefore, despite the pleas for integration, the Horn does not exist as a firm, easily definable geographical, political or economic unit.

The formal policy structure that has emerged since the transition of the Organization of African Unity into the African Union (AU) in 2002, places responsibility on the AU for developing the broad policies for Africa's development. The policies of the Regional Economic Communities (RECs) should then follow the AU lead, but with regional adaptation suited to context. However, many countries are members of more than one REC – Kenya and Uganda are members of the Common Market for Eastern and Southern Africa (COMESA), the Intergovernmental Authority on Development (IGAD), and the East Africa

Community (EAC); while Djibouti, Ethiopia, Sudan and Eritrea are members of both COMESA and IGAD. In addition, the importance of trade linkages across the Red Sea is illustrated in other alliances and groupings, such as the trade-based Sana'a Forum for Cooperation, comprising the four countries of Sudan, Ethiopia, Somalia and Yemen and, notably, excluding Eritrea. Despite the complexity of these relationships, the common language of regional economic integration, and the free movement of goods, services and people may offer opportunities for pastoralism. While pastoralists might now be marginalized in terms of national economies, within RECs they can become more formally recognized as being central to regional economies. However, there are important caveats. The imperatives of regional integration proclaimed by the World Bank, the African Development Bank and repeated by many national governments, and highlighted especially by IGAD, EAC and the AU, are centred on the presumed benefits of economic growth, modelled on groupings such as the European Union (African Development Bank, 2010; Mattli, 1999; Healy *et al.*, 2009). Yet the wider political economy question of 'integration for whom?' is rarely asked. Of course, it depends on where your locus of power and economic activity lies. Pastoralists have long been integrating economies across borders, linking production systems and markets, in ways only dreamed about by the economic planners. Yet such efforts have often fallen foul of national regulations, border restrictions and laws created by national policy elites, who are often culturally, economically and politically distant from pastoral people and areas.

Although pastoralists are often omitted from most official documents on regional economic integration, an important exception is the 2010 AU Policy Framework for Pastoralism in Africa which recognizes the economic, social and cultural contributions of pastoralists both historically and into the future (African Union, 2010). At the highest level of policy-making in Africa, the framework directly addresses many of the myths surrounding pastoralism, and formally calls for national and regional processes that prioritize the involvement of pastoralists and their institutions in policy-making. In the following section we discuss the vibrant and substantial market activity in and out of pastoralist areas and, contrary to many national policies, the AU framework recognizes this activity and aims to develop it further. While there is clearly much work to be done to align national and regional policies with the AU policy, for the first time Africa has a continent-wide and progressive policy on pastoralism.

Trade matters

One of the most persistent policy and development myths around pastoralism has been the picture of the conservative herder, bound by a primitive cultural imperative to build his herd for the sake of ego and prestige, and sell as few animals as possible (Herskovits, 1926). It is a story that is still heard today in government and donor meetings, and underpins the misguided programmes that aim to make pastoralists understand markets and behave more rationally. Yet, as the first section of this book shows, the livestock trade networks emerging from pastoralist areas of the Horn are so massive that Sudan, Somalia and Ethiopia can be categorized as 'high export' countries (Aklilu and Catley, this book). The significance of pastoral trade becomes clearer when our gaze shifts again, away from the capitals and towards the flows of people, livestock and commerce that emanate from the places at the borders of the nation state. Connecting huge hinterlands to key terminal markets, in Nairobi, Addis Ababa, Khartoum, and outside the region to Kinshasa to the south or Cairo and the Arabian Peninsula to the north and east, the livestock trade, and the huge range of economic activity associated with it – transport, marketing, finance, processing and so on – portrays a very different economic geography.

This makes a broader regional perspective on 'the Horn' much more real, envisaged as a complex network connecting producing areas with intermediary markets and ports and terminal markets. Almost without exception, these vibrant commercial routes cut across borders. They involve the movement of camels, cattle, goats and sheep which are traded in vast numbers across the region and inter-nationally (Catley and Aklilu, this book; Mahmoud, this book). Consider estimates of livestock exports from Sudan, which for decades has been exporting around 1.5 million pastoral sheep, 200,000 camels and 100,000 goats annually (apart from 2007 and 2008) (Aklilu and Catley, 2009). Similarly, the Somaliland port of Berbera receives livestock from the Somali Region of Ethiopia and locally, and exported 1.6 million sheep and goats, 136,000 cattle and 97,000 camels in 2010 (Somaliland Chamber of Commerce, Agriculture and Industry, 2010). To these figures we can add the formal livestock and meat export values from Ethiopia for 2010–11 (Catley and Aklilu, this book) – derived mainly from pastoralist areas – and reach a provisional total livestock export value from these three countries that exceeds US$500 million in 2010. However, to this figure we should also add the cattle exports from southern Somalia into Kenya, valued at US$8.8 million in 2000 (Little, 2003), but rising to around US$13.6 million in 2007.[3] In addition, there are livestock exports from other large and small ports along the Somali coast, from Djibouti and from Mombasa, plus a substantial domestic livestock trade in Djibouti, Ethiopia, Eritrea, Kenya, Somalia, Sudan and Uganda. It seems feasible, therefore, to propose a pastoral livestock and meat trade value approaching US$1 billion for the Horn in 2010. Yet this trade remains under-valued at national level, with countries such as Kenya and Ethiopia continuing to misrepresent the livestock economy, and there-fore the pastoral economy, in national planning processes. In Kenya, comprehensive assessment of the contribution of livestock to gross domestic product valued livestock 150 per cent higher than government figures (Behnke and Muthami, 2011), whereas in Ethiopia, a similar study valued livestock at 350 per cent higher than government figures (Behnke and Muthami, 2011). This analysis points to the wider challenge of understanding the total economic value of pastoralism, given the diverse range of goods and services that pastoralists provide (Hesse and MacGregor, 2006).

Pastoralists have adapted to, rather than ignored, market demands and oppor-tunities. In the 1980s, Somalis shifted the species composition of their herds away from camels to cattle in response to export demands (Al-Najim, 1991), whereas the last few years have seen a shift back to camels and, indeed, a boom in camel prices and expansion of trade (Mahmoud, this book). In Ethiopia, a substantial internal camel trade has evolved in response to demand for camels in the highlands, involving networks that cover 2000km and cross four regions of the country (Aklilu and Catley, 2011). Also linked to camel exports to Sudan, this trade was valued at US$61 million in 2010 and evolved without aid or government programmes. Other local initiatives include the emergence of private abattoirs in pastoral areas of Somalia and Somaliland, with exports of chilled meat to the Gulf States using privately owned aircraft. Engagements with the private sector, sometimes under the banner of 'corporate social responsibility' are growing, with a diversity of marketing and service provision relationships being developed (Morton, this book). Further types of pastoral market-based adaptations are seen in the area of milk marketing, as pastoralists organize themselves to supply milk to growing urban populations within pastoral areas (for example, see Abdullahi *et al.*, this book) but also to those who out-migrated and reside in cities such as Nairobi, Addis Ababa, and even London. In eastern Ethiopia, camel milk is collected from pastoral producers and flown to the Gulf, while recent developments in Kenya include the processing and packing of camel milk for sale in supermarkets and other outlets. All these changes do not depend on aid or government, are dramatically assisted by technological change in, for example, the expansion of mobile phone networks or milk processing and packing, and reflect a market response to changing consumer preferences in importing countries. In other words, new pathways are emerging, responding to changing conditions, but often under-the-radar, and outside the influence and control of aid interventions or state policies, yet facilitated by changing technological and market contexts.[4]

Some of the fastest growing urban areas in Africa are linked to these pastoral trade activities. The town of Garissa in north-eastern Kenya has grown from 14,076 people in 1979[5] to an estimated 250,000 people in 2008, driven by the livestock trade, but also, refugees from Somalia and destitute pastoralists locally (Gedi *et al.*, 2008). The price of goats/sheep, camels and cattle for export from the Port of Bosasso increased threefold between 2000 and 2006.[6] And the growing wealth of cities like Addis Ababa, Nairobi, Khartoum and Kampala, as well as regional towns such as Mbarara, Nakuru, Isiolo, Kassala, and Adama provide a burgeoning demand for meat and animal products. The 'livestock revolution' (cf. Delgado *et al.*, 1999) is happening in Africa, and is centred on the Horn. Yet this revolution does not follow the standard prescriptions. This trade is largely unregulated, and run by a vast network of producers and traders, financiers and transporters who must continually find ways round customs restrictions, excessive taxation, border restrictions, outdated veterinary controls and conflict in order to make their businesses profitable. They are the quintessential 'free marketeers' so lauded by the liberalizers at institutions like the World Bank, yet are rarely given necessary support or encouragement. At the same time, major 'contraband' trade routes flourish, where vast quantities of clothes, electronics, cigarettes and household utensils are imported unofficially into cross-border pastoral areas. Typically, central governments link this trade to the apparently wayward and illegal tendencies of pastoralists, and overlook the fact that much 'contraband' does not stay in pastoral areas, but finds its way to capital cities and major towns with the involvement of government officials, politicians, well-connected business people, as well as the police and military. The political economy of this trade, and its links to the pastoral economy, remain both under-researched and highly sensitive. But any analysis quickly reveals how the maintenance of illegality and instability at the margins in pastoral areas reaps benefits for many non-pastoral and government actors.

Development challenges: seas of failure, islands of success

Driving through pastoralist areas of the Horn in 2011, a common sight is that of a dilapidated irrigation scheme, cattle dip tank, livestock market or borehole, all constructed by aid programmes. In some places, a series of defunct facilities of the same type are positioned right next to each other, and in various states of decay, depending on the decade in which they were built – often by the same donor. It seems that not only did development planners fail to understand pastoralism and its opportunities in the 1970s (Sandford, 1983), but the same trend continues today. Taking the example of the highly dynamic and successful pastoral livestock trade networks outlined above, almost inevitably, a Western aid response is to formalize and organize, cleanse and control. Rather than seeing a billion dollars of dynamic trade activity in one of the most hostile regions in the world, the misperception is one of inefficiency, disorganization, disease risks and tax avoidance.

We must ask: should pastoralists really be forced to comply with a set of international standards developed for European markets with different disease dynamics and consumer preferences, especially when those same standards are based on outdated science?[7] Even if European consumers wanted meat from pastoral areas, will African countries ever really compete in these high-value markets when exporters from Brazil, Argentina, Australia and New Zealand are already so dominant? Furthermore, what is the appropriate market infrastructure and support required in pastoral areas if so much trade already takes place in simple market yards anyway? Would high-cost holding pens and abattoirs, designed for Texas or Utah, add significant value, or instead is there something more appropriate to the flexible, low-cost marketing systems of the region? If there is one area of development where the concept of 'appropriate technology' was lost for decades, it is pastoral livestock marketing.

In the same vein, substantial policy and extension effort has been invested in range management in the dry rangelands of Africa with the aim of replicating the managed ranches of the US or Australia, with fencing, rotational grazing and other approaches. Yet traditional mobile pastoral systems have consistently shown themselves to be more productive than ranch systems in African settings (Western, 1982; Breman and de Wit, 1983; Behnke, 1985a; Cossins and Upton, 1988; Hogg, 1992; Abel, 1993), and external models have consistently failed (Scoones, 1995a; De Jode, 2010).

Thus development pathways, defined by regulatory, market and technological dimensions, are repeatedly being constructed through ill-informed and outdated policy framings, which are out of kilter with the emerging alternative pathways on the ground. But, while poorly designed projects will inevitably fail, more appropriate investments may make a big difference. Where designs have taken account of local circumstances and priorities, and where pastoralists themselves have been involved, the success rate is much higher. Examples include the development of privatized community-based animal health worker systems in pastoral areas of Ethiopia and official endorsement of these systems in 2004 (Admassu, 2002), and, related to these approaches, the eradication of rinderpest in the Afar region of Ethiopia and South Sudan in the 1990s (Catley and Leyland, 2001). Other livestock examples include support to small-scale women's dairy groups in northern Kenya (Aklilu, 2004), the introduction of commercial destocking to Ethiopia (Abebe *et al.*, 2008) and working with pastoralists to design and evaluate livestock feed supplementation during drought (Bekele and Abera, 2008). Although difficult to design and implement well, restocking projects after drought can help to shift pastoralists away from food aid, especially when drawing on traditional restocking systems (Lotira Arasio, 2004; Wekessa, 2005). Livelihood-based approaches to drought response, such as destocking and restocking, livestock feed supplementation, and veterinary voucher schemes, have been incorporated into the global standards and guidelines for humanitarian crises (LEGS, 2009), offering potential for good practice to be further applied in pastoral areas. There have also been numerous community-based peace building initiatives in pastoralist areas, focusing on conflict management between groups within and across borders. These approaches can lead to local peace agreements and reductions in conflict during project implementation, but the gains are fragile and often undermined by higher-level political interference (e.g. Minear, 2001). Siele *et al.* (this book) highlight another type of innovation: a distance learning system for the education of nomadic children developed by the Kenyan government using a combination of radio programmes, mobile tutors and audio/print materials. As they explain, the initiative is emblematic of an important shift in the mindset of state planners in Kenya towards tailoring service delivery approaches to the fundamental requirements of nomadic pastoralists to be flexible and mobile.

Despite such bright spots demonstrating the possibilities of alternative pathways, overall, mainstream pastoral development is a litany of failure, involving substantial sums of wasted resources (Hogg, 1987, 1988; Baxter, 1991; de Haan, 1994; Anderson and Broch-Due, 1999). For many in the aid industry and in national governments, pastoral areas are poor investments, destined for failure, where no 'quick wins' are possible. With such a track record this view appears, on the surface, to be justified. The response from the capital cities and the donor or NGO headquarters has been either to abandon such areas, or impose radical new solutions, including privatization of the rangeland to foster the emergence of a commercial ranching sector, forced (or semi-voluntary) sedentarization in towns and in irrigation schemes, large scale infrastructure investments (such as dams) to attract alternative uses (such as irrigated plantations) or selling the marginality of such places as a tourist destination, with exotic people, charismatic wildlife and dramatic, 'empty' landscapes.

As reflected in the chapters of this book, a hot debate exists today about the relative merits of 'traditional' land uses such as mobile pastoralism and 'modern' interventions such as irrigated farming. Of course the simplistic contrast between tradition and modernity does not wash, given that pastoralism has been fast-changing and responding to contemporary contexts, and irrigation has always been an important if small component of livelihoods in dryland areas (Anderson and Johnson, 1988; Sandford, this book). But this debate raises many issues, including what are the comparative returns from different land uses and the forms of productive activity that may be taxed more easily by states. As explained above, the weight of evidence suggests that 'modern', commercialized forms of livestock-keeping and irrigated farming are not as productive as customary forms of pastoralism (Behnke and Kerven, this book); although it is equally true that there are severe resource and practical constraints to continued reliance on 'traditional' mobile pastoralism: 'too many people and too few livestock' (Sandford, this book).

This raises the question of why governments seek to replace pastoralism with alternative land uses? An important reason is the interest of governments in raising tax revenue and, more generally, to exert greater control over economic and political life at the margins. By controlling economic activity in the pastoral margins through resource grabs, ruling regimes are able to capture economic wealth for national development (see Behnke and Kerven, this book).

Borders and boundaries: sites of innovation

The processes of incorporation, assimilation and integration have long been at the centre of the politics of the pastoral areas, driven by the imperatives of national elites located far from the margins. The control of borders and the taming of the borderlands has been a significant part of both colonial and post-colonial state building (Young, 1994; Herbst, 2000).[8] Indeed, the very identity of the central state, and its visions and plans, is often presented in opposition to these areas. The central state thus offers modernity and progress, security and stability, shaped by a settled highland, crop-farming culture and practice. This is projected as a counter to the backward, primitive, war-like and threatening mobile livelihoods of the lowlands. The civilizing mission of development thus becomes associated with settlement projects, irrigation schemes, road building and the provision of 'modern' services. Such interventions have a political dimension. Settlement means ordering and control, irrigation means profit and taxation, roads allow for the extraction of surplus to the metropolitan centres and service provision means disciplining, educating and incorporating citizens through the attractions of schooling and services. 'Seeing like a state' (cf. Scott, 1998) thus takes on a particular form in the relationship between a highland-centric state and its peripheral territories in the drylands.

Thus state identity and processes of state formation must be seen in terms of the relation between the centre and the periphery, the core and the margins, the metropole and the hinterland. Charles Tilly (1992) argues this in relation to the origin of nation states in Europe, whose establishment depended on the incorporation of the margins through population control and the generation of capital to support the creation of armies. The capture of land, the appropriation of agricultural production and the extraction of surpluses provided the wealth to establish city states, their infrastructure and military force. The very origins of the state were thus reliant on the control of the margins. And the tools of statecraft (and development) – taxation, statistics, bureaucracy and military might for example – were all deployed to this end (Hagmann and Peclard, 2011). In the process of imperial conquest in Africa, or the establishment of independent states more recently, the processes have been similar. It is thus no surprise that tensions exist – politically, economically and culturally – between these poles of authority, despite long periods of attempted assimilation and incorporation.[9]

These pastoral borderlands are, in some important senses, beyond the reach of the state, and so the development industry. Historically, these areas have been seen as both *threats*: sites of famine, destitution and impoverishment, and so the origins of mass migrations to cities, and *threatening*: undermining political stability through forms of rebellion and insurrection, as well as a source of demands for services and basic welfare from the central state, while contributing little tax or tribute to state coffers.

As Peter Little shows for Somalia (2003, 2005), even when a central state is effectively absent, daily life, relationships and particularly markets are still governed. Here segmented lineage systems, linked to complex clan-based hierarchies, operate (Leonard, 2009), providing order amongst apparent disorder. Disintegration of the Somali Republic precipitated a distinctively Somali-type of economic integration, in which the free movement of livestock, people, goods and information across Somali-inhabited territories of the Horn was helped – or was at least unhindered – by the segmentary clan system (Little, 2003). As discussed earlier, the dynamic cross-border cattle trade between Kenya and southern Somalia has responded to shifts in state power and influence: from feeding the export market through Kismayo in Somalia before the war to supplying Kenya's domestic markets through Nairobi after state collapse (Little, 2003, 2005, 2007).

Physically, culturally, economically and politically removed from the calculus of power of the central state, these people and areas have always resisted incorporation, avoiding taxation, resisting external imposition, and maintaining an apparently aggressive war-like stance in relation to state efforts. With reference to the mobile swidden agriculturalists of the south-east Asian highlands, James Scott explains that they have developed the 'art of not being governed' (Scott, 2009) – or at least not being governed in ways that the central state desires. A similar story applies to pastoralists of the Horn of Africa. Scott argues that in south-east Asia, hill peoples operate outside the reaches of state authority, or at least resisting it at every turn. He argues that this grouping of peoples requires its own history which needs to be counterposed with the standard national histories of the rice-growing valley states. Although in the Horn the topographic distinction is reversed, the differences are further accentuated by deep, historically rooted cultural and religious differences:

livestock-keeping, nomadic (mostly Sufi-adhering) Muslims at the margins, confronting a highland agriculturally based orthodox Christian state in Ethiopia or a Wahabi-influenced Islamic state in the former Sudan, having to deal with animist or Christian pastoralists in the south. The borderlands can thus be seen as places of opportunity, with borders being a resource, a conduit for exchange, not a threat or constraint.[10]

Yet despite the impacts of globalization and shifting notions of territory and sovereignty (Appadurai, 2003; Ferguson, 2006), borders still have real meaning, especially as such divisions become the focus for trans-national struggles over security (Clapham, 1999; Newman, 2006). Thus cast at a global scale, the relationships with other centres of power and these 'marginal' areas have been central to some of the broader geopolitical struggles of recent times. In the Cold War era the alliances between east and west were all-important in the playing out of interventions in the region, with the Derg regime of Ethiopia backed by the East, especially the former Soviet Union, until the fall of the Berlin Wall, while by contrast Kenya and Uganda were closely allied with the West (Ottaway, 1982; Luckham and Bekele, 1984). And, particularly since 9/11 and the emergence of the network of groups associated with Al-Qaida, the borderlands of the Horn have become a site for a global struggle over values, identity and power. In the Bush era this was dubbed the 'war on terror', and presented as an epic and defining struggle for Western civilization in the face of barbaric forces inspiring terrorism, located in the marginal pastoral lands of the Horn or the Sahel (Howell and Lind, 2009; Lind and Howell, 2010; Bradbury and Kleinman, 2010; Goldsmith, this book).

Pastoral areas are thus seen as a threat, not just to peripheral states in the global system, but to the political, security and commercial interests of leading industrialized countries. US Special Forces operations inside Somalia since 2001, and drone warfare launched from bases in Djibouti and southern Ethiopia against suspected terror leaders in southern Somalia, as well as US support to Ethiopian proxy forces to remove the Islamic Courts Union (ICU) from power in Mogadishu in 2006 under the guise of 'counter-terrorism' (Barnes and Hassan, 2007; Menkhaus, 2007), indicates the importance of this region to the post-9/11 global security regime. The ongoing conflict with the Al Shabaab group who occupied the vacuum of power in Somalia, has helped exacerbate the impact of the 2011-12 famine in southern Somalia (McVeigh, 2011; LaFranchi, 2011). The stand-off in the region between the West and the pastoral margins creates a precarious politics, and with this a rationale for highly top-down development, and sometimes draconian military intervention (Hagmann and Mulugeta, 2008; Bradbury and Kleinman, 2010).

These geopolitical engagements with the margins have therefore given rise to a plethora of new 'development' projects in pastoral areas, funded by a combination of US/European conventional aid agencies, foreign affairs and defence/security ministries. Labelled as 'peace building', 'good governance' or 'conflict resolution' efforts, they are often aimed at ensuring that the interests of a larger political-security regime are upheld, and that development is the best remedy for countering terror and destabilizing forces.

Thus, to outsiders, whether based in Addis Ababa, Nairobi, London or Washington, the pastoral borderlands are at once baffling, unruly, threatening and backward, and in need of taming, controlling, incorporating and civilizing. The development enterprise over the past century or more has been geared to this transformation, and informed by these perspectives to modernize the backward borderlands and banish primitive practices that give rise to rebellion, insurrection and, in extreme cases, terror. But a perspective that sees the margins as the centre, borders as zones of exchange, and borderlands as sites of creativity and innovation in response to adversity, offers an alternative, although one that requires both new research methods and development practices (Little, 2006).

Future pathways: diverse livelihood options

What is the future for pastoralism in the Horn of Africa? This book is full of examples of how pastoralists are responding to the diverse drivers of change that are impinging on them. But, critically, not everyone succeeds, and processes of quite extreme differentiation are unfolding in some places, with dire consequence for those who lose out. A much more complex understanding is needed to provide insight into the nuances and complexities of change.

A first step is to recognize that 'pastoralism' does not represent one form of livelihood. All forms are broadly connected to mobile livestock production, but pastoralists may have more or fewer animals, different combinations of species, different levels of engagement with markets (local, cross-border or export), different types and entry points into livelihood diversification and varying objectives for production. And these different pathways vary from place to place and over time.[11] Some pathways are pushed by long-term processes (such as encroachment of pastoral lands by agriculturalists or game parks) and some are shaped by sudden shocks, such as disease epidemics or a large livestock raid. Many are shaped by a series of shocks and stresses, acting sequentially or in combination, including climatic events such as droughts and/or floods, trade bans imposed by veterinary regulations, wars and conflicts, or sudden shifts in market opportunities. But these cannot be easily predicted: future pathways are highly contingent and deeply uncertain – pastoralists must live with uncertainty (Scoones, 1995a) and continuously adapt and innovate (Scoones and Adwera, 2009).

Given this context, it is useful to think about future scenarios – possible pathways that might be followed by different people in different places. Figure 1.2 offers a simple schema for thinking about this. It was originally developed in a workshop with Ethiopian policy-makers, development practitioners and pastoral leaders (UNOCHA-PCI, 2007), and proved a useful heuristic tool for thinking about both the past and the future. The diagram contrasts four 'ideal type' livelihood strategies which are created through the interaction of two different axes: resource and market access. Of course, access to resources and markets is in turn affected by multiple intersecting drivers. Thus, for example, climate change may reduce resource access by reducing effective rainfall (or increasing its variability) and so affect grass/browse

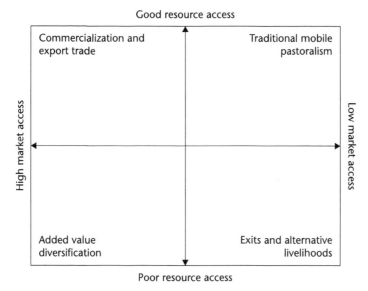

FIGURE 1.2 Four scenarios for the future of pastoralism (adapted from UNOCHA–PCI, 2007).

production and surface water access (Ericksen *et al.*, this book). Resource access may also be affected by 'land-grabbing' where particularly important 'key resources' are removed for other uses, including private enclosures, irrigated agriculture, game parks and so on (Tache, this book; Galaty, this book). Market access, in turn, may be affected by disease outbreaks, preventing access to particular markets, especially across borders. The quality of roads, holding grounds and port infrastructure may also affect market access, as well as patterns of demand from urbanizing centres affected in turn by changing consumption patterns (Catley and Aklilu, this book). Conflict – long-running rebellion, large-scale raiding and disorganized banditry – may affect both resource and market access (Goldsmith, this book).

Over time for a particular place, we can use Figure 1.2 to trace the changes in livelihoods. What is clear is that, even if we go back 50 or even 100 years, not everyone was involved in what is labelled 'traditional' or 'pure pastoralism'. While the anthropological accounts perhaps focused on the dominant (male) occupations of the majority (Evans-Pritchard, 1940; Lewis, 1988), pastoralism has always been much more complex. For example, the long-term engagement of pastoralism with agriculture, including irrigated agriculture, is well documented (Sandford, this book), as is the differential participation in markets, including across national borders (Dietz, 1993; McPeak and Little, 2006). Taking the example of Somalia as a country long-associated with pastoralism, it also has the longest coastline of any country in Africa, and from the 1830s Somalis were travelling overseas to find work and send money home to relatives (Geshekter, 1993). Due to links with Arab traders and merchants, Somalis regularly travelled to the Gulf States in the colonial period, and were employed as sailors and other workers. Pilgrimages to Islamic centres also helped to ensure that Somalis were not isolated from news and experiences from other countries. Rather than describing a nation of nomadic herders, the International Labour Organization characterized Somali families as multi-occupational, multi-national production units whereby a family grazing their livestock on the Ethiopian border could, via the clan system, receive support from relatives abroad (Geshekter, 1993). These remittances were estimated at US$825 million per year, or around 60 per cent of GDP in 2004 (Economist Intelligence Unit, 2006) although some reports value remittances at up to US$1 billion (Lindley, 2005).

Pastoral systems have long exhibited a boom and bust cycle (Dahl and Hjort, 1976). However, such dynamics are even more important today, and the scenarios, and associated livelihood options, are both more constrained and more differentiated. As the chapters in this book show, the past dominant livelihood practice characterized as 'traditional mobile pastoralism' is increasingly rare. While in pastoralist discourse there is a vision of such a lifestyle, and it remains wrapped up in constructions of identity, the options of regular mobility and reliance on livestock for subsistence and limited exchange are constrained. Of course, in some more remote areas, where market access is poor and options of commercialization are limited, and where resources are still relatively plentiful, this scenario remains important, now and into the future. Cases might include the various societies within the 'Karamoja Cluster' of north-western Kenya, north-eastern Uganda, and the far south-eastern corner of South Sudan, as well as neighbouring groups in the Omo River Delta of southern Ethiopia. But, overall, these are the exceptions, rather than the rule. In other areas, a combination of factors, all with historical precedents, but now with greater force, influence and impact, are shaping pastoral livelihood options and opportunities.

For example, the phenomenon of 'land grabs', discussed by Babiker, Galaty, Letai and Lind, and Nunow in this book, has increased in intensity in recent years. A combination of crises – of food, fuel and finance – has driven speculative investment in land. The land that new investors want is invariably the best watered and the most valuable, as their projects focus on irrigated agriculture, for food, fuel and other commercial cash crops such as sugar cane (Borras *et al.*, 2010, 2012). In Ethiopia, for example, the government has committed up to three million hectares of land to 1300 foreign investors with licenses for commercial farms (Graham *et al.*, 2009, p44; Galaty, this book; Lavers, 2012). In Kenya, a range of domestic and foreign investors have targeted the Tana Delta, the largest wetland in the country, and a vital drought-grazing reserve for pastoralists from across northern and eastern Kenya (Nunow, this book). And such investments are not only for agriculture or biofuels, but also for tourism, a burgeoning and highly profitable industry in Kenya, as Letai and Lind (this book) discuss in reference to the Laikipia Plateau in Kenya, for example. External investors may be a combination of local elites, including pastoralists and foreign nationals, operating with the support of national governments, who see a vision of a green, irrigated land or a wild, natural space in what they regard as barren, idle drylands. At a smaller scale, range enclosures, where individuals fence off areas of rangeland for private use, have grown dramatically, as fodder becomes scarcer and more valuable. This has resulted in the disruption of traditional, common property-based range management practices, as described by Tache (this book) for Borana, Ethiopia.

Such land grabs – small and large – remove 'key resources' from pastoral production systems (Scoones, 1991; Oba, this book). Even if they remove only a fraction of the overall rangeland area, the removal of key resource patches, such as riparian strips, wetlands and hilltops, undermines the functionality of the whole system, increasing risk and vulnerability, as Babiker (this book) explains in his assessment of the impacts of the grabbing of seasonal grazing lands in Gedaref state in Sudan.

Another factor that has affected future pathways is the changing nature of conflict in pastoral areas. Armed violence is a historical condition of many pastoral societies, and localized disputes over water and grazing are altogether normal features of most pastoral production systems. However, far from being skirmishes of little consequence in distant peripheries, pastoral conflicts in the Horn today are closely entwined with the dynamics of wider political and economic contexts. Further, as Goldsmith (this book) explains, the future of pastoral conflicts in the region will closely mirror the transitional dynamics overtaking all but the most isolated corners of the region. The closer incorporation of pastoral areas into national and regional economies, the shifting calculus of power in the wake of national political change and the concomitant emergence of new actors in these areas, as well as the spread of small arms and light weapons linked to conflicts in the region (Gray, 2000; Mirzeler and Young, 2000; Pike, 2004; Mkutu, 2008), have all changed the timbre of conflict and violence in the pastoral margins.

Forms of conflict vary across the region. Conflict in the Ogaden region of eastern Ethiopia is subsumed in a long-running insurrection by various armed factions as well as counter-insurgency operations by the Ethiopian military (Markakis, 1994, 2011; Lyons, 2008). Conflict in Isiolo, an emerging regional hub in northern Kenya, pits members of several ethnic groups against each other against a backdrop of a booming local economy and political-administrative transition under Kenya's new constitution (Amani Papers, 2010; Salesa, 2011). In Karamoja in north-eastern Uganda, the state has played a critical role in the latest phase of armed violence through a disarmament operation by the Ugandan People's Defence Forces, which has involved confining livestock belonging to disarmed communities in the shadow of military barracks where they are assumed to be secure (Stites *et al.*, 2007). However, the picture of pastoral conflict in the region is not one of ever-escalating violence. There are examples of effective stabilization and peace-building efforts that build on customary institutions. The government that has developed in Somaliland is a mix of traditional and modern, and this mix helps to explain the relative stability of an entire 'pastoral state' (Bradbury, 2008). Elsewhere, the transitional dynamics shaping pastoral conflicts in the Horn favour innovation and reform that promotes the incorporation of minorities and marginal areas, which might reduce armed violence in the future (Goldsmith, this book; Scott-Villiers *et al.*, 2011).

The growth of the livestock trade and the opening up and consolidation of a series of important trade routes building on centuries of trading and exchange across the region, is a further driver of change. As already discussed, the growth in demand for meat from rapidly urbanizing centres in the region, and increasingly wealthy, oil-rich regions such as the Middle East, has helped the formation of strong trade routes. These mirror older routes in some cases, but others are new. In 2009, importing countries for pastoral livestock from the Horn included Egypt, Libya, Chad, Yemen, Saudi Arabia, Oman, Bahrain, Qatar, United Arab Emirates and Mauritius (Aklilu and Catley, 2009, this book).

One consequence of a growth in commercial trade is that a number of livelihood opportunities open up. As several chapters in this book show, pastoralists are taking full advantage of closer incorporation into national and regional economies to move livestock and goods across long-standing geopolitical, ecological and land-use boundaries. This expanding trade is having multiplier effects, promoting diversification pathways in the drylands, with increasing demands for trekking and transport of livestock to fattening lots, sale yards and abattoirs; high value fodder to fatten livestock for sale; and milk to supply towns where increasing numbers of pastoralists are moving to engage in trade, marketing and related enterprises (Fratkin, this book). As Livingstone and Ruhindi (this book) explain, there are gendered dimensions of such expanding forms of economic life, with women taking on many of the newly important value added activities.

The net result is that there is a greater spread of livelihood pathways across the diagram in Figure 1.2. While in the past, the majority concentrated on traditional, mobile forms of livestock-keeping, with some specializing in supplying larger markets, others diversifying into enterprises associated with keeping herds, and many dropping out, today there is even greater differentiation. In particular, as Catley and Aklilu show (this book), there is a growing gap between those who are able to profit from the growing opportunities of commercialization and those who cannot, and so are unable to stay in the traditional pastoral system. These people must exit to other livelihood activities in the area, or in increasing numbers become reliant on aid agency support, sometimes in camps, or in the constant movement out of pastoral areas to towns. For others, exit means movement out of the country into the diaspora. While data on these processes is difficult to come by, estimates of population growth and poverty levels in pastoral areas (Catley and Aklilu, this book) are consistent with estimates of increasing urban populations, both within and outside pastoral areas of the Horn (Anon., 2010), as the poorest move out of pastoralism. Stephen Sandford argues persuasively that there are 'too many people and too few livestock' in pastoral areas, and that the prospects are bleak.[12] He argues that the value of growing trade and the opportunities for diversification are too small to sustain the growing number of people. The result is a growing pattern of differentiation: some moving up, others moving out. Catley and Aklilu (this book) thus explain the trends in high-export pastoral areas of Sudan, Ethiopia and Somalia, less in terms of the demise of pastoralism in the Horn, more as an expected transfer of livestock from smaller to larger herds – a process of classic class formation – as commercialization advances. Forms of mobile pastoralism will continue, they argue, for those who are able to commercialize while others will seek options elsewhere, as labourers, entrepreneurs and service providers; a process in common with changes in pastoralism in other parts of the world (Steinfeld *et al.*, 2010) and agricultural development in general (Bryceson *et al.*, 2000).

What is certainly clear is that this process of differentiation – the creation of a relatively elite commercial class within pastoral societies – is occurring at a rapid pace in some areas. The main herd owners may often be absent, employing labour or loaning out animals through social networks (Little, 1985a). This process absorbs labour to some extent, creating livelihoods for those unable to socially reproduce on the basis of traditional modes of production, such as through contracted herding, being enlisted as labour on farms owned by pastoral elites, or trekking/transporting livestock to distant private ranches and sale-yards. With this, we see the expansion and entrenchment of new pastoral elites, who are well-connected economically and politically with the centre, as a result, often losing their connections with the 'margins'.

The implications of this rapid process of socio-economic differentiation are evident in the erosion of customary safety nets, as Lind and Letai (this book) explain in the case of the Laikipia Maasai. Nunow (this book) similarly describes the loss of cooperative herding arrangements in the Tana Delta in Kenya. He explains that, whereas in the past wealthier and poorer herders would combine their herds and hire labour to move these to distant grazing, and would be compensated in kind with an animal belonging to a better-off herder, wealthier herders are now backing out of such arrangements and paying in cash hired herders to move livestock being reared for the market. The implication is that poorer herders are losing out, unable to afford to pay cash to hired herders.

In the past such processes of extreme differentiation were not so evident in pastoral areas. A tradition of sharing and equity was linked to a 'moral economy' reinforced by cultural and religious mores of inclusion and preventing destitution, embedded in a strong lineage and clan-based social fabric (Broch-Due, 1990; Storas, 1991; Waller, 1999). There were of course elites, but they often represented positions created through clan and lineage connections, religious affiliation and age, rather than the harsher dynamics of class formation in a commercializing economy under pressure. This of course has implications for rural politics. Clan elders may or may not be coincident with the new economic elites. Traders, brokers, transporters may be the 'big men' today and, while negotiating their position with traditional elites, they may have other routes to access power and resources via alliances with the central state. Operating outside the local moral economy, they may also have fewer obligations and reduced qualms about exploitative labour and market practices, and less commitment to others who drop through any safety net once provided.

It is in this context that aid agencies, NGOs and governments must struggle to provide 'social protection'. However, as Catley and Aklilu (this book) indicate, safety net programmes may be fundamentally flawed in high export pastoral areas if the objectives include either returning substantial numbers of destitute herders back to pastoralism, or if the expectation is that many people can find alternative livelihoods in these areas. Although livestock commercialization does provide some new employment opportunities and there are also economic spaces for alternative livelihoods to develop, the demand far exceeds the supply. Similarly, the level of assets provided by safety nets and similar programmes may meet some immediate food security needs (rather like food aid), but in terms of herd re-building are insignificant (Catley and Napier, 2010). In addition, as the gap between poorer and richer households widens, larger herds are needed to enter into and stay in the commercialized system. Still, Devereux and Tibbo (this book) suggest that in pastoral areas there is a role for other types of 'social protection', which they use more broadly to refer to social insurance, livelihood support, employment guarantees and conflict resolution.

Some development programmes focus on 'livelihood diversification', attempting to create alternative livelihoods to help people diversify out of pastoralism. But the design of these programmes often fails to understand the intimate economic and cultural connections between diversified livelihoods and the core pastoral economy. Many people have the ambition of returning to pastoralism, and will use town-based livelihoods to accumulate animals, which may be herded by relatives out on the range. The small towns that are scattered across the pastoral areas are, as we have already noted, growing fast. This is driven by the pastoral economy locally and often complemented by diaspora investments in these places – involving not only real estate and business development, but also, crucially, investments in livestock (Horst, 2004; Lindley, 2007, 2009). Such small towns offer numerous opportunities for small-scale entrepreneurs, as in the camel milk trade described by Abdullahi *et al.* (this book). Such opportunities are especially important for women who are able to gain independent sources of income (Ahmed, 1999; Hodgson, 2000; Livingstone and Ruhindi, this book). The connections between economic activities are thus essential, and the interaction between the four quadrants in Figure 1.2 is important to highlight, both for individual people at a particular moment, but also across time.

The future of pastoralism?

The central proposition of this book is that by making the margins the centre of our thinking, a different view of future pathways emerges. A perspective centred on 'the margins' unmasks the continuous innovation, adaptive practices, complex governance arrangements and entrepreneurial dynamism of these areas. This is not to say that there is no role for development supported by outside actors, or no need to improve livelihoods and human development for the vast majority of herders; far from it. But it does mean that the forms and styles of intervention need to be very different indeed, and result in a more effective negotiation and accommodation between the (multiple) centres and the diverse peripheries, in the margins of the Horn.

As we have seen, the pastoral drylands of the Horn of Africa are simultaneously sites of accumulating wealth and downward spirals of destitution and displacement.

They are places of increasing specialization in commercial livestock production as well as foci for entrepreneurial diversification. They are places where social and technological innovation is constantly happening, but more often than not undetected by official development agencies. They are places where change of various types is always unfolding, increasingly in connection to the broader dynamics of political and economic transition that are sweeping the region. They are today places of sometimes extreme contrasts and stark differentiation. They are places full of hope, yet with pockets of real desperation and despair, as the famine crisis in southern Somalia in 2011–12 makes clear. The contradictions and complexities of multiple, competing pathways of change make these places difficult to understand, especially with the mindsets, perceptions and framings of the development elite from the metropolitan centres, both north and south.

What then needs to happen? How can the hope and optimism, the dynamic entrepreneurialism and ingenious innovation be capitalized on, spread and multiplied? And how can the crises, failures and cycles of destitution and human misery be avoided? The challenges are conceptual and practical. Conceptually, as emphasized throughout this book, we need to change the way we view the pastoral areas of the Horn. This requires some very fundamental 'flips' in the way problems are framed, and solutions envisaged. Table 1.1 provides contrasting views of a number of important development challenges, as seen from 'the centre' and 'the margins'; shifting from 'seeing like a development agency' to 'seeing like a pastoralist'. Of course the world does not exist in bipolar opposites, and shades of grey always represent the complex reality in between. But as a challenge to normative perspectives of mainstream development, Table 1.1 offers some contrasts for debate. Critically, it means changing the way we think about development, not as a singular pathway to be introduced or pushed by states in the region and their aid partners, but rather as a plural set of pathways unfolding on multiple fronts in the margins, driven by the wider dynamics of transition and a diversity of actors, both men and women: livestock keepers of all types, market traders, foreign and domestic investors, local entrepreneurs, rural middlemen, customary leaders, armed agents and youth, among others. But such plural pathways are also thoroughly shaped by pastoral innovation, ingenuity and aspiration. Thus, by consciously moving our gaze from the centre to the margins the world begins to look different.

Practically, there are a number of steps that aid agencies and government departments can take. A first step is to work with and through existing policy frameworks that support entrepreneurialism and innovation in pastoral areas, and which suggest moves towards a different configuration of markets and governance. In particular, as already mentioned, the AU policy framework on pastoralism provides a progressive vision of development pathways in pastoral areas, and can be built on by efforts to develop complementary policies – and crucially, resulting resource allocations – through regional economic bodies and national governments. Development actors can buttress these efforts by helping to shape strategies for very different pastoral contexts in ways that resonate with the core ideas of the AU policy.

TABLE 1.1 Contrasting visions of development at the margins

Issue	View from the centre ('seeing like a development agency')	View from the margins ('seeing like a pastoralist')
Mobility	Pre-sedentarization, nomadism as a stage in the process of civilization.	Mobility as essential for modern livelihoods – of livestock, people, labour, finance.
Climate and environmental change	Pastoralists as villains and victims: environmental degradation needs to be curtailed, and pastoralists are in need of support for climate adaptation.	Responding to non-equilbrium environments and adaptation to climate variability as a way of life.
Markets	Uneconomic, weak, thin, informal, backward, in need of modern facilities and upgraded value chains, and so formalized, regulated.	Vibrant commercial trade, cross-border, linked into regional/global markets, constrained by state. Informality as a strength.
Agriculture	The future, a route to settlement and civilization, and more profitable return.	A temporary stop-gap, but linked to pastoralism, especially if based on flexible locally controlled small-scale crop production.
Irrigation	A sound investment, a profitable enterprise, especially if large-scale and linked to infrastructure development of the region.	A risky investment that undermines the core economic opportunity (livestock production), especially if externally owned and controlled and large-scale. A land grab, not a land investment.
Technology	Backward, primitive, requiring modernization (range management, breeding, fences, abattoirs and so on).	Appropriate technology, mixing old (mobile pastoralism) with the new (mobile phones, Internet etc.).
Services	Simple to supply, but difficult, resistant customers unwilling to take up education and health services.	Huge demand for health care and schooling, but requires new forms of service delivery compatible with mobile livelihoods.
Diversification	A way out of pastoralism; a coping strategy.	As a complement to pastoralism, adding value, gaining business opportunities, a route 'back in' to livestock-keeping through investment of new income.

Social protection	Aid programmes and safety nets, externally designed and imposed, difficult to get out once in the net.	Focused on mutual support networks and informal interactions, culturally rooted and highly dynamic, movement in and out of 'support'.
Small towns	Sites of destitution, dropping out; in need of 'development' (services and infrastructure).	Commercial hubs, foci for growth and private investment, including from diaspora networks.
Borders	The edge of the nation, to be controlled and protected.	The centre of extended livelihood and market networks.
Conflict	Destructive, violent and in need managing; external peace building efforts through disarmament and 'development'.	Linked to local peace initiatives, rebuilding clan and ethnic identities and promoting and improving the inclusion and representation of pastoralists in national political fora.
Identity	Tribes, the 'other', not us. In need of development, civilization, incorporation into the nation.	Trans-national linking clans and groups across nations, into the diaspora; diverse citizenships.
State	Fragile, weak, collapsed, failed.	New networked forms of governance, linking local organization (clans) and wider polities beyond the state.
Class	Homogenous, tribal.	Highly differentiated, different socio-economic groups.
Gender	Regressive, anti-women.	Women as key innovators and agents of diversification, promoting peace by building a network of contacts across social and ecological borders through trade and exchange.
Youth	Dangerous, idle, impoverished – caught up in banditry and raiding, and potential recruits into extremist groups.	Important connectors to newly important economic activities, exploiting new political spaces to negotiate and contest better terms for pastoral societies in national debate.

A second step is to gear organizations to work over the long-term in the margins. To shift the vision from the centre to the margins will require more people spending more time in places such as Gode, Garsen and Gambella. Our knowledge and understanding of the dynamics shaping development at the margins is constrained by the fact that so many agencies have their staff concentrated in the region's political and commercial centres. Many organizations with national offices make their decisions based on the limited and sometimes poor quality information availed by field staff in regional towns or consultants who visit for rapid assessments. For development organizations seeking to shift to the margins, this means creating new partnerships with local civil society in these areas, such as customary authorities, church missions, mosque committees and trade-based groups. Partnerships need to be less concerned with 'implementation' of preconceived plans and more focused on finding workable ways of 'entrusting' local actors to identify problems, opportunities and ways of working on these.

A third step is that development actors need to support more long-term analysis and learning. Under conditions of dynamic uncertainty, adaptive responses, experimentation, piloting and above all research and learning are critical. Yet research effort, and the resulting evidence base, is limited, due to insecurity, the difficulties of working in such environments and the relative lack of funding. Most donor/ NGO-supported assessments are localized and provide only a snapshot of a very complex reality, and many extract unreliable information, without building relations of trust with local communities that allow researchers and development practitioners to gain 'a view from the margins'. Development actors need to reinvest in sustained, high quality participatory analysis with communities which, when done well, incorporates a differentiated analysis by gender and wealth group and thereby begins to probe the key issues of social difference; moving beyond a uniform view of pastoralism to an appreciation of diversity and difference. This change would also benefit from wider use of participatory approaches for reviewing and assessing the impact of projects (Catley *et al.*, 2008), especially when impact assessment is linked to reshaping organizational or government policies.

A fourth step must be an acceptance that many of the issues that remain challenges at the margins are political. While adopting policies, changing resource allocations, shifting staff locations, building local partnerships and improving research and learning processes through participatory approaches are all important, in the end a rethinking of development at the margins will require some fairly fundamental changes in power and politics. This requires a renegotiation of the relationships between the central state – and the associated international development apparatus – and the margins. Given the long histories of conflict, secession and wider distrust that exist, how can this be possible? Surely the very vibrancy of life at the margins is based on the 'art of not being governed', escaping the disciplining strictures of state control? And will not an accommodation with the central state likely result in capture, incorporation and exploitation? These are all certainly risks. But maybe the centre now needs the margins more than before. There is a growing acceptance of the importance of the livestock trade as a source of national economic growth, with positive multiplier linkages across the economy. There is mounting evidence that small towns in pastoral areas are centres of livelihood creation, stemming the flow of migrants and reducing levels of destitution, both substantial costs to the central state. Processes of political decentralization and regionalization also offer autonomy and self-determination in the context of a more enabling central state, recognizing that issues of conflict and development can only be dealt with at a local level (James et al., 2002; Samatar, 2004; Turton, 2006; Scott-Villiers et al., 2011; Goldsmith, this book). The geopolitical and strategic interests of the margins are increasingly evident. This brings with it the dangers of heavy-handed intervention, as we have discussed, but it also offers opportunities for making the case that sensitive development can build peace and stability. With increasing numbers of pastoralists part of an educated national elite, they are now part of political, business and diaspora networks with considerable influence. While this has its downsides, the potentials for articulating interests and advocating change at the margins have certainly increased (Lister, 2004; Morton, 2005). The state, and its implementing agencies and donor partners, must wake up to these new relationships, and pastoralist advocacy organizations equally need to make use of them to leverage resource allocations and policy influence. Thus, in time, the margins would become more central, opening up opportunities for making the case for new, more appropriate pathways of development in these areas.

Thus, in thinking about the future of the margins in the Horn of Africa, very different potential pathways become apparent, with different practical challenges. Returning to our scenario diagram (Figure 1.2), a pessimistic outlook might foresee a dramatic split between the top-left scenario (commercialization and export trade) and the bottom right (exit and destitution). This would entail large-scale out-migration and increasing numbers of pastoralists exiting, but with few opportunities for making a decent living outside of livestock-keeping. This would entail the need for relief assistance and externally provided safety nets for many years to come, to sustain a large, destitute population living in camps and on the outskirts of regional centres and small towns. This implies that very few will remain in pastoralism; perhaps just those who are vertically integrated into national and regional markets and follow a ranching-to-abattoir model. There would be limited multipliers outside of this commercialized form of pastoralism in the way of economic activities and opportunities that add value to local livelihoods. Much herding would be contracted out, with absentee livestock owners living in towns or in irrigation schemes, where they have acquired high-value plots. By contrast, a more optimistic view would foresee pathways emerging across all the quadrants of the diagram, with the growth of a broad-based commercialization, rooted in many forms of livestock production, linked to expanding options for local enterprise and livelihood diversification. This would provide more opportunities for pastoralists to stay in pastoral areas, through adapting traditional forms of pastoralism, such as by engaging in value-added activities, as well as through better service provision in regional towns and centres for those who opt to abandon livestock production.

Which of these scenarios is most likely, where and for whom? In all probability the future of pastoralism in the Horn of Africa region will include elements of all potential pathways. This underlines the need to develop far greater knowledge and understanding of the different development pathways at the margins, and their contextual particularities. Policy and development actors need to work on multiple fronts to encourage the most sustainable and secure outcomes possible for pastoralists whose existing livelihoods and future prospects are necessarily very different. This book provides detailed examinations of innovations, entrepreneurialism, dynamism and cooperation to inform more effective use and investment of political, security and development inputs at the margins. If the progressive ideals of development are to have purchase and positive change take place with wide benefits, we have to take the visions and perspectives from the margins seriously.

Notes

1 The book builds on a substantial literature that has explored the future of pastoralism in Africa over time (see, *inter alia*, Monod, 1975; Galaty *et al.*, 1981; Jahnke, 1982; Sandford, 1983; Galaty and Johnson, 1990; Scoones, 1995a; Zaal, 1998; Anderson and Broch-Due, 1999; Nori *et al.*, 2005; De Haan *et al.*, 1997, 2001; De Jode, 2010). In addition, there have been more focused treatments on, for example, pastoral ecology (Dahl and Hjort, 1976; Behnke *et al.,* 1993; Homewood, 2008), mobility (Niamir-Fuller, 1999), gender and culture (Hodgson, 2000), history (Anderson and Johnson, 1988; Smith, 1992), settlement (Fratkin and Roth, 1990), marketing (Kerven, 1992; McPeak and Little, 2006) and conflict (Doornbos *et al.,* 1992; Fukui and Markakis, 1994). There have also been important local studies from Kenya (Spencer, 1973; Fratkin, 1991; Homewood and Rodgers, 1991; McCabe, 2004; Homewood *et al.*, 2009), Ethiopia (Markakis, 2011), and Somalia (Lewis, 1961; Little, 2003).
2 In the Greater Horn of Africa, we include Sudan, South Sudan, Eritrea, Djibouti, Ethiopia, Somaliland, Puntland, Somalia, Kenya, Uganda, and Tanzania. Hereafter, we refer to this region as 'the Horn of Africa' or, more simply, 'the Horn'. See Figure 1.1.
3 Based on Garissa market data in 2007 of 105,667 cattle and 25,457 sheep and goats.
4 While increasing, these are of course not new phenomena: see Herren (1990a) and Little (1989, 1994) on milk marketing in Somalia in the 1980s.
5 www.citypopulation.de/Kenya.html, accessed 8 December 2011.
6 www.scribd.com/doc/4185744/Puntland-Facts-and-Figures-MOPIC- 'Puntland Facts and Figures' September 2007, Ministry of Planning and International Cooperation, accessed 8 December 2011.
7 See the discussion surrounding 'commodity-based trade': Thomson *et al.* 2004, 2009; Scoones and Wolmer, 2006; Scoones *et al.* 2010; Brückner, 2011.
8 See Baud and Van Schendel, 1997; Lugo, 1997; Anderson and O'Dowd, 1999; Roesler and Wendl, 1999; Diener and Hagen, 2009; and Johnson *et al.*, 2011 for reviews of different understandings of 'borders' and 'borderlands'.
9 See discussion on Ethiopia in particular in: Schlee and Watson, 2009; Hagmann and Mulugeta, 2008; James, 2007; Abbink, 2006; Young, 1999; Donham and James, 1986.
10 See for example, Asiwaju and Nugent, 1996; Baud and Van Schendel, 1997; Barth, 2000; Nugent, 2002; Feyissa and Hoehne, 2010.
11 See www.future-agricultures.org/index.php?option=com_content&view=article&id=7544: timelines&catid=1549:future-of-pastoralism&Itemid=981, accessed 8 December 2011.
12 See the e-debate on 'Pastoralism in crisis?', Future Agricultures Consortium, see www. future-agricultures.org/index.php?option=com_content&view=category&layout=blog& id=39&Itemid=534, accessed 8 December 2011.

PART I

Resources and production

2

THE SUSTAINABILITY OF PASTORAL PRODUCTION IN AFRICA

Gufu Oba

Introduction

How can pastoral production be sustained in the drylands of Africa, particularly in the context of the rapid changes being seen? This chapter discusses in particular the implications of the loss of pastoral mobility, asking what sustaining mobility might imply in current contexts. The chapter is informed by the increased sedentarization of pastoralists, the loss of key grazing and drought reserve resources to alternative uses and the radical transformation of pastoral land use overall. The chapter argues that an understanding of dynamic rangeland ecologies is essential, yet traditional responses involving long-range transhumance may also no longer be feasible. A range of processes that undermine mobility and access to 'key resources' are identified, including increasing crop production, sedentarization, dam building and exclusion due to land grabs. The chapter argues that, despite such constraints, pastoralists are continuously adapting and innovating, responding in new ways to shocks and stresses. New forms of pastoralism are emerging which still have mobility and response to non-equilibrium systems at their core, but they must now take on new forms.

Understanding rangeland ecologies

Many debates about African pastoral development in the 1980s cast pastoralists as largely responsible for land degradation (Lamprey, 1983; Sinclair and Fryxell, 1985). It was claimed that this degradation was so severe that it threatened the very survival of the system. Researchers and policy-makers used measures of rangeland carrying capacity to regulate the problem of herd stocking rates (Sandford, 1983). The impact of overstocking was gauged in terms of changes in composition of the herbaceous layer, shrub encroachment, declines in the diversity of plant species and the degradation of the soil (Abel, 1997). An additional assumption was that rangelands protected from livestock grazing would benefit from reversals of these conditions, and that livestock population densities were the key variables driving rangeland dynamics (Westoby et al., 1989). For dryland ecosystems, the effect of biotic factors, such as grazing intensity, on plants was overemphasized, while the effects of abiotic influences, independent of livestock densities, notably spatial and temporal variability in rainfall, were ignored (Behnke et al., 1993; Ellis and Galvin, 1994; Angassa and Oba, 2007). In arid environments, stochastic climatic events have a greater impact on rangeland production than grazing alone (Ellis and Swift, 1988; Oba et al., 2000a, b; Kraaij and Milton, 2006; Hein, 2006; Anderson and Hoffman, 2011). Yet the dust from discussions on 'carrying capacity' has not settled.

The most obvious weakness of the carrying capacity paradigm, based on equilibrium understandings of ecosystems, is that it assumes spatial and temporal homogeneity of rangelands, ignoring the importance of 'key resources' within wider landscapes (Scoones, 1991, 1995a; Hary et al., 1996). It also fails to recognize that in multi-species livestock management systems, such as those of African pastoralists, there is no fixed carrying capacity. Instead, any assessment must reflect the different nutritional requirements of different livestock species during different seasons of the year and across years (Illius and O'Connor, 1999; Oba et al., 2000b) and landscape characteristics (Rutherford and Powrie, 2010; Tefera et al., 2010). Such systems exhibit high levels of resilience (Robinson and Berkes, 2010). For example, in northern Ethiopia and northern Kenya, research shows that extended periods of protection from grazing did not necessarily promote plant biodiversity, but only increased biomass (Oba et al., 2001a; Asefa et al., 2003; Abebe et al., 2006).

With accumulating evidence pointing to the limitations of the conventional paradigm by the 1990s, discussions moved from a narrow range management focus to a wider interdisciplinary dialogue. The importance of non-equilibrium systems was increasingly being recognized, with more nuanced understandings of degradation processes in dryland areas (Behnke et al., 1993; Scoones, 1995a; Vetter, 2005; O'Connor, 1994). However, disagreements between the equilibrium and non-equilibrium hypotheses persisted (Vetter, 2005), as well as debates about opportunistic and other stocking strategies (Campbell et al., 2000; Sandford and Scoones, 2006). But too often interpretations relied on short-term studies, lack of control sites and poor understanding of pastoral systems. To understand longer-term dynamics, studies must cover sequences of both wet and dry years (Oba et al., 2000a), and a spatially sensitive approach is also required which reflects patterns at a landscape rather than plot level (Pickup, 1995; Oba et al., 2003).

At larger scales the role of human effects on environmental change of dryland areas is also disputed (see Ericksen et al., this book). For example, large-scale global climate variability dominated by the North Atlantic Oscillation (NAO) and El Niño Southern Oscillation (ENSO) were used as predictor variables for the expansion and contraction of the Sahara desert (Oba et al., 2001b). Eleven years of environmental data was used to analyse the role that large-scale climate variability played by correlating the indices of the NAO with rangeland production and vegetation Normalized Difference Vegetation Index (NDVI) across sub-Saharan rangelands. It showed that the combined effects of NAO and ENSO accounted for 75 per cent of the inter-annual variability of the expansion and contraction of the southern borders of the Sahara Desert and 40 per cent of the variability of range production in Africa, with most of the variances explained by NAO alone. The study contradicted the common perception that the southern expansion of the Sahara desert indicates a progressive trend (Lamprey, 1975). On the contrary, the fluctuations of the southern borders of the Sahara Desert and fluctuations in rangeland productivity were a response to the cyclical dry and wet episodes; these are more strongly influenced by global climate variability than by local human agency (see Ericksen *et al.*, this book).

Herds, flocks and droughts

In dryland environments, livestock numbers seldom exceed any carrying capacity because frequent die-offs maintain the stocking density at lower levels (Ellis and Galvin, 1994; Moritz, 2008). But what are the impacts of these often dramatic die-offs?

A series of studies in Ethiopia and Kenya give some indications. First, herd die-offs influence herd structure, with immature livestock, e.g. calves and reproductive females, being most affected and males and steers least affected (Oba, 2001; Desta and Coppock, 2004; Angassa and Oba, 2007). Second, different droughts cause different die-off patterns. The increase in mortality recorded during some droughts was often a result of a combination of feed scarcity and animal diseases (Desta and Oba, 2004). Third, mortality patterns between ranches and herds on communal rangelands were comparable (Angassa and Oba, 2007). Fourth, drought recovery rates were related to levels of herd die-off, but not to pre-drought stocking density, as livestock population variation is mostly related to lagged rainfall variation (Ebei *et al.*, 2008).

However, such patterns are not universal. In relatively wetter areas, such as Borana in Ethiopia, long-term data reports varied herd die-offs based on the drought frequency (Desta and Coppock, 2004). Population recovery depends on whether droughts occur within 10–15 year intervals (Coppock, 1994) or whether the drought return time is 3–5 years (Oba, 2001). In periods when there is a rapid succession of drought events (as in 2010 and 2011), the impacts can be very dramatic. This has important consequences for pastoralists, as 'opportunistic systems' are no longer able to respond with rapid recovery to droughts. This has resulted, across pastoral areas, in high rates of dropping out with households moving from the pastoral system into alternative livelihoods (Fratkin, this book).

Mobile livelihoods

While mobility is at the core of pastoral livelihoods, traditional patterns of pastoral migration are increasingly under threat. Niamir-Fuller (1999, p1) asks a critical question: 'Is pastoral mobility an archaic remnant of the past . . . or the foundation of future sustainability?' Pastoral mobility entails the rotational use of spatially varied resources by diverse species of livestock. For families managing smallstock, cattle and camels, each situation requires different patterns of mobility, the choices reflected by different livestock nutritional requirements (Oba and Kaitira, 2006; Roba and Oba, 2009). Whereas mobility is associated with environmental variability, traditional herd mobility is also a result of different socio-economic status (Bassett and Turner, 2007; Turner, 2011). Pastoral herd migration takes into consideration labour scarcity and the distances moved in space and time (Robbins, 1998), with migration being an important way of reducing herd losses (Homan et al., 2008).

Nomadic systems are embedded in deep local understandings of dynamic ecologies at local, landscape and regional scales. Pastoral migrations are traditionally preceded by herder assessments of rangelands, which are usually conducted at a landscape scale (Oba et al., 2008b; Roba and Oba, 2008, 2009). The scales of movement vary enormously between locality and region. In traditional systems, migration might not be driven by scarcities alone, but by herder preferences or the dietary needs of livestock (Behnke et al., 2011). Herders have developed systematic landscape classifications according to grazing resistance gradients (Bauer, 2009; Roba and Oba, 2008). Unlike ecologists, herders can distinguish between landscapes that are vulnerable to heavy grazing and degrade rapidly, and those that resist degradation. Where there is greater risk of degradation, landscapes are grazed for brief periods during the wet season (Oba et al., 2008a, b; Roba and Oba, 2008). Using the trajectories of vegetation change, herders are able to alter their herd composition and modify grazing movements. The shift in ownership from cattle to camels is one such example. Extensive bush cover that reduces herbaceous biomass production is undesirable for cattle management (Angassa and Oba, 2008); by contrast, camel pastoralists consider bush encroachment to be highly desirable (Desta and Coppock, 2004).

These knowledge systems are central to sustainable pastoral herd mobility. They help to determine the distribution of spatial and temporal resources. Different cultural specializations and individual migration topologies exist (Henry et al., 2004). For example, the Gabbra and the Borana, who are neighbours in northern Kenya, rely on different systems of mobility. The Borana practise orbital mobility with their cattle, where the distribution of water points determines the seasonal movements and the distances moved, while the mobility of the camel-owning Gabbra is influenced by access to pastures rather than by distances to water. Their camels are able to tolerate thirst for as long as 14 days, allowing them to trek nearly 100km to water (Roba, 2010). For the Borana, the distance to water during the dry season hardly exceeds 20km (Helland, 1982).

When herd movements are in response to environmental stress, different families may adopt different strategies (Homan et al., 2008). The wealthier herd owners are likely to be the first to respond. For these families, one way of spreading the risk is to diversify their herds. They build networks with the less wealthy in order to obtain extra labour to manage diversified multi-species herds. By contrast, less wealthy herders without access to labour often choose to adopt local management strategies, rather than resort to long-distance migration or herd diversification. Owners of small herds pay attention to individual animals: the weakest ones are nursed by hand-feeding with bundles of grass or tree branches, while the stronger ones are allowed to fend for themselves. Wealthier owners take a herd-level approach. For example, in order to maximize the survival of the reproductive females, wealthy herd owners may kill off the calves during periods of severe stress, thereby ensuring the survival of the dams (Tache, 2008).

Disruptions of these differentiated response strategies, and the indigenous knowledge that underpins them, expose pastoralists to much more severe stresses. The impacts and consequences of this are explored in the following section.

Pressure points: the loss of key resources

Pastoral herd survival is critically dependent on the availability of dry season pastures, often along river courses and in floodplains. These 'key resources' (cf. Scoones, 1991) enable transhumance (Scholte et al., 2006), and offset drought risk (Ericksen and Lind, 2009). For example, in the Turkwel River in Turkana, Kenya, 30 per cent of the total human and livestock populations are found within 5km of the floodplain (Oba et al., 2002). The Turkana pastoralists, who have customary ownership of trees, conserve pastures near the river during the wet season for use during the dry season (Stave et al., 2001). Equally, for the Orma, the floodplain of the Tana River (Terer et al., 2004) and for the Afar, the floodplain pastures of the Awash River, are critical resources during drought years (Getachew, 2001).

However, the flow of many of these rivers is being regulated by dams for commercial irrigation and hydropower, and this competes directly with pastoral land use. Yet transforming river ecosystems has huge ecological implications (Scudder, 2006). Dam construction influences flooding regimes and therefore the availability of dry season grazing (Stave et al., 2005). In most cases of irrigation systems, there is no attempt to integrate seasonal grazing patterns with commercial agriculture (Unruh, 1990; Behnke and Kerven, this book). Other sources of threat to floodplain and riverine ecosystems include invasive species (Stave et al., 2007).

In many instances, the loss of critical dry season grazing resources is due to a failure of governance. Inappropriate development policies, the introduction of invasive species, or the lack of attention to multiple resource access in the design of crop irrigation all add to the problem (Behnke and Kerven, this book). This often leads to conflict, and a further undermining of livelihoods (Facius, 2008). Ethnic and political conflicts have also contributed to land use changes. For example, the Obbu Borana in northern Kenya were removed from their grazing lands by the *Shifta* conflicts of 1964–77. The population was removed from almost 95 per cent of their traditional grazing lands and forced into 'security villages'. For nearly a decade livestock grazing was restricted to a radius of 10km. In the process they lost all their pack animals, thereby losing the means of mobility. Overgrazing around the settled villages completely transformed the natural vegetation from perennial grasslands to a situation of bush encroachment over a period of three decades. Subsequent droughts caused the loss of herds, resulting in impoverishment of families. The Obbu Borana began crop cultivation but because their environment was not suited for growing crops, they ended up enclosing large areas of communal grazing lands as fodder reserves. Four decades later, with the return of peace, the Obbu residents have resumed a mobile lifestyle in areas from which they had earlier been displaced through insecurity. However, encroachment of the rangelands by invasive bush has undermined the potential of former grazing lands (Oba, forthcoming).

Yet at the local level there may often be institutional arrangements between different pastoral and agro-pastoral groups to share resources that lead to inclusion of others in mutually beneficial arrangements (Beyene, 2010). Such 'non-exclusionary' systems of resource use operate where local institutions create entitlements shared with neighbouring pastoral groups (Bogale and Korf, 2009). Policies that ignore these delicate social relationships create a crisis for pastoral herd mobility (Johnson, 1993).

Responding to new shocks and stresses: adaptable livelihoods

In response to changing land-use systems – such as increased sedentarization, the practice of agro-pastoralism, non-herding pastoralism, commercial pastoralism and peri-urban pastoralism – different forms of mobility are emerging (Moritz, 2010), associated with different tenure regimes and resource use (Tache, this book). Today, pure forms of pastoralism, where families rely entirely on livestock produce for their livelihoods, are diminishing, with declining livestock per capita (Desta and Coppock, 2004; Homan et al., 2008). Alternative modes of resource exploitation are emerging, with multiple forms of innovation among pastoralists in response to new shocks and stresses (Scoones and Adwera, 2009). Yet, given the ecological particularities of dryland settings, mobility, opportunism and the management of key resources are all central, though in new and different ways to the past.

Among the new livelihood possibilities, agro-pastoralism has offered traditional pastoralists new opportunities to integrate the production of herds and the cultivation of crops (Pedersen and Benjaminsen, 2008; McCabe et al., 2010; Tache and Oba, 2010). Yet, they face different problems from those which confront the traditional herding families. While agriculture provides alternative livelihoods, it has not necessarily reduced the need for herd mobility. Agro-pastoralists are moving towards the exclusive use of resources, especially in the exploitation of grazing reserves (used by settled families) that excludes their mobile neighbours (Tache, this book). The conversion of the grazing lands into land used for semi-private crop cultivation is undermining traditional systems of herd mobility. Crop cultivation takes up quality grazing land that is traditionally set aside for dry season grazing (Coppock, 1994), thereby exposing pastoralists to greater risks. Yet the integration of pastoral herding with crop cultivation can be an advantage, especially where livestock/farm owners use crop residues as grazing reserves (Toulmin and Gueye,

2003). Where such agro-pastoral families developed new strategies, they put their livestock on the communal pastures during the wet season, before returning to their enclosure reserves, for which they have exclusive access during the dry season (Angassa and Oba, 2008; Fabusoro, 2009). Nonetheless, because of their smaller sizes, crop plots and range enclosures have not offset the need for herd mobility, although the regularity of the transhumance has been significantly transformed (Samuels *et al.*, 2008).

Indeed, in several areas of the Horn of Africa where agriculture, wildlife conservancies and private range enclosures obstruct migratory routes, the changes have brought about new ways of negotiating access to private pastures (Letai and Lind, this book). Commoditization of forage in private ranches and grazing fallows has forced the migrating herders to pay grazing fees (Lengoiboni *et al.*, 2011; Tache, this book). However, in increasingly resource constrained settings, resilience has decreased and even minor environmental stresses have a disastrous effect on local economies (Tache, 2008).

Commercial pastoralism, by contrast, is another livelihood pathway (Catley and Aklilu, this book). This centres on a capital accumulation strategy, focusing on non-reproductive herds which are sold when the market environment improves. Commercial pastoralists have two options if their investment is threatened by droughts. They can invest in trucking to ferry their herds to commercial ranches, or they can rent grazing reserves during periods of stress (Mahmoud, 2006; this book). However, commercial cattle pastoralists will not risk long-distance migration because of a greater risk of huge financial losses when the herds are lost as a result of environmental stress (Adriansen, 2006). Wealthy urbanized pastoralists or commercial traders, rather than subsistence herders, are able to offset such risks. This type of pastoralism has strong links to consumer markets in cities and rural towns and is less regulated by the need for conventional mobility. By contrast, commercial camel pastoralists engage in long-distance mobility to capitalize on markets, with herds moving from Kenya through Ethiopia to Sudan (Catley and Aklilu, this book)

Today, not all pastoralists are on the move, living out on the range. Non-herding families live in peri-urban and urban environments, and engage in retail trade or have regular jobs, while also maintaining herds on the rangelands (Fratkin, 1998; Galaty, this book). They often hire labour to herd their livestock; in this way maintaining the traditional herd production system but with a difference, using their past herding experience to guide them in making critical decisions (Khalif, 2010). The novelty of these new strategies is that they build linkages between urban consumer markets and mobile herds. In northern Kenya, for example, dairy camels present an economic opportunity for non-herding urban households: their role in supplying milk to urban residents has promoted a new way of tapping into the pastoral economy, although the mobility of these dairy herds has been reduced (Khalif, 2010). The hiring of labour by the non-herding pastoralists creates employment opportunities for young herders who use the opportunity as transitional employment before relocating to rural towns and cities as watchmen for urban businesses and elites (Doti, 2005).

The emerging trends in these new forms of pastoralism therefore contradict the assumption that pastoralism ends when families stop practising mobile herd management. The rapid transformation of former herders, who, even after leaving the pastoral environment, still consider themselves to be pastoralists, indicates that pastoralism is not a dying system banished to the margins (Moritz, 2010). Instead, it is characterized by adaptation, innovation and dynamism, but also increasing differentiation between different livelihood strategies – all of which are linked to a reliance, in some form, on highly non-equilibrium rangeland environments. Linking our understanding of such dynamic ecological settings with new forms of livelihoods is a key challenge for future pathways of pastoralism in Africa.

3

RANGELAND ENCLOSURES IN SOUTHERN OROMIA, ETHIOPIA

An innovative response or the erosion of common property resources?

Boku Tache

Introduction

The rangelands of the Horn of Africa are undergoing major changes influencing access to and control of resources. Rangeland enclosures – the closing off of previously common property land – are on the rise. This chapter asks: is this an innovative response to resource scarcity, facilitating private investment and new forms of production, or a detrimental erosion of once common, shared resources? Rangeland enclosures in African grazing lands have received research attention since the 1980s (e.g. Behnke, 1985b, 1988), indicating gradual changes in the property regimes for grazing lands. This chapter looks at rangeland enclosures (*kaloo*) in Borana and Guji Zones of Oromia Regional State, southern Ethiopia.[1] The chapter provides an overview of the processes, trends, typologies, rationales, status and early impacts of enclosing rangeland resources, along with implications of the practice for resource tenure security. Findings show the existence of enclosures in various forms, created due to a multiplicity of objectives and motives and involving various wealth groups. The result is a pattern of land fragmentation and privatization, resulting in a decline in land under common property resource tenure. This has major implications for future development pathways, as changes in tenure result in options opening up for some and closing down for others.

Pasture reserves in pastoral land use

Reserving a section of the communal rangeland for later use is an integral part of pastoralist practice. Fluctuations in rainfall impose resource mosaics over different but functionally interconnected landscape units (Tache, 2009), thus making it necessary for pastoralists to move in order to access these patchy resources, sometimes involving long-distance trekking (Niamir-Fuller, 1999; Oba, this book). Mobility is augmented with homestead pasture reserves that target those physically weaker and more drought-vulnerable herd classes (immature calves, emaciated milk cows and selected breeding bulls), particularly in stress periods. The objective is to enhance drought survival by protecting the nucleus herd, thereby contributing to herd growth and household food production.

Some enclosed pastures are a collective responsibility and utilization is for communal purposes. In southern Oromia, drought reserves have been widely practised among Borana, Guji and Gabra Oromo communities long before the arrival of externally funded pastoral development projects. These communal pasture reserves, locally known as *kaloo*, provided an important response to drought. Customary institutions oversaw their closing and opening at appropriate times and places so as to ensure sustainable management and utilization of grazing. Among the Borana, these restricted areas were not fenced in the past. Word of mouth was sufficient to restrict access. Everyone knew that a particular area was an enclosure for calves, not to be used by other herd classes.

But what is the situation today? In recent decades, pastoralists in the southern Ethiopian rangelands have witnessed a dramatic shrinkage of the resource base, resulting in major land use changes. For example, dry season wells and associated grazing in eastern and south-eastern territories have been lost to competing groups (Bassi, 1997; Tache and Oba, 2009). In addition, large-scale bush encroachment has reduced available grazing (Brocklesby *et al.*, 2010), as has the grabbing of land for large-scale investments, as in the Liban plain (Tache, 2010). Proliferation of crop cultivation has resulted in further reductions in communal grazing areas (Tache and Oba, 2010; Berhanu and Colman, 2007). In some instances, people have enclosed areas ostensibly for crop cultivation, but actually for *de facto* pasture reserves (Tache, 2000).

The overall result is the shrinkage in available dry season grazing, a reduction in communally managed grazing reserves and growing individualization of land use rights through privatization. While there certainly are still places in Borana where communal enclosures are not physically fenced, and indigenous local institutions manage their use, these are becoming much rarer. The local institutional arrangements are becoming weaker, and the pressure to individualize and enclose land for private use has grown.

The drivers of change

What is driving this shift to enclosure of the rangelands? The *de facto* private enclosures relate largely to the expansion of crop cultivation in the rangelands. Historically, farming in Borana areas used to be restricted to sub-humid rangelands near towns and cultivators were largely non-Borana immigrants (Coppock, 1994). The Borana inhabitants used to buy food crops from these areas in dry years. The large-scale expansion of crop cultivation is a recent phenomenon, especially since 1997 – an El Niño year with good rainfall. People who had cultivated that year had a great harvest. Since then, it has been rare to find a Borana household that is not involved in crop cultivation. Frequent drought is also an important factor to consider. As the frequency of droughts increases, the need to maximize options for drought survival also increases (Tache and Oba, 2010). Since 2000, the Government of Ethiopia and NGOs have been transporting dry hay from the highlands to pastoralist areas as emergency relief during major drought episodes. This relief largely targeted nucleus herd protection. The increased drought frequency, and the corresponding increase in demand for hay, also gave impetus to the crop-associated 'private' pasture reserve.

Growth in livestock marketing opportunities has also triggered *de facto* private enclosures. For example, Moyale is an important point for livestock trade that provides an international business outlet for herders and traders from southern Ethiopia and northern Kenya (Mahmoud, this book). Thus animals (camels, cattle, small ruminants and even equines) are trekked to Moyale town for sale every day (except Sunday) from different parts of Borana and Guji zones and the neighbouring Somali Region. In recent years, this trade has increased significantly (Mahmoud, 2008, this book; Catley and Aklilu this book). Given the opportunistic nature of livestock marketing in pastoralist areas and the unpredictability of selling, animals are often backlogged. So the communities adjacent to the towns are enclosing land to rent to provide grazing for animals that come from long distances. Suburban communities, driven by income generated from the land rentals, have caused land fragmentation in the town's vicinity, with the emergence of multiple private plots dedicated to fodder production (Mahmoud, this book).

Concerning the NGO-supported enclosures, the rationale was to improve hay availability in critical times and to replace the expensive hay transported from the highlands to the lowlands. Community enclosures were therefore aimed at improving local drought coping capacities. In Liban District, for example, some of the communities had benefited tremendously in terms of drought survival, in terms of saving women's labour (hay collection), availability of milk in dry periods for children and availability of cosmetics (butter) for women in the dry season (Tache, 2010). There are also a few fattening bulls at some sites for marketing purposes.

The new enclosures: patterns of innovation

In the Borana rangelands today, grazing reserves exist in various forms. One is customary enclosure where a group of villages reserve pasture on a communal basis. The second is enclosures used by the community, but introduced or supported by NGOs. This particular category emphasizes hay availability during critical times. The third involves individually managed closed areas. Under this category, individuals fence out a large area for crop cultivation. They cultivate a part of it and leave another part untilled. The latter aim is to reserve 'private' pasture in the 'farm plot'.

Pasture is a key resource which is customarily perceived as 'God given'. The society owns and uses it according to the customary rules that guarantee use rights to the inhabitants under regulated access. Enclosing pasture reserves for private use is like making an island in an ocean. Those individuals reserving 'private' pasture on 'farm plots' make reference to private holding rights to the cultivated land – a concept which has its roots among the farmers of northern Ethiopia, where land has long been cultivated and individually owned and inherited (Dessalegn, 1984). This type of land holding system was introduced in the rangelands following the Abyssinian conquest of the South in the late nineteenth century (Donham and James, 1986). Even in pastoralist areas, farm plots became individually owned, although local customary laws did not recognize private holdings.

At a day celebrating a new community reserve site supported by Save the Children USA and the district administration near the town of Nagelle Borana in Liban District, the community told of the difference between before and after the enclosure. They proudly described their local innovations in detail. Heaps of hay were covered with tarpaulins for protection from rain and sun for later use, while the community fodder bank was for use only in the elongated dry season and a drought year. In some communities (e.g. Kurkurru), each household cuts their own share and stores the hay at home. In other communities (e.g. Simminto and Kobadi), communal hay is heaped on the site. Some communities enclose a 'degraded' area and allow natural regeneration, so improving overall rangeland quality (e.g. Qawa).

In all types of enclosure, the most important change is the physical fencing of areas. Traditionally, to 'own' an enclosure, the legitimate minimum geographic unit is a village – comprising a number of households or families. Such systems still exist, particularly in places far removed from urban influences. However, there is a tendency whereby rich pastoralists fence an area. They have huge herds and need extra pasture to sustain their increasingly commercial enterprises. The marked differentiation in pastoralist communities – between rich herd owners and the rest – is a pattern seen in many places (Catley and Akilu, this book), and is certainly becoming an important factor in Borana. The rich also have influence in different arenas of politics and decision-making, allowing them to subvert 'tradition' and capture resources. This process is triggering discussions among community members, with disputes and conflicts emerging.

There is also a remarkable interdependence between the communities. People travel long distances with pack animals to receive hay gifts from friends. The recipients reciprocate later when their hosts face grazing scarcity. Those who sell hay are those who live close to town. The closer the community is located to the town, the greater their interaction with the urban population around hay sales. The practice is not observed in places far from town, where hay sale is still a social taboo.

Winners and losers from innovation

Driven by a variety of factors, the process of rangeland enclosure – by communities, projects or individuals – is changing the pattern of resource tenure and access on the rangelands. These innovations, responses to changing patterns of resource scarcity and shifting demand, have diverse implications. Some people gain, while others lose. Shifts in tenure away from traditional common property resource management have differential impacts, on richer and poorer pastoralists, men and women.

Pasture is a vital material and social resource in pastoralist communities. In community discussions, questions are regularly raised about pasture sales. While some look at it as a positive innovation – obtaining cash income from the sale of what is locally available – others raise the bigger issue of the erosion of common property resource access. The main concern is that this previously shared resource finds its way into the market as a commercial commodity. This runs counter to the resource sharing tradition – based on accommodation, reciprocity and symbiosis – within and between pastoralist communities, the very basis of the social fabric that constitutes pastoral production in Borana (Legesse, 1973; Tache, 2000; Bassi, 2005; Bassi and Tache, 2011). It is therefore no surprise that the enclosure of these key resources has caused conflicts between and within pastoralist communities.

Yet some argue that there is no choice: traditional systems used in the past can no longer cope with today's pressures. The fragmentation of the rangeland eco-system, the decline in mobility and the privatization and marketization of land and resources are perhaps inevitable, if pastoral production is to survive. But such trends have social and political ramifications for pastoral society. If rich herd owners can spontaneously fence an area, using their connections to politicians, civil servants and merchants, what does this imply? Those who can buy the hay will survive, but those who cannot, will be excluded. What will happen if these resources are openly commercialized? What are the implications for social relations and resource sharing?

Discussions with communities reveal a number of responses. In areas where enclosures exist in their traditional form, there are few problems around property rights. The problems are with *de facto* private enclosures and farm-associated enclosures, as people are especially worried about enclosures for private use, acting to exclude others from the community. A continuation of this trend would result in socio-economic differentiation, whereby the rich get richer and the poor poorer. Informant Borbor Bule explains his observations and concerns:

> Pastoralism in Borana today is tending towards more exclusion in terms of property rights in the rangeland and shifts in decision-making. Rich business-men and the *kebele* leadership are increasingly influencing local government officials and customary institutional leaders to achieve exclusive gains from the land. This will gradually push out the poor families and expose them to difficulties to survive.[2]

These discussions are reflected in more formal fora. For example, at a cross-clan meeting of Borana elders and 16 customary leaders (representing the top Gadaa leaders, the Laduu and Gadaa councillors) in December 2009, the following declaration was made, condemning private enclosures:

> In our culture, rangeland is the property of the community as a whole and our customary law does not recognize and allow making and holding of private pasture reserves in any form. However, the communities in different

districts have repeatedly complained about *de facto* private enclosures that are spontaneously flourishing in our common property resource areas. The control of the best grazing lands by self-interested individuals has resulted not only in degradation of the non-enclosed communal areas but also has caused internal conflicts at different times in different places. Having consulted with community representatives from different districts in our Zone, government line departments and NGOs involved in pastoral development here, we hereby issue our directives that as of today December 7, 2009, there will be no private enclosures recognized in any part of our rangeland. Only the calf reserves enclosed for the purpose of supporting the more drought vulnerable herd classes (such as calves and weak cows), through public consensus, for communal utilization by *ardaa* and *reera*, are recognized by our customary law. Community leaders, district and PA (peasant/pastoralist association) leadership in different places where the problem exists are expected to implement the opening up of all the privately controlled enclosures for equitable public access in the manner that ensures peace and security of all concerned.

(Tache, 2009, p25)

The leaders appealed to all authorities, formal and informal, to take these issues seriously. These community-level policy directives have received support in several places. Some families voluntarily opened 'their' enclosures for public use following the directives, as in the case of Arero where some villagers around Qaqallo Waraba changed their reserves from private to public domain. By contrast, others showed systematic resistance and dragged out the implementation process by accepting the decision in principle, but requested a grace period until the next rainy season, as in Dharrito (Yaballo District) and Funnan Birressa and Hallona (Arero District).

The following section takes the unique case of Moyale to explore these issues in more depth.

Enclosures in Moyale District

In the 30 villages of the 11 rural *kebeles* in Moyale District located along the Yaballo–Moyale highway, people keep 'private' enclosures that range from 1 to 10 hectares of land. These enclosures, fenced out of the communal grazing areas, have existed since 1992 according to informants. They first emerged as farm land, as people took up maize cropping on an occasional basis, but they then evolved into 'private' grass reserves when the intended crop production repeatedly failed. According to local informants, the dramatic expansion of enclosed sites has eco-logical, economic, demographic, social and political explanations.

Over recent decades, the area suffered a series of crop failures due to failed rains. Repeated droughts also affected the livestock sector. This increased poverty levels for the majority of the community, although some were able to survive with large herds. Poverty was further exacerbated by rampant conflicts, including raids and counter raids among the neighbouring groups (Borana, Gabra and Garri). This affected movement and marketing of livestock, especially access to Moyale, which is a regional hub for livestock marketing (Mahmoud, this book).

Conflicts have also arisen over regional boundaries. Moyale District has been claimed by the Somali Region over the last two decades, and uncertainty over local jurisdiction has affected conflict resolution processes. The district has also witnessed a growing population pressure due to a high influx of people into Moyale town and its environs by groups who identify themselves with the Somali Region. This has been encouraged by regional authorities who anticipated control of the area through the winning of a referendum to determine the regional identity of the territory (Bassi, 1997; Tache and Oba, 2009).

In rural parts of Moyale, therefore, politically motivated spontaneous enclosures are common features, aiming at exclusive resource control. By warding off rival groups, land is claimed and so effectively incorporated into the regional state's area. For example, along the Moyale-Goofa route, all the lands left and right, have been fenced and thus 'a tired passerby would have no place to release his pack animal to rest for a while, as there was no piece of God's land', as one informant explained.[3]

The spontaneous expansion of land enclosures is indicative of weakened customary governance institutions. Moyale is one of the places where the directives discussed above were not implemented. In this area, there is a replacement of the customary resource management institutions by statutory ones (e.g. the *kebele*). This has resulted in weakened customary resource governance, which in the past regulated resource use, including the making of pasture reserves.

Who is enclosing the land in Moyale? According to local informants, individual families from all the 'ethnic' groups practise land enclosure regardless of their wealth status, as measured in livestock holdings. The immediate economic objectives in land enclosure are threefold, summarized in the Oromo language as: *tokko looniin bitataa jaara, tokko loonii jaara, kaan qotiif jaara*, meaning, respectively and in ranked order, that people build herds with the proceeds from the grass sales; people fence the land to graze their own herds; and people fence the land to produce food crops.

Who buys the reserved grass? Buyers include better-off pastoralist families who still pursue mobile pastoralism to ensure drought survival, animal traders who purchase emaciated animals for a cheap price in order to fatten them and sell them later for higher prices, and itinerant livestock traders who rent the sites as temporary holding grounds until the animals are all sold. Hay price varies, depending on quality of the grass and size of the reserved site. If the grass quality is good, the lowest price for one hectare of land is 2500 Birr (about US$150). As prices easily double with the progress of the dry season, the reserved grass is usually kept standing until such time as the open range is completely used up, usually just prior to the onset of the rains.

In sum, in the Moyale area, a pattern of privatized range enclosure has emerged, supporting a vibrant trade in hay. This has been driven by a range of factors, but the result has major consequences for the pattern of pastoral production and its long-term future, as discussed in the following section.

Consequences and implications

One of the most immediate consequences of enclosures and the concentration of animals in non-enclosed areas, especially near roads and towns, is the reduction in above ground vegetation cover in the non-enclosed areas, due to fierce competition over limited resources. At the peak of the long dry season near Moyale, nearly all the grass reserves in the enclosed sites had been sold. There was no available fodder, as in open range areas which are grazed sequentially. This was making it difficult for herds close to town to survive.

Local residents have switched to alternative livelihoods. They generate income from firewood sales, petty trade in consumable items smuggled from Kenya and retail business in *kat* grown in the Sidama highlands. Businesses range from well-established and capitalized operations, such as those that use lorries to transport and sell firewood like good quality *Acacia sayal*, to the majority who operate on a much smaller scale, bringing half-dry twigs transported by women or donkeys.

Pastoral production in Moyale District is in deep crisis, and spontaneous enclosures have contributed to the worsening of the situation. As observed elsewhere (Catley and Aklilu, this book), pathways of pastoral livelihoods are diverging – with some able to continue pastoral production with capital intensive investments (purchase of feed, lorries for moving animals to market, water tankers for watering, etc.), while others struggle with more labour intensive subsistence systems. It is the latter that are particularly under threat. As pasture scarcity increases, even in a normal dry season, richer, large herd owners are forced to buy expensive animal feed, and transport it from around Addis Ababa, more than 770km away. During the field research in Moyale (February 2010), an 11kg hay bale cost 70 Birr (about US$5), a 50kg bag of wheat husk cost 160 Birr (US$10), while an emaciated cow was sold off at a throwaway price of 200 Birr (about US$12). Such terms of trade are expected to further disfavour herders when the drought situation worsens, as in the 2011 drought. Under such conditions, livestock production becomes very precarious economically.

Another consequence of range enclosures relates to the escalation of violent internal conflicts over infringement of 'private' enclosed lands. Reported cases include verbal abuse, fighting with dangerous weapons and the killing of animals by shooting, beating, stabbing or hamstringing them. Correspondingly, an unprecedented culture of litigation is in the making. Informants cited some examples (Table 3.1).

Conclusion

In Southern Ethiopia, the community rangelands are changing, and with this, pastoralism, and its traditional institutions. Through an incremental land grab for private interests, pastoralists are living with more uncertainties – greater both in scope and depth than the ecological uncertainties inherent in the arid environments that they have responded to for so long (Scoones, 1995a). Living 'at the margins' has become increasingly challenging. Yet such challenges result in new experiments

TABLE 3.1 Examples of violent internal conflicts over enclosures in selected kebeles, Moyale District in 2009 and 2010

Incidence	Immediate consequence	Response taken	Remark
Killing of the only milk camel found by the enclosure owner on 'his' land in Dambi *kebele*	Shock-induced miscarriage and hospitalization of the lady owner	Fine of two camels	Incident took place between two Borana families
Fighting with machetes in Dambi *kebele*	Mutual physical disability	Not reported	As above
Killing of the only milk cow found in the enclosure in Lagasure *kebele*	Disrupted milk production and child starvation	Fine of one pregnant camel and 700 Birr	Incident took place between two Gabra families. The victim's family supports 20 dependent children
Nine camels, goats and dogs found dead in various enclosed sites in Lagasure *kebele*	Suspicion, mistrust and heightened insecurity in the community	Public inquiry by local leaders	Incident occurred among Gabra community

and innovations, each with winners and losers. This is a very dynamic setting, where old patterns and long-held traditions are being transformed.

How do pastoralists themselves see these land-use changes in relation to the customary resource tenure and the future of pastoralism? They respond by stating that pastoral production requires open space to allow mobility and to mitigate seasonal resource variability over a landscape, allowing resource sharing beyond 'ethnic' boundaries. However, in many areas of Borana, and especially in Moyale, such practices and institutions hardly exist today due to conflicts over land, intensified by political conflicts, range enclosures and settlement, among other factors. Given these factors, pastoralists foresee a conflict-ridden future.

In the rangelands, initially it was livestock that was commoditized and monetized, then livestock products (milk, meat, hides), but now it is the range resources to support production. The entire production system is apparently heading towards the market domain. This has dramatic social and political consequences, creating new pathways of change. When the production system is marketized in this way, poorer pastoralists may be forced out, pushed towards livelihoods not based on livestock, or towards migration or destitution. Those able to benefit from the monetized system will be few. A more commercialized, elite system, reliant on capital inputs, market relations and business acumen will emerge. This is more akin to western industrial ranching systems; traditional mobile pastoralism, reliant on customary institutions and with only elements monetized, will be increasingly difficult to sustain.

What can be done about this? Pastoral development policy in Ethiopia empha-sizes sedentarization as a way out of poverty. Yet, past experiences of such efforts have often been disasters. Shifts to diversified livelihoods in pastoral areas are cer-tainly important, but diversification is often reliant on a core economic activity based on livestock production to provide demand for products and services. Overall, these policy directions fail to recognize the centrality of mobility for food production in Ethiopia's arid lands. A more commercialized mode of production equally relies on mobility, even if this is complemented by trucking of feed and animals. And, for many, mobile pastoral production is perhaps the only route to improved livelihoods, managing the changing resource patterns, with new institutions to guarantee access, critical for supporting a mobile production strategy while, at the same time, pro-moting social development.

Acknowledgements

This study was financed by Future Agricultures Consortium (FAC) to which I am grateful. I have also used some interview data from a study I had conducted earlier on the subject. I thank Save the Children USA for commissioning that particular study. I am also indebted to my colleagues in the Pastoralism Theme of FAC, informants and field assistants for their time and valuable ideas.

Notes

1 The data is based on observation and interviews conducted with key informants during visits to various reserved sites in Gorodola and Liban districts (Guji Zone), Arero, Yaballo, Dirre, Dillo, Taltalli and Moyale Districts (Borana Zone) in 2010 and 2011.
2 Borbor Bule, interviewed in Dubuluq, 23 February 2010.
3 Ibrahim Ali, interviewed in Moyale, 25 February 2011.

4

PASTORALISTS AND IRRIGATION IN THE HORN OF AFRICA

Time for a rethink?

Stephen Sandford

Too many people, too few livestock

This chapter is a plea for a rethink about the potential of irrigated agriculture to be a valuable alternative or additional livelihood to pastoralism.

For many years the average levels – and the equity of inter-household distribution – of wealth and welfare among pastoralists in the rangelands have been getting worse (Waller, 1999; Desta and Coppock, 2002; McPeak, 2006; Devereux, 2006). This is a consequence of a growing imbalance between the extent, productivity and sustainability of the rangelands, the number of people dependent on them for their livelihood, and the number of livestock needed to support people living from pastoralism. That number is, in turn, determined by the productivity of the land and animals, the proportion of different types of output which are bought and sold, and their relative prices (Dietz *et al.*, 2001; Sandford, 2006; ODI, 2010).

If both the growth of the human population and primary dependence on a pastoral livelihood are to continue, and if mass poverty is to be avoided, the net value of total pastoral output (i.e. animal products) needs to increase. This is unlikely to occur as a result of real price increases of pastoral products (OECD–FAO, 2011) and, despite claims to the contrary, I do not believe that we have the technology available substantially to increase the primary productivity of rainfed rangelands. The burden of the current situation falls principally on the already-poor. They have herds that are too small to sustain them. Consequently, they have to supplement their income in other ways. This leads to the neglect of their herds which shrink yet further as a result (Lybbert *et al.*, 2004).

The decline in the welfare of pastoralists will not be halted or reversed by focusing only, or even principally, on livestock-based pastoral livelihoods.[1] Diversification into other production options – creating alternative livelihood pathways – is essential.

Diversification is happening

Diversification in pastoral areas is already happening fast and affects different social groups in different ways (Fratkin, this book). The poor have been forced to diversify out of pastoralism, but the opportunities for diversification that they have are very poor, offering minimal returns (Devereux, 2006). The returns to rainfed cropping in a pastoral environment are low and uncertain and continuing the switch from pastoralism to cropping will become less and less feasible as climate change worsens conditions. The local opportunities for casual labour and petty trade are limited. Such labour and trade is mostly dependent on demand by pastoralists, financed by sales of their livestock output. But most goods consumed – such as cereal flour, sugar or veterinary medicines – are imported from outside pastoral areas. There is thus limited demand for locally produced goods and services which the growing number of pastoralists attempting to diversify livelihoods could supply. The inevitable result is intense competition and very low remuneration rates. For many higher-return livelihood opportunities, pastoralists, particularly the poor and women, suffer a disadvantage in selection for entry, arising from relatively poor education and linguistic skill. The same is true if they migrate to urban or non-pastoral rural areas (Little et al., 2001; Homewood, 2008; Randall, 2008) where an additional constraint is often ethnic prejudice.

In contrast, as I argue below, opportunities for an (ex-)pastoralist in irrigated agriculture in their own area will be favourable, and the reward relatively attractive. The following sections explain why such an alternative livelihood pathway is possible and desirable, despite the poor track record of past interventions.

Irrigation possibilities

The size of the pastoral population in the Horn of Africa is estimated at between about 12 million (ICRC, 2005, p2) and 22 million people (Morton, 2008, p6), depending on source and on definition. The total estimated amount of irrigable (including already irrigated) land in or immediately adjacent to pastoral areas is 2.2 million hectares. Table 4.1 shows the figures for individual countries. At an estimate of the population near the upper end of the range given above, and at a standard household size of six persons, the irrigable land/pastoral-household ratio (shown in the right hand column of the table) ranges from near zero in Djibouti to 1.25 hectares/household in Ethiopia.[2]

In comparison, the total extent of the area which is already regularly irrigated with the involvement of pastoralists in the Horn of Africa may be about 120,000 hectares of which Somalia accounts for 55 per cent, Ethiopia 28 per cent and Kenya 14 per cent. A typical figure for the amount of irrigated land farmed by households in these pastoralist-related irrigation schemes is 0.25 ha/household.

TABLE 4.1 Irrigable land and the number of pastoralists in the Horn of Africa

Country	Pastoralists (persons in millions)	Extent of irrigable land in pastoral areas ('000 ha.)	Irrigable land (ha.) per pastoral household
Djibouti	0.1	1	0.06
Eritrea	1.7	137	0.48
Ethiopia	8.0	1,673	1.25
Kenya	4.5	173	0.23
Somalia	5.0	240	0.29
Horn of Africa total	19.3	2,224	0.69

Sources: Awulachew *et al.*, 2007 (Table 9); USAID, 2008; FAO Aquastat (Kenya), 2006; FAO Aquastat (Somalia), 2005; FAO Aquastat (Eritrea), 2005; FAO, 1997.

Failures, successes and their causes

Irrigation involving pastoralists is not new. Prior to the colonial era there was already such involvement. Ghebremariam and van Steenbergen (2007) and Gomes (2006) record that, in Eritrea and Somalia respectively, pastoral people have taken part in irrigated agriculture for at least a century. Adams and Anderson (1988) have shown that indigenous irrigation – irrigation designed, implemented, managed and resourced by pastoralists – was often of considerable engineering complexity and involved parts/groups of the Maasai, Samburu, Pokot, Il Chamus and Turkana pastoral people in Tanzania and Kenya. Much of this irrigation appears to have lasted continuously for a century or more; and some for over 500 years. Although the involvement of any one pastoral household in irrigation may have originally been involuntary and intended to be temporary, the persistence of these patches of irrigation without outside subsidy shows that they have been important for the pastoralists concerned.

Interventions by outsiders to irrigation in pastoral society – by government or international organizations, NGOs or commercial companies – over the past 50 years have a chequered history. Some of the failures occurred in cases in which the intended role of pastoralists was to be operators of small irrigated farms. In cases of interventions by commercial companies the pastoralists were not expected to play any significant role in irrigated agriculture, but were seriously affected by the loss of their prime grazing land and/or access to water points for their livestock (e.g. in the Middle Awash area in Ethiopia, see Getachew, 2001, and Behnke and Kerven, this book). In this chapter both kinds of case are referred to as 'pastoralist-related' irrigation. The technical performance of commercial companies was often good, but their impact has been determined, in Somalia and Ethiopia, more by national political developments than by their local performance.

Systematic monitoring and evaluation of many past irrigation schemes has not been done and so the conditions and causes of success or failure have not been rigorously assessed. However, many people have expressed strong opinions on these issues. The most commonly cited causes of failure or extreme difficulty in these outsider-sponsored irrigation schemes in pastoral areas include:

- Technical deficiencies in design and construction of the irrigation works (e.g. in Turkana, Isiolo, and Garissa districts in Kenya; Farah *et al.*, 2001) and/or in the agricultural and organizational skills required for efficient irrigated farming (e.g. in the southern part of the Wabe Shebelle Basin in Ethiopia; Gedi, 2005; SCUK *et al.*, 2002).
- Incompatibility, for those households trying to practise both traditional pastoralism and irrigated farming, in both the overall and seasonal demands for labour of the two livelihoods. The extent of this incompatibility and the potential to resolve it may vary between social, age and gender categories (Little, 1992).
- The tendency of pastoralists to abandon the irrigated plots allocated to them, and to revert to being full-time pastoralists as soon as they have been able to rebuild their herds to the minimum size needed (e.g. Anderson, 1999 for Kenya; and Gomes, 2006 for Somalia). This may be linked to the cultural aversion pastoralists are often believed to have for agricultural work, but may also be due to the higher returns available to capital invested in pastoral livestock compared to the alternatives (McPeak, 2005).
- Unfavourable economics, due to the high initial investment in irrigation structures (e.g. Turkana and Perkerra in Kenya, see Hogg, 1983 and Adams and Anderson, 1988) and/or in the unfavourable price ratios between inputs and outputs due to national or international markets factors, deficiencies in the systems for marketing output, e.g. in Garissa (Farah *et al.*, 2001) and for delivering inputs, e.g. in Turkana (Watson and van Binsbergen, 2008).
- Governments' inability to provide the recurrent expenditure or other working capital (e.g. fuel for pumped irrigation) needed to carry out their self-selected roles (Hogg, 1983). Many schemes reflected donor interest but lacked government support and simply vanished as soon as the funds for the expansion of physical structures were exhausted (Ngigi, 2002a).
- Violent conflict as a result of rival claims on resources or loss of access to resources, for example in the Middle Awash basin in Ethiopia (Abule *et al.*, 2005).
- The spread of human diseases among the pastoralists and labourers involved in the expansion of irrigated agriculture. For examples of this in the Middle Awash Basin in Ethiopia, see Kloos *et al.* 1981; and on the Bura Irrigation Scheme in Kenya, see Scott-Villiers, 2005.

It is frequently claimed that the design and implementation of irrigation schemes in pastoral areas has suffered from inadequate legal protection for the land rights of pastoralists, who run the risk of losing the irrigated land originally available to them, to urban dwellers and other politically favoured interest groups, e.g. in Somalia (Samatar, 2007) or to neighbouring ethnic groups or to other immigrant outsiders, e.g. along the Tana River in Kenya (Umar, 1997). Another major tenure-related risk is of losing access to traditional water supplies and grazing areas which are essential for their continuation as viable pastoralists, e.g. in the Middle Awash Basin (Getachew, 2001). However, as we shall see later, the severity of the problems caused by land tenure depends on the context.

Not all irrigation interventions by outsiders in pastoral areas have been disastrous failures. Some schemes which were established 30 or 40 years ago, and for which 'irreversible decline' (Hogg, 1983) was predicted soon after their opening, are still in use today; for example the Melka Daka scheme amongst the Borana on the lower Waso Nyiro river (National Assembly, 2010).

In recent years there has also been a growth of small-scale, privately-led irrigation activity, some of it community- and subsistence-based, but some of it much more profit-oriented, led by a thriving entrepreneurial class. For example, in the Mandera Triangle, where the boundaries of Ethiopia, Kenya and Somalia meet, there is now a total irrigated area estimated at 22,000 hectares (Nyangaga *et al.*, 2009, p21) which is used by three socio-economic groups: tenants who do most of the actual field work, land-owners who have been successful in getting their title to land accepted and pump-owners who supply the pumps, fuel and technical expertise in pumping. Irrigation in the Mandera Triangle has its problems, however, including land tenure on the Ethiopian side (Gedi, 2005), flooding on the Kenyan side (Mohammed, 2008) and insecurity on the Somali side. But it is a very dynamic area which has shown remarkable growth of pastoralist-related irrigation, much of it privately or self-financed, in the last two decades.

Similarly, small-scale private, pump irrigation along the Wabe Shebelle River in the Somali Region of Ethiopia has also been quite successful (USAID, 2010), although with problems both of flooding and land tenure (Ayele, 2005). The essentially private pump-irrigation systems are not only expanding and diversifying, but are also finding ways of integrating fodder production for surrounding pastoralists into their production system, of developing new governance mechanisms for arbitrating disputes between pastoralists and irrigating farmers and of equitably distributing irrigation water and its costs between holders of land close to and far from water sources.

Despite this record of success of indigenous irrigation and the recent growth in small-scale, privately-led irrigation by (ex-)pastoralists in pastoral areas, the history of past failures of outside interventions has led to a very negative image and created an almost automatic rejection of new proposals for irrigation involving pastoralists by most of those who have had a long-term involvement in pastoral development. Thus Peter Little (2009, p1) comments: 'Pastoral areas are littered with failed development projects, particularly expensive irrigation schemes.' John Markakis (2004) regards small-scale irrigation as part of a massive incursion into the pastoral domain that will inevitably be grabbed by cultivating peasants with ominous implications for the pastoralist economy. IUCN (2011) believes that those who advocate irrigation regard it is as a relatively secure 'panacea' and quotes Richard Hogg approvingly in his statement that 'they have failed disastrously, encouraged further marginalization of already poor pastoralists and increased pressure on areas of vital importance in times of drought'.

Changing prospects for irrigation

But are these negative views, allegedly founded on past experience but based on very few cases, now becoming outdated? As conditions change do we need to update our ideas on the potentials for irrigation for pastoralists? Below I shall examine three of the most commonly cited causes of failure.

First, the early irrigation schemes often suffered acute technical and organizational problems. And there was very little information available to decision-makers at field or higher levels about how to avoid or resolve them. Mistakes were inevitable. By contrast today, the volume of technical and socio-economic knowledge easily available is immense.[3] Access to the results of past experience worldwide is now available to those who wish to use it.

Second, in the past there was a tendency for pastoralists to take up irrigation at times of crisis and then to return to a predominantly pastoral livelihood again when they had built up their herd. This may be due to a cultural aversion to agriculture, to an overall shortage of labour or to a seasonal incompatibility of the labour demands of different alternative livelihoods. The cultural aversion may be less important now than it was. Surveys of Afar men and women show that the attitude to wage labour as an alternative to pastoralism was less negative than it had been (Getachew, 2004, pp61–63).

Third, the competition between pastoral and irrigation activities for the labour of the poorer sections of society in some irrigated areas, now seems to be resolved in favour of irrigation. For example, among irrigated share-cropping tenants in the Mandera Triangle, both on the Ethiopian side of the border (SCUK et al., 2002, p14) and, although less markedly, on the Kenya side (ALRMP, 2001, p7), the dominant opinion expressed in survey interviews of (ex-)pastoralists is that they are better off as irrigating share-croppers than they were as pastoralists, and that they have no intention of returning to pastoralism. In contrast, in Garissa district of Kenya, Farah et al. (2001, p273) found that a majority (62.9 per cent) of the irrigation scheme households had settled to farming in the last five years, showing a very high turnover in the irrigated areas. People moved between irrigation and pastoral production over short time periods, and the demands for labour for irrigated farming led to a less profitable and environmentally benign pastoral system of land use.

The pattern of labour shortage and consequent choice of alternate livelihoods therefore seems to vary widely, but the overall decline in the average size of household herds and the increasing concentration of ownership of livestock has led to an increase in the number of households for whom a pastoral livelihood is no longer an option and their commitment to irrigation more likely.

The economic returns from irrigation

The generally accepted impression of failure associated with past attempts to involve pastoralists in irrigation relates to an assumption that they provided very poor economic returns to the investment, although, in practice, this return has not often been rigorously calculated (Behnke *et al.*, 2007b, p32).

Cost-benefit analysis is the most appropriate tool for calculating such returns. In principle, good cost-benefit analysis includes not only the costs and benefits directly accruing to the beneficiaries of the scheme, but also the other indirect local, national, even global, costs and benefits. In practice it has not been possible to include these indirect effects in the analysis here, as the information needed to do so is simply not available.

The results of a highly simplified cost-benefit analysis of three irrigation schemes are presented below. This approach involved the calculation of the margins between the annual costs and benefits received by 'typical' irrigating smallholder households. The assumption is made that the annual costs and benefits recorded for these smallholders cover all the costs involved, and there are not any additional costs paid by, for example, a government subsidy. These margins are then expressed per ha. and the margin for each year is then discounted (at 5 per cent and 10 per cent) to give a net present value (NPV) at year zero (the year of decision about whether to undertake the scheme or not) (Table 4.2).

Significantly, the costs of the schemes shown in Table 4.2 do not include any opportunity costs of the land put under irrigation or the labour costs of the households involved. If those two factors have no opportunity cost then the NPVs shown represent the maximum economically justifiable value (per ha.) of the initial capital

TABLE 4.2 Benefits and costs of irrigated smallholdings on four pastoralist-related irrigation schemes

	Title and location of scheme		
Output and annual recurrent outputs/costs	*Katilu Turkana, Kenya*	*Kelafo on Wabe Shebelle, Ethiopia*	*Dawa-Ganale Riverine, Ethiopia*
Gross value of annual output/ha (US$)	120	400	1,199
Cost of irrigation (US$)	1	121	66
Other costs excl. labour (US$)	0	14	28
NPV of costs and benefits (excl. capital costs) at 10% discount rate (US$)	852	1,863	7,801
NPV of costs and benefits (excl. capital costs) at 5% discount rate (US$)	1,429	3,140	13,155

Sources: Watson and van Binsbergen (2008); USAID *et al.* (2010); SCUK *et al.* (2002, Appendix 2).

costs of installing the irrigation system. However, if the land brought under irrigation or the family labour used to operate the farms have opportunity costs then that cost, duly discounted, should be deducted from the NPVs, thereby reducing the maximum justifiable capital cost of irrigation.

The declining economic welfare of pastoralists and the very low rewards they get for diversification of livelihoods imply that the opportunity cost of their labour is very low. The opportunity cost of land depends on the use which would be made of it if not developed for irrigation. Calculations made for Ethiopia (Hagos *et al.*, 2009, p22) of the differences in gross margins of rainfed and irrigated agriculture by smallholders on the same piece of land indicate that the values of the NPVs shown in Table 4.2 might be reduced by as much as 50 per cent if the alternative (to irrigation) use for the land is productive rainfed agriculture. If the land used for irrigation is too dry to be used for rainfed agriculture it may nevertheless have an important role as a 'key resource'; as a dry-season feed source or as a source of water for pastoralists' herds. If so, this role should be given a value and a corresponding deduction made in the NPV calculation.

Given these important caveats, NPVs in Table 4.2, representing the maximum justifiable capital costs of pastoralist-related schemes (ranging from US$852/ha. in Turkana to US$7801/ha. on the Dawa-Genale rivers on the Ethiopian side of the Mandera triangle), at a 10 per cent discount rate, can now be compared with the actual capital costs of irrigation. Unfortunately we do not have data on the actual capital costs incurred on these particular schemes but 'typical costs' have been estimated for small-scale schemes in Kenya at 2002 prices and exchange rates (Ngigi, 2002b).[4] They are US$1200/ha. for gravity-fed open canal conveyance and distribution schemes and US$2200/ha. for pump-fed open canal conveyance and distribution schemes.

The actual capital costs of spate irrigation schemes in Ethiopia have been reported (Van Steenbergen *et al.*, 2010, p164) as lying between US$170 and US$350/ha., but the nature of spate-irrigation schemes is that low capital costs are matched by very high annual maintenance costs to repair the damage done by floods. Capital costs of irrigation on large-scale commercial developments in Ethiopia have been estimated as ranging between US$437 and US$7728/ha. (Hagos *et al.*, 2009, p14).

The comparison between the NPVs shown in Table 4.2 and the 'typical' capital costs incurred in Kenya indicates that, with the exception of the example from Turkana, the level of net benefits that can be achieved on pastoralist-related schemes is broadly compatible with the level of capital costs actually incurred in installing the irrigation systems, although there is no great margin to allow for opportunity costs of land and labour which are excluded from the calculations. On this basis, depending on the context, investment in irrigation makes sense.

But the context clearly does matter. Opportunity costs of labour and land have already been mentioned. Land tenure issues are a significant factor in areas where the total amount of irrigated land is large enough to seriously affect access to the river by watering livestock as in the Awash Valley, the Wabe Shebelle River or on the Ethiopian side of the Mandera Triangle. Here, the traditional tenure system is breaking down and different groups are jostling to improve their claims (Ame, 2002; Gedi, 2005). This leads to violent conflict and to a failure to take up the opportunities to improve economic welfare. Land tenure, however, does not seem to have been such a significant factor in determining the success or failure of many of the *small* irrigation schemes in which pastoralists have been involved. Such small (and often private schemes) are able to negotiate ways out of both internal disputes and ones with their neighbours. They are also able to draw and enforce extremely complex and detailed rules to optimize both the efficiency and equity of water use (Ghebremariam, 2006).

Conclusions

The first part of this chapter notes the rapid and serious impoverishment of pastoralists that is taking place in the Horn of Africa arising from population growth and the absence of technology to improve the productivity of rangelands. It stresses the urgent need to find other livelihoods, not dependent on rainfed agriculture or on demand from a stagnant pastoral economy, for those pastoralists whose herds are too small to practise viable mobile pastoralism. This applies to a high proportion of current and recently ex-pastoralists.

The chapter then draws attention to the significant amounts of irrigable land that occur in the pastoral areas of several countries in the Horn, and to the relative success of traditional indigenous and modern privately-led, pastoralist-related irrigation compared to the poor record of interventions by outsiders to pastoral society. In contrast to the large-scale schemes, it is the dynamism of the private sector in the development of small-scale irrigation where much potential is shown, as in along the Wabe Shebelle River, and in the countries on all three sides of the Mandera Triangle. The private sector has been the source of much of the capital investment, especially for the purchase of pumps, and has the incentive to continue to maintain infrastructure and productive systems. An important future challenge is to harness this dynamism of the small-scale private sector to facilitate a transition to a new livelihood pathway based on irrigation. But larger scale schemes should not be rejected outright. Some of the factors which caused the past failures in outsider-promoted schemes have changed for the better. The potential level of economic output on these schemes, where pastoralists are both the irrigating farmers and also play a major role in on-site management and managing relations with pastoral or non-pastoral groups, justifies investment at levels of capital cost which countries in the Horn of Africa can achieve.

The development of successful pastoralist-related irrigation is not easy. However, the scale of the need for pastoralists to diversify is immense; much additional land can be irrigated and many (ex-)pastoralists can be involved. An irrigation scheme in a pastoral area centred on food production can sell much of its output to surrounding pastoralists, thus retaining within the pastoral areas earnings which would otherwise have gone elsewhere. This provides a necessary condition for growth in demand for diversified local activities. The expansion of irrigation will take place in areas where pastoralists form a large part of the population and consequently are not at a comparative disadvantage for jobs and other resources.

All these factors add up to a conclusion that the seemingly automatic aversion to pastoralist-related irrigation should be replaced by a much more positive attitude that recognizes its positive potential.

Notes

1 See the elaboration of this argument at: www.future-agricultures.org/index.php? option=com_content&view=category&layout=blog&id=39&Itemid=534, accessed 29 November 2011. See also supplementary text at: www.future-agricultures.org/toomany people, accessed 11 January 2012.
2 The calculation of these figures includes an estimate by the author of the proportion of the total irrigable area in different river basins that are in or immediately adjacent to pastoral areas. The figures are extremely rough, but they offer an idea of the scope and potential of irrigation in these areas.
3 Examples on the more technical side are: Brouwer *et al.*, 1985; Van Steenbergen *et al.* 2010. On the socio-economic and management side are the Research Reports and Briefs of IWMI (International Water Management Institute, www.iwmi.cgiar.org/) and the irrigation-oriented publications of CAPRI (Collective Action and Property Rights, www.capri.cgiar.org/).
4 These estimates are not based solely on pastoralist-related irrigation, and in practice costs vary substantially. Price levels today will be about twice the 2002 levels due to inflation.

5

COUNTING THE COSTS

Replacing pastoralism with irrigated agriculture in the Awash Valley

Roy Behnke and Carol Kerven

Introduction

The development of hydropower and the availability of irrigated land per capita are lower in sub-Saharan Africa than in any other major region of the world. After several decades of avoiding investment in large infrastructural projects, particularly big dams, international donors are under pressure from African governments to remedy this situation or are themselves looking forward to doing so (You *et al.*, 2010). Accelerated dam development would have an impact directly on pastoral welfare and livestock productivity. With the exception of the Congo, all of Africa's major river flood plains – the Niger, Nile, Zambezi, Senegal, Volta, Okavango and Lake Chad basin – support significant numbers of pastoralists. In East Africa alone, 56 per cent of the Nile Basin is used by pastoralists (Amede *et al.*, 2011), and smaller river systems used by pastoralists include the Tana, Omo, Jubba-Shebelle and Awash. Few other systems of land use can survive in the empty expanses of rangeland that pastoralists can profitably exploit, but it is also clear that African pastoralists rely upon access to valuable riverine areas, and new dam building will intensify competition for these key resources (Scudder, 1991).

Key resources – often relatively small but extremely productive areas that serve as drought and dry-season refuges for pastoral herds – are the assets that allow mobile pastoralists to exploit vast, erratically productive rangeland areas (Oba, this book). The economic performance of pastoralism, its capacity to support human populations and to ride out droughts, depends on continued access to these key assets, especially river valley lands. Across Africa and Asia, many pastoralists lack secure land rights, and the loss of pastoral access to small pockets of highly productive land and the alienation of this land to other uses is a widespread occurrence (Behnke, 2008), with the rate of loss currently being accelerated by so-called 'land grabs' in pastoral areas (Galaty, this book). These changes are frequently justified *a priori* by unrealistic projections of the increased income that will be generated by irrigated agriculture, or by simply ignoring the opportunity costs of excluding pastoral users (Adams, 1992; cf. Sandford, this book).

Because it has been used so intensively for so long, the Awash valley in north-eastern Ethiopia provides a realistic yardstick for evaluating the benefits and liabilities of irrigated agriculture. The valley contains only 4 to 5 per cent of all the land area that is suitable for irrigation in Ethiopia (Awulachew *et al.*, 2007). But over a third of all Awash valley irrigable land is already irrigated, which amounts to just about half of all the land that is presently under irrigation in Ethiopia (48,311 irrigated hectares out of a national total of 107,265 hectares) (Awulachew *et al.*, 2007). Some of this land has also been under irrigation for four or five decades and long-term effects are now apparent.

Until the 1960s, Afar pastoralists retained unimpeded access to the Awash River valley as a source of grazing for their livestock. Their herds congregated in the valley in the dry season or during droughts and spread out onto the surrounding plains when it rained. This oscillation provided the herds with access to two feed sources – abundant riparian grazing supported by the flooding of the Awash river, and sparse but extensive grazing dependent on local rainfall. Rainfall in Afar is low and highly variable from year to year (Cheung *et al.*, 2008). Floodplain grazing supported by river water drawn from more reliable highland sources was essential for stabilizing the system and preserving life whenever the local rains failed.

By the early 1970s pastoralists along the Awash were rapidly losing their riverine grazing due to upstream hydroelectric projects that regulated river flow and to land concessions granted by the then Imperial Ethiopian government to international agricultural companies for the development of irrigated cotton and sugar plantations (Kloos 1982; Gamaledin, 1993). Much of the riparian forests that once supported traditional Afar pastoralism have been bulldozed under and replaced by irrigated or abandoned fields. It is difficult to conceive of these areas – many of them now damaged by soil salinity and bush encroachment – ever returning to natural vegetation and pastoral use. For the Awash valley there probably is no turning back. An evaluation of agricultural development in the Awash is nonetheless important because the Awash exemplifies general development trends in Ethiopia (Kloos and Legesse, 2010), and more broadly across semi-arid Africa (Adams, 1992). Unlike any other part of Ethiopia, the Awash valley illustrates what lies in store for pastoral areas if African governments pursue a policy of modernizing agriculture by displacing mobile livestock production in favour of irrigated crop agriculture.[1]

Clearing the river floodplain for plantations

The object of this study is to compare the economic returns derived from devoting the Awash valley to pastoralism as opposed to irrigated cotton or sugar cultivation. Our unit of comparison is a hypothetical hectare of riverine floodplain left to pastoralism as opposed to the observed returns per hectare from various forms of cotton and sugar cultivation in the Awash valley.

The following analysis will show with reasonable certainty that pastoralism is either economically comparable or more advantageous than either cotton or sugar cane cultivation. While a well-run private cotton farm can achieve rough productive parity with pastoralism, state cotton farms lost money for decades. Current development programmes suggest that the Ethiopian government is aware of this situation. For some time it has been either turning the operation of its cotton holdings over to private interests – the Afar clans or investors – or transforming old government cotton farms into sugar plantations. The state's sugar estates are more profitable than its old cotton estates, but whether farming sugar cane is more profitable than livestock production is doubtful. Pastoralists in Afar are nonetheless currently losing additional land to expanding state-owned sugar plantations. Later sections of this paper clarify the economic returns and losses in this conversion.

The research study area roughly corresponds to the middle Awash (Figure 5.1), a stretch of river between the towns of Awash and Gewani, an area traditionally inhabited by the Afar people and now part of Afar Region within the Ethiopian federal administrative system.[2]

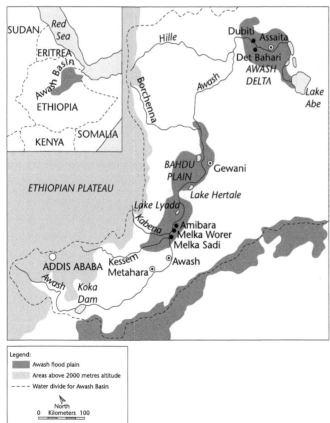

Legend:
- Awash flood plain
- Areas above 2000 metres altitude
- – – – Water divide for Awash Basin

North
0   Kilometers 100

Redrawn from Kloos 1982, Kloos et al. 1981

FIGURE 5.1 The Awash Basin.

Livestock production

The first step in this analysis is to estimate the returns to pastoralism from the seasonal use of a hypothetical average hectare of Awash valley grazing land. To do this we build a model of Afar herd performance based on a body of field research stretching back over the last four decades.[3]

Prior to the transformation of the valley by irrigated agriculture, most Afar pastoral herds spent only a portion of their year grazing on floodplain vegetation (Cossins, 1983). For the purposes of this calculation, we have assumed that herds spend six months of the year feeding on floodplain grazing, with the rest of the year spent on rain-fed pastures outside the river valley. No attempt has been made in this analysis to describe where herds go or how much rangeland they use when they leave the valley. It is instead assumed that herds without seasonal access to valley grazing simply cannot survive, and that the loss of valley grazing entails the loss of a herd's entire, year-round output. In short, we have assumed that herds depend on valley pastures for their existence, and that the opportunity cost of denying access to valley pastures is the loss of all their productivity.

Based on the characteristic Afar herd composition and the feed requirements of each species, we can calculate the species mix, the number of animals and the average number of breeding females that will be supported by a single hectare of valley grazing for six months at high and low stocking rates. This calculation is summarized in Table 5.1.

Including both the imputed value of home consumed products and income from sales, the estimated gross value of livestock production per hectare at 2008–09 prices for two stocking densities is presented in Table 5.2.

TABLE 5.1 Head of stock and breeding females supported per hectare of valley grazing alternate stocking rates

Herd species	Scenario (a) low stocking rate			Scenario (b) high stocking rate		
	TLU/ha.[1]	Head/ ha.[3]	Breeding females/ha.[4]	TLU/ha.[1]	Head/ha.[3]	Breeding females/ha.[4]
Cattle	1.252	1.75	0.81	2.504	3.51	1.61
Camels	0.786	0.786	0.36	1.572	1.57	0.72
Sheep	0.252	2.52	1.08	0.504	5.04	2.17
Goats	0.337	3.37	1.45	0.674	6.74	2.90
TLU	2.63[2]			5.25[5]		

Sources:
1   Getachew (2001) for herd species composition.
2   MAS (1991) for feed estimate and Jahnke (1982) for feed requirements.
3   One Tropical Livestock Unit (TLU) equals 1 camel, 1.4 cattle or 10 sheep or goats, Jahnke (1982).
4   Estimates of breeding component from Davies (2004).
5   Cossins (1983) for feed estimate and Jahnke (1982) for feed requirements.

TABLE 5.2 Gross value in 2009 of live animal, meat and milk for human consumption, EB per hectare per annum at two stocking densities

Herd species	Output EB per breeding female	Scenario (a) low stocking rate		Scenario (b) high stocking rate	
		Breeding females/ha.	Gross value EB/ha.	Breeding female/ha.	Gross value EB/ha.
Cattle	2,651	0.81	2,147	1.61	4,268
Camels	6,551	0.36	2,358	0.72	4,717
Sheep	651	1.08	703	2.17	1,413
Goats	758	1.45	1,099	2.90	2,198
Total			6,307		12,596

Source: Behnke and Kerven (2011)

By far the most important cash cost of herding is the provision of security, which requires the purchase of an automatic weapon. The other cash costs of livestock husbandry – the purchase of stock water, health care or feed supplementation or the expense of transporting animals and their products to markets – are low. Table 5.3 summarizes herding costs exclusive of weaponry and security provision, which varies markedly as 'front line' communities facing hostile non-Afar neighbours bear the brunt of protecting Afar territory (Rettberg, 2010; Unruh, 2005).

TABLE 5.3 Husbandry costs in 2009 exclusive of weaponry and security provision at two stocking rates in EB

Herd species	Total costs per head	Scenario (a)		Scenario (b)	
		Head per ha. (a)	Costs per ha. (a)	Head per ha. (b)	Costs per ha. (b)
Cattle	82.9	1.75	145	3.51	291
Camels	107.7	0.786	85	1.57	169
Sheep	18.1	2.52	46	5.04	91
Goats	18.1	3.37	61	6.74	122
Total			337		673

Source: Behnke and Kerven (2011)

Deducting the costs of production (Table 5.3) from gross output (Table 5.2), the annual net returns to Afar pastoralism per hectare are slightly less than 6,000 Ethiopian birr (EB) (about US$543[4]) at the lower range of potential riverine stocking densities, and slightly less than 12,000 birr (about US$1084) at the upper range of potential stocking densities (Table 5.4).

TABLE 5.4 Net returns in 2009 to one hectare of riverine land under seasonal pastoral land use in EB

Scenarios	Value of gross output	Husbandry costs	Net returns
Low stocking rate (a)	6,307	337	5,970
High stocking rate (b)	12,596	673	11,923

Source: Behnke and Kerven (2011)

In sum, at 2009 prices, 6,000–12,000 birr is the opportunity cost per year of excluding pastoralism from a hectare of Awash valley grazing, i.e., the economic contribution of pastoralism that is forgone with the conversion of a hectare of valley grazing to another land use. The following sections of this analysis examine the ability of cotton and sugar farming to compensate the national economy for this loss in livestock output.

Cotton cultivation and processing

Cotton cultivation produces a raw agricultural commodity – unginned seed cotton – that is then processed into lint cotton and seeds. Seed cotton is comparable to the live animals and milk production used in this analysis to calculate the returns to pastoralism – all are lightly processed agricultural commodities that producers might sell onward for further processing.

Table 5.5 shows the returns to seed cotton farming on the Middle Awash Agricultural Development Enterprise (MAADE), a large, irrigated state-owned cotton farm in Amibara District. The farm was set up in 1969, nationalized when the Derg came to power in the mid-1970s, and expanded to over 13,000 ha. in the mid-1980s following high levels of government investment (Said, 1992; Nicol, 2000; Getachew, 2001). Table 5.5 summarizes the performance of the farm in the 1980s, when it reached its greatest size and was strongly supported by government.

Despite respectable yields of 2,615kg/ha. on average between 1980 and 1990, the farm was unprofitable in this decade, losing money seven out of the 11 years covered in Table 5.5. Including operating and administrative expenses, interest, and corporate overheads, average annual losses per hectare from 1980–90 were EB - 2,412 or the equivalent of a loss of US$ -1,165/ha. at 1990 exchange rates. The farm was also losing annually between 200 and 300 ha. of cultivated area to salinity, a cost that is not reflected in these figures since reclamation was not taking place. According to estimated reclamation costs at that time, about half of the gross revenue of the farm would have been spent on land reclamation in order to maintain a stable farm size – around EB7600/ha. at 1985 prices (Said, 1992).

By 2009 MAADE had shrunk in size, had ceased to be a state farm and was instead leased to a private investor. This smaller, privatized farm slipped in and out of profitability in the period between 2004 and 2009, with yields averaging 2,159kg/ha. and average profits of EB1,349 (about US$135) per hectare (Table 5.6).

TABLE 5.5 MAADE yields, operating expenses and revenue from seed cotton, 1980–90

Year	Area (ha.)	Yield, 100 kg/ha.	Production costs, EB/ha.	Gross revenue, EB/ha.	Profit or loss, EB/ha.
1980	6,337	31.7	4,267.9	4,021.0	−247
1981	7,940	29.4	4,255.7	3,730.0	−526
1982	9,268	24.9	3,554.6	3,158.0	−397
1983	11,169	24.6	2,898.0	3,124.0	226
1984	13,000	32	3,476.2	4,060.0	584
1985	12,470	32.8	3,499.3	4,170.0	671
1986	12,998	32.4	3,541.2	4,118.0	577
1987	12,998	26.6	3,547.1	3,380.0	−167
1988	12,058	23.7	3,736.0	3,012.0	−724
1989	12,696	21.8	3,843.1	2,774.0	−1069
1990	12,318	17.7	3,526.0	2,250.0	−1276
Average	–	26.15	3,650.0	3,402.0	−248

Source: Said, 1992, appendix 5 and tables 6.4 and 5.3

TABLE 5.6 MAADE yields, costs and revenue from cotton production and processing, 2004–09

Year	Area (ha.)	Yield, 100 kg/ha.	Production costs, EB/ha. for seed cotton	Gross revenue, EB/ha. from seed cotton	Profit or loss, EB/ha. seed cotton	Profit or loss, EB/ha. lint cotton
2004–05	6,569	16.40	5,348	4,920	−428	−941
2005–06	6,569	19.57	5,868	5,382	−540	−1,745
2006–07	6,515	24.88	6,037	6,966	929	4,240
2007–08	6,448	19.95	5,283	8,977	3,694	5,555
2008–09	6,368	27.16	8,318	11,407	3,089	

Source: Unpublished MAADE records, 2004–09

This modest improvement in economic performance was achieved despite the lower yields that were the consequence of long-term underinvestment in farm and irrigation infrastructure. Land was still being lost to salinity and overall soil fertility was probably declining, irrigation canals and equipment were under-maintained and ground water levels were elevated, no land reclamation was taking place and in some years no fertilizer was used, and for decades fields had not been re-leveled to promote efficient irrigation (MAADE, 1997/2005; also unpublished estate records and interviews with farm management, March and November 2009). In short, after about 40 years of cultivation, the MAADE farm was showing its age. Even with conscientious management, at this point the farm appeared to be incapable of internally generating income sufficient to cover its own rehabilitation, and any stable improvement in farm performance was dependent on an infusion of fresh capital.

Our final case study comes from Gewane District where abandoned and bush encroached cotton fields were handed back to their original Afar clan owners. Instead of contracting the management of their land to outside investors, one clan formed a cooperative and farmed the land itself. By early 2009 the cooperative farm had been in operation for five complete cropping cycles, growing annually from 16 to 27, 42, 64 and 70 hectares, with further expansion planned for subsequent years. In 2009, both yields (4290kg/ha.) and net income per hectare (EB6,774 or about US$616 per hectare) were roughly double those achieved by MAADE even in good years. Seed cotton production was therefore profitable, but the profits from cotton farming were nothing compared to the exceptionally high profitability of exporting ginned lint cotton, which yielded a profit of about US$2,800 per hectare and was the cooperative's sales strategy in 2009.

These are exemplary results; indeed we are almost certainly looking at the financial returns to one of the best-run cotton farms in Afar Region. Like the other private 'investor' cotton operations in this region, however, the cooperative is indirectly subsidized by government expenditure, paying nothing for the main-tenance of irrigation infrastructure, for water or for the initial costs of land develop-ment. A comprehensive assessment of the economic performance of the cooperative would need to take account of these largely hidden costs.

The preceding case studies underline the economic variability inherent in cotton farming, depending on factors such as management skill, the age of the farm, and the overhead costs that the farming operation must support. MAADE has spent the better part of four decades either losing money or barely breaking even. In contrast, with good management, newly opened fields and low overheads, private farms like the Gewane cooperative can at least match the lower estimates of the returns per hectare to pastoralism. This assessment is based on a like-for-like comparison of relatively unprocessed agricultural and pastoral output – unginned cotton versus live animals, milk and home-preserved milk products. The real profitability of cotton farming arises not from farming itself but from the value added by industrial processing and export – the transformation of raw cotton into lint cotton that can be sold on high-priced international markets. As the next section will show, much the same results emerge from an analysis of sugar cane cultivation.

Sugar cane cultivation and refining

Located on the Awash River near Lake Beseka, the Metahara Sugar Factory began producing sugar in the 1960s under the management of a Dutch firm Handels Vereniging Amsterdam (HVA), was nationalized under the Derg and has remained a wholly state-owned operation (Nicol, 2000). Two other large sugar estates are located elsewhere in Oromiya Region, and two additional factories are currently under construction in Afar Region, all under government ownership (Girma and Awulachew, 2007; Awulachew *et al.*, 2007; interviews with Metahara managers and Ministry of Water Affairs, Metahara and Awash, November 2009).

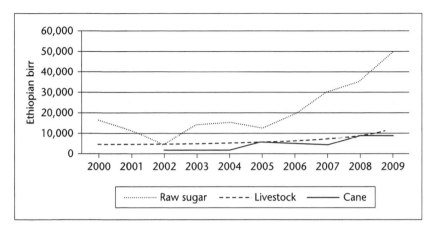

FIGURE 5.2 Revenue per hectare – cane cultivation, livestock production and sugar processing (source: Behnke and Kerven, 2011)

Like cotton, sugar production begins with a raw agricultural commodity – sugar cane – that is comparable to the live animals and dairy produce sold by pastoralists. The first stages of processing turn cane into three intermediate products – raw sugar, molasses and bagasse (cane residue after pressing). Using cane grown on its own fields, an on-site factory at Metahara produces these three products which are then sold.

Estimated returns from cane cultivation and the actual returns from the processing and selling of raw sugar and molasses at the Metahara factory over the last ten years show average cane yields of 162 tons/ha., mean net revenue from cane cultivation of EB4,874/ha. (about US$500 in 2009) and mean net revenue from raw sugar and molasses of EB20,976/ha. (US$2,100).[5] Figure 5.2 (above) graphically illustrates the relative profitability of livestock-keeping relative to cane cultivation and the processing of raw sugar. Cane cultivation was roughly as profitable as livestock in two years and less profitable in six out of the eight years in which this comparison is possible. As with cotton farming and processing, the real profits were to be made not from cultivating cane but in adding value by refining it and marketing raw sugar.

Livestock, cotton or sugar?

In the decade from 2000 to 2009, Figure 5.3 summarizes the relative returns per hectare from livestock and plantation agriculture in the Awash floodplain. As long as the comparison is with large-scale farms, livestock is consistently more profitable than cotton farming and routinely more profitable than sugar cane cultivation. The situation is more complex if we extend our comparison to include the performance of the state cotton farm in the 1980s or the Afar cooperative farm in 2009. Compared to the historical performance of state cotton plantations, pastoralism is unequivocally the more productive use of the valuable floodplains and river water of the Awash and its tributaries. At least up to the mid-1990s, state-owned cotton

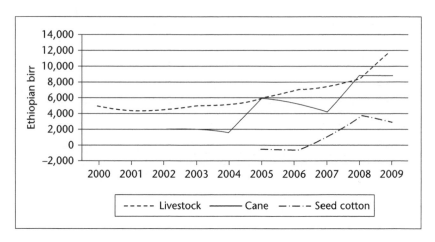

FIGURE 5.3 Revenue per hectare – alternative uses of the Awash floodplain (source: Behnke and Kerven, 2011)

plantations in the middle Awash have provided a clear example of dysfunctional development – a country investing in making itself poorer. The situation is more equivocal when pastoralism is compared to private cotton cultivation on the Afar cooperative farm, which can give net returns that are roughly equivalent to those of pastoralism. There would, therefore, appear to be approximate productive parity between pastoralism and well-managed private cotton farming. This implies that the opportunity costs of excluding pastoralism from sections of the Awash valley are roughly comparable to the revenues generated by the cotton farming that might replace it. The promotion of cotton farming has radically changed the ecology, the agricultural production systems and the ethnic background of the people that exploit the valley, but despite years of investment, there is little evidence that it has significantly improved agricultural income per unit area.

Sugar cane presents a better argument for irrigated agriculture than cotton, but there are reasons to be cautious about using Metahara as justification for expanding sugar production. One of the principal reasons for Metahara's success is its favourable location on a broad, alluvial plain with rich volcanic soils high in the course of the Awash River where water supplies are reliable. As a consequence, a very low proportion of Metahara's fixed assets – only 16 per cent – is tied up in investment in irrigation infrastructure (Metahara Sugar Factory, 2008). To put this into perspective, more of the estate's capital is invested in buildings and office furniture than in irrigation infrastructure.

The estate's favourable circumstances also hold down the cost of bringing new land into production. Using 2008–09 development costs and sales figures, the investments needed to bring a new hectare of unirrigated land into cultivation at Metahara could be paid off with the profits of 1.6 years of raw cane and molasses sales from that land – a remarkably rapid return on a long-term agricultural investment (unpublished records, Metahara). But these figures refer to incremental additions to the existing plantation, not a major expansion onto a new site. Such a major expansion is underway adjacent to Metahara using the water of Awash tributaries, and the economics of this project look very different from those of Metahara itself. When this new land has been brought into full production (a process that will take some years), it is likely to require more than a decade of raw sugar and molasses sales to simply recoup the initial capital investment, irrespective of additional financing, operating or overhead costs. Metahara sits on an extraordinarily favourable site, maybe the best in the Awash valley, and produces probably some of the most profitable sugar in Ethiopia. It therefore provides little indication of the likely returns from future sugar cultivation at less favourable sites elsewhere along the Awash or on other Ethiopian river systems.

Stability, risk and water scarcity

In an unpredictable natural environment, the reliability of a production system may be as important as its profitability. Stability of income may therefore provide a second yardstick against which we can judge the suitability of alternative agricultural production systems for the Awash valley.

The Ethiopian government views the agricultural development of the Awash as a means of both increasing and stabilizing incomes to reduce dependency on food relief. The government officials responsible for promoting the development pro-gramme assert that mobile pastoralism was an economically appropriate use of the valley 30 or 40 years ago, but that falling rainfall levels and recurrent droughts now make it necessary to abandon pastoral mobility for settled livestock and crop farming.[6] The accuracy of this narrative is open to doubt.

With respect to rainfall, a recent study of 13 Ethiopian watersheds found no strongly significant changes in annual rainfall levels for individual watersheds, including the Awash, or for Ethiopia as a whole between 1960 and 2002 (Cheung et al., 2008). The problems of pastoralism in the Awash cannot, it would seem, be attributed to documented changes in rainfall levels or to an increase in the meteoro-logical incidence of drought. There is, on the other hand, a broad scientific con-sensus that drought and famine in Afar are exacerbated by government-sponsored development programmes that have deprived pastoral communities of access to the key riverine resources that they need in order to adapt to variable rainfall levels (Gamaledin, 1993; Desta, 1996; Gebre and Kassa, 2009).

Finally, there is little evidence that the agricultural systems that have displaced pastoralism – huge, integrated plantations and processing complexes – have actually increased the stability of agricultural performance in the valley. The current performance of the privatized MAADE farming and processing complex illustrates the risks. Between 2004 and 2009 the processing of lint cotton both increased profits in good years and magnified the financial losses to the farm in bad years, as compared to raw seed cotton cultivation (Table 5.6). The economic performance of the Metahara Sugar Factory between 1999 and 2009 replicates this pattern. Using international producer prices for sugar cane to estimate the net revenue from cane cultivation at Metahara, we can compare the annual variability in revenue derived from cane to that from raw sugar and molasses. The coefficient of variation (CV, a measure of variability), for annual sugar and molasses income was nearly six times higher than that for the imputed income from unrefined cane – 65 per cent for sugar and molasses versus 11 per cent for cane. Apparently, refining adds considerable value to raw cane in good years, but the high fixed costs of maintaining a factory are a risk in poor years when the factory works at reduced capacity. Like cotton ginning, sugar refining may be more profitable than farming alone, but it would also appear to be more risky, and vertical integration may exacerbate income instability.

Distinctive environmental problems are associated with each of the production systems reviewed here, but quantification of the economic costs of these environmental hazards is beyond the scope of this analysis. Water scarcity issues that are just now emerging in the Awash valley also alter fundamentally the framework for evaluating alternative land use systems. As a result of increased levels of water extraction following the completion of the Kesem extension to Metahara and the rehabilitated Tendahu plantation near Logia in Afar Region (downstream from the study area), the availability of water across the Awash drainage system as a whole is becoming an issue. Up to this point we have compared different systems according to how efficiently they utilize scarce river bottom land. The emergence of water scarcity suggests the need to look at water use efficiency as well as land use efficiency in calculating the dis/advantages of alternative agricultural systems (Adams, 1992). Calibrating returns in terms of cubic metres of water rather than hectares of irrigated land would reduce the apparent advantages of water-demanding agricultural production systems and emphasize the advantages of natural grazing which uses less water, adds few chemical pollutants to it and leaves the remainder available for other purposes.

Conclusions

Throughout the 1960s and 1970s there was a blueprint for African range and livestock development projects: the ranching model. Improved levels of livestock production were one of the many benefits that ranching projects promised to deliver, and at first this claim seemed so self-evidently true that no one critically examined it. When researchers did compare ranch and pastoral productivity in the early 1980s, their studies revealed that, contrary to expectations, pastoralism was the more productive of the two systems (Oba, this book).

Like the older work on ranch and pastoral productivity, the results of the present study could not have been foreseen. That an indigenous African pastoral production system would produce returns per hectare equal to or greater than those from state-subsidized irrigated cotton and sugar farming runs counter to reasonable expectations. Whether these results are anomalous or indicative of a broader trend remains unclear and will only become apparent when additional comparative work is available.

Until then, the one conclusion that does emerge unequivocally from this analysis is the remarkable continuity of Ethiopian irrigation policy for the Awash valley, across half a century and despite radical changes in political regimes. What is now Afar Region was formally annexed by the Abyssinian Empire late in the nineteenth century but retained a degree of independence until the middle of the twentieth century (Harbeson, 1978). Irrigation schemes along the Awash were part of the incorporation process, a way for the central government to control resources by putting immigrant Ethiopian highlanders on those resources and by reengineering the environment to provide labouring jobs that accommodated their farming backgrounds – cutting cane and picking cotton.

Plantation agriculture has been a consistent feature of the incorporation process. In the Imperial period the concessions went to UK, Dutch, Israeli and Italian firms. The Derg government nationalized the plantations and turned them into state farms (Nicol, 2000). Borrowing from each of its predecessors, the present Ethiopian People's Revolutionary Democratic Front (EPRDF) government is both expanding its sugar estates – at Wonja, Metahara, and Tendaho – and contemplating the leasing of thousands of hectares of concessions in Afar Region to Egyptian, Saudi, Turkish and Israeli commercial interests.[7]

The advantages of this policy for government are illustrated by the finances of the Metahara Sugar Factory in 2007–08, a year in which we have complete annual accounts (Metahara Sugar Factory, 2008). In that year the government, which was the combined estate owner and taxing authority, used a variety of different account- ing devices – excise tax, Sugar Development Fund, State Dividend, Industrial Development Fund – to claim for itself 65 per cent of the sales turnover of the Factory, about 541 million birr or the equivalent of US$58 million at the then exchange rate (Metahara Sugar Factory, 2008). Whatever else it does, Metahara makes a lot of money for government. Despite their importance to the Ethiopian national economy, pastoralists almost certainly do not match; and would not want to match, this level of contribution to the state treasury. Indeed, the recurrent complaint by the authorities against the informal cross-border trade in livestock is that this trade escapes taxation, despite its obvious contribution to the wealth and welfare of Ethiopians (Catley and Aklilu, this book).

Plantation agriculture may or may not be good for the Ethiopian environment and economy, but it has been good for the government. It has transformed a fiscally sterile grazing environment into a fiscally productive agricultural one, and displaced independent pastoral producers with tractable taxpayers. James Scott has drawn a distinction between gross domestic product and what he has termed state-accessible product. It was, he has argued, not the size of the total economy but the size of that portion of the economy that the authorities could appropriate, that animated pre- modern state behaviour in Asia (Scott, 2009). Scott's observation may also explain the great attraction of vertically integrated plantations and processing facilities for Ethiopian governments irrespective of their different ideological backgrounds. The real advantage of plantation agriculture may not be its purported efficiency, productivity or contribution to the national economy. Its greatest virtue may be that it makes money that is accessible to government. Don Donham has argued that the modern Ethiopian state survives largely through the exploitation of its margins, the 'subsidy of the core by the periphery' (1986, p24, quoted in Pankhurst and Johnson 1988). The lopsided contest between development pathways based on pastoralism and plantation agriculture in the Awash conforms to this pattern.

Acknowledgements

Many people and organizations generously supported this study. The International Institute for Environment and Development (IIED) funded the initial field research and Ced Hesse of IIED has provided consistent encouragement as our results slowly emerged. The Feinstein International Center of Tufts University supplied logistical support and funded fieldwork by Gezu Bekele, who investigated sugar production and prices at the Wonji-Shoa Sugar Estate and contributed the information on those topics used in this analysis. Research on sugar production was funded in part by the UK Department for International Development (DFID), and supported by the Ethiopian Development Research Institute (EDRI). Herrie Hamedu Ali and Kassa Negussie Getachew introduced us to Afar Region and Mohamodu Duwod and Mohammed Awel served ably as translators and field assistants. Mintewab Bezabih, Steve Mandel, John McPeak, Essam Mohammed, Ian Scoones and Peter Little all commented on various drafts of this paper. Finally, we wish to thank numerous staff at the Metahara and MAADE estates and the Afar pastoralists and farmers whom we interviewed for their open and helpful responses to our questions. The content of this paper represents the views of the authors, and does not necessarily represent those of our funding or implementing partners. We are solely responsible for any errors this paper may contain.

Notes

1 Although Sandford (this book) offers a more positive scenario, especially for small-scale private-led irrigation development in pastoral areas.
2 Fieldwork on cotton farming and livestock production was carried out in 2009 and 2010 in three districts of Afar Region – Awash Fantale, Amibara and Gewani. Data on sugar cane cultivation was collected from the Metahara Sugar Factory which is located in Metahara District on the Oromiya-Afar regional border. The current Metahara sugar estate is located in Oromiya Region; the Kesem extension to the estate is located in Awash Fantale District of Afar Region.
3 For details of this model, and its results, see the longer version of that paper at www.future-agricultures.org/index.php?option=com_docman&task=search_result&Itemid=965 (Behnke and Kerven, 2011), accessed 5 December 2011.
4 Using an approximate average exchange rate for 2008–09 of EB11 = $1.00.
5 Source: Based on unpublished data from the Metahara Sugar Factory and Wonji-Shoa Sugar Estate.
6 Kesem-Tendahu Integrated Development Project, interview with staff, Awash town, November 2009.
7 Interview with Ministry of Water Resources staff, Awash town, November 2009.

6

CLIMATE CHANGE IN SUB-SAHARAN AFRICA

What consequences for pastoralism?

Polly Ericksen, Jan de Leeuw, Philip Thornton, Mohammed Said, Mario Herrero and An Notenbaert

Introduction

Managing climate variability and climate risk is not new to pastoralism. Both traditional nomadic or mobile pastoralism and mixed or agro-pastoral systems have been highly effective responses to cycles of drought, floods and 'normal' rainfall years, most often in areas that do not receive more than 600mm rainfall annually and more often make do with 200–300mm (Ellis and Swift, 1988; Ellis and Galvin, 1994; Scoones, 1995b; Oba, this book). Pastoral herders balance herd size, species and breed composition, grazing patterns, as well as other livelihood options, with an eye to managing climatic risk, even if other risks such as social, economic or conflict are more immediate (Coppolillo, 2000; Vetter, 2005; Homewood, 2008). Decisions to crop in wet years or areas are also in part influenced by climate variability. The consequences and implications of twenty-first century global warming and the resulting changes in climatic patterns that will occur are therefore of paramount importance to the future pathways of pastoral livelihoods, production systems and landscapes. Choices made now will have implications for the coming decades, as climate change unfolds and pastoral communities continue to transform, adapt and innovate.

In important respects, pastoral peoples are at the forefront of responses to climate change, given their experience managing high climate variability over the centuries. Insights from pastoral systems are critical for generating wider lessons for climate adaptation responses (Scoones, 2004; Davies and Nori, 2008). This chapter explores the current state of research knowledge about climate change and its consequences in pastoral areas of East Africa. Gaps and uncertainties in knowledge are very apparent. The key question is how to make choices today given uncertainties of the future.

We first review traditional and current pastoral climate risk management strategies in a changing economic and political context. Second, we present downscaled climate projections to 2050, describing several different types of impact thresholds. The interpretation of, as well as the uncertainties in, these projections are explained. Third, we present evidence on how climate change might affect pastoral systems through changes in vegetation, frequency of drought and livelihood transitions in marginal cropping areas.

How do pastoralists manage climate risk?

Climate risk in pastoral landscapes is a product of low precipitation that is highly temporally and spatially variable. Water is always an underlying scarce resource, since rainfall varies between years, with variability increasing with aridity (Homewood, 2008). Hence, the more arid a pastoral environment, the less predictable the rainfall (Le Houérou, 1989). Additionally, in most of East Africa (including the pastoral lowlands) rainfall is bimodal, with the short rains from October to December and the long rains from March to May, due to movement of the inter-tropical convergence zone (ITCZ). Further north, over much of Ethiopia, Sudan and Eritrea, at the most northerly limit of the ITCZ annual cycle, there is a unimodal annual precipitation cycle with the primary rainy season falling during June to September (Giannini *et al.*, 2008). Additionally, over much of Ethiopia there are preceding rains from March followed by a pause before the main rains begin (Verdin *et al.*, 2005). In the bimodal areas, the short rains exhibit more interannual variability than the long rains (Mutai and Ward, 2000), with the El Niño Southern Oscillation (ENSO) having more influence on the former. The underlying process is that variability in rainfall between years is related to temperatures of the southern oceans, with a series of drier and wetter years associated with the ENSO cycle. In much of East Africa, El Niño (warmer southern oceans) brings more precipitation during the short rains, but less during the long rains (Mutai and Ward, 2000; McHugh, 2006), while La Niña events (cooler ocean temperatures) bring less precipitation during the short rains. Additionally, Indian Ocean temperature anomalies also influence precipitation patterns and thus dry and wet years can also occur in the absence of an ENSO event (Mutai and Ward, 2000). Overall, the ENSO cycle is more influential on the short rains in East Africa.

Rainfall in pastoral areas is a primary driver of vegetation in variable arid and semi-arid climates, and hence vegetation growth closely follows rainfall amount, frequency and duration (Vetter, 2005; Ellis and Galvin, 1994). The primary production of rangelands is variable in time and space, primarily in response to water available for transpiration and plant production (Vetter, 2005; Oba *et al.*, 2000a; see Oba, this book). Normalized Difference Vegetation Index (NDVI) is a remotely sensed index that indicates how green the biomass in a landscape is. It is highly correlated with rainfall in arid and semi-arid areas and, as there is a 30 year record of it with full spatial coverage, it is a better tool for analysing the impacts of climate variability on rangeland vegetation than precipitation data in locations with few rain stations. Investigation of a 28 year time series of NDVI data (Figure 6.1) for Kajiado district in southern Kenya, for example, reveals that droughts (e.g. 1984, 1995, 2000,

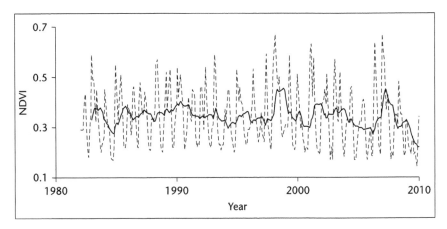

FIGURE 6.1 Variation of monthly (dashed line) and 12 month running average (solid line) of NDVI for Kajiado district from 1982 to end of 2009 (source: Zwaagstra *et al.*, 2010).

2005–06) occur at irregular intervals, with periods with above normal NDVI associated with El Niño years (for example 1998, 2006).

The relation between above ground biomass and rainfall is about 8 kg.ha⁻¹ for every mm of rainfall above 20mm in East Africa (Deshmukh, 1984, p181). Availability of forage and shortages (whether from drought or constrained access or change in palatability, as well as differences in soils) are the primary drivers of variability in livestock production in pastoral areas, and most rangelands include a mix of vegetation types and productivity.

In severe or prolonged droughts, forage and water scarcity combine and livestock mortality rates increase. Nkedianye *et al.* (2011) report mortality rates of 14–43 per cent in southern Kenya in 2005, while livestock losses were as high as 80 per cent in 2009. Huho *et al.* (2011, p780) cite 30 per cent losses in 2001 and losses in northern Kenya of 30–40 per cent of cattle and sheep/goats in 2005. Here we present the relationship between total livestock biomass and NDVI to assess how droughts affect livestock populations. Figure 6.2 shows that in Kajiado, Kenya, total biomass was surprisingly poorly related to short-term variation in NDVI, which is a good indicator of drought, but related very well to a five year running average of NDVI.

Livestock population dynamics in such areas are therefore not only determined by short-term losses of livestock during drought, but also track the history of resource condition over a longer time period. For example, given low reproduction rates, it may take four or five years for a herd to recover after a major drought. Data from the Kadjiado rangelands show cycles of livestock biomass, connecting to El Niño events in 1989, 1998 and 2006, with peaks of one Tropical Livestock Unit (TLU) per four hectares and troughs of one TLU per eight hectares. Higher forage availability around El Niño (or other wet) years (reflected in NDVI measures) results in population growth and so a phase of higher biomass density. However, this

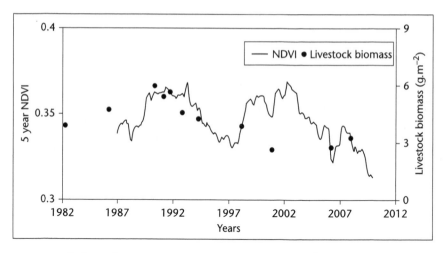

FIGURE 6.2 Relation between total animal biomass (dots, g.m^{-2}) and the five year running average of NDVI from 1987 to 2009, Kajiado district, Kenya. A livestock biomass of 6 g.m^{-2} corresponds to a stocking density of about 1 TLU1/4 ha. (source: unpublished International Livestock Research Institute (IRLI) and Department of Resource Surveys and Remote Sensing (DRSRS) data)

pattern did not occur following the El Niño year of 2006. But this event was preceded and then followed by severe droughts that lasted more than one rainy season. This rapid succession of droughts, although interrupted by an El Niño year, kept the livestock population in a low biomass phase. The cattle in Kadjiado district were severely affected by the 2008–09 drought with an estimated mortality of 70 to 80 per cent (Worden, pers. comm.). Such mortality would have reduced the live-stock biomass further to around 1 g.m^{-2}, or one TLU per 25 ha, the lowest stocking density in memory. By contrast, for Laikipia in northern Kenya, the relationship between livestock biomass and NDVI was better for a two, rather than five, year running average (International Livestock Research Institute (ILRI) unpublished analysis). All this suggests that multiple factors, such as herd composition, access to remote grazing areas, as well as stocking densities and migration from other areas, affect the NDVI and population density relationship (Nkedianye *et al.*, 2011).

While we currently have a good understanding of interannual variability in East Africa, longer-term trends in rainfall are difficult to assess for East Africa. Although Nicholson (2001) reported a 5–10 per cent decline generally for much of Africa (except West) in the latter part of the twentieth century, this does not hold for localized areas of East Africa. Hulme *et al.* (2001) reported a slight wetting of 5–10 per cent in East Africa. Schreck and Semazzi (2004) assessed long-term trends in the October–December rains (1979 to 2001) and their analysis suggests the northern part of the region is getting wetter, while the southern is drying up. A very recent analysis by Washington *et al.* (2011) of multiple data sets finds disagreement in precipitation trends from 1961–2000. One data set shows an annual drying trend of 0 to −1.1mm per day/decade, while another indicates no trend on an annually averaged basis. Additionally, research by Funk *et al.* (2008) and Williams and Funk (2010) presents evidence of a recent historical drying trend in parts of Ethiopia, Kenya and Tanzania, a result of warming in the Indian Ocean.

In sum, climate risk is a core driver of livestock population dynamics. Due to high interannual and interseasonal variability, rainfall influences fodder availability and, depending on the context, patterns of herd growth and mortality. This may occur in cycles, or as a consequence of repeated extreme climatic events (Vetter, 2005; Angassa and Oba, 2007; Homewood, 2008). This pattern of non-equilibrium herd dynamics has been extensively documented, particularly for the more arid regions of sub-Saharan Africa (Ellis and Swift, 1988; Behnke *et al.*, 1993; Sullivan and Rhode, 2002; Oba, this book). But what about longer-term change? Can such cyclical and opportunistic responses be sustained in the face of secular changes in the climate?

What about longer-term climate change?

In preparation for the Fourth Assessment Report of the Intergovernmental Panel on Climate Change (IPCC), the scientific community undertook a large coordinated global coupled climate model experiment, using 19 models, in order to provide a comprehensive multi-model perspective on climate change.[2] The use of multiple models improves predictive ability, because no single model captures all of the climate features for any region of the world. Indeed, different models, with different parameters, based on different sources of data, often throw up very different conclusions, with temperature much easier to model than precipitation. Thus predictions of future patterns must be made with caution. This section reviews the evidence from a range of modeling efforts, and explores the implications for East Africa and the Horn.

Historically, temperature across Africa has increased by 0.5°C per decade (Desanker and Magadza, 2001). For East Africa specifically, Christy *et al.* (2009) suggest no change in maximum temperature but an increase in minimum temperature between 1964 and 2004. Washington *et al.* (2011) averaged observations from two data sets between 1961 and 2000 and found that most of the domain showed a warming trend of between 0.1 and 0.6°C per decade. Models of surface warming for different climate scenarios show increases of about 1–2°C to the 2050s and about 1.5–3°C for the 2080s globally (Meehl *et al.*, 2007, executive summary).[3] Such trends could have dramatic impacts on pastoral areas, given their high exposure to climate variability, although the general models do not indicate with any precision what impacts will happen where. To illuminate this, the results of multiple GCM scenarios can be explored by downscaling them to different regions (Jones *et al.*, 2009; Washington *et al.*, 2011). Results indicate that climate change will bring about three types of possible change on pastoral systems: increases in maximum and minimum temperatures; changes in the duration, frequency and intensity of precipitation events; and increases in the CO_2 concentrations in the atmosphere (above 350 ppm).

Multiple climate change exposure thresholds can be calculated from such downscaled GCMs. Using the means from four GCMs, we calculated places in the global

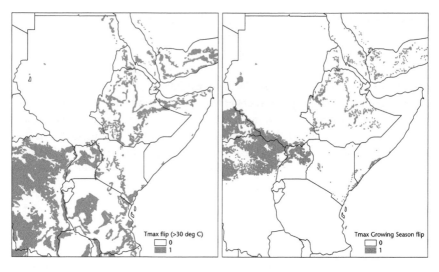

FIGURE 6.3 Areas in East Africa that may undergo a flip in maximum temperature overall and during the growing season (source: Ericksen *et al.*, 2011, p36).

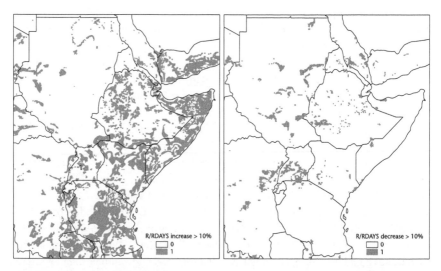

FIGURE 6.4 Areas in East Africa where a) rain per rainy day may increase by more than 10 per cent and b) rain per rainy day may decrease by more than 10 per cent (source: Ericksen *et al.*, 2011, p37).

tropics where maximum temperatures are predicted to flip from less than 30°C to greater than 30°C by 2050. This temperature threshold is a limit for a number of staple crops, including maize, beans and groundnut. Heat stress also affects grass and livestock productivity (Desanker and Magadza, 2001). Large areas in East Africa may undergo this flip, according to these models (Ericksen *et al.*, 2011, p36; see

Figure 6.3, opposite). If we confine the threshold only to places that experience an increase in maximum temperature during the growing season, the exposed area decreases.

A different sort of threshold is shown in Figure 6.4 (opposite). The most difficult characteristic of precipitation patterns for the GCMs to simulate is variability (Washington *et al.*, 2011). Here we show two approximate indicators: increases in rainfall per rain event, and decreases in rainfall per rain event, for East and West Africa (Ericksen *et al.*, 2011). According to these models, large areas of East Africa will experience greater rainfall intensity, while decreases in rainfall per rainy day are less common.

Another measure of how climate change will affect production systems is the length of the growing period. This is the average number of growing days per year, and can be interpreted as (among other things) a proxy for the number of grazing days.[4] Thornton *et al.* (2009) show where more than 20 per cent reductions in the LGP are predicted to occur. This analysis suggests that significant changes are possible across livestock production systems in Africa.

Major uncertainties

A major difficulty in interpreting and using climate change model results is the uncertainty in the calculations and predictions. This arises not only from the different greenhouse gas emissions scenarios and GCM combinations used, but also the uncertainties associated with downscaling. Table 6.1 shows the level of agreement among the IPCC AR4 ensembles by region and by season for precipitation – a feature which, as already noted, is much harder to predict than temperature.

Except for southern Africa, projections were inconsistent in all regions for the December to January period and in west and southern Africa for the June to August period. In other words, predictions remain highly uncertain.

To assess the pattern of agreement among GCMs, Thornton *et al.* (2010) estimated the standard deviation of the mean estimate of change in LGP for each pixel using 14 climate models and three emission scenarios. These represent the variability of LGP estimates primarily due to the different climate models, as there is only limited difference between the three emission scenarios in the first half of the current century. The results show that variability among the climate models is relatively

TABLE 6.1 GCM consistencies in regional precipitation projections for 2090–99 (SRES A1B)

Region	Jun–Aug	Dec–Jan
Sahara	Small decrease (5–20%)	Inconsistent
West Africa	Inconsistent	Inconsistent
East Africa	Small increase (5–20%)	Inconsistent
Southern Africa	Inconsistent	Large decrease (>20%)

Source: Wilby *et al.*, 2009, p1198

small for large areas of central and eastern sub-Saharan Africa (20 per cent or less), higher (up to 40 per cent) for the crop and agro-pastoral lands of West Africa and parts of southern Africa, and highest (>50 per cent) in arid and semi-arid rangelands in south-west Africa and the central desert margins in the north, where LGP is short and highly variable anyway (Thornton *et al.*, 2010, p122). These results highlight a reasonable consensus among the climate models for shifts in conditions in East Africa, but a lack of consensus as to changes in agricultural conditions in some of the higher-rainfall areas of West Africa in particular.

All this uncertainty suggests that, as regional climate models improve, earlier GCM results may become outdated, and both models and predictions will have to be revised. While evidence for climate change resulting in surface level warming is incontrovertible, the consequences this will have for pastoral production systems are less clear. Impacts are likely to be highly spatially heterogeneous, influenced by diverse factors on the ground. As we have shown, major uncertainties are inherent in the modelling efforts, resulting in often divergent predictions. While there is growing consensus on the impacts on temperature, there remain uncertainties around precipitation, particularly extreme events and overall seasonal and inter-annual variability. The next section then turns to evaluating the potential impacts of climate change in pastoral areas.

The impacts of climate change

The impacts of climate change are thus likely to be varied, site-specific and uncertain. The specific impacts for pastoral systems pertain to vegetation, herd dynamics and herd composition. These will of course have broader implications for pastoral livelihood options and strategies.

Increases in maximum and minimum temperatures, combined with increased CO_2 which improves water use efficiency, could increase net primary productivity in rangelands in the presence of more rainfall. However, the impact on species composition is much more dependent on precipitation and evapo-transpiration. The proportion of browse could also increase in combination with more competition if dry spells are more frequent (as they are predicted to be in southern Africa). The overall impact is made more complex still by the difficulty of estimating livestock response and the corresponding interactions with vegetation. Changes in variance may be more important than changes in means as grazing systems are so hetero-geneous to begin with (Thornton *et al.*, 2009). Doherty *et al.* (2010) used a dynamic global vegetation model to estimate impacts of a warmer, wetter climate on rangeland vegetation in East Africa, where the GCM predictions are fairly consistent. These results indicate that C4 grasses are likely to decrease in productivity, while tropical broadleaf growth increases. A decrease in grass cover could mean more competition among grazing species for forage (Doherty *et al.*, 2010).

Changes in herd dynamics can also be expected from climate change. Thornton and Herrero (2010) investigated the impacts of increased frequency of drought on livestock herd dynamics. They ran a herd dynamics model (Lesnoff, 2007) to investigate the impacts of increased drought frequencies on herd dynamics and livestock numbers, based on baseline information on mortality, reproduction and herd structures from pastoralist herds in Kajiado, Kenya. The model was run for 20 years assuming a herd baseline size of 200 animals, of which 60 were adult females. Two scenarios were run: a baseline scenario simulating realistic weather variability of one drought every five years (Orindi *et al.*, 2007) and an alternative scenario of increased frequency of droughts – one year in three. Their results indicate that drought every five years keeps the herds stable as it allows sufficient time for the herds to re-establish. A once in three year drought interval by contrast drives livestock density to lower levels, as a result of increased mortality and poorer reproductive performance. Hence, if there is a greater frequency of drought under climate change, this might have a lasting impact on stocking density, and the productivity of pastoral production systems. The results were extrapolated to all arid and semi-arid districts in Kenya and estimated that 1.8 million animals could be lost by 2030 due to increased drought frequency, with a combined value of US$630 million due to losses in animals, milk and meat production (Herrero *et al.*, 2010, p56).

One way of dealing with increased frequency and impact of drought is to change herd species composition. Figure 6.5 shows the change in the ratio of shoats to cattle across Kenya between 1977-1978 and 2005-2010. Goats, as well as camels, are more

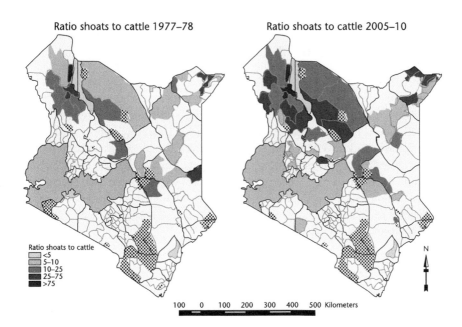

FIGURE 6.5 Changes in ratio of shoats (sheep and goats) to cattle 1977–78 and 2005–10 in Kenya. Hatched areas indicate protected areas (source: DRSRS aerial census 1977–78 and 2005–10, cited in ILRI report to Association for Strengthening Agricultural Research in Eastern and Central Africa (ASARECA) African Biodiversity Conservation in Drylands Project, forthcoming).

drought tolerant than cattle, and also have different fodder preferences, preferring browse to grasses.

Such changes in species mix and distribution will have important implications for overall livestock productivity and nutrition, as well as milk production (Sellen, 2000; Fratkin *et al.*, 2004), and will define the possible pathways for livestock-based livelihoods in different areas (Little *et al.*, 2008; McPeak *et al.*, 2011). However, without more sophisticated dynamic rangeland vegetation models we are not yet able to estimate these combined impacts (Asner *et al.*, 2004; Soussana *et al.*, 2010), and exact outcomes remain uncertain.

Conclusion

Potential, if still uncertain, climate change impacts could well bring about major social and economic transitions in pastoral systems, shifting livelihood pathways in new ways. Although pastoralists living 'at the margins' are very accustomed to dealing with change, their options are restricted in many places, as mobility is constrained, and herd sizes are decreasing for many. Pastoral households may also find themselves settling, for various economic and social reasons (Fratkin, this book). While climate change may present significant challenges for the future of pastoralism, it may open up opportunities too. For example, Jones and Thornton (2009, p432) examine the areas where climate change could produce shifts in growing seasons sufficiently large that cropping would become too risky and livestock production might become the best alternative source of livelihood. These included mid-altitude zones and parts of coastal areas in East Africa.

Pastoral systems in Africa are highly complex and undergoing rapid change. Shifts due to climate change may result in greater risks as the climate becomes hotter and more variable. But in other areas opportunities may open up. Future patterns remain highly uncertain, although the predictive capacity of models is improving slowly. As we contemplate 'development at the margins', scientists, modellers and pastoralists must work together. Due to the significant complexities and deep uncertainties, it will be important to engage pastoral populations in debates about how to respond to climate change. Building on significant expertise and past experience, adaptation and response strategies in increasingly variable environments must emerge from grounded local experience and knowledge, as well as be informed by increasingly sophisticated modeling efforts.

Notes

1   TLU – Tropical Livestock Unit, a unit used to represent the total amount of livestock, of various species and body mass, present in an area. One TLU corresponds to cattle of 250kg.
2   This is the World Climate Research Programme (WCRP) Coupled Model Intercomparison Project Phase Three (CMIP3), which uses multiple general circulation models (GCMs) (Meehl *et al.*, 2007; Randall *et al.*, 2007) that are hosted centrally at the Program for Climate Model Diagnosis and Intercomparison (PCMDI). This archive is referred to as 'The Multi-Model Data set (MMD) at PCMDI'.

3 These models predict means of surface warming (relative to 1980–99) for the Special Report on Emissions Scenarios (SRES) A2, A1B and B1 from IPCC.
4 A growing day is a day in which the average air temperature exceeds 6°C and the ratio of actual to potential evapo-transpiration exceeds 0.35 (Jones and Thornton, 2009).

PART II

Commercialization and markets

7

MOVING UP OR MOVING OUT?

Commercialization, growth and destitution in pastoralist areas

Andy Catley and Yacob Aklilu

Introduction

In mid 2010, two contradictory narratives were prominent in policy dialogue around pastoralism in the Horn of Africa. Within governments, regional bodies and aid actors with a more long-term development mandate, a common perspective was the link between pastoral livestock exports and economic growth. Here the development strategies assumed a simple causal pathway between higher levels of livestock exports and broad-based poverty reduction in pastoralist areas. In part, this thinking underpinned investments aiming to modernize pastoral livestock marketing, such as repeated efforts to develop the kinds of market infrastructure and formal certification systems used in the US or Europe. In contrast, humanitarian actors continued to present the view that pastoralism was in crisis and non-viable, as evident from increasing levels of pastoral destitution. Strongly associated with this perspective was an emerging sub-narrative around climate change, and the argument that declining rainfall and more severe droughts were drivers of vulnerability in pastoralist areas. One aid response to this kind of analysis was the introduction of relatively large-scale safety net programmes in northern Kenya and some pastoral areas of Ethiopia, and renewed interest in alternative livelihoods.

The two broad narratives outlined above were contradictory because although pastoral livestock exports from the Horn were increasing, there was a corresponding increase in poverty indicators in pastoralist areas. These trends indicated that the association between more exports and poverty reduction was flawed. Also, if the supply of export livestock from pastoral areas was increasing, how could pastoralism as a production system be in crisis?

This chapter analyses pre-existing literature and data from 'high-export' pastoralist regions of Ethiopia and surrounding areas to examine why it is possible to see a dynamic and growing pastoral livestock export trade from the Horn but also, increasing levels of destitution. A core aspect of the analysis is wealth differentiation in pastoralist communities, and how processes such as commercialization and population growth impact differently on different wealth groups. This approach draws on research that highlights the importance of viewing poverty in pastoralist areas not from an area-wide position, but according to the assets and behaviours of different wealth groups (Little *et al.*, 2008). The chapter also draws heavily on two recent studies on commercialization in pastoralist areas in the Horn of Africa (Aklilu and Catley, 2009) and Ethiopia (Aklilu and Catley, 2010), which examined the benefits of the livestock export trade by wealth group.

History lessons

Long before the era of the global climate industry and related aid funding, in-depth field research had explained co-existing pastoral poverty and wealth by describing economic behaviours by wealth group. As early as the 1980s it was shown that commercial herding depends on the attainment of a large herd. Poorer owners with small herds aimed to both maintain a reliable income and maximize long-term herd growth, such that 'Once domestic needs have been met, the successful herd operator is free to engage in a spiralling process of sales, reinvestment and herd expansion' (Behnke, 1987). However, not all poorer pastoralists achieve the levels of herd growth needed for commercial herding. For example, after seven years of project implementation and research by GTZ in the central rangelands of Somalia, again during the 1980s, the economic analysis concluded that:

> Economic parameters, calculated for differently sized pastoral herds, support the evidence that herders with undersized herds are subjected to a displacement process: a household's income increases with the number of animals owned . . . It is shown that households organize and utilize their resources to achieve not only subsistence but also a surplus for commercial use; the latter however is only possible for pastoral households with large herds.
>
> *(Abdullahi, 1993)*

Driving this 'displacement process' was commercialization, with Somali herders and traders responding to a growing demand for live animals in the Middle East. In Ethiopia, long-term research studies in Borana, also during the 1980s, were prophetic:

> Human population growth, drought, inappropriate water development, land appropriation, peri-urban influences and even livestock commercialization have reportedly contributed to an increased pauperization, wealth stratification and the cultural alienation of pastoralists.
>
> *(Coppock, 1994)*

Looking specifically at drought, poorer households suffer proportionately higher losses of livestock and take longer to rebuild their herds. For example, net drought-related cattle losses in Borana households between 1980 and 1997 averaged 37 per cent (Desta, 1999). However, poor households experienced net losses of 60 per cent while middle-class and wealthy households had losses of only 25 per cent:

> Although the wealthy suffer larger absolute losses compared to their poorer counterparts, they usually retained a sufficiently large nucleus herd to rebound in an efficient manner while the poor may lose enough to be *pushed out*.
>
> *(Coppock, 1994, our emphasis)*

So poor pastoralists were being 'displaced', 'pauperized' or 'pushed out' from pastoralism for many years, as commercialization trends set in, as populations grew, and droughts continued to occur.

Livestock export trends – who sells?

While governments and some aid actors claim that pastoralism has no future, Somalia, Ethiopia and Sudan can be categorized as 'high export' countries in terms of live-stock, and critically, most of these animals are sourced from pastoralist areas (Aklilu and Catley, 2009). In Ethiopia the export trade is growing with revenues of US$211 million from meat and live animal exports for 2010–11 (Table 7.1). This level of formal export earnings from the livestock sector (excluding exports of hides and skins) is unprecedented, and represents a five-fold increase compared to 2005–06. Key supply areas are Borana (mainly for cattle and chilled sheep and goat carcasses, and to some extent, camels), and the Somali Region (mainly for live camels, and sheep and goat exports). Other supply areas include the lowlands of Bale (for camels and cattle), Southern Nations, Afar and mid-altitude agro-pastoral zones of Oromia (for sheep and goats channeled to export abattoirs). In Borana, the major pastoral livestock markets supplying the formal export trade are located in Harobake, Dubluk, Negele, Teltele and Finchowa along the main roads, and the bush markets of Surupa and El Waya. These markets have grown in prominence in the past few years, and a recent study showed average price increases between 2009 and 2010 of 34 per cent for cattle, a staggering 86 per cent for camels, and about 32 per cent for

TABLE 7.1 Volume and value of livestock exports from Ethiopia

Year	Live animals	Value (US$1,000)	Meat (tons)	Value (US$1,000)
2005–06	163,000	27,259	7,717	15,598
2006–07	234,000	36,507	7,917	18,448
2007–08	298,000	40,865	5,875	15,471
2008–09	150,000	77,350	6,400	24,480
2009–10	334,000	91,000	10,000	34,000
2010–11	472,041	148,000	16,877	63,200

Source: National Bank of Ethiopia/SPS-LMM

small ruminants. These changes were explained by growing demand, which far outweighed inflationary trends (PLI Policy Project, 2010).

Absent from these figures is the larger informal trade of livestock from Somali Region in Ethiopia, through the northern Somali ports to the Gulf. These trends, together with pastoral livestock sourced in Somaliland, are reflected in the export figures for Berbera (Table 7.2).

Looking specifically at who sells livestock within the main pastoral supply areas, data from different areas consistently supports earlier research (e.g. Abdullahi, 1993), with wealthier owners with larger herds selling far more animals than other wealth groups (Table 7.3). For example, the number of sheep or goats sold by middle and better-off groups was seven and 19 times higher than the very poor in Mandera (Kenya), and 14 and 24 times more in Wajir (Kenya) (SCUK, 2007). In Teltele, Dillo, and Dier (Ethiopia), the middle and better-off income groups sold six and 18 times more small ruminants than the very poor (LIU, 2008).

TABLE 7.2 Livestock exports from Somaliland

Year	Camels	Cattle	Sheep and goats	Chilled sheep and goat carcasses (tons)
2008	18,517	59,519	940,976	–
2009	34,274	121,845	1,640,065	193
2010	97,165	136,001	1,569,094	145

Source: Somaliland Chamber of Commerce. These figures exclude the additional cross-border trade into Djibouti, and also exclude Ethiopia-Somali livestock consumed domestically within Somaliland.

TABLE 7.3 Annual pastoral household income from livestock sales in Somali areas of Kenya, and Borana and Guji areas of Ethiopia

Area	Household income (US$) by wealth group			
	Very poor	Poor	Middle	Better–off
Mandera, Kenya	105	229	702	1,787
Equivalent sheep or goats	3.5	7.5	24	60
Wajir, Kenya	42	169	677	1,105
Equivalent sheep or goats	1.5	5.5	22	37
Teltele, Dillo, and Dier, Ethiopia	114	202	714	2,100
Equivalent sheep or goats	5	8.5	31	92
Borana-Guji, Ethiopia	132	231	768	1,500
Equivalent sheep or goats	5.5	10	34	66

Source: Compiled from SCUK (2007) and LIU (2008)

Moving up or moving out?

Commercialization mainly benefits wealthier herders, who not only acquire larger herds, but also use their influence to gain more control over key resources such as water and grazing. These actors have financial and political capital to secure control of resources, especially where formal institutional arrangements for tenure are vague or overlooked locally. As hitherto communal resources become privatized, poorer herders are excluded or struggle to make the payments needed to access these resources. Hence, their ability to stay in the pastoral system is further reduced. Accounts of rangeland enclosures and private water development in these areas are numerous and go back many years. Examples include the massive expansion of private water *berkads* in parts of the Somali Region of Ethiopia (Sugule and Walker, 1998; Devereux, 2006; Aklilu and Catley, 2010), and the emergence of private rangeland enclosures in Borana since the 1970s (Kamara *et al.*, 2004; Angassa and Oba, 2008; Aklilu and Catley, 2010; Tache, this book). In some areas, these resource access problems are worsened by bush encroachment and in all areas population growth means that increasing numbers of households need to acquire a minimum herd to exist as pastoralists. Although these general trends are well described in the literature, few researchers have looked specifically at declining natural resource access in terms of wealth groups, and who is most affected. The apparently robust and growing livestock export trade indicates that at least so far, wealthier herders are not unduly hindered by limited access to water or grazing which, in turn, indicates that poorer herders are relatively more affected.

Positioned in eastern Ethiopia adjacent to the Djibouti and Somaliland borders, pastoralists in Shinile Zone have multiple trading options, from the informal export of livestock to Djibouti, through to various internal domestic markets in Ethiopia (Catley and Iyasu, 2010). Using data on livestock holdings by wealth group (Kassahun *et al.*, 2008), we visualized changes between two 30-year periods, before and after 1974 (Figure 7.1). Despite droughts, conflict, bush encroachment and population growth, wealthier herders maintained or increased their livestock holdings over 60 years, assisted by a shift in ownership away from cattle to camels and goats. In contrast, the lowest wealth group described by local informants as 'below medium' in the period before 1974 disappeared after 1974, being replaced by two new wealth groups called 'poor' and 'very poor'. The livestock holdings in these groups were far below the level needed to maintain a pastoralist household. Essentially, these two groups would be labeled as destitute pastoralists or 'pastoral drop-outs' in 2010. This kind of analysis clearly explains the contradictory narratives we offered at the start of the chapter. Pastoralism remains viable and productive for wealthier herders, as they are best placed to engage in livestock trade and adapt to changing market demands and resource trends, e.g. by shifting from cattle to camel production.

Data from other parts of Somali Region over a much shorter time period shows comparable trends. For example, data from early warning surveys for the lowland Hawd area is shown in Figure 7.2, with wealthier and middle-wealth groups increasing their livestock assets over about ten years, whereas the assets of the poor

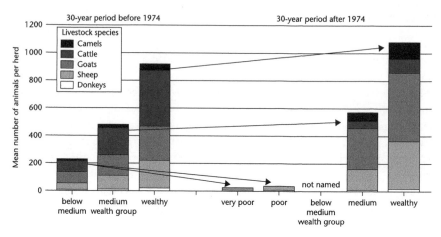

FIGURE 7.1 The 'moving up, moving out' scenario – trends in livestock ownership by wealth group over 60 years (1944–2004), Shinile zone, Somali Region (source: Catley and Iyasu, 2010, using data adapted from Kassahun *et al.*, 2008. Data based on interviews with 300 households. The year 1974 separates the two time periods as this was a year of particularly bad drought and famine among the Issa pastoralists in Shinile zone, and therefore, easy to recall as a point of reference among informants).

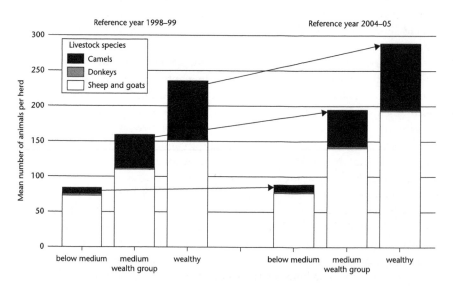

FIGURE 7.2 Short-term trends in livestock ownership by wealth group, lowland Hawd area, Somali Region (source: adapted from SCUK, 1998, 2005).

remained constant. These trends also illustrate the growing asset gap between richer and poorer households, and indicate that poorer households have to attain higher livestock holdings to 'stay in' the commercializing system.

The other impacts of commercialization include the decline of traditional social support systems as more and more people need assistance. According to Boran elders in 2010, the traditional *busa gonofa* support system provided only about a fifth of the household support needed compared to the past, and now it takes years before a household receives this support due to a long list of intended beneficiaries (Aklilu and Catley, 2010). Commercialized production also contributed to behavioural changes around *busa gonofa*, as individualism crept in. Desta *et al.* (2008) reported that Borana communities used to have positive attitudes about 'dropouts', since they provided labour as hired herders (notably, for the wealthy). However, such people are increasingly seen as a nuisance as their numbers have grown in excess of the labour needs of the communities they live in, and they require assistance in the form of food, milk, loans and so on. In the Somali Region of Ethiopia, early warning survey data for the Shinile agropastoral zone in 1998–99 showed that gifts of food and cash accounted for up to 15 per cent of the income of poor households, whereas in 2004–05 this figure was only 5 per cent (SCUK, 2005). In addition, no food gifts were recorded since 1998–99 in the lowland Hawd pastoral livelihood zones, and since 1999–2000 in the Shabale riverine livelihood zones, no cash gifts were recorded for Harshin and Degahbur East pastoral livelihood zones. However, *zakat* contributions could be higher in some rural areas, and Devereux (2006) reported that *zakat* contributions were important for Somali pastoralists between 1995 and 2005, after drought and livestock disease outbreaks.

Trend analysis not only needs to consider livestock ownership by wealth groups over time, but also the *absolute number* of people moving between wealth groups. Early warning survey reports provide some insights by providing proportions of households in each wealth group in each livelihood zone (SCUK, 2005; SCUK and DPPC, 2008). We re-analysed these wealth group proportions by applying an estimate of 2.5 per cent annual population growth to the proportions from ten livelihood zones in Somali Region, with a 'start' reference year of either 1996–97 (for five locations) or 1998–99 (for five locations), and all locations with an 'end' reference year of 2004–2005.[1] The results were an absolute 2.5 per cent annual increase in the number of wealthy households, a 0.8 per cent annual increase in the number of middle-wealth households, but a 4.1 per cent annual increase in the number of poor households. In other words, the number of poor households increased at around five times the rate of middle-wealth households, and 1.6 times the rate of wealthy households.

Climate change (or not)

The ecological and economic logic of pastoralism in Africa, and especially pastoral mobility, can be explained by the high temporal and spatial variability of rainfall in these areas (Scoones, 1995a). Marked rainfall variability is normal in these environments, and rainfall is the main determinant of the quality and availability of vegetation, and therefore, livestock survival and production. Given the fundamental importance of rainfall in pastoralist areas and the possibility of climate change leading to altered rainfall patterns, contemporary analysis of trends and vulnerability in pastoralist areas has to consider rainfall tends. However, this topic is characterized by very mixed views, and in Ethiopia for example, a string of rapid surveys have reframed pastoralist vulnerability around climate change. In late 2009 a group of NGOs concluded that for some pastoralist areas, 'communities and local governmental and non-governmental agencies are presently observing unprecedented climate variability and extremes' (Anon., 2009). In contrast, objective analysis using rainfall data from 134 rain gauge stations over 42 years, including pastoralist areas, concluded that, 'since we failed to see any significant changes in inter-annual rainfall at the watershed or national level, it is unclear whether climate change is driving any systematic trends in Ethiopia's rainfall' (Cheung et al., 2008).

For our analysis, we considered cross-border areas of Ethiopia, Kenya, Somalia and Somaliland as a regional system that was influenced by climatic events over the Indian Ocean and atmospheric features such as the inter-tropical convergence zone and anticyclones (Cheung et al., 2008). This approach also took account of the similarity in livelihoods across national borders (Crosskey and Ahmed Ismail, 2009). Annual rainfall patterns are shown in Figure 7.3 and a trend analysis is shown in Table 7.4. This analysis indicates that only Kenya had a sufficient body of rainfall data for long-term analysis, and here no trends were evident. Only Teltele in Ethiopia showed a negative rainfall trend but for this location data for 18 out of 37 years was omitted from the analysis due to gaps in the data for those years. Overall, the data shows the typical marked variation in rainfall in dryland areas and does not show that droughts are becoming frequent or more severe, if drought is defined using rainfall measurements.

When compared to other trends affecting vulnerability in pastoralist areas, the occurrence of drought is still a major factor – as it was 100 years ago or more. However, with increasing numbers of poorer herders with relatively few animals per household and with reduced access to resources, the impacts of drought will be more evident and in part, this explains the concerns of humanitarian actors. In addition, increasing appropriation of communal water and rangeland by wealthier pastoralists and commercial owners further limits the capacity of poorer herders to respond to drought, while also enhancing the drought resistance of the wealthier herders. In part, this explains why the livestock export trade continues to grow despite recurrent droughts and increasing levels of destitution.

Visualizing the trends

By drawing on a mix of old and new data, we attempted to show some of the main trends in a hypothetical high export pastoralist area. We developed a simple model that assumed an annual population growth of 2.5 per cent, and used the kind of commercialization history seen in Somaliland. Here, substantial livestock exports were recorded in the 1920s (Hunt, 1951) but in the 1960s and 1970s they increased due to demands in the Gulf States, such as those associated with the oil boom (Reusse, 1982). For the sake of the model, we started in the early 1920s but introduced substantial commercialization from the mid 1960s, and used export figures from the FAO Statistical Database (FAOSTAT) and later, the Somaliland

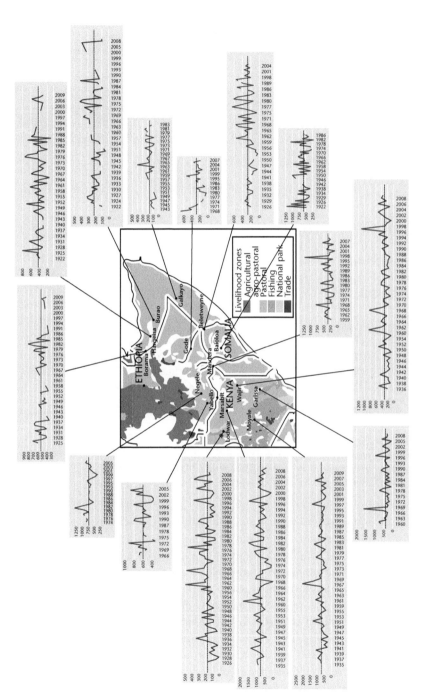

FIGURE 7.3 Mean annual rainfall patterns in pastoralist areas of Ethiopia, Somalia, Somaliland and Kenya. On each graph, rainfall is shown on the y-axis in millimeters and years are shown on the x-axis (data sources: see Table 7.4. Map of livelihood zones from Crosskey and Ahmed Ismail, 2009).

TABLE 7.4 Trend analysis of annual total rainfall by location, Kenya, Ethiopia and Somalia

Location (period)	Number of years covered by analysis (missing years)	Kendall tau (p-value)[1]	p-value: interpretation
Kenya[2]			
Lodwar (1926–2008)	84 (2)	0.132 (0.079)	> 0.05; no trend
Marsabit (1935–2009)	75 (3)	-0.156 (0.054)	> 0.05; no trend
Moyale (1935–2009)	75 (2)	-0.075 (0.351)	> 0.05; no trend
Mandera (1959–2009)	51 (0)	-0.042 (0.673)	> 0.05; no trend
Wajir (1935–2008)	74 (1)	0.141 (0.085)	> 0.05; no trend
Garissa (1960–2009)	50 (0)	-0.115 (0.242)	> 0.05; no trend
Somalia[3]			
Borama (1925–2009)	84 (41)	-0.022 (0.840)	> 0.05; no trend
Hargeisa (1922–2009)	88 (21)	-0.045 (0.592)	> 0.05; no trend
Burao (1921–88)	68 (25)	0.021 (0.852)	> 0.05; no trend
Galkayo (1943–84)	42 (16)	0.200 (0.160)	> 0.05; no trend
Beletweyne (1926–2005)	80 (13)	0.132 (0.115)	> 0.05; no trend
Baidoa (1922–88)	67 (12)	-0.076 (0.416)	> 0.05; no trend
Ethiopia[4]			
Yabello (1966–2005)	40 (13)	-0.08 (0.573)	> 0.05; no trend
Teltele (1970–2006)	37 (18)	-0.368 (0.029)	< 0.05; negative trend
Mega (1966–2003)	35 (12)	-0.217 (1.000)	> 0.05; no trend
Negele (1974–2006)	33 (7)	-0.298 (1.000)	> 0.05; no trend
Moyale (1971–2006)	36 (11)	-0.200 (1.000)	> 0.05; no trend
Gode (1968–2007)	39 (16)	-0.051 (1.000)	> 0.05; no trend

Notes:
1 Mann-Kendall trend test, XLSTAT 2010.3.01 software.
2 Data sourced from Kenya Meteorological Office.
3 Data sourced from Somali Water and Land Information Management.
4 Data sourced from Ethiopia Meteorological Office.

Chamber of Commerce, to show the long-term trends as well as early export data from the Somaliland Protectorate (Hunt, 1951). For rainfall trends, we used data from the Somalia Water and Land Information website, some of which dated back to 1921. For rangeland access, we estimated a 1.5 per cent annual loss of rangeland access for poorer herders from the onset of commercialization. This figure was a 'best guess' and aimed to represent changes such as the introduction of private enclosures. We then used the estimates of population change by wealth group derived from early warning survey reports, presented above.

The overall intent was to visualize and compare long-term trends, and some of the key features were: a gradual increase in livestock exports over about 50 years; high rainfall variability between years, but no overall change in mean annual rainfall between 1922 and 2009; an increase in wealthy herders in line with overall population growth, but a far greater increase in the population change of the poor

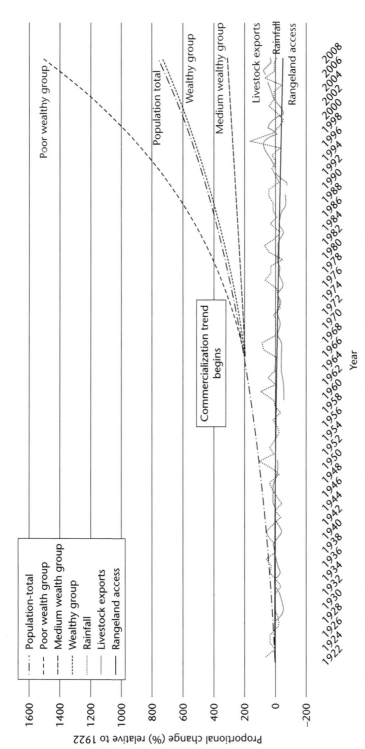

FIGURE 7.4 Simple modeling of long-term trends in high export pastoralist areas and impacts on wealth groups.

wealth group. There are many other factors that could be added to this kind of model, such as levels of governance and conflict. However, even if different types of conflict are considered, ranging from local resource-based conflicts to large-scale war between countries, it is notable that livestock exports continue – this would be the case for both the trade from the northern Somali ports, and the trade from Sudan. Rather like drought, it is wealthier actors who are better able to respond to, or even benefit from, certain forms of conflict.

We propose that this kind of simple modeling and the market-access/resource-access framework shown in Catley *et al.* (this book) are the kinds of tools that policy-makers need to understand the relative importance of long-term trends in pastoralist areas. For high export areas, the key questions are the futures of the increasing numbers of people leaving pastoralism either voluntarily or due to the combined impacts of commercialization, drought and conflict. Recent demographic studies indicate that many of these people are moving to urban centres (Anon., 2010). For example, in Ethiopia, urban populations within pastoralist regions grew at about twice the rate of rural populations between 2006 and 2008.

Conclusions

If we stand back from the Horn of Africa and look at pastoralism in other parts of the world, some common trends are evident. As commercialization advances, there is nearly always a redistribution of livestock from smaller to larger herds. In some ways, this is the history of global agricultural development and is not that dissimilar to, for example, family-owned dairy farms in the UK being acquired by transnational retailers. Commercialization of agriculture is characterized by the absorption of smaller units by larger units. In Libya and some Middle East countries, pastoral commercialization was driven by growing demand for meat in urban centres, which in turn, grew due to 'boom industries' such as oil. In these areas, the same industries absorbed some potential pastoral 'drop outs' as the commercialization of pastoralism took place. The end state, roughly speaking, was the continuation of pastoralism in a commercially orientated form, and employment in new industries for some of those who opted out, or who were forced out of pastoralism (e.g. Evans-Pritchard, 1949; Barth, 1961). At the same time, social mechanisms within some pastoralist societies acted to alienate those who lacked the wherewithal to acquire or maintain sufficient livestock to stay in the system. Socially, such people were ostracized and forced out – a very different dynamic to the more widely reported traditional safety nets in pastoral areas. Being 'forced out' not only refers to a disengagement from pastoralism, but also a physical separation, because non-livestock related economic opportunities in these areas were so limited. Hence the trends in seeking work in cities and other countries.

In high export pastoral areas of the Horn, commercialization provides some new employment opportunities, such as contract herding, and creates users of new services such as fodder supply and veterinary services. In addition, pastoralist areas have various economic potentials such as the wildlife conservation and tourist business in Kenya, production of dryland products, and different types of small business. To varying degrees, the safety net, asset-building and alternative livelihoods-type programmes of governments and aid organizations are a response to these opportunities, or aim to return substantial numbers of people to pastoralism. However, returning poor herders to an increasingly commercialized system needs far better analysis of where the economic spaces may be, if anywhere, given the capacity of wealthier actors to secure these spaces for themselves. Similarly, there will be limits to the new economic activities that will arise from commercialization of livestock, or alternative livelihoods, and these limits need to be far better understood. At present, safety net-type strategies seem to assume that increasing numbers of destitute pastoralists can either return to pastoralism or develop a viable alternative livelihood *in pastoral areas*. For many people, however, the opportunities will be outside of pastoral areas or in other countries, and access to these opportunities requires both a rapid acceleration of quality education, and policies that support movement in search of work both within countries and regions. At worst, large-scale safety net programmes may provide incentives for destitute herders to stay in pastoralist areas simply to receive modest amounts of food or cash, but when there are few long-term economic opportunities in either the pastoral or non-pastoral sectors.

Acknowledgements

The original analyses behind this chapter were funded by the IGAD–FAO Livestock Policy Initiative, the Foreign and Commonwealth Office, United Kingdom and UKAid from the Department for International Development. The authors also appreciate the support of the United States Agency for International Development in Ethiopia under the Pastoralist Livelihoods Initiative. We are also grateful to Francis Chabari for sourcing the Kenya rainfall data.

Note

1 The livelihoods zones were Hawd pastoral, Fik pastoral, Shinile agropastoral, Shinile pastoral, Degahabur agropastoral, Afdher pastoral, Gode agropastoral, Liban pastoral, Filtu-Dolow pastoral and Moyale Wayamo pastoral.

8

PASTORALISTS' INNOVATIVE RESPONSES TO NEW CAMEL EXPORT MARKET OPPORTUNITIES ON THE KENYA/ETHIOPIA BORDERLANDS

Hussein Abdullahi Mahmoud

Introduction

Although cattle marketing has been studied extensively in the Horn of Africa (e.g. Aklilu, 2002; Little, 2003; Mahmoud, 2008), camel marketing has received relatively limited attention. Some very recent studies are now available, such as the description of the commercialization of camels in Ethiopia (Aklilu and Catley, 2011), but in general, camel marketing is still an under-researched topic. In contrast to marketing, camel husbandry and production has attracted more research in the Horn and Eastern Africa (e.g. Bollig, 1992; Simpkin, 1996; Getahun and Belay, 2002). Also, much work has been done on camel diseases in the Horn of Africa (e.g. Abdurahman and Bornstein, 1991; Catley and Mohammed, 1995; Dirie and Abdurahman, 2003).

While camels, sheep, and goats are traded in both smaller and larger livestock markets in the region, cattle sales dominate many markets and particularly, the southern Somalia-Garissa route in north-eastern Kenya and the Moyale market in northern Kenya. In contrast, small stock dominates routes such as from Somaliland and Puntland to the Gulf States. Although the number of camels traded may be comparatively low, the value is high relative to small stock. Indeed, camels have not been a prominent market commodity in the Horn of Africa until fairly recently, partly because these animals have not been offered at competitive prices, and the demand has been low in the growing meat markets in major towns and cities of the region.

The Horn of Africa has the largest concentration of camel herds in the world, with Somalia estimated to have the highest population globally. Large camel populations are found in the eastern lowlands of Ethiopia, northern, western, and north-eastern Kenya, and in most parts of Somalia. According to the Food and Agriculture Organization, Somalia had seven million camels in 2008, while Ethiopia and Kenya had about 2.4 and 0.95 million camels in 2009, respectively. Therefore, the combined estimated camel population of Ethiopia, Kenya, and Somalia is slightly over 10 million head, which is a substantial population. Somalia alone holds more than twice the combined camel populations of Ethiopia and Kenya.

Historically, camels in pastoral areas of the Horn of Africa have been used mainly for milk and meat production, and as pack animals, with modest sales at local markets. Camel meat is less expensive than beef, mutton or goat meat. Camel meat and milk consumption is popular among Somalis in the region and so is consumed over a wide area covering Somalia, Djibouti, eastern and southern Ethiopia, northern and north-eastern Kenya, and among Somali populations in Kenya's major towns, such as Nairobi, Mombasa and Nakuru. While cattle have largely remained a commodity for local and national consumption, camels are now being exported to Middle Eastern countries in larger numbers. In fact, the news of lucrative camel prices at the Moyale livestock market in Ethiopia continues to elate many pastoralists and residents of northern and north-eastern Kenya, and in other pastoral areas of the country.

This chapter examines the newly emerging and vibrant camel marketing activities in the northern Kenya/southern Ethiopia borderlands that have become an attractive economic activity only in the past few years. These changes relate to the growing interest in pastoral innovation systems and the many new ideas that are being generated from among pastoral communities (Mahmoud, 2006; Scoones and Adwera, 2009). Pastoralist innovation is key to risk mitigation and survival in an uncertain environment, and livelihood improvement. The emergence of an increased demand for camels and camel meat in Arabian countries and the over-whelming response from pastoral communities in the Horn supports the premise of an ongoing pastoral innovation in livestock marketing. The current camel trading activity in the region is a good example of a promising enterprise with potential to further strengthen the livestock-based economy with direct benefits to local herders. Focusing on the Moyale market on the Ethiopia/Kenya border and through extensive fieldwork and the use of secondary data, the chapter describes this dynamic and innovative marketing enterprise and the ways in which herders and traders respond to emerging market opportunities.

Livestock trading dynamics

Moyale is the second largest cattle market in northern and north-eastern Kenya after Garissa. Although the market only handles about half the number of cattle passing through the Garissa market, it is becoming a large camel market in the region and continues to be a center of prominence for cross-border livestock trade. So while Moyale has long been an important conduit for southern Ethiopia cattle to Kenya, a more prominent role has emerged in recent years – as one of the leading channels for camel exports to the Arab world.

In southern Ethiopia, pastoral livestock are trekked from villages and primary markets to the secondary market of Moyale. The northbound livestock from these areas are trucked to markets, such as Addis Ababa, the capital city of Ethiopia, and other major consumption areas. The volume of cattle trekked is much larger to secondary markets than between the smaller routes. In general, trekking livestock from numerous smaller villages and markets is more cost efficient than trucking.

Livestock trade directions on the Kenya-Ethiopia-Somalia borderlands have been changing depending on the market and political circumstances in the border areas and further afield, for the past century or so. During this time many shifts in trade flows have been attributed, for example, to conflicts between the Somali and the Boran, and sometimes between Somali clans and the prohibitive policies of the colonial administration. The current change of direction in camel trade from northern and north-eastern Kenya and southern Somalia to the border town of Moyale for onward trucking to Ethiopian feedlots and eventually to Arab markets, seems to be demand driven.

Prior to the collapse of the Somali state in 1991, the livestock trade movement was from Kenya and Ethiopia into Somalia for export to the Middle East, principally through the port of Mogadishu. The Somali state collapse instigated a reversal in the direction of livestock trade leading to an increased flow of livestock to Kenyan markets. Cattle from southern Ethiopia had regularly been moved to Kenyan markets while camels and the small stock had been heading toward Somali ports for exports (see Little, 2003; Mahmoud, 2010). These trends were illustrated by a camel trader in Moyale, who stated that he used to trade in camels from southern Ethiopia to Mogadishu, but has now changed the direction by sourcing camels from southern Somalia, north-eastern Kenya, and south-eastern Ethiopia to supply the Moyale market.

To reiterate, the push behind the current expansion of camel trading on the Kenya/Ethiopia border is the growing demand for camels in the Middle East, including Egypt. One explanation for the expanded camel trade to Egypt from the Horn is that Egypt used to purchase from unstable countries, such as Somalia and the Sudan, particular from the Darfur area. These countries cannot supply adequate camels now because of insecurity, which has prompted Egypt to seek alternative sources of camels. Other Arab countries also used to depend, to some extent, on the Somalia and Sudan sources, which have now turned to Ethiopia for their supplies. It is important to note that not all camels being sold and transported to the Middle East through Ethiopian markets and territories are Ethiopian animals, as many are trekked to the Moyale market from as far as southern Somalia and north-eastern Kenya.

When Egyptians used to purchase from Somalia, some of the current Somali camel traders in Moyale would supply camels from southern Ethiopia and trek them to Mogadishu for onward shipment to Egypt. Camel traders state that several factors have reversed the direction of camel trade in favor of southern Ethiopia, including the widespread piracy activities along the Somalia coast, and increased insecurity in Somalia. It should be noted that commercial livestock treks from southern Ethiopia to Mogadishu did not halt after the 1991 Somali government collapse, but the political situation is complex and the area is extremely insecure.

In addition to these regional factors, the Kenyan economy is regarded as bureaucratic and corrupt in all the sectors, and these factors deter investors in the pastoral livestock marketing sector. For example, in February 2003 a group of pastoralist livestock traders in Kenya exported 750 camels to Egypt. It was reported that the Egyptian importer was extremely upset by the unnecessary harassment and delays from the Kenya livestock officials (Mahmoud, 2006). It is highly probable that the disappearance of the camel importer from the Kenyan scene led to his and fellow importers' appearance in Ethiopia.

Markets and brokers

The Moyale livestock market on the Ethiopian side of the border has three major divisions, for camels, cattle, and sheep and goats, but the camel market is the most prominent and lively of all. It is a relatively modern facility supported through USAID funds, and contrasts sharply with the market on the Kenyan side of the border, which can best be described as dilapidated. It is important to note that the drivers of the trade are rising demand and prices, and not necessarily the improved market facilities on the Ethiopia side. Pastoralists are responding to emerging markets irrespective of improved roads and market places, although these facilities are appreciated. The sustainability of the new market facilities on the Moyale, Ethiopia side need to be considered for the long-term service for pastoralists.

Trading activities in Moyale begin early in the morning and end before noon each day, except when the market is closed on Sundays. There are several tea kiosks in the market area, mostly operated by women – one of the key groups that indirectly benefit from camel trade. Also, the tea kiosks are meeting places used for negotiations and information sharing among the various market actors. Police officers watch over the market to maintain order and ensure the safety of partic-ipants. The officers may also be called upon to mediate between disputing parties in addition to enforcing tax payments to local authorities.

As is the case with most pastoral livestock markets in the Horn of Africa, the pricing, sales, and other activities of the camel market in Moyale, Ethiopia are heavily dependent on brokers. Sudanese traders in Moyale praise the role of their brokers for helping them in the market place and reward them with payment. Brokers are an invaluable link between Sudanese exporters and local traders and herders and sometimes act as guarantors for both sides. Brokers are paid between KSh200–500 (US$2.3–5.8) per camel sold. Livestock brokers are so influential that they can determine livestock prices in the market on a daily basis, sometimes keeping prices high and at other times lowering the prices. Different market actors forge relationships that are based on such factors as ethnicity, kinship, patron-client, and livestock loaning. Ethnicity is important in camel marketing in the Moyale market as herders tend to trust brokers from their own ethnic groups. Thus, the general trend is that most brokers sell for herders and traders of their ethnic groups.

However, not all brokers are honest with herders, especially if those herders have very little experience with the market prices and transactions. Some brokers are said to be extremely greedy and raise their fees for unwary traders and herders. Incidents are common in which, for example, a broker would sell a young camel for

Ksh25,000, give the herder only Ksh20,000 and keep Ksh5,000 for himself. When challenged about the high fees, the broker would not hesitate to threaten the trader that he would sell the animals to other traders. Most brokers in the Moyale, Ethiopia market are from Ajuran, Boran, Degodia, Gabra, and Garri groups.

Significance of the camel trade to herders and traders

Camel trading at the Moyale, Ethiopia market is a good example of an emerging enterprise which is strengthening the livestock-based economy with direct and improved benefits to local herders. Numerous factors explain the significance of this growing trade. First, the response of camel herders to the demands for camels is overwhelming. Herders are supplying camels to Moyale from as far as Rendille, Tana River, and Chalbi areas in Kenya, as well as from southern Somalia. This remarkable response is driven by the high prices offered at the market place in Moyale. Table 8.1 shows the range of camel prices at the Moyale, Ethiopia livestock market, with prices reaching US$1,400 for a large, grade one adult. Grading is based on body size and general body condition and this assessment is done locally by brokers, herders, and traders to determine the worth of the camels that are brought to the market for sale.

Second, it is believed that the number of camel herders and traders going for Hajj in Saudi Arabia has increased dramatically in recent years. The increased incomes for camel herders and traders could be enabling more people to afford the trip to Mecca for the Islamic Hajj ritual. One key informant stated that four years ago only about eight people could afford to go for Hajj from Moyale annually, but now over 100 people are making the trip.

Third, camel trade is becoming a mechanism that is facilitating restocking and herd building among pastoral communities that participate in the trade. For example, a herder sells an adult camel for Ksh80,000 and immediately purchases two or three immature camels from the same market for about Ksh20,000 each. After these purchases the herder is left with about Ksh20–40,000 to buy foodstuffs and meet other obligations. Finally, the Moyale camel trade is an activity of both regional and international dimension attracting participants from various places in the region and also from abroad.

TABLE 8.1 Grades, body description and prices in Moyale, Ethiopia market, 2010

Grade	Description	Price range
Grade 1	Adults 8–9 years old, large in body size	Ksh80–120,000 (US$923–1400)
Grade 2	Immature camels, medium in body size	Ksh50–60,000 (US$583–700)
Grade 3	Immature camels, small in body size	Ksh25–40,000 (US$291–466)

Source: author's field notes

The impact of the Moyale camel market on camel trade in Kenya

The Moyale camel trade undoubtedly has a significant effect on both household incomes and other regional livestock markets such as Garissa. The trade influences camel movements to other destinations in Kenya, the availability of camel meat locally, and camel production practices in the region.

Increased camel sales, increased incomes

The turnover of sales at the Moyale market is significant, which may be an indicator that herders are earning more from the sale of their camels than in the past. For example, daily camel sales at the Moyale, Kenya market fluctuate depending on the demand for camels on the Ethiopian side, plus a host of factors on the supply side in the countries and regions that deliver the camels. General estimates indicate daily sales of some 100–300 camels at the market, six days a week. Working with a sales figure of 100 camels daily sold at an average price of Ksh50,000 for four weeks a month and 12 months a year, Table 8.2 provides an estimate of the value of the trade. The table indicates a substantial flow of money into a small border economy in a short period of time. For example, daily sales of Ksh 5 million (US$58,275) of camels alone in Moyale, Ethiopia is significant.

The recent increase in camel prices in Moyale was confirmed by price data collected on the Ethiopian side and a comparison of prices in 2009 with 2010 (PLI Policy Project, 2010a). Whereas in June 2009 the average camel price was EB 3,995, in June 2010 the average price was EB 10,200 – a 2.6 fold increase. This dramatic increase was attributed to increased demand for camels, in line with the findings of research on the Kenyan side of the border.

The market also generates income for the local administration. The Moyale, Ethiopia local authority collects taxes on each camel sold from both the buyer and the seller. The current market tax is EB 13 charged on both the buyer and the seller. Thus, one camel generates EB 26 (US$1.55). For an annual turnover of about 30,000 camels, the total tax collected would amount to EB 780,000 (US$46,512).

TABLE 8.2 Estimating the value of camel sales at Moyale, Ethiopia market[1]

Time period	Value of 100 camel sales		
	Value (Ksh)	Value (EB)	Value (US$)
Daily	5,000,000	977,271	58,275
Weekly	30,000,000	5,863,626	349,650
Monthly	120,000,000	23,454,504	1,398,600
Annually	1,440,000,000	281,454,048	16,783,200

Source: author's field notes

Declining domestic camel sales: the case of Garissa

The Moyale camel market is believed to have an effect on regional livestock markets, especially for camels. For example, it seems that a large number of camels normally destined for the Kenyan urban markets in Nairobi and Mombasa are being diverted to meet the rising Arabian demand for camels. Consequently, the Garissa market has been affected through reduced camel sales. According to official market records, no camel movements were recorded to major Garissa livestock clients, such as Nairobi and Mombasa, while several thousand cattle, sheep and goats were moved to these and other towns during 2007–09. Although there could be unrecorded or unofficial movement of camels to these destinations, the impact of the Moyale camel market may be considerable.

Livestock destined for Kenyan markets for immediate slaughter or fattening are usually recorded by the relevant institutions issuing movement permits. When livestock move in the opposite direction, as is the case with camels trekking from Tana River and Garissa to Moyale, no permission or recording of the movements is necessary. These movements are similar to seasonal migrations that pastoralists usually undertake in search of range resources in the region, including crossing into neighbouring countries. As more camels are destined for the Moyale market for export to Egypt and the Middle East, large livestock markets such as Garissa are deprived of their share of camels. This may have serious implications for local camel meat availability and consumption in Kenya's major urban centres as illustrated in the following section.

Camel meat consumption in Garissa

Garissa is one of the fastest growing towns in Kenya, principally from livestock wealth (see Little, 2003; Mahmoud, 2010), the presence of UN missions in refugee camps in the area, and investments from the Somali diaspora. Garissa residents consume huge quantities of camel meat and mutton. Figure 8.1 shows the trend in

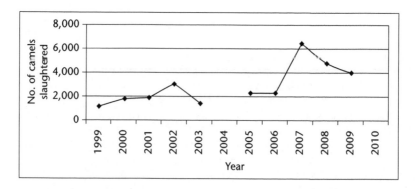

FIGURE 8.1 Camels slaughtered in Garissa town, 1999–2009 (source: Data obtained from the District Veterinary Office, Garissa, Kenya, the author did the analysis).

the number of camels slaughtered in Garissa town during the period 1999–2009. Although the 2004 estimates are missing, there is a gradual increase in the amount of camel meat consumed in the town. However, after reaching its peak in 2007, the trend in butchered camels starts to decline.

Camel exports and implications

There are concerns about the escalating shipment of camels to Arab countries in recent years. Generally, camel herders and traders are responding overwhelmingly to the new market forces to meet the ever increasing demand for camels in Egypt and the Middle East channeled through Ethiopian markets. However, traditionally, the camel helps desperate pastoral populations move away from drought-stricken areas, and camels are slaughtered for sacrifices during communal rituals. Critically, camels provide the much needed milk and meat for family sustenance. The newly emerging use of the camel in the Horn of Africa is its exchange for cash, taking advantage of the best market prices ever offered for camels in the region. Further research is needed to examine how the booming camel trade is affecting other uses of camels, especially for milk production, and to understand how the income from camel sales is used.

As Catley and Aklilu (this book) point out, the benefits of pastoral livestock commercialization need to be understood in terms of wealth groups as, in general, wealthier herders sell more animals. In the case of camels, it seems likely that the dynamic response to the increasing demand is largely a response from relatively wealthy pastoralists who have more camels to sell, or who can adapt their herd composition and management more easily than poorer pastoralists. Again, this aspect of the commercialization trend warrants further study.

Concerns of cross-border camel trade

While camel traders are generally content with the growing business, there are a few, still significant concerns regarding the trade. Indeed, some of these concerns include the general trickle-down effect that the trade should have and raise the question of who benefits more from the trade and what herders ought to gain from the trade. A major concern shared across the pastoralist and trader community is summed up in this trader's statement:

> These are our livestock, but a larger portion of the profits go to others while we just remain as brokers. At the feedlots on the highlands they have feed and water for the animals so those traders have become millionaires through value addition on our camels. As primary producers we would like to fatten the camels here and sell them directly to the Middle East. In that way we shall reap the full benefits of our produce. But this is not the case at present. Although we can buy the feed, we have no adequate water sources here in the lowlands and there is not much help from the government in this regard.

We really need the exporters to come and buy directly from us, only then we can gain maximum benefits from our livestock.

Conclusions and policy implications: opportunities for pro-pastoralist policies

While the pastoral areas of the Horn of Africa are endowed with animal resources, several factors have hindered the full benefits to be gained from market access and livestock sales. These include poor policies, poor roads and communications, inappropriate regulatory mechanisms, insecurity emanating from communal conflicts and political instability, state failure, livestock diseases, poor prices, and marketplace exploitation. However, pastoral livestock trading has grown tremendously in recent years as a result of expanding markets and networks. The sale volumes of key pastoral livestock species of camels, cattle, sheep, and goats have soared as regional markets have grown to accommodate the rising sales. For example, the rapid growth of Garissa in north-eastern Kenya near the border with Somalia and Moyale on the Kenya/Ethiopia border is largely attributed to expanding cattle sales since the 1990s (Little, 2003; Mahmoud, 2010).

While the Ethiopian government seems to show interest in the emerging camel trade in its southern region, Kenyan policy-makers appear to be indifferent to the new developments on the northern border areas. The lack of access to information regarding pastoral trading activities and the general apathy towards the pastoral sector could be depriving the Kenyan economy of massive economic benefits, due to the surge in the value of camels in the country's northern borderlands.

In its policy statement, the government of Kenya acknowledges that it hosts a sizeable population of camels and that the animals are suited to the fragile environment of pastoral territories of the country. It also recognizes the important role that camels play in pastoral food security. Currently, the Kenya government's priority is to popularize camel milk and meat consumption in the rest of the country. It argues that a lot of camel milk is wasted because of lack of markets and poor connections between camel milk production areas and urban centres. It stresses the need to invest in dairy milk processing facilities. While these are positive steps, it is important to recognize that the camel marketing industry is becoming a multi-million dollar business and camels are increasingly becoming an international commodity. A refocus of policies in the light of new developments is not only timely, but crucial, as Kenya is certainly losing on this channel of trade to Ethiopia.

This chapter has demonstrated that an increasing number of camels are being sold in Moyale market for onward shipment to Egypt and Middle Eastern countries. Pastoralists in the region have responded to the growing markets by diverting camels from other markets to the new destination. A lot has been written about pastoral marginalization at the hands of the pro-farmer Ethiopian and Kenyan regimes. The long-held premises of anti-pastoralist policies including low productivity of the pastoral sector and unresponsiveness to markets have been challenged for a long time. The arguments for new directions in pastoral development include promoting pastoral livestock marketing (Scoones and Graham, 1994; Little, 2002). Each of the countries that provides and facilitates the camel trade has different policy regimes which need to be examined with respect to the new ideas that are being developed in the trading network. Generally, this is an excellent opportunity for the Ethiopian and Kenyan governments to review their anti-pastoralist policies and initiate a strong pro-pastoralist policy path to support pastoral involvement and innovations in the emerging market opportunities.

Note

1   The price of camels in the Moyale market has remained almost the same in the past six months or so, but the dollar has gained substantially against the Ethiopian Birr and Kenyan Shillings. The currency conversion rates are, as of March 16, 2011, 1US$ = EB 16.77; 1US$ = Ksh85.8; 1EB = Ksh5.12; obtained from www.finance.yahoo.com.

9

'RESPONSIBLE COMPANIES' AND AFRICAN LIVESTOCK-KEEPERS

Helping, teaching but not learning?

John Morton

Introduction

Much work in pastoral development in recent years has been around increasing pastoralist voice or representation and improving dialogues between pastoralists and other stakeholders in pastoral development: with the national and local state, with NGOs and civil society, and with researchers. However, there has been a relative absence of work that seeks to link pastoralists with the private sector (beyond the vital but distinctive case of veterinary services), and increase private sector engagement in pastoral development. This is surprising for two reasons.

First, pastoralists are not 'subsistence producers', nor are they 'isolated' from national and global trade (McPeak *et al.*, 2006). Livestock trade has been an important feature of most pastoral societies in Africa for centuries (Kerven, 1992) and pastoralists increasingly use purchased inputs, especially veterinary drugs, and are consumers of many other goods and services purchased from the market. In a globalizing world, they are increasingly involved in global value chains involving the corporate private sector. Given all this, the lack of a body of understanding and practical experience on relations between pastoralists and the corporate sector is increasingly problematic.

Second, 'Corporate Social Responsibility' (CSR), a concept that evolved in the context of 'developed countries', has become an important idea in development programmes and debates. For example, the UK Department for International Development suggests that, 'by following socially responsible practices, the growth generated by the private sector will be more inclusive, equitable and poverty reducing' (DFID, n.d. cited in Jenkins, 2005).

In his book on Fulani pastoralists in Senegal, Vatin (1996) describes the failed attempts by the Swiss dairy multinational, Nestlé, to establish a collection system for fresh milk and to mould pastoralists into a different kind of producer. Here, investments in CSR, like so many aid programmes, overlooked the pastoralist context and multiple objectives of livestock rearing. Other than Vatin's work, there appear to be no other accounts of CSR-type experiences in pastoralist areas.

This chapter examines two case studies of recent private sector involvement in pastoralist areas of Ethiopia, and extensive mixed crop-livestock systems in Uganda. The case studies had different geneses and objectives, but a theme of the private sector 'teaching but not learning' emerged independently from both.

Corporate Social Responsibility in development

CSR is an evolving and contested concept, especially in developing countries. Definitions of CSR are various, and can relate to commercial viability, wider values, or both. Critically, CSR is generally seen as a voluntary commitment by business, rather than compliance to external rules. A broad definition of CSR is:

> An umbrella term for a variety of theories and practices all of which recognize the following: (a) that companies have a responsibility for their impact on society and the natural environment, sometimes beyond legal compliance and the liability of individuals; (b) that companies have a responsibility for the behaviour of others with whom they do business (e.g. within supply chains); and (c) that business needs to manage its relationship with wider society, whether for reasons of commercial viability or to add value to society.
>
> *(Blowfield and Frynas, 2005)*

Although some analysis of CSR in developing countries is available (Blowfield and Frynas, 2005; Blowfield, 2005; Prieto-Carron *et al.*, 2006; Hamann, 2007; Edward and Tallontire, 2009), this work focuses on northern companies in developing countries, or on CSR among indigenous companies in the larger 'emerging economies' (Frynas, 2006), with less on how CSR might be understood and played out by indigenous firms in smaller, poorer economies. It seems evident that further research is needed in developing countries, with emphasis on indigenous corporate sectors, and taking care to consider the socio-cultural context of CSR, including local traditions of philanthropy (often differentiated from CSR in a Western context). The other key area of discussion on CSR in development is the question of 'the business case' for CSR and whether this privileges the fundamental values of business, and over-rides a whole raft of questions about the role (or not) of business in poverty reduction (Blowfield, 2005, p524).

Ethiopia: complexities of responsibility

This case study is based on interviews and workshops with four meat export companies and six livestock export companies (out of five and 12 companies respectively then operating) in Ethiopia in 2007. The companies were all Ethiopian-owned and formally registered, and all but one were small, solely owned or family businesses.

During the interviews we used an inclusive view of CSR and did not assume that CSR was a familiar concept in Ethiopia, or that it should be framed according to definitions in the north. We tried to capture a range of perceptions and behaviour that might loosely translate into CSR, including philanthropy.

The international meat and livestock trade is central to Ethiopian pastoralism, as well as providing two of the country's largest exports. Government sources value 2002/03 national official livestock exports at $US606,437 and meat exports at $US2,896,782, with most exports directed to the Gulf States. It is estimated that pastoralist-owned livestock account for 20 per cent of the national cattle population, 25 per cent of the sheep, 75 per cent of the goats and almost 100 per cent of the camels. However, they account for the great majority of the country's official meat and livestock exports (Greenhalgh and Orchard, 2005). Pastoralists are also engaged in unofficial cross-border trades with neighbouring countries, with trade volumes that dwarf official exports.

Pastoralist livestock marketing in Ethiopia is complex, with a dynamic set of actors, such as local traders and agents (Solomon *et al.*, 2003; Saperstein and Farmer, 2006; Umar with Baulch, 2007; Aklilu and Catley, 2009). There is variation between value chains in different regions, and exporters have different preferences and practices. Most of the meat and livestock exporters operate mixed strategies for purchasing, using their own salaried staff, small traders and brokers. Both the meat and livestock exporters also use cooperatives and pastoral livestock marketing groups, especially in Borena zone (e.g. Desta *et al.*, 2006).

Attitudes to Corporate Social Responsibility

The exporting companies were generally unfamiliar with the concept of CSR, and expressed mixed, complex views that were hard to summarize. Some direct quotes from informants illustrate the complexity of the issues:

- 'Business is not a charity.'
- 'Creating an export market could be considered as social responsibility because the pastoralists benefit.'
- 'Our real competitors are not each other, they are India, Sudan, Australia.'
- 'As a company we have a responsibility: if the pastoralists do not survive, we do not survive.'

These quotes show how within quite a small group, views range from a very orthodox view that business has no responsibilities, through views that by doing business the exporters benefit either pastoralists or the national economy, to a more nuanced view of the specific vulnerabilities of pastoralism, and consequent vulnerabilities of the sectors that depend on it.

In practical terms, several exporters had made philanthropic donations (about US$500 to US$5,000 annually) to educational and other causes in pastoral areas. Some companies had engaged in two closely related activities within this general field that could be labelled CSR, specifically drought-time destocking, and educating pastoralists on the requirements of the livestock market. Each of these is discussed in more detail below.

While the concept of CSR was generally new to exporters, they seemed to accept some overall connection between their business and the issue of pastoral development, and were willing to enter into a dialogue about the relationship between their survival as businesses and their responsibilities towards pastoralists.

However, both meat and livestock exporters felt that if they were to implement responsible practices, this would be easier through their respective trade associations than as individual companies. They also took a strong view that the livestock and meat industries were in an early stage of development, and still dependent on government and donors for guidance and capacity-building. At this early stage, government, not companies, needed to take the lead in pastoral development. The livestock exporters had a specific angle on this, as they see government policy as favouring meat export as more 'progressive' – one livestock exporter was vociferous in stating he had no reason to be concerned with pastoral development since the government has a discriminatory policy. The companies want government to take action on a number of pastoral development issues: improving animal health service delivery, providing livestock market infrastructure, providing businesses with soft credit. In these suggestions they were very much in line with current international orthodoxy on pastoral development. Some companies, however, supported further-reaching policies that are more controversial, such as sedentarization of pastoralists and restructuring of land tenure in the direction of more fixed individual or small-group title.

Drought and destocking

The frequent droughts in pastoral areas of Ethiopia have serious effects on the meat and livestock export companies, but also present an opportunity to examine the way these companies engage with pastoralists in ways that might be considered to show 'corporate responsibility'. As a generalization, one of the most important responses of pastoralists to drought is to sell livestock. However, during drought animals are often in poorer condition, and prices are low due to increased market supply and distress sales. The poor condition of animals hinders trekking to markets, and so pastoralists are more dependent on livestock traders who come with their own transport. In Ethiopia, there is good evidence that pastoralists wish to sell more animals during drought than they currently do.

For meat-exporting companies (at least in Ethiopia), droughts affect the quality of meat and may disrupt supply and therefore long-term market share. Drought also seriously affects live animal export through the declining condition of animals, and consequent need for extra fattening before they can be exported. However, the business impact for both groups is generally one of a reduction in profit rather than an actual loss.

In Ethiopia, NGOs and international donors have involved private companies in purchasing livestock during drought that would otherwise go unsold, a practice variously referred to as 'destocking', 'commercial destocking' or 'emergency live-stock marketing interventions' (Morton, 2006). During the 2005–06 drought in southern Ethiopia the Livestock Marketing Department and Save the Children US (SCUS) supported familiarization tours of the rangelands for meat and live animal exporters, and later, offered soft credit (Abebe *et al.*, 2008). The *livestock exporters* became involved on a large scale, with at least two companies buying 20,000 head of cattle. A thorough impact assessment has concluded on the basis of this experience that 'commercial destocking is a viable and useful drought intervention' (Abebe *et al.*, 2008). Companies bought more animals than they would otherwise have done, bought from communities more distant from tarmac roads, and bought animals in worse condition. It appears that the tours organized by SCUS, and continuing discussions between SCUS and the traders, were the triggers – loans were only taken after the purchasing was underway. The companies most involved freely admit that they were able to build their reputations among pastoralists to their long-term commercial advantage. The manager of the most active company said, 'we did it to strengthen our relationships with the pastoralists: now everyone in Borana knows the name of [the company owner]'. But it is clear from outside observers (such as the responsible officer at SCUS) that something more than even long-term commercial motives was involved.

Ethiopian *meat export companies* assisted pastoralists during drought by buying marginally more livestock than they would have done based only on short-term profits, temporarily overstocking their holding grounds to do so. Two of the four companies interviewed told us they had bought 2,000 cattle and 2,000 smallstock respectively, in excess of their holding ground capacity. Any additional buying has been limited by the lack of fattening facilities, and the fact that Borana pastoralists sell mainly cattle during drought, while the meat export companies deal mainly in small stock carcasses. Representatives of the only large company in the sample told us that they had bought additional stock during the 2006 drought that they had then sold into domestic meat markets, but this does not appear to have been the case for other companies.

Training pastoralists for export markets

Exporters also show a strong desire to influence the supply of livestock for sale by pastoralists. In practice this has taken, and is likely to continue taking, two overlapping forms: hosting, in conjunction with development agencies, 'study tours' of export abattoirs; and encouraging certain sorts of 'well-performing' cooperatives. All four of the meat exporters we interviewed and one of the livestock exporters had been involved in hosting study tours of abattoirs and other locations associated with the export trade. Participants were variously identified as 'clan leaders', 'tribal elders', leaders of cooperatives or pastoral marketing groups, or ordinary pastoralists. It is important to note that exporters saw their hosting of the tours as collaborating with aid projects rather than being beneficiaries of them, of fitting into the category of 'responsibility for pastoral development' we were exploring with them, and being of a piece with both destocking activities during drought and with philanthropic donations. Exporters made small monetary outlays to host the pastoralists.

Project reports and publications by those involved give a sense of the objectives and underlying assumptions of the tours. The organization Agricultural Cooperative Development International/Volunteers in Overseas Cooperative Assistance (ACDI-VOCA) reports on tours in early 2006 as follows:

> Over the course of these trips and meetings, seller groups ... obtained information on buyers' requirements in terms of weight, sex, age and other parameters, and buyers were informed of the timing frequency and market days.
>
> *(ACDI-VOCA, 2006, p6)*

This is referred to as an 'exchange of information' but the information *imparted to pastoralists* appears to have been fuller and more fundamental than the information *obtained from them*. Similarly, for earlier tours organized by the Pastoral Risk Management (PARIMA) programme:

> The pastoral participants, overall, were selected based on their potential to serve as community mentors and role models to increase the chance they could pass knowledge on to others . . . the two tours allowed the pastoralists to better grasp what an export market network entails and exposed them to various events along a marketing chain from production and processing to final sale of a wide variety of products. The tour members learned about required quality, size (i.e. 6–10kg dressed carcass weight), and health criteria that export markets demand, associations between grading and pricing, and the growing demand for specific grades of small ruminants for export.
>
> *(Desta et al., 2006, p114)*

While this report notes that pastoralists also were able to express their concerns about marketing, the language used ('mentors', 'pass on knowledge') and the very specificity of the knowledge passed on ('6–10kg dressed carcass weight') suggest a process where the balance of real communication was distinctly uni-directional.

From our own interviews there were similarly revealing comments. The manager of one export abattoir stated: 'VOCA brought the pastoralists here – we gave them our specifications'. In response to a question on whether he felt responsibility for pastoral development, one livestock exporter replied emphatically that he did. Pastoralists, he said, do not want to sell old animals and replace them with younger animals in order to be 'business-oriented'; he himself was prepared to contribute to the costs of communicating to them that they should do so.

Uganda: creating new channels for veterinary drug supply

South-east Uganda is an endemic zone for acute human sleeping sickness, and cattle are the main reservoir for the parasite *Trypanosoma brucei rhodesiense* that causes the disease. The parasite is transmitted between cattle and humans by tsetse flies. In 1998 there was an outbreak of acute sleeping sickness in Soroti, north-west of the traditional endemic zone. National and international concern increased, not only because of the human suffering involved, but also due to a perceived risk that acute sleeping sickness would spread further and merge with foci of chronic sleeping sickness, caused by *T.b. gambiense*, in north-west Uganda, greatly complicating the work of correct diagnosis and treatment (Morton, 2010a).

Research carried out among others by Makerere University, the University of Edinburgh, and the Natural Resources Institute, provided possible solutions to the outbreak. Modelling results showed that a mass synchronized treatment of cattle with injectable trypanocides called Veridium® and VerebinB12® would clear the cattle reservoir of trypanosomes, while a recurrent programme of mass spraying (or painting) cattle with insecticide would prevent reinfection by killing the tsetse fly. A suitable insecticide was marketed as Vectocid®.

The sleeping sickness campaign

In 2006 the 'Stamp Out Sleeping Sickness Campaign' (SOS) started in five districts north-west of Soroti. These districts, inhabited mainly by Teso and Lango people, are characterized by mixed farming, including use of draft cattle; cattle were also extensively grazed at some distance from villages. The SOS partners included the government of Uganda, Makerere and Edinburgh universities, and two private companies. One was the French-based multinational veterinary pharmaceutical company Ceva, the manufacturer of Veridium® and Vectocid®, and the other was the Swedish-based private equity company Industri Kapital (IK), at that time the majority shareholder in Ceva. Both donated veterinary products, but also supported activities that relate to CSR. IK aimed to bring private sector management expertise to the project, and stated a strong interest in 'education and training'. Similarly, Ceva described its involvement at this early stage as 'pure altruism'. It claimed not to seek publicity and saw the control of sleeping sickness as something it could and should do. It was also keen to get government blessing for the initiative.

Initially the campaign achieved a major drop in trypanosome prevalence, but by late 2007, levels were increasing again. It was felt that cattle-owners needed to be encouraged to spray regularly with Vectocid®, rather than relying on mass treatment campaigns, and a second phase of the programme was planned.

Introducing project veterinarians – the 3Vs

In the second phase, IK had divested itself from Ceva, and funded the operation essentially as philanthropy through IKARE, its in-house UK-registered charity. Alongside one further round of mass treatment, five new veterinary graduates would be sponsored by IK to establish themselves in the programme areas, both to raise the awareness of cattle-owners on the importance of regular spraying, and specifically to build sustainable market channels for the sale of Vectocid®. They became known as the '3V vets' after Veridium®, VerebinB12® and Vectocid®.

The 3V vets were employed by a private company called High Heights Services (HHS). Some of the documentation suggests that those funding and leading the programme intended the 3V vets to become self-sustaining businessmen following initial support from the programme, but the objectives of various actors were complex and ambiguous. The programme contract with HHS gives a key objective, 'to initiate and co-ordinate the establishment of a commercial logic for livestock owners to purchase [the three products and] to ensure the products are widely available at all key points in the SOS area'. For Ceva the main objective was to 'fully test whether there was a viable market' for the insecticide, whereas the IK representative stated that initially there was 'no clear vision', but that the main tasks were 'messaging' and 'mapping' the complex landscape of small businesses and NGOs that might act as channels for sales.

By October 2008, the 3V vets were spending most of their time on 'farmer sensitization' and saw themselves as 'people educators' and 'preachers of the gospel'. They were doing some spraying demonstrations and trying to train farmers in the longer term. The problems they faced included large areas to cover, lack of co-operation from local leaders, a 'handout' mentality among farmers and others, fluctuating drug availability, rivalry with local traders, limited collaboration from District Veterinary Officers and lack of business training. At this point the margin they were making on drug sales was only about 10 per cent of the amount they received as salary.

Evolving the business model

In late 2008, IK and Ceva committed themselves to longer-term support and a vision of the 3Vs as self-sustaining businesses. The 3Vs had identified untapped markets, and IK and Ceva extended their support to include basic business training, and advance payments for the 3Vs to rent small shops. The 3Vs also continued to receive some salary support. These moves indicated that IK and Ceva were keeping themselves well-informed about progress and obstacles, and responding with real flexibility.

The new shops were started in relatively remote locations, and sold a wider range of veterinary drugs, rather than only trypanocides and insecticides. Not only did these shops look like enhancing the 3Vs businesses, they also gained the favour of local leaders and District Veterinary Officers. Over time, drug sales increased, and by mid 2009 the 3Vs were dealing with a large and diversified customer base of at least 100 customers, including at least 17 drugstores and 39 private sprayers. At the time of writing, the programme is expanding to new areas to the south-east (*New Agriculturalist*, 2011).

Changing commitments

Despite these improvements, the 3Vs still faced high business running costs and these constraints became exacerbated when Ceva decided to increase the cost of

Vectocid®, and offered franchises to the 3Vs. This created distrust, with the 3Vs seeing Ceva as increasingly profit-orientated and 'tightening everything', compared to IK, whose representative continued to be flexible.

The 3Vs rejected Ceva's franchise offer and instead sourced drugs from Kampala. However, they still struggled with high transaction costs and various external factors that affected farmers' capacity to buy drugs. These included impoverishment from the brutal insurgency of the Lord's Resistance Army, a long dry season in 2008–09, and livestock trade restrictions due to an outbreak of foot and mouth disease.

By May 2009, the 3Vs were highly uncertain about their future, could not envisage becoming self-sustaining businesses, and still needed salaries from IK. The option of commercial loans was closed due to the stringent requirement for collateral, such as buildings. In response, the 3Vs sold increasing amounts of non-project insecticides, which were not effective against tsetse.

Teaching and messaging

In SOS there was a strong emphasis on farmer education and training. The *IK News* article on the campaign uses the terms 'training' and 'teaching' eight times in around 1,500 words:

> This project has a big teaching and training element. We want to build awareness and transfer knowledge on the interaction of human and animal health as well as sickness prevention techniques.
>
> (IK News, 2006)

'Messaging' was also a dominant theme and a key term of campaign rhetoric. These activities were overwhelmingly conceived as education and training *of* farmers, or messaging *to* them. There is undoubtedly much to teach farmers, and much thought needed on how to do so, but the critical approach of learning *from* or *about* farmers was absent. Farmers' objectives for keeping cattle were not understood, nor were farmers' constraints. The business plans of the 3Vs, developed with the help of the Institut Européen d'Administration des Affaires (INSEAD), the internationally renowned business school near Paris, failed to take into account what should have been foreseeable risks such as displacement, drought and market closures.

Conclusions

A number of conclusions can be drawn from the case studies. First, there is a real potential for engaging the private sector in pastoral development, in ways that go beyond companies' short-term business interests, and appeal to what could be called CSR. The destocking activities of the Ethiopian livestock exporters, and the generous funding by IK and Ceva of sleeping sickness control in Uganda, were both at the end of the day very positive interventions on a considerable scale. Both stories demonstrate the decisiveness of the private sector at its best, and also its flexibility to respond to circumstances and try new approaches in ways that development donors would find difficult. NGOs, CSOs, development donors and researchers can and should look for dialogue with the private sector. It will be important not to assume that there is any straightforward or obvious relation between useful CSR-type activities and the size, origin or level of formality of companies. The most effective action came from the 'unprogressive' Ethiopian livestock exporters and from the private equity company.

The case studies also highlight more problematic tendencies of the private sector: to resist learning about pastoralism; to assume that corporate rationality can be used to design pastoralist interventions; and to assume that pastoralists can and should be trained in that corporate rationality. The Ethiopia case study indicated a desire to mould pastoralist marketing behaviour, chiefly by educating them in market requirements for livestock – what was significantly absent was any sense that the exporters themselves needed educating on pastoralists' herd accumulation, off-take strategies, and selling behaviour. The assumed information deficit was entirely one way: pastoralists being ignorant of business. The private sector players in Uganda taught and trained the 3V vets, and indirectly cattle owners, trying to make them conscientious practitioners of scientific preventive animal health and modern business practices, but not acknowledging farmers' profound vulnerability to shocks that made that so difficult.

Suggestions that CSR activities are generically prone to these sorts of blindnesses are found in the literature, with questions over the capacity of corporations to take on community development roles that require 'soft' social science skills of the kind sometimes used in aid management (Prieto-Carrón et al., 2006, p984). Similarly, Blowfield and Frynas (2005, p507) claim that 'stakeholder engagement' – a key concept of the private sector and CSR – 'presents particular challenges in a developing-country context where factors such as language, culture, education and pluralistic values can all affect the process of negotiation and decision-making'. As a result, companies may fall back on 'learning' from market signals only, and in other tightly defined ways.

These are very general questions, but they may become sharpened when private-sector bodies attempt to deal with developing-country livestock-keepers, pastoralists or others, who balance multiple and complex objectives when they keep livestock (Kitalyi et al., 2005). The intersection of what is possibly an intrinsic trait of CSR with the complexity of pastoral systems severely limits the potential development contribution of CSR.

Elsewhere (Morton, 2010b) I have argued for an expanded view of 'power' and 'government' and the way they are exercised over pastoralists, quoting Dean and Hindess (1998, p8) on:

> a whole host of mundane and humble practices, techniques, and forms of practical knowledge which are often overlooked in analyses that concentrate on either political institutions or political thought.

The study tours, incentives, training courses and business plans described in the above cases are just such 'mundane and humble practices', and the ways they are spoken about are such 'forms of practical knowledge'. Detailed attention to these practices and discourses can help reveal what is happening when companies act in the name of CSR or development or both, and thus identify options for other forms of development based on dialogue and mutual respect, in which pastoralists can teach as well as being taught.

Acknowledgements

Several acknowledgements are due. My reading on and analysis of CSR issues in development has been greatly influenced by Dr Anne Tallontire. The study in Ethiopia was funded under the Wellcome Trust's Livestock for Life Programme and carried out in collaboration with Dr Mohammed Mussa, and in part by Dr Mohammed on his own according to a checklist we had agreed. I would like to thank all the exporters and other stakeholders who agreed to be interviewed and to attend workshops. The Ugandan study was funded under DFID's Research into Use Programme. I would like to thank all who agreed to be interviewed, especially Anne Holm Rannaleet, Martin Mitchell and the '3V vets'. My understanding of the sleeping sickness campaign was greatly assisted by Dr Charles Waiswa and many other collaborators, as detailed in the acknowledgements to Morton, 2010a. I would emphasize that the use made of these interviews in this paper is my responsibility alone.

10

TOWN CAMELS AND MILK VILLAGES

The growth of camel milk marketing in the Somali Region of Ethiopia

Abdi Abdullahi, Seid Mohammed and Abdirahman Eid

Introduction

Although pastoralists are often perceived by policy-makers as conservative and resistant to change, Somali herders in the Horn of Africa have a long history of market responsiveness and adaptation. For example, from the 1950s to the mid 1980s, pastoralists in the Bay Region of Somalia shifted the composition of their herds due to the growing demand for beef in Saudi Arabia and Somalia's increasing cattle export trade (Al-Najim, 1991). Another example is from the mid-1970s, when pastoralists around Mogadishu started to supply camel milk to the city (Herren, 1990a). This supply reached 1.5 tons of camel milk daily by the 1980s, and used a network of women milk traders to buy milk from mobile camel herds up to 150km away. With increasing interest in livelihoods support and livelihoods diversification for pastoralists, it is notable that both these examples of innovation occurred without any external support from aid programmes.

In the Somali Region of Ethiopia, there are many explanations for why former pastoralists have settled in towns, including the loss of herds due to drought or disease, the growth of services and markets in towns, and in some cases, wealth as better-off herders settle and seek to diversify their production while enjoying the amenities of town life. The growth of these has encouraged a wealth of innovation, often small in form and quite localized, but which has spread as pastoralists seek to strengthen ties to these important new urban markets.

One innovation that has become widespread is the marketing of camel milk in towns throughout the region, as well as in Addis Ababa to serve its expanding Somali population. Camels, traditionally animals that are husbanded in more remote bush far from settlements, are increasingly kept in and near to towns. These 'town camels' support a growing camel dairying industry to supply milk to town populations. This chapter explains why small towns have grown in Somali Region, and describes the emergence of town-based camel dairying in Gode in the far south of the region. The chapter details the drivers of camel milk marketing in Somali Region and the growing prevalence of 'town camels' and 'milk villages'. By examining the growth of marketing in camel's milk in Gode, the research examines change in the provision of fodder and labour, land use planning of rangelands near to town, and cultural attitudes that support this growing enterprise.

The chapter draws on field research in Gode beginning in May 2010, and visits to several towns to speak with camel-keepers and milk sellers in towns, other townspeople, bush pastoralists, as well as government officials. The research included a household survey and informal discussions with 'town pastoralists', including an elder who was the first camel-keeper to begin selling camel's milk in Gode.

The growth of small towns and new opportunities for pastoralists in Somali Region

Pastoralism in the Somali region of Ethiopia has been changing for some time, and the growth of small towns is one manifestation of the changes. In recent history, towns began to expand with the return of Ethiopian refugees of Somali origin from Somalia in the late 1980s and early 1990s. Towns like Dollo, Filtu, Nagelle, Moyale, Charati and Gode were swollen by returnees. The returnee population, while originally from pastoralist backgrounds, had resided in camps and settlements in Somalia. Being accustomed to town life, and lacking livestock and knowledge of herding to return to a customary pastoralist livelihood, most returnees chose to settle in the outskirts of towns where they could better access basic services such as education, health and water. Crucially, the returnee population, although they owned very few or no animals, sought milk and other livestock products, particularly from camels. However, camel milk remained scarce in towns since camels are typically kept far from towns in bush areas.

Over time, these towns continued to expand, drawing an ever growing population of Somalis who have settled. The introduction of regional autonomy in Ethiopia from the mid-1990s led to greater devolution of power and resources to local people at district (*woreda*) level. Relative to any other time in Ethiopia's history, urban centres started to be administered by ethnic Somalis who were directly related to pastoralists on the rangelands, who spoke the Somali language, and who had cultural, social and economic ties to pastoralism. It seems likely that this shift made towns more attractive to pastoralists. In addition, to have better access to food aid, political representation and basic human services, pastoralists not only moved into existing settlements but also established new villages and settlement centres to get the attention of local administrations and NGOs.

Most research tends to view the growth of small towns negatively, as either symptomatic of worsening poverty levels among the pastoralist population or because pastoralists have been pushed to give up livestock-keeping for alternative livelihoods. While it is true that towns are expanding as more pastoralists move out of full-time livestock keeping, the growth of towns has also brought new opportunities for marketing, livelihood diversification and accessing services. It is important therefore to better understand the phenomenon of small-town growth in pastoralist areas to help identify how pastoralists can capitalize on this important yet poorly understood trend.

Many factors other than destitution help to explain the growth of small towns in Somali Region. District (*woreda*) capitals such as Gode have experienced tremendous growth as development planning and resource distribution has become focused at the district-level. A large infusion of development funding along with improved infrastructure and connections to larger regional centres has spurred growth in these remote centres. The commercialization of livestock in Somali Region has been evident for many years (Catley and Aklilu, this book) and in part, small towns grow as wealthier herders move from the rangelands to the town and diversify their activities. Similarly, commercialization attracts traders who in turn, need hotels and restaurants, and the demand for products such as milk and meat increases. Prominent traders are procuring camels from these towns to supply the booming export markets in Egypt, Sudan and the Arabian Peninsula (Hussein Mahmoud, this book). The spread of network coverage for mobile phones means that herders can access more accurate market information on livestock prices in the region. With markets being established closer to 'home', herders no longer have to trek animals to distant sale yards, which causes animals to lose weight. This means that the animals can fetch a better price. The growth of small towns also supports the commercialization of livestock production, with holding pens and livestock sale yards being established in *woreda* centres.

Another broad factor that pulls people towards small towns is the better provision of social services relative to rural areas. In common with many other pastoralist areas in Africa, in Somali Region the accessibility to health and education is far better for people in urban centres (Devereux, 2006). Schooling has improved, giving youth from poorer pastoralist backgrounds more options to move into non-livestock work and as government offices expand, many have aspirations to gain employment in the public sector (Jackson, 2011). NGOs and the UN also have offices in towns, and employment by these organizations is seen as highly lucrative.

Small town expansion is also related to land uses in some areas as deeper connections develop with regional and international markets, as government and private investment rises, and as growing numbers of pastoralists move out of full-time livestock keeping. Domestic and overseas investment is transforming areas such as Negelle and Medawolabu, where large commercial wheat farms have been established. These farms are eating away at prime grazing lands and poorer herders who are less able to manage these worsening restrictions on access to pasture are moving out of livestock-keeping and into different livelihoods. However, youth from poorer pastoralist families, previously with few or no options to make a living, are seeking work as labourers on the commercial farms.

In some areas adjacent to the highlands, small farms are mushrooming on the sub-humid rangelands as pastoralists seek to diversify beyond the herd. Small towns help to make such diversification more productive as they provide: better access to markets; extension support and other inputs to improve production; and opportunities to add value to farm products. The provision of electricity to towns like Negelle and Medawolabu has supported new cottage industries in baking and milling. In times past, wheat was milled in Awassa or Shashamene and sold to pastoralists at a very high price. Local milling in pastoralist areas has helped to rein in the costs of grain, particularly for townspeople who depend more on grains and less on livestock products in their diets. Keeping camels in and near to towns is part of these changing trends in livelihoods, markets and society in the lowlands of Somali Region.

Camel dairying in Gode

Background to Gode

The town of Gode is situated in the far south of Somali Region. It is the former capital of the region, but currently is a zonal and district (*woreda*) centre. The area is a typical, low-lying arid and semi-arid pastoralist area with annual rainfall of only around 200mm and mean annual temperature of 28°C. According to government statistics in 2007, the population of Gode district was 109,584, with 43,134 people living in Gode town. The town is quite close to the border of Somalia, and had strong links ethnically and economically with Somalia. Another important defining feature of Gode is its position next to the Wabi Shabelle river. The people in the rural areas are a mix of crop farmers and pastoralists. The pastoralists tend camels, small ruminants, cattle and donkeys through seasonal movements between the wet season grazing areas in the interior and the dry season grazing areas along the river. The farmers depend mainly on growing maize, produced under gravity or pump-fed surface irrigation along the river banks, and sorghum which is traditionally grown in the two rainy seasons – the main *gu* rainy season and the shorter *deyr* rainy season. The area has a long history of irrigation dating back to the 1960s (PLI Policy Project, 2010b). Although the area is among the most drought-affected pastoral areas in Ethiopia, at the same time, the communities located in the low-lying areas along the river are also affected by regular flooding caused by heavy rainfall in the highlands. The floods destroy crops and livestock, but also provide an opportunity to practice flood recession agriculture.

The camel dairying innovation

> He who has goats has a garment full of corn;
> A milch cow is a temporary vanity;
> A he-camel is the muscle that sustains life;
> A she-camel – whoever may have her – is the mother of men.[1]

Customarily, camels are the most important signifier of wealth and determinant of status within Somali society. Camel keeping has also been the preserve of pastoralists living in the bush. Camels were kept far from settlements, especially during the dry season, and the milk produced by camels was used mostly for direct consumption by herders or in the household. In the past, the sale and exchange of camel milk in the region was not really part of the many connections that bonded pastoralists with town, although they would bring fermented camel's milk (*susa'i*) to give as gifts to family and friends they visited when travelling to towns.

The innovation of keeping camels around Gode town to supply milk was traced back to a single 75-year-old man called Afi Mes'ud, an elder from the Abul Wak clan, who had lived in Kenya and Somalia as a refugee before returning to settle in Gode. The idea had very modest origins and arose from his attempts to sell a she-camel to pay a bill at a local health centre:

> One day in early 1990s, I took a she-camel to the market in Gode. But I could find no buyer willing to pay me a fair price. I could not return the animal to the bush. So I decided to keep it with my family in Gode. In Kenya and Somalia where I had lived, people in towns kept camels and sold milk at high prices. So it came naturally to me to see the opportunity, and begin settled dairy camel production, and capitalize on high prices for camel milk. That was how the new scheme started.

Thus, selling camel's milk to townspeople began with one innovator who was responsive to an emerging market and needed new income. For a while, no other townspeople sought to follow Afi Mes'ud's new idea. Newcomers to Gode, being mostly poorer pastoralists who were no longer able to move with their herds, were the first to try selling milk in town. They often came to town with one or two camels and, like Afi Mes'ud, were looking for new ways to make a living in a context that was unfamiliar.

Over the next 20 years, keeping camels and selling milk in Gode town spread from a single innovator to over 100 households. The Somali Region Pastoral and Agro-pastoral Research Institute estimated that there were between 100 and 150 camels living in the centre of Gode, and hundreds more camels lived on the periphery of Gode in so-called 'milk villages', where the camels could be moved more easily to nearby rangelands. Our research shows that urban camel-keepers had relatively small livestock holding compared to pastoralists, and on average kept only two to three camels, four sheep and goats, and less than one cow or donkey. The camels consist mostly of lactating females and calves. The she-camels are milked twice a day and much of the milk is sold, but there are marked seasonal variations in production and prices (Table 10.1). During the wet season, milk supply increases because the camels have better feed, but the price decreases due to the extra supply.

Comparison of the levels of milk off-take in urban camels with camels managed traditionally on the rangeland is not straightforward, because many studies in pastoralist areas do not distinguish between milk production (or milk yield) and milk off-take. The former measures both milk consumed by calves and milk taken during milking, whereas the latter measures only the milk volume at milking. In Somalia,

TABLE 10.1 Urban camel milk production in Gode, Somali Region

Urban production indicators	Wet season	Dry season
Average milk off-take per camel per day (litres)[1]	3.38 (2.68–3.70)	2.39 (1.70–2.66)
Average price (Ethiopian birr/litre)	10[2]	15[2]
Milk off-take per household per day (litres)	6.26	3.90
Home consumption per day (litres)	1.27	0.98
Sales per day (litres)	4.52	2.90

1   Milk off-take figures do not take account of the milk consumed directly by camel calves, hence total
    milk production is greater than milk off-take.
2   Equivalent to US$0.59/litre and US$0.88/litre in wet and dry seasons respectively.

camel milk off-take is estimated to be about 4 litres/day during the wet season and
1 litre/day during the dry season (Herren, 1993), indicating that the Gode urban
camels produce less than the traditional system during the wet season, but more
during the dry season. Relatively high season off-take in urban camels might be a
result of supplementary feeding (see below).

It is difficult to estimate the total number of camels involved in the urban dairy
system and milk villages, but higher estimates were around 800 camels. If correct,
this number would result in an average daily revenue from milk sales of around
Ethiopian birr 30,000 (US$1765). Petty traders, mostly women, purchase the milk
from producers and sell to small shops and restaurants in town.

As indicated earlier in the chapter, the spread of urban camel dairying from the
originator of the approach to other households was a slow process, and took place
over 20 years or more. Those who adopted the approach early on explained that
many people did not support the idea of keeping camels in the town, and various
beliefs were mentioned that hindered adoption. Traditionalists in Somali society
believe that towns are unhealthy environments for camels because of the existence
of strange 'odours' and the 'evil eye' of the poor living in towns. Therefore, camels
exposed to towns were thought to suffer from ill-health or die. Others who opposed
the system argued that the traditional camel husbandry system and culture of the
pastoral community should be protected. These attitudes have slowly changed as
townspeople have become accustomed to camels living in towns, and this attitudinal
change is part of the innovation process.

Husbandry changes related to urban camel dairying

Innovations in accessing feed and looking after camels were also necessary to support
small-scale camel dairying in Gode. For feeding urban camels, owners used a mix
of communal rangeland, privately enclosed land and additional supplementary feeds.
During the wet season, use was made of communal areas up to about 8km from the
town, whereas during the dry season, similar areas were accessed 10–17km from
town. Dry season enclosures were either owned by the camel-keepers, or rented

from others. In addition to using dry season feeds such as hay, camel-keepers have developed their own feeds, such as boiling a 'soup' made from the meat of shoats, oil and sugar. The chaff of wheat was also boiled with sugar and fed to camels during drought. As towns become more important in pastoralist areas, some herders and townspeople produce fodder on enclosures near to town to sustain 'town camels' as well as livestock brought to towns for sale.

Herding camels is skilled work and requires time when camels living in towns must be driven to rangelands to find sufficient feed. Furthermore, camel-keepers in town, who are mostly quite poor, have other demands on their time and little spare labour within their household. Camel-keepers handle these constraints by setting up informal cooperatives in which camels are herded in a larger group, and the households rotate responsibility for looking after the larger herd. Sharing the burden in this way frees up time for camel-keepers to pursue complementary activities in towns, since herds are small and do not provide for all of a household's needs. Although town herders call this an 'innovation', sharing labour and mutual help is a practice that runs deeply in Somali society.

Urban camel dairying retains many linkages with traditional pastoralism, and to some extent was dependent on these linkages. Somali society is based on strong ties between clan members, and this allowed urban camel-keepers to keep dry female camels in the rural areas, either with direct family members or clan relatives; only the milking camels and their calves were kept in or around the town. Also, the urban producers did not keep bull camels and so used the bulls of relatives for breeding their females. In these ways, the new system allows pastoralists to make best use of both urban and rural centres, with easy access to markets in the town, and more abundant fodder on the rangelands. The connection between the old and new systems also made the new system less alien to pastoralists, and disruptive to traditional institutions and beliefs.

Growing networks of milk trade

The growth of urban camel dairying in Gode illustrates a trend towards increasing camel and cattle milk trading in Somali Region since the arrival of returnees in the pastoral areas some years ago. Cattle milk used to be more popular in towns than camel's milk, whereas that preference has now been reversed and the price of camel milk far exceeds cow milk.

At least four milk trading routes are well-established (Figure 10.1): the Finchawa to Moyale route in Borena zone of Oromia Region of Ethiopia covers a distance of 360km to the Kenyan border; the Boqol-manyo to Suftu route in Liban zone of Somali Region covers 120km and links to Mandera town in Kenya; the Awash to Addis Ababa in the eastern Shawa zone of Oromiya serves mainly Somalis in Addis Ababa about 200km away; and the Babile to Tog-wachale route passing through Jijiga links to the markets in Somaliland and the Gulf states. Further study is needed to determine the volume of trade and milk prices on these routes.

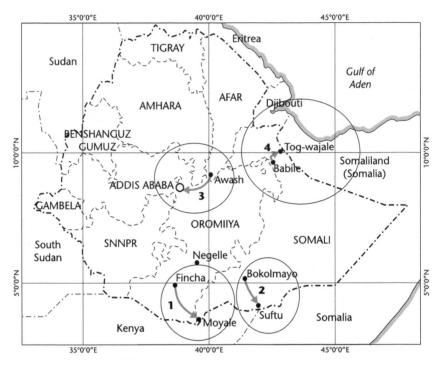

FIGURE 10.1 Map showing milk trading routes (source: author).

Reflections on the importance of town camels and milk villages

Camel dairying began with a few individuals who exploited an emerging market in growing small towns, as many newcomers to towns came from pastoralist back-grounds and preferred to drink camel milk. Typically, commercialization processes start with – and mainly benefit - relatively wealthy pastoralists and others who become more market-orientated (Catley and Aklilu, this book). The camel dairy-ing in Gode followed a rather different pathway, beginning with poorer, more town-based herders who were seeking new sources of income. Many of these people were forced out of pastoralism due to drought and other factors. Although started by poorer, former pastoralists, it was notable that some wealthier individuals were also beginning to keep camels in towns, seeing the benefits of diversifying their production into new areas. Significantly, the objective of keeping camels in towns is very different from bush pastoralism, where breeding and maximizing the size of the herd is an objective shared by many. Instead, small-scale dairying and tapping new markets is the primary objective of those who keep camels in towns.

Selling camel's milk in towns has proven lucrative for some town-based owners, who have used their income to purchase plots in town and build houses. Furthermore, keeping camels in towns has created new income for women, who are the main buyers of camel milk and sell this in the market as well as to restaurants. Urban camel owners explain that herding in and near to towns has some advantages, such as easier access to markets, veterinary treatment for livestock, and diversification to complement keeping few livestock. Pastoralists in towns also note that they were able to organize themselves more easily than when they lived in the bush to lobby the government to provide treatments for camel diseases, a still neglected issue.

For aid donors and policy-makers, the growth of urban camel dairying illustrates local innovation of former pastoralists who responded to market demands. The new approach is likely to continue to grow as urban populations increase. There may also be opportunities to expand camel milk marketing by looking more at markets in neighbouring countries and the Middle East.

Note

1   A well-known poem, translated from Somali.

PART III

Land and conflict

11

THE FUTURE OF PASTORALIST CONFLICT IN THE HORN OF AFRICA

Paul Goldsmith

Introduction

Conflict is a form of disorder intrinsic to development processes. The impacts of violent conflict on economy and governance represent both a set of costs and specific indicators of serious problems on different levels of the system. Pastoralist conflict has for decades acted as a source of positive feedback reinforcing perceptions of pastoralism as a static and anti-modern mode of production. More recently, however, it has become a critical source of negative (or system-changing) feedback for contemporary socioeconomic processes. Pastoralist exclusion and the militarized responses resulting from it are now taken seriously as a destabilizing force across the region. Pastoralist conflicts have exposed state policy biases, highlighted issues of resource management, reaffirmed the instrumental value of indigenous cultural institutions, and contributed to the increasing involvement of regional and supra-state organizations working with local civil society.

The Horn of Africa is undergoing a capitalist transition. High rates of demographic growth, technology change, accumulation of indigenous capital, contested rights and popular support for legal-constitutional reforms, state-supported initiatives for regional economic and institutional integration, and a host of other developments all point to such a transition. Such transitions are by definition uneven and often accompanied by conflict. They provide the primary context for assessing the direction of future pastoralist conflicts explored in this chapter. Commercial forces are penetrating the livestock economy, pastoralists are seeking greater inclusion *via* diverse political and social channels, and governments are belatedly realizing the importance of the range livestock sector as a critical source of economic and human capital. Future conflicts will reflect the transitional dynamics overtaking all but the most isolated pockets of the larger rangeland region.

The region's capitalist transition has reached the point of no return, but the wide disparities among regions and communities remain an obstacle. The feedback generated by pastoralist conflict during the current phase transition may ultimately be seen as a vital contribution to regional socioeconomic transformation, at least in some cases. But the patterns of internal conflict detailed by Krätli and Swift (1999) remain, and chronic resource and political frictions can also result in economic relapse in pockets of the region, or even contribute to the collapse of national political systems – the situation in Somalia exemplifying the complicated influence of internal Somali factors on the region's political economy over time.

While pastoralists' ability to negotiate change will be a critical determinant of future outcomes, this chapter considers various off-range forces and dynamics that are likely to condition new forms of resistance and conflict in the coming years.

Drivers and trends of future pastoral conflict

The global processes associated with the current phase of 'late capitalism' provide a context for assessing trends in pastoralist conflicts. Grono (2011) identifies five drivers of future trends in conflict in this context, including:

1 Weak states with low capacity.
2 Tensions between authoritarian regimes and popular demands for greater political space.
3 Competition over scarce resources, exacerbated by climate change.
4 Extremist religious movements seeking violent political change.
5 The growing reach and power of transnational organized crime networks.

He went on to observe that, 'in many cases it's not about doing things differently, but doing better the things we already know should be done . . . The starting point is that policymakers need to have a sophisticated understanding of the key dynamics of the countries they are dealing with.'

So what are the 'key dynamics' in the case of the Horn of Africa's rangelands and pastoralist societies – and how do they articulate with the five 'drivers' listed above? There are a number of overlapping factors specific to pastoralist regions that heighten the prospects of future conflict.

• Higher population growth rates exacerbating declining total livestock units (TLU) ratios, environmental degradation in many areas while increasing the numbers of unemployed males within pastoralist communities.
• The developmental gap, including biased policies and terms of trade, that inhibits capital accumulation and reinvestment while increasing social and environmental vulnerability to system 'shocks' like climate change and spiking food and fuel prices etc.
• The 'tax' imposed by high transaction costs, high input costs, outside investment in commercial ventures, and other factors reducing the profits realized through export of livestock and other new and old rangeland commodities.
• Spatial and environmental factors militating against monitoring, policing, and other state and/or components of conflict management.

- Exposure to open source innovations and technological inputs contributing to the adoption of new military strategies, tactics, and weaponry associated with fourth generation warfare. This trend also includes piracy and other new forms of social banditry and ideologically justified participation in black market economies and globalizing criminal networks.
- The negative influence of the state despite the rhetoric of regional integration, e.g. the impact of securitization policies and traditional counter-insurgency methods in regions with Muslim populations.
- The potentially negative impact of Asian capital in marginal regions, which is aggravated by reform-dampening political patronage at the centre.

The picture emerging from this analysis indicates that pre-existing patterns of conflict will continue to be problematic, while new variations based on the factors noted above will present new practical and policy-related dilemmas. But the shifting equation also includes a number of positive trends and potential mitigations that are enhancing the productivity and efficiency of the rangeland sector:

- The role of civil society and capacity of local communities to project their voice on the national and international level.
- De facto and formal policies of subsidiarity promoting devolved decision-making, management of resources, and indigenous conflict management.
- The potential of information and communications technology for closing the economic and infrastructural gap between highland and lowland regions.
- Diversification of household economies underscoring the growing economic productivity of pastoralist women.
- Development policies mandating community participation, utilization of traditional technologies and knowledge, and evaluation of the environmental and social impacts of projects and interventions.
- The shift in public perceptions and attitudes supporting national agendas promoting minority inclusion.
- The continuing role of remittances from overseas diaspora, and permanent and cyclical returnees' contribution to social welfare, service delivery, and building local economies.
- Improved resilience and capacity for adaptation to uncertainty that comes with revitalization of the pastoralist cultural endowment.
- Incremental implementation of conflict early warning systems and other elements of peace infrastructure under the aegis of the Intergovernmental Authority on Development (IGAD) and the African Union (AU).

It is difficult to anticipate how these factors and other less predictable phenomena like the populist Arab reawakening in North Africa – will articulate across the region. From the perspective of this analytical frame, global warming is not a new phenomenon; the shock administered by the great Sahel famine of 1974–76 initiated a basic reordering of household strategies in the rangelands. In contrast, the reform process engenders some new conflicts of its own. In southern Ethiopia, for example, economic incorporation is promoting the 'politicization of kinship relations' while communities rush to stake out 'parochial' claims to territory (Hagmann and Mulugeta, 2008).

Ensminger (1992) traced the success of Orma herders of Kenya's coastal hinterland to reduced transaction costs, yet commercialization also instigates new forms of criminality and conflict as Mahmoud (2009) documents for the Kenyan–Ethiopian cross-border zone. Insecurity significantly raises the transaction costs for pastoralist producers and traders. His analysis of marketing-related costs shows that security accounted for 7 per cent of the cattle transport costs on the Moyale-Isiolo route, 5.7 per cent on the Samburu–Isiolo route, and 7.4 per cent on the Wajir–Isiolo route.

While the value of animal protein has risen apace with population growth over the past decade, these costs, increasingly severe droughts, rising energy prices, and other factors at least partially negate the gains on the household level. These trends question the ability of the livestock sector to replicate the role of agricultural commodities as an engine of pastoralist household accumulation and development (Goldsmith, 2008).

Long-standing differences among individual states and issues such as transnational water management within the larger Common Market for Eastern and Southern Africa (COMESA) region will also continue to be critical variables. Factoring for the most tangible drivers of future conflict at this juncture, however, inevitably leads us to focus on how the neo-classical economic regime of international capital impacts in the region.

There is no evidence the neo-liberal policy frame has arrested the longitudinal trend of declining terms of trade between the small-scale agriculture and livestock sectors (Zaal and Deitz, 1999). Neo-liberal policies have also reduced the provision of the same state services that fostered agricultural diversification after independence. Contrary to the promise of increased employment and income for the poor, critics have documented how the free-flow of international capital has increased their vulnerability by eroding communal access to resources (Zoomers, 2010). Indigenous rangeland populations rarely enjoy legal ownership complementing customary usufruct rights to their lands. Policies promoting the commoditization of land justify their fears of losing control over vital natural resources.

Where some see raiding as a threat to pastoralist cultural survival (Gray *et al.*, 2003), pastoralist activists often note that internal conflicts had the unintended benefit of preserving their land and resources from state exploitation. Coping with the influence of international capital may prove more difficult to fight in comparison.

The China foreign investment model

Eliciting some important elements of the Chinese Model helps us to better understand the implications of their rising profile across the continent for marginal areas. The rapidly growing role of China in Africa can be seen in its growing influence on internal political and inter-state power relations, unencumbered capacity to parlay patronage resources into government tenders and concessions, and alternating positive/negative aspects of its role as an alternative to Western donors and their policies (Large, 2008).

The Chinese alternative, although a positive development in many ways, is also exerting a dampening effect on internal forces of democratization. If the policy of working through sovereign governments and support for repressive leaders (Robert Mugabe in Zimbabwe and Omar Bashir in Sudan) highlights the illiberal dimension of their African interventions, the Chinese are contributing to regional economic integration through their emphasis on infrastructure development. It remains to be seen if this will benefit pastoralists and other vulnerable minorities over the longer term.

Ideologically, the Chinese Model conflates the dominant role of the state with Confucian emphases on harmony and stability. Participation in Western institutions of global economy is conditioned by the autonomy conferred by the country's large population and historical episodes of self-imposed isolation. They joined the World Trade Organization only recently, and at this stage of their national development they appear reluctant to adopt growth-tempering rules and standards that come with many international treaties and protocols.

Access to oil and natural resources define China's primary national interests in Africa, and this is typically secured by entering into long-term contracts with national governments. The Chinese foreign investment model generally follows the government's domestic developmental strategies, which is backed by an ethnic monoculture (the Han Chinese are 92 per cent of China's 1.2 billion population) organized within a rigid hierarchical system. China's foreign policy focus on national sovereignty accounts for the seemingly invisible quality of local communities, and minorities in particular.

We should nevertheless point out that where Western human rights policies focus on individual rights and political freedoms, the Chinese concept of human rights is based on satisfying the need for basic food, health, and housing on the population level – and that China has successfully reduced the global population of people living beneath the poverty level by several hundred million in a relatively short space of time. Building local hospitals and schools is the most visible manifestation of their human rights policy in Africa.

China watchers attribute the large increase in the 2012 military budget and rapid development of a blue water navy to the dangers facing the growing population of Chinese abroad. The indication is, they see attacks on oil facilities in Sudan and the Ogaden, and events like recent labour riots in Zambia, as harbingers of a larger future trend.[1]

These factors and the kind of power relations that come with a US$60 billion foreign currency surplus suggest it will be difficult for China's decision-makers and policy analysts, who are overseeing the most successful phase of economic growth in the country's history, to appreciate the narrative of multi-ethnic competition, lateral power structures, and the lopsided qualities of African politics in place of their own models of African polities. These observations are qualified by the fact this is a relatively early phase of Chinese global involvement.

The more serious concern over the resource extraction and infrastructure focus of Asian international capital is that its positive effects will once again bypass range-land and minority communities. Pastoralists may be at the forefront of major future conflicts if this scenario comes to pass; the ultra-ambitious Lamu Port South Sudan and Ethiopia Transport Corridor (LAPSSET) project is likely to be an important test case for minority and national civil society advocacy.

Implications of the LAPSSET land bridge

LAPSSET is a US$20 billion infrastructure initiative, whose first phase involves constructing a new port located in Magogoni in Kenya's Lamu District, and infra-structural linkages connecting it to Juba and Addis Ababa. China has used its connections with the Kenyan government to emerge as the lead financier. The lack of transparency and consultation attending the award of initial tenders, large land allocations in the Tana River/Lamu region, and contracts for oil exploration in the hinterland have raised alarms among pastoralists and coastal minority groups. Speculators have acquired large chunks of land in Lamu and Tana River, and secretly along the corridor's proposed route. Uncontrolled in-migration has swollen the Lamu District population by 17.8 per cent since 1999 while Kenya's national rate of demographic increase over the same period was 2.8 per cent.

The issues raised by LAPSSET and the Magogoni port contradict the content and spirit of the reformist agenda at a time when implementation of Kenya's new constitution is fostering perceptions that historical injustices will be rectified. Although release of the feasibility study undertaken by a Japanese firm and discussion of its contents in Parliament are supposed to precede implementation, the govern-ment proceeded to issue tenders for the construction of the first three berths.

The network will open up the isolated coastal hinterland and large expanses of rangeland to capital investment. Pastoralists rue the irony of massive investment occurring just when their traditional livestock economy is beginning to generate a measure of monetary value and institutional respect. Many pastoral leaders fear that the influx of foreign capital and infrastructural development will be the Trojan Horse dooming their identity and way of life. After decades of political passivity, the Swahili and their pastoralist neighbours now talk about violent resistance. The influence of foreign capital in marginal areas is likely to catalyse prolonged resistance before this happens.[2] If this occurs, linkages with other conflict zones in the Islamic world will drive new insurgencies utilizing the 'open source' methods associated with fourth generation warfare (4GW), the sophisticated all-systems model of resistance that evolved in response to the marginalizing effect of globalization on ethnic communities elsewhere. This will likely extend the conflict to urban areas, include attacks on civilians and foreign targets, and feature *systempunkt* attacks on critical nodes in electricity, water, transport, and other infrastructural systems – while exploiting black market and criminal networks to sustain the insurgency (Ronfeldt and Arquilla, 2001; Robb, 2007).

Actors within the larger trans-national Somali community are familiar with many of the 4GW methods and strategies waged by non-state actors, and like the case of small arms proliferation, this could lead to their adoption by other pastoralist insurgents in the future.

The Somali factor

Somalia continues to be the region's most problematic and unpredictable area. The collapse of the Somali state lent credence to the conveniently named 'crescent of crisis' (Keenan, 2007), while catalyzing one of the planet's most robust global economic juggernauts. Small ports dotting Somalia's long coastline harbour the world's most notorious pirates; Djibouti hosts the US army's Advanced Frigate Consortium (AFCON) hub. In the north, the Republic of Somaliland recovered from a period of clan warfare to emerge as an exemplar of indigenous governance; similar conditions in southern Somalia support a conflict system that is impacting across the larger eastern Horn of Africa region.

Since independence Somali has featured as the epicentre of rangeland conflicts in adjacent countries. The effects of the Shifta war in Kenya extended into the 1980s as herders raided each other to restock. Subsequent episodes of raiding in Kenya reflected periodic political disturbances in Somalia. The collapse of Syad Barre's government triggered a wave of banditry and communal clashes while providing many of the weapons pastoralist communities acquired during the 1990s. A prolonged insurgency continues to challenge the Ethiopian government's control and legitimacy in large areas of the Ogaden.

Somalia emerged as an incubator of Islamist militancy in the mid-1990s. Foreign trainers in the Al-Qaeda training base across the Kenyan border in Ras Kiamboni operated in the open before dispersing after the Kikambala attacks in 2002. Although the Islamic Courts Union (ICU) sheltered several known Al-Qaeda agents and received support from external jihadi networks, it was essentially a nationalist movement. The transition from movement to a proper government would have diminished the role of Somalia as a terrorist safe haven. Instead, covert CIA support for the Warlord alliance and the US-backed Ethiopian invasion had the opposite effect. The subsequent rise of Al Shabaab increased the threat of terrorism across the region.

The US government is now funding soft-power initiatives like the Mandera triangle project and the construction of schools in Lamu District to balance the radicalizing feedback generated by counter-insurgency interventions in southern Somalia and their securitization policy equivalents on the Kenyan coast. These include the rendition of innocent civilians following the 2006 invasion that saw Faizul Mohammed and other 'high value' Islamic Courts Union leaders flee towards the Kenya border.

Bradbury and Kleinmann (2010) discuss the problems and some of the positives of American hearts and minds interventions in Lamu and North Eastern Province. The goals of the programme – which was also designed to extend the reach of the state into areas where it has traditionally had a weak, intermittent, or predatory presence – are defined as the '4Ps': preventing conflict, promoting regional security, protecting coalition interests, and prevailing against extremism. However, the large¹ localized projects carried out by the US military civil affairs team have not won hearts and minds, had any discernible impact on regional security dynamics, or addressed the causes of persistent human securities, which related to far deeper state–society relations and development failures (Bradbury and Kleinmann, 2010).

The Islamists' activities suggest that ideologically justified opportunism and criminal economic incentives are equally if not more important motivators than opposition to American foreign policy. And as the network behind the Kampala 2010 World Cup bombings revealed, the more dangerous radicalization may occur among segments of the population not related ethnically or culturally to the aggrieved groups; many of the actors behind the operation were non-Somali Muslims from predominantly Christian ethnic groups.[3]

These factors underscore the view that civil society is the best arena for mediating the fierce and bloody contest for the hearts and minds of the Muslim *umma*, and other non-Muslim inhabitants of the rangelands by extension. However, the security imperative has negatively affected the position of minorities and Muslims in general, and has constrained their contribution to the civil society movement in different national arenas (Howell and Lind, 2009). This presents a basic contradiction in respect to the ostensible objectives of securitization policies that Lind and Howell (2010) explore in respect to the constraints imposed on CSOs in Kenya and the larger region. Perceptions of Muslim civil society organizations' position on the root causes of terrorism, however, fuel suspicions about their motives and those who support them. The growing clout of Somali capitalism, however, may prove to be more influential over the long term.

The 'mystery' of Somali capital

The security issues raised by Somalia's state collapse tend to obscure the Somali community's dynamic response to the new opportunities arising in its wake. Their contemporary success in accumulating capital underscores the resilience of Somali lineage organization, spatial mobility, risk taking and rapid adaptation to new opportunities, and how this cultural endowment has replicated the dynamics of traditional pastoralism within the global economy.

Clan identity is still a driver of conflict inside Somalia. However, in the larger economic domain augmented by the post-1991 diaspora, lineages serve as stable units in wider networks that dramatically increase returns to labour and investment. Cultural and behavioural traits bred in the rangelands – mobility, resilience, and a propensity for risk-taking in uncertain conditions – generate new synergies within free-scale networks exploiting multiple off-range resource patches.

Salafi networks tapping into the Middle Eastern oil wealth were a critical factor in the spread of Somalia's Islamist movement. Many thousands of Somalis are employed and running businesses in the diaspora, and there are many other income streams. Kenyan Somalis have distinguished themselves in high-income professions and the private sector. Somali transporters are active in a region spanning the Congo, South Sudan, the Horn, and southern Africa. That much of the monies provided by both Western and Islamist financiers for weapons and military operations is diverted into more productive activities – and not Islamist radicalism – reveals the real import of the Somali factor in global networks.

Lineage-based social organization provides a vehicle for Somalis in Africa and abroad to pool their financial resources. This entrepreneurship, and traditional pastoralist resilience and risk-taking – and not the profits of piracy and banditry – go a long way towards explaining the mystery of Somali capitalism (Goldsmith, 2010). The piracy problem, in contrast, began as isolated incidents of social banditry before morphing into a highly organized form of criminal predation complete with share-issuing syndicates.

lineage-based org'n!

The profits generated by piracy are often invoked to explain the rise of Nairobi's Eastleigh neighbourhood as a thriving commercial hub and the high profile of Somali investment in Kenyan real estate. The value and distribution of ransom payments, however, do not support this hypothesis. Annual pirate ransom payments have leveled off after passing US$100 million in 2008 – a fraction of the profits generated by legitimate Somali businesses and the funds remitted by the Somali diaspora (Abdulsamad, 2011).

piracy

Where Ethiopia has maintained its role as a military bulwark against Somali irredentism, Kenya chose to act as a safe haven, initially for Somali refugees and later for Somali investment. The latter strategy has promoted ethnic integration while allowing the Kenyan government to walk the tight line between security and repression fairly successfully.

In any event, a World Bank study (Maimbo, 2006) indicates the resources and technical skills accumulating within the Somali diaspora will be a powerful engine for reconstruction and development when conditions inside Somalia permit. This is already occurring in Somaliland, albeit on a modest level, where the revived tuna fish cannery in Las Khoreh and new soap powder and beverage factories in Burao are producing goods for export. There are also cases where returnees have sparked new and long-dormant clan frictions.[4] The eventuality of a large-scale repatriation of people and investment capital is bound to generate a new set of problems and conflicts roiling the internal political *status quo*. The government of President Kahin, for example, rejected a proposal by Somalilanders abroad to rehabilitate the dormant cement plant outside Berbera.

The new Somali economy provides a counterpoint that appears to be lessening the role of clan identity as a driver of conflict over time. The Somali ability to adapt their pastoral cultural endowment to the off-range economy may or may not have a galvanizing effect on how the larger pastoralist and minority community copes with issues like the LAPSSET project. Somali and other nodes of pastoralist capital will provide a powerful alternative to the influence of international capital in rangeland areas over time.

Security as a public good: international forces and indigenous responses

Local security, as the matrix of issues responsible for the rise of Somali piracy and other related drivers of conflict demonstrate, is necessarily a global concern. Yet, local security is in turn related to wider drivers of political and economic incorporation and integration.

The neo-liberal economic policy has unleashed powerful forces expanding the sphere of economic competition, fostering technological innovation, and enhancing more efficient production. But neo-liberal democracy has also increased inequality, weakened collective management of the environment, aggravated social problems, distorted political power relations, undermined the institutional capacity to regulate the circulation of capital, and heightened the conditions of economic insecurity that increasing numbers of people live under (Bujra, 2005; Armbrust, 2011).

The distortionary effect of the neo-liberal regime recalls the problems of the state's economic hegemony before it. Small groups of strategically located elites typically capture a disproportionate share of surplus generated by occasional spikes, leaving most of the population to absorb the impact of the corresponding shocks.

Gundel (2006) illuminates how cultural institutions and traditional structures of Somali governance, although not without their problems, have functioned remarkably well in very difficult circumstances. Other pastoral communities have similar structures for internal governance that are critical for maintaining peace on the grassroots level. Dynamics on the ground highlight Ruttan's (1982) argument that a society's cultural endowment is an essential if often neglected element enabling the synergetic function of its resource base, technological capacity, and economic institutions. Reinforcing the efficacy of local problem-solving processes is at least one part of the puzzle.

A networked civil society can exert a multiplier effect within local communities. The movements based on networked individuals operating independent of formal opposition parties that are revolutionizing governance in the Arab world are a yet more virile exemplar (El Shakry, 2011), but the spread of information technology requisite for it to work in the rangelands is lagging in the margins of this region.

Conclusion: exit or devolved sovereignty?

The evolving situation in the region's rangelands demonstrates clear parallels with the transnational area of autonomous indigenous peoples popularized by James C. Scott's 2009 study of *Zomia*. Conflict has been the primary driver of developments weakening state control in the region, and outright collapse in Somalia. Across pastoral areas of the Horn of Africa, there is a common legacy of biased policies, unsecured land rights, and economic marginalization (Goldsmith *et al.*, 2009).

In many cases, the militarization of ethnic relations Jok and Hutchinson (1999) reported for the Dinka and Nuer replaced the generations of co-evolutionary clan and social dynamics documented by Schlee (1989) in northern Kenya. In contrast to the cynical exploitation of conflict by some elders and local elites, livestock raiding and banditry revealed a trend towards cultural anomie or normlessness among the youth in the north Rift Valley, Somalia, and southern Sudan. Both trends accompanied the weakening of state control in remote regions and the lapse of traditional mechanisms that formerly limited the impact of communal violence.

The surge in communal conflict spurred civil society advocacy, the critique of state neglect and marginalization. The subsequent adoption of participatory conflict management and the revival of cultural protocols governing it have restored a measure of internal equilibrium to the rangelands in many areas. The success of the Wajir Peace Committee in reducing the endemic insecurity prevailing in Kenya's North Eastern Province prompted the implementation of district peace committees across Kenya, and the creation of a special conflict monitoring body in the Office of the President (Menkhaus, 2008).

The influence of cross-border factors, the impact of conflicts beyond the rangelands, and expanding circulation of firearms spurred a corresponding development of regional security institutions. Although the on-the-ground impact of bodies like CEWARN, a conflict monitoring and early warning body based in Addis Ababa, remains limited, improvement in the peace infrastructure and implementation of a regional livestock branding and tracing system will mark a new threshold in institutional capacity in addition to curbing the incidence of rustling (Ekuam, 2009).

Local benefits notwithstanding, securing the peace serves the larger prerogative of making rangeland regions safe for in-migration and settlement, international investment in resource extraction, export agriculture, and new transport corridors to the sea. The problem of centralized state sovereignty remains.

Interventions combating Islamist terrorism have often emphasized their opponents' rage against the West when the real drivers of minority discontent are much closer to home. Their grievances have more to do with the hegemony of ethnic majorities, and economic inequities responsible for reducing proud and formerly self-reliant communities to highly vulnerable wards of the region's states. Efforts to redress the equation will have to go much further than reforms currently on the table if the centre is to hold. Provisions in Kenya's new constitution that provide for legalization of customary communal tenure and recognition of historical injustices appear liberal by the standards of the current legal order. But they are largely negated by the government's Vision 2030, a blueprint for national development that threatens to reduce pastoralists to herders on pockets of range and indigenous communities on the coast to minorities in their own homelands.

In 2008 a group of peasant intellectuals in the coastal region of Kenya began challenging the legal agreements facilitating the incorporation of the ten-mile strip, which was a Protectorate separate from the Kenya Colony under British rule, into independent Kenya. The state claimed the Mombasa Republican Council (MRC) was an armed gang and banned it. By 2011, the MRC campaign to reestablish coastal autonomy through the courts and other non-violent means had morphed into a social movement enjoying massive support in Mombasa, rural areas and other coastal towns (Goldsmith, 2011). Similar sentiments prevail in northern Kenya where pastoralist communities voted overwhelmingly against unification with Kenya in a 1962 referendum. The same applies for many other pastoralist-inhabited areas of the Horn. After five turbulent decades, the negotiation of devolved control over land and resources with local communities may yet produce an adaptive model of governance for the rangelands. Failure to do so will reinforce the secessionist sentiments long present in many rangeland areas.

Notes

1 The Ethiopian government rejected China's demand to station soldiers in the Ogaden after Somali rebels attacked an exploration site and killed several Chinese nationals. The Chinese reportedly do maintain a military presence guarding oil facilities in the Bentiu area of Sudan.
2 Several years ago the Chinese financed the development of a modern port in Gwadar, a traditional Pakistani dhow harbor, and transport links transiting the hinterland of central Asia. Hyped to promote prosperity and regional integration, the project spawned massive corruption, land-grabbing by state elites, and fuelled a still-raging insurgency waged by Baluchi secessionists (Robert Kaplan, Pakistan's Fatal Shore, *The Atlantic Monthly*, May 2009). China recently signed an agreement with Pakistan to turn the unused Gwadar facility into a naval base.
3 'Kenya: Suspected Al Shabaab terror squad named', *Nairobi Star*, Kamore Maina and Abdilatif Maalim, 8 March 2011.
4 Mahdi Abdille, unpublished dissertation research.

12

LAND GRABBING IN THE EASTERN AFRICAN RANGELANDS

John G. Galaty

Introduction

The appropriation of rangelands by a variety of actors who use political means to achieve what would normally be socially and economically impossible is one of the most critical factors undermining pastoral productive land uses and innovation in the Horn and east Africa. 'Land grabbing', which has become a general idiom of African politics as salient as the 'politics of the belly' (Bayart, 1993), is especially striking in dryland locales because of the scale with which it is pursued. Within the large setting of African modernity and political economic change, this chapter examines recent large-scale land acquisitions in East Africa, identifying factors that make pastoral landholding vulnerable and the strategies used by those who have seized pastoral lands. What is in question is the disappearance from under the feet of local inhabitants of the resources that provide them livelihood security now and represent their stake in innovations for the future (Vidal, 2010).

For reasons intrinsic to drylands and herding, pastoral lands are vulnerable to being grabbed. On a scale never before envisioned, the most valued pastoral lands are being acquired through state allocation or purchase for two purposes: by agro-industrial companies or foreign states promising to use it for highly efficient commercial agriculture, and by conservation groups and entrepreneurs who vow to protect wildlife and propagate high-end lucrative tourist ventures (European Civil Society, 2009; Friis and Reenberg, 2010).

The fragmentation of rangelands, through changing forms of property and land use, has proven a global phenomenon, with important impacts on dryland ecology, and livelihoods of resident communities (Galvin *et al.*, 2008). Formal shifts in tenure have made landholding vulnerable, but informal factors initiated by population growth and land scarcity have led enterprising individuals to move to landholding frontiers, building on networks, friendships or opportunities to gain slivers of land by leasing or purchasing small farms or simply squatting in areas seen as 'under-utilized' (Berry, 2009).

The notion of pastoral land rights was considered an oxymoron during the early colonial period when the requirement of 'productively transforming' the land meant that cultivators were granted rights that hunters and foragers and pastoralists were not, territories of the latter deemed Crown lands or state holdings. But if we consider 'tenure', legally a modern notion, to derive from historical 'holdings' (from the French, *tenir*), then pastoralists clearly gained, maintained and defended rights – like imperialists – through force of arms, and – as witnessed throughout the literature on pastoralism – the threat of violence (Kurimoto and Simonse, 1998; Schlee and Watson, 2009).

Given pastoralists' martial talents, the reciprocal dynamic of husbandry entrains in herders the need to defend their property. But while pastoralists claim and recognize pastoral territories, access has been socially mediated through an inclusive process of management, other herders welcomed or at least tolerated in times of stress. Herders rarely felt constrained to remain in core territories when drought demanded that they find pastures elsewhere (Homewood, 2008). The motility of the herding process reflects the unpredictability of rainfall and the spatial dispersion of pastures across drylands, and the opportunism and spontaneity shown by herders (Galaty, 1993, in press).

Pastoralists' vulnerability to losing land can be attributed to their systematic refusal to embrace a bounded, alienable and exclusionary notion of landed property, or to attitudes of the land seekers. Stereotypical views of pastoralists have disarmed them in debates over how rangeland should be held and used: that they are traditionalists, keep livestock for cultural rather than economic reasons, maintain herds as customary wealth rather than for instrumental reasons, tend to overgraze and degrade land, and refuse to market their animals (Roe, 1994; Galaty, 2002). While research has thoroughly refuted these views (Sandford, 1983; Behnke and Scoones, 1992; Scoones, 1995a; McPeak and Little, 2006) they persist in public perception and policy-makers' minds, in part because such perspectives seem to justify attempts to grab land for other ostensibly more 'productive' uses.

What follows is an examination of three forms of land grabbing experienced in East Africa in recent years: the appropriation of enormous amounts of fertile land through 'agrarian colonialism' by states and commercial agro-businesses; the acquisition of wildlife-rich range areas by entrepreneurs practicing a sort of 'environmental imperialism' to create private game parks and high-end tourist attractions; and loss of Maasai land in Kenya via what I call 'legal theft' during the privatization process.

The new agrarian colonialism in Ethiopia

Africa has recently experienced unprecedented acquisition of land by international agro-businesses, purporting to enhance food security in their own countries by developing land elsewhere (World Bank, 2010). Ethiopia now has 1,300 foreign investors (the majority from India, China, Europe and the Middle East) with licences for commercial farms, and promises to make up to 3 million ha. available to them (Graham *et al.*, 2009, p44). Investing US$40 million, an agricultural development company acquired 200,000 ha. to grow export crops, with the aim of expanding its holdings to 500,000 ha. over the next decade, and acquired 150,000 ha. for a livestock project (Cotula and Vermeulen, 2009). Although a small proportion of total land in Ethiopia (1 per cent) (Graham *et al.*, 2009, p10), the lands taken are among the country's most fertile areas, representing crucial dry-season refuges in the rangelands.

A recent article in Ethiopia's *Fortune* (Asfaw, 2011 p30), dated 20 March, notes that the Ministry of Agriculture 'has identified and added 1.9 million hectares to its land bank, which it plans to lease out for development'. The 'land banking procedure' involves earmarking arable land 'until such time as it is profitable for the land to be developed' (Asfaw, 2011 p30). 'The government has been especially active adding more arable plots from hot and arid (*kolla*) areas of the country'. The government land bank has now reached 3.6 million ha., of which 342,099 ha. have been leased to local and foreign investors, especially those intending to grow 'priority produce'. It is claimed that 'the investments will be designed in a way that will not harm local communities or the environment', according to a code of practices that many question. Ethiopia has generated US$91.3 million from exporting flower horticulture and vegetables in the last six months, the Minister testified to Parliament, but this only represented 59 per cent of expected revenues. In fact, the article claimed, with a potent critique hidden in the reportage of facts, expectations were not met due to 'inefficiency, lack of quality, poor management among companies, production cost increases, and the decline of the international market due to global climate change' (Asfaw, 2011, p30).

The countries involved are wealthy but lack abundant agricultural land (e.g. Saudi Arabia) or have very large populations to feed (e.g. India). But global agricultural markets have stimulated this 'outsourcing' of agrarian production, both for foodstuffs and for agro-fuels, for which subsidies have created what appears to be an 'artificial demand' that is moving land from food to fuel production (Asfaw, 2011, p20).

Underpinning the Ethiopian Government's policy of making large-scale lands available for foreign acquisition is the argument that the lands being allocated to foreigners are not under cultivation, that is, are 'underused' (Tolossa, 2011), despite the longevity of occupation and continuity of use.

Most importantly for our purposes, is the process by which these acquisitions are taking place. The form of tenure normally defines how land can be transmitted to commercial landholders. Rangelands occupied by pastoralists are variously held under customary rights, under private title, or by the State. Some acquisitions occur through purchase of titles or leaseholds, but some lands are allocated directly by the state. The mediation of the state is invariably central to land acquisitions (Quan, 2000).

Often customary rights are not codified in law, and though locally recognized, have little status in courts. Most importantly, customary systems often regulate rights of access and use over lands formally held by the State, which often retains the right of allocation (Berry, 1993). After shifts in tenurial systems over many decades, customary rights are often embedded in forms of legal pluralism which both empower land users and undermine recognition of their claims, leading to conflict. However, pressures on existing landholders and pastoralists by the State to acquiesce in their own displacement, regardless of the status of their landholding, show that 'security' of tenure offers no certain protection against appropriation, except where effective court systems operate. As a result, 'focusing primarily on formal aspects of tenure security as a response to land grabbing is not sufficient' (Graham *et al.*, 2009, p24), although the evocation of land rights is invariably a key plank in protests and conflicts that do arise. For Ethiopia, the government maintained that when pastureland was allocated to international investors, 'pastoralists who used this land would not be compensated, as "they should go somewhere else"' (Graham *et al.*, 2009, p46).

Often companies and host governments take advantage of the lack of tenure formalization in localities where customary systems are in force. In Ethiopia, companies first gain a licence from the Ethiopian Investment Commission, then seek out land to acquire, often negotiating with local leaders not empowered to enter into agreements that bind their communities. After the capital to be invested is confirmed and a feasibility study prepared, a leasehold is signed with a regional office, sometimes with the agreement of local elders, after which land is acquired (Cotula and Vermeulen, 2009).

Without implying that foreign investment is intrinsically undesirable or that foreign firms should play no role in stimulating growth in the agricultural economy, it is important to point out that contraventions in the processes followed often result in investments being carried out at the expense of landholders for whom land is scarce and indispensable for local food security. On a continent where most land is not held under formal title, whether by individuals or collectivities, landholding is remarkably stable since it rests on customary systems of rights underpinned by relatively transparent recognition of rights holders by neighbours who share boundaries (Cotula, 2010). Where rights are ambiguous or overlap, it is through negotiations and compromises forged through local figures of authority that solutions are often found that mitigate conflicts (Berry, 1993; Von Benda-Beckman *et al.*, 2006). In some countries, including many formerly under socialist systems of governance, the state is the landholder of last resort. But just as local elders have claimed individual titles over clan lands for which they hold titular or symbolic responsibility, so states often claim the unilateral right to allocate land only nominally under their authority, ignoring all but perfunctory local consent and compensation. Local landholders – especially mobile herders – are often completely unaware that their lands are being acquired in ways that transgress their rights to retain, use or receive compensation for parcels that they hold through local consent and with clear collective recognition. The fragility of customary rights not only makes local landholders vulnerable to land grabbing, but makes foreign investments quite risky if investors believe local rights can simply be ignored (Cotula and Leonard, 2010). The story of land grabbing in Africa is not just a drama involving local landholders and inside or outside investors but implicate officers of the state, who are the inevitable mediators in large-scale allocations of land, gripped by twin motives of trying to control events through eroding local autonomy (and perhaps realize their frustrated ambitions to facilitate 'development') and to draw from a river of benefits themselves.

Environmental imperialism in Tanzania

In Tanzania, the intention was to put land under the management of villages, which, shortly after the Arusha Declaration in 1967, became the foundational unit of socialist administration and resource management. But after neo-liberal reforms had taken hold in the late 1980s, it was realized by state officials that were villages recognized as radical owners of lands, there would be no additional land available for national projects and allocation (Shivji, 1998). During this period, government unilaterally allocated lands in Loliondo to the National Breweries, which alerted local Maasai leaders to the dangers of community lands being lost for local purposes. Arusha Regional authorities encouraged people and investors to pursue agriculture in Loliondo; 100 requests for land in the Loliondo Division in 1985 became 264 in 1989, claiming up to 140 per cent of Loliondo as a whole (an area of 5,755km^2, over 575,000 ha.), creating great insecurity regarding Maasai land rights (TNRF, 2011, p11).

The first pastoral NGO, Korongoro Integrated People Oriented to Conservation (KIPOC), was instrumental in urging Ngorongoro District to 'register' village lands in Loliondo in order to make land in this well-watered highland area less susceptible to appropriation, and this was accomplished in the early 1990s (Hodgson, 2011). But the receipt of title deeds essentially meant that ownership passed to village governments, whose answerability to Village Assemblies or communities was unclear (TNRF, 2011, p12). In 1992 it was with surprise and controversy that the entire Loliondo hunting block was leased to an army officer from Dubai, through the Ortello Business Corporation (OBC) (TNRF, 2011, p16). Villagers felt they had neither been consulted, nor had given their permission. It was considered not by chance that the president of the day was from Zanzibar, which to the chagrin of many mainlanders had recently joined the Arab League. The 'Loliondogate' scandal was heightened by reports of leaseholders shooting rare animals from helicopters, failing to provide promised local assistance, and ejecting herders from the hunting block, which occupied most of the dry season pastures of the Loliondo Maasai. The 1994 Shivji Commission on Land Matters described the Loliondo arrangement with the Arab consortium as a dubious land deal that undermined the land rights and legitimate livelihood pursuits of locals (Shivji, 1998). Numerous conflicts have occurred between the company and both the villages and the government, in particular over continuing range use by pastoralists and the environmental destruction perpetuated by the company in its hunting pursuits (TNRF, 2011, p17). The OBC has, however, guaranteed a continuous flow of annual revenues to governments (US$560,000 to the central government, US$109,000 to Ngorongoro District

Council, US$150,000 to villages), as well as support for anti-poaching and local development projects, mainly in health and education (TNRF, 2011, p18).

Ecotourism and photographic tourist initiatives that villages entered into had originally been encouraged by government to advance community conservation ties, but the OBC objected to these village-level leases and on occasion forced tour companies to leave the area, depriving villages of the considerable revenues they had been receiving (TNRF, 2011, p19). Loliondo (together with the neighbouring Sale Division) had been declared a Game Controlled Area (GCA) since the colonial period, creating an overlap between the GCA and village lands. The Wildlife Conservation Act of 2009 prohibited all agriculture and animal husbandry within a GCA, in principle bringing the 'village' as such into direct conflict with the GCA administration, were that prohibition to be enforced. This eventuality in fact occurred when, in July 2009, government forces evicted Loliondo residents from the OBC hunting area that has long served as dry season grazing for Loliondo villages. Hundreds of homesteads were reported burned, affecting up to 20,000 residents and their 50,000 head of cattle that were ejected from their grazing and water resources at the very time a very serious drought was impacting the entire region (TNRF, 2011, p20). This military operation was justified on environmental grounds, since the region had indeed been affected by the combination of drought conditions and grazing, but no more than would be expected during a period of severe rainfall shortage.

Given the payments made by the OBC for privileged hunting rights to this large sector of land immediately adjacent to the Serengeti National Park, there might be economic reasons to suppress the use of these villages for photographic safaris and livestock production. But figures demonstrate the opposite. In 2007, annual revenues realized on the basis of land area from the OBC Hunting Concession were US$546/km^2. Photographic safaris brought in US$240/km^2 to six Loliondo villages while potential expansion of Serengeti National Park revenues could be expected to generate US$1,418/km^2. However, actual livestock revenues generated US$2,010/km^2. In short, in the absence of the hunting concession, Loliondo could combine livestock production with enhanced earnings both from ecotourist and photographic tourism to generate over six times as much revenue for the Tanzanian nation as OBC provides (TNRF, 2011, p25).

Were village and conservation activities to be integrated through the option of creating a Wildlife Management Area (WMA), tourism, pastoralism and wildlife conservation could coexist with a combination of investments being pursued, ensuring continuing access to grazing while supporting the development of non-hunting tourism.

Exactly the opposite strategy has been pursued on the western side of the Serengeti National Park, where in 2003 an American investor founded Grumeti Reserves, a 140,000 ha. concession created out of Ikorongo Game Reserve, Grumeti Game Reserve and Fort Ikoma Open Area (PR Newswire, 2011). These reserves were originally created as multi-use protected areas to provide catchment areas for wildlife from the Serengeti National Park, with cooperation between the goals of conservation and local livelihoods. By granting a concession over this vast area to an outside investor, Tanzania essentially privatized not only a significant national reserve of wildlife but also lands held by several Tanzanian communities (including Sukuma, Ikoma and Maasai) that were ceded to the concession with the understanding that continuing productive use could be made of the region by locals (cf. Mayunga, 2009).

Why and how have investors been able to gain such enormous amounts of land in Tanzania? While developing a system of economic management and political governance informed by the socialist experiment may have provided Tanzania with a system of administrative organization and a humanitarian ethos, it also left a legacy of centralized decision-making, a philosophical denigration of the capacities and rights of the peasantry, and a ruling party that feels it has both the responsibility and the privilege of unilaterally determining policies that affect every local community. Out of the combination of a dominant ruling party and the onset of market liberalization has emerged a nervousness about ceding too much power to localities and sense of entitlement, that government and party deserve to benefit from the liberalized economy, which in the absence of real growth means access to flows of foreign investment (Chabal and Daloz, 1999). So in considering why lands should be allocated on such a large scale to outside investors, even for non-competitive returns, we must consider that funds invested in Tanzania provide 'rents' for officials (Bayart et al., 1999). Perhaps the key factor to be considered is that a critical amount of the hunting concession revenues from Loliondo and tourist revenues from Grumeti are received by the central government, which finds itself now in competition with its own citizens for sources of revenue. Given a certain amount of statutory devolution to villages of rights over certain tourist activities, the federal government finds that its most direct access to revenues comes from leasing land to foreigners, land that is appropriated from local Tanzanians (UCRT, 2010).

Legal theft: insecurity and land loss in Kenya

The lands held by Maa speakers from central to southern Kenya and northern to central Tanzania are especially illustrative of pastoral land loss, given the sheer diversity and inventiveness of the strategies that have been used to seize their territories. Privatization of rangelands has been carried out under the spurious rubric of making landholding secure (cf. Lesorogol, 2008), while in fact it has done the opposite: it has destabilized local systems of tenure, opened the door to corruption and speculators, and stripped land from pastoralists on the grounds that they were not using the land well and so deserved to lose it (Rutten, 1992). Land loss in Maasailand has involved a progressive hemorrhage of 10, 20, 50, 100 to 1,000 acres at a time, either accumulated by richer herders from poorer, or transferred to outsiders (Homewood et al., 2009). Outsiders, often completely unaware of where land that they have grabbed actually lies, may seek the title-deed, rather than the relatively dry land itself, to use as collateral for loans that are often never repaid, or as long-term investments. So until the fateful day when all obligations are called in, many Maasai have both the money and the land to use. What I will present here is a remarkable case of legalized theft, involving the court-ordered auction of two Group Ranches in their entirety, which may anticipate future ventures in land grabbing on a scale not previously witnessed.

On 15 July 2010, the Kenyan newspapers included a notice given by Njoka & Njoka (K) Ltd regarding the 'Proclamation of Attachment and Sale of Immovable Property', that declared that the Ol Kiramatian and Shompole Group Ranches would be sold at auction at noon on 27 August 2010 at the Kajiado District Land Registry. Ol Kiramatian Group Ranch comprises 20,531 ha., and Shompole 64,989 ha. The two parcels were to be sold to recover a fine of Kshs 5 million (c. US$63,000) against members of the Group Ranch for trespassing on another adjacent land parcel (variously called the Komorora or Nguruman Limited). When compound interest and fees were added, the total came to came to Kshs 18.7 million, or approximately US$235,000. At the judicial proceedings, when the case was finally heard, the counsels for the defendants (two Group Ranches) were not present, nor did they forward the judgment of 2 December 2009 to the authorities of the Group Ranches they were representing (Kenya, 2009). In fact, the final hearing had been moved to a distant court at Kitale, far from the site in Narok where the case originated, and was quickly completed. Only when the auction was announced in the press did leaders of the Groups Ranches hear about the finalization of the case, the unpaid fine, and the upcoming auction. They approached a judge to have the orders stayed.

The case had been running for 20 years since the purported offences had occurred. The original plaint had been registered in 1991, concerning the entry of members of Shompole and Ol Kiramatian Group Ranches into properties of the Nguruman Limited on 'diverse days of December 1990, notably 4th, 7th, 8th, and 27th days of December 1990' (Kenya, 1991). That had been a drought year, and the trespass was carried out by herders seeking to use what had always been part of their dry season grazing, high up on the Nguruman Escarpment, part of the western Rift Valley escarpment that divides Kajiado from Narok District, and the Lodokilani section of Maasai from the Loita section. The trespass was on an area that was originally constituted as a Group Ranch, called Kamorora, which in 1973 had been registered in the name of the 14 members of the adjudication committee. None were in a strict sense resident on the land, but saw an opportunity to intervene to claim the land prior to the time when the larger adjudication process that would create two Group Ranches in the area, Ol Kiramatian and Shompole, was to proceed. Of the fourteen members of the Kamorora group, five were from the Transmara region, two from Kajiado Central (i.e. Lodokilani), six from Loita, and one from Tanzania. The members were primarily civil servants, then serving in diverse governmental positions, including as provincial range manager, Clerk of the County Council, two Councilors (one from Narok, one from Kajiado), and a member of the Presidential Security Service. It appears that when the original Land Certificate was received in 1975, the Nguruman-Kamorora Group Ranch included only 6,970 ha. but, strangely, was enlarged to include 26,993 ha. when the title deed was finally received in 1984.

Lodokilani had been declared an adjudication section in 1969, with the aim of sub-dividing the section into nine Group Ranches, though in the end only seven Group Ranches were created since two irrigation schemes along the Nguruman escarpment were finally incorporated into Shompole and Ol Kiramatian Group Ranches, with the new boundaries taking this change into account being declared in 1970. At that time, there was no mention of a Kamorora Group Ranch, and the land in question was included in the two Group Ranches just mentioned. The Nguruman-Kamorora Group Ranch received the title deed in 1984, the same year that a certain Mr Hermus Philipus Steyn changed the name of the Rift Valley Seed Company to Nguruman Ltd. In 1986, the Nguruman-Kamorora Group Ranch was dissolved and its title and all of its assets transferred to Nguruman Ltd, with its members becoming shareholders in the company, along with Steyn. Steyn was an investor in and main source of capital for the company, but over time he bought out most of the other members, who proved unable to provide the capital they would have owed as shareholders. Steyn built up a tourist camp, under a 20-year lease. This was the enterprise that he claimed incurred serious losses at the time of the Maasai trespass in 1990, since he maintained that clients with whom he had contracts refused to visit while Maasai herders were living in the area (Kenya, 2007).

In the meantime, a suit was brought forward in 2006 by the two major Group Ranches, challenging the ownership of the Kamorora lands, first by the Nguruman-Kamorora Group Ranch, subsequently by Nguruman Ltd (Kenya, 2006). In effect, Shompole and Ol Kiramatian were questioning whether trespass could obtain on lands that they claim belonged to them anyway. Their argument was that the original adjudication of Nguruman-Kamorora was carried out without the knowledge or permission of the residents of Shompole and Ol Kiramatian to whom the land had originally been allocated. Attestations maintain that the group of 14, led by a former government chief of Lodokilani, aimed to defraud locals, some of whom were settled on the land in question, who had rights to the land through residence or via membership in the Group Ranches within which the Nguruman/Kamorora area was located. The former Chief, 'who was not even entitled to own a portion of the disputed land, used his position as a local Chief, and an elite of the community to grab the community's land behind their back' (Njoroge to Kamau, 2003). They were said to have fraudulently obtained a title deed on the basis of disputed documents, on the strength of which the area was leased to the investor. It was, however, the decision of Steyn to bring a suit against the two Group Ranches, so we must question what his motives and strategy were.

If the two Group Ranches were auctioned for amounts that will far exceed the amount due to the court, who would acquire it? One must suspect that the same investment group will, directly or indirectly, end up with extensive lands of the two Group Ranches, thus considerably expanding the zone given over to conservation and high-end tourism. The 2009 census reports that in Shompole there were 8,226 people in 1,629 families, and in Ol Kiramatian there were 7,947 people in 1,755 families, all of whom would be seriously affected if the ranches were auctioned. It was estimated that, if eviction were to be carried out, numerous security personnel would be needed (200 general service unit officers, 200 policemen, 100 administration policemen, and 100 anti-stock theft personnel), and that the exercise 'would cause a lot of bloodshed and destruction of property as the people on the ground feel that their land has been taken unjustly and thus are not willing to vacate without putting up a fight' (Njoroge to Attorney General, 2003). In interviews I carried out in late February 2011, residents of Ol Kiramatian reacted with dismay and apprehension at the prospect of their lands being auctioned and themselves being evicted: where would we go, what would our children do, what would happen to our livestock?

The legal issues at stake are too complex to be addressed here, but it is pertinent to question how the purported trespass by individuals from two Group Ranches on the Nguruman-Kamorora land could have resulted in charges being brought against the entire Group Ranch? How could the lands of a collectivity be used against the alleged offences of a few individuals? One suspects that court cases mounted for minor trespasses always had a larger aim, to grab the land of the defendants. Once in the Kenyan courts, unfortunately, the end result would be subject to politics, corruption and bribery, which would give the richer individual an advantage over time. It may have taken 20 years, but from the perspective of the foreign investor, the cases achieved the aim of legally challenging the right of an entire community, of some 16,000 people, in nearly 3,400 families, to inhabit the land in which their ancestors had settled hundreds of years before. Land grabbing in Maasailand is often justified by the economics of competing land use, but advantages given to outside investors merely undermine the local opportunities to combine livelihoods and forms of land use in optimum configurations. In Ol Kiramatian and Shompole today, households combine animal husbandry, cultivation and wildlife conservation and tourism. The aim of the Karomoro case is not just to eliminate trespassing on the Karomoro land but also to eliminate competition in the form of community pursuits of conservation and tourism.

Conclusion

While the corrupt nature of some land grabbing in pastoral areas of eastern Africa is indicated by its covert and surreptitious nature, some is carried out under the progressivist and triumphal banners of development, national progress, the preservation of natural resources, conservation, regional diversification, anti-traditionalism, and anti-conservatism. Land grabbing is strategized and justified, in discourse and policy, on the basis of capital that will be invested purportedly to the ends of more productive agriculture or more effective wildlife conservation. Yet, justifications for land grabbing on the basis of prospective but invariably elusive outcomes (see Rawls, 1971) underestimate the potential effectiveness of local land users who may be able to accomplish the same ends as foreign investors claim they will.

Almost always underestimated is the importance of productive use of rangelands by pastoralists/ranchers, where mobile livestock husbandry has long defined the most effective strategy for extracting value out of otherwise marginal lands, and in so doing feeding growing millions. As other contributions in this collection show, the impact of land grabbing on rangeland societies seriously challenges their resilient forms of land use, as pastoralists are increasingly squeezed into smaller territories, while their reputation for innovatory husbandry is put into question. For the states of East Africa to foreclose options for resident rangeland populations by accommodating and encouraging large-scale foreign acquisition of their lands cannot be justified by prospective returns on commercial agriculture and tourism which will never flow to the energetic local populations that are most in need of economic opportunities. States in the region should demonstrate greater confidence in their people's ingenuity by seeing them as the agents of arid and semi-arid land change and potentially enhanced prosperity, rather than looking elsewhere for eager hands of investors in which to place the lands of the future and the future of the land.

Acknowledgements

Information was obtained through the McGill-based research project on Pastoral Property and Poverty, pursued through the Centre for Society, Technology and Development in cooperation with Mainyoito Pastoral Development Organization. The research was carried out with the support of the Social Sciences and Humanities Research Council of Canada and the Québec Fonds pour la Formation de Chercheurs et l'Aide à la Recherche, and in affiliation with the Ethnography Unit of the National Museums of Kenya (Kenyan research authorization #: OP/13/001/ 25c 261/8). I am indebted to Stephen Moiko and John Kamanga for information concerning the Kamorora case at Ol Kiramatian in Kenya, and to Corey Wright for information and help in accessing materials on the Tanzanian case studies.

13

LAND DEALS AND THE CHANGING POLITICAL ECONOMY OF LIVELIHOODS IN THE TANA DELTA, KENYA

Abdirizak Arale Nunow

Introduction

Successive governments in Kenya have excised key resource pockets in areas inhabited by pastoralists to establish large plantations and other schemes to settle landless households from the densely populated central highlands. These land grabs have happened with no regard for the significance of these areas to pastoralist production systems and livelihood security. In the past, herders managed the greater restrictions on mobility and key resource access resulting from such land expropriations by longer distance movements in search of fodder and water, which required greater labour and wealth. However, as human and livestock populations have expanded over time, and an increasing proportion of key resources in drylands have been poached for plantations and settlement schemes, pastoralists have found it increasingly difficult to cope.

While land expropriation by the state in Kenya's drylands is a historical phenomenon, the scale of recent and proposed land deals is unprecedented. The deals involve a range of investors, both domestic and foreign, state and non-state, to acquire high-value pockets of land and resources in drylands for plantation agriculture, the establishment of settlement schemes, wildlife conservation and tourism, and mining. They signify the intensifying encapsulation of drylands that were once regarded as being low-value and inconsequential to national economic growth. The details and impacts of current land deals are largely unknown, not least because of the secrecy that surrounds many deals and the reluctance many officials have to divulge the particulars of proposed acquisitions. This chapter seeks to provide greater insights into the likely impacts of land deals on pastoralist production and livelihoods by focusing on the Tana Delta, a large wet rangeland ecosystem in eastern Kenya that is ground zero for many deals that are in the pipeline. The impacts of land deals on pastoralists are socially differentiated and need to be understood in the context of broader changes in the political economy of drylands and pastoralist responses to such change.

Geography of pastoralism in the Tana Delta

The Tana Delta is a vast wetland where the Tana River, Kenya's largest river beginning in the highlands of central Kenya around Mt. Kenya and the Aberdares Range, empties into the Indian Ocean. It is an unusually fecund pastureland cut by numerous waterways. It is starkly different from the surrounding extensive dry rangelands of eastern Kenya and southern Somalia. Rainfall in the delta is variable across time and space and often unreliable. Different groups have adapted to the complex agro-ecology of the delta. Orma and Wardey herders have long supported mixed-species herds by fanning out over the rangelands of the wider delta region after the long rains in April before moving back to the banks of the Tana River and wetlands in the dry season. Over time, some Orma have combined mobile livestock-keeping with cultivation, and many Orma now live side by side next to Pokomo farmers, who customarily inhabit the thin riverine strip along the Tana River as it flows in a south-easterly direction across north-eastern Kenya (Figure 13.1). They practice irrigation to cultivate crops mostly for home consumption and local barter and trade. Relations between the Pokomo and pastoralist groups have wavered between cooperation and exchange on the one hand and conflict on the other. Typically, tensions flare when Orma and Wardey herders seek to access the river during the long dry season, which has become increasingly difficult for pastoralists as the area under small-holder cultivation has expanded year on year.

The delta borders Tsavo National Park to the west. The customary grazing range of the Orma extends from the border of Tsavo National Park up to Garsen, the administrative centre of Tana River County, and to Witu on the eastern edge of the delta near Lamu. The Galana Ranch, operated by the Agricultural Development Corporation (ADC), lies to the south of the delta, an unfenced area covering 1.4 million acres that stretches up to the town of Voi on the Mombasa-Nairobi highway. Customarily, the Orma move non-milking herds (*fora*) toward the ranch following the rains to reduce pressure on delta pastures and return when dry conditions take hold. The Kenyan President visited the delta in 2010 and agreed to set aside 200,000 acres of Galana Ranch for pastoralists to use for grazing. However, the part of the ranch delineated for pastoralists is infested with tsetse fly and has not been used. The Orma are negotiating access to a different area of the ranch, claiming that the ranch boundary has moved progressively northwards over time into the Orma customary grazing range.

Historically, the delta has served as an important drought grazing reserve for local Orma and Wardey pastoralists as well as herders from the more distant reaches of north-eastern Kenya and southern Somalia. Locally, the delta is referred to as '*chafa langana*', meaning an 'ocean that can accommodate everyone'. It is estimated that 50 per cent of Kenya's potential irrigable land lies in the Tana Delta, underlining its value not only to local pastoralist production systems but also its appeal to outside

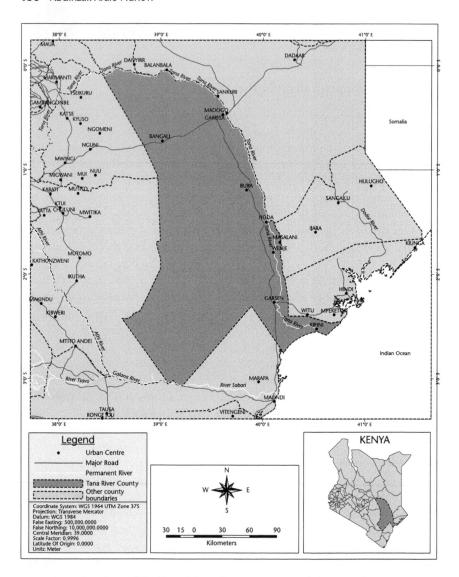

FIGURE 13.1 Location of the Tana River County in Kenya (source: author).

domestic and foreign investors. During the 2009 drought crisis, which local elders regard as having more severe impacts than the 1984 drought, it is estimated that there were 3 million head of livestock in the delta, coming from as far as Wajir in North Eastern Province. Pastoralists, mainly Somali, were welcomed on the condition that they would return when drought conditions eased, which they did and, hence, the influx happened with little conflict.

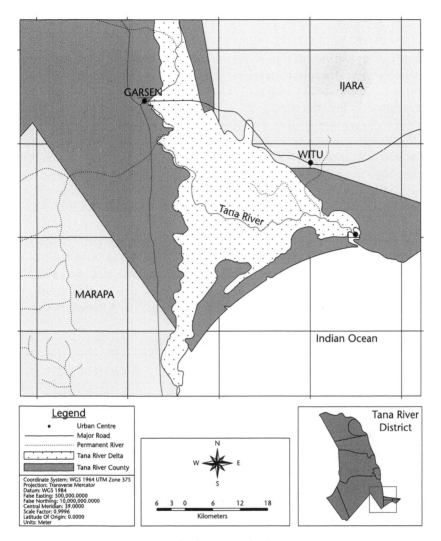

FIGURE 13.2 The Tana River Delta (source: author).

Excision, extraction and economic restructuring in the Tana Delta

Like elsewhere in the Horn (Ahmed, 2001; Pankhurst and Piguet, 2004; Galaty, this book; Babiker, this book; Tache, this book), the Tana Delta sits at the precipice of an unprecedented transformation as a range of investors seek to acquire large tracts of land to produce food and biofuels and extract minerals, often at the expense of pastoralists' access to key resources. In recent years, the Tana Delta has been increasingly absorbed into a wider political economy both through its deepening connections to national livestock markets as well as land deals that involve a range of state and non-state domestic and foreign investors to excise the highest value land

and resources. While a few are benefiting from these changes, a majority of the delta's pastoral and small-holder population stand to lose greatly.

Already, large expanses of land in the delta were set aside by previous governments for commercial farming purposes and as settlement schemes for farmers coming largely from upcountry areas. However, the scale of recently completed and proposed land deals dwarves any prior expropriation. These deals are secretive and authorities are reluctant to provide accurate details of pending applications to acquire land. Details of deals reported here were gained from knowledgeable informants in the delta as well as Kenyan media outlets (see Table 13.1). Most deals are still in the planning stages but if they were to materialize they would significantly reduce the area of the delta available for pastoralism. Efforts so far through the courts to halt deals have been unsuccessful. For example, a local conservation group challenged the acquisition of 40,000 ha. by the Tana Athi River Development Authority (TARDA – a state parastatal) and the Mumias Sugar Company, the largest completed deal to date which will displace 25,000 people. However, the Court dismissed the case based on a technicality and the local lobby was asked to bear the entire cost of the suit.

Other lands were expropriated to establish settlement schemes, some dating to the 1960s in the aftermath of independence when Kenya's first President settled

TABLE 13.1 Known details and status of proposed land deals in the Tana Delta

Investor	Foreign investment	Details of land deal	Status of deal
TARDA and Mumias Sugar Company		40,000 hectares, sugar	Title deed issued. Farm being enclosed with electric fence.
Tiomin Kenya Ltd.	China, Canada	50,000 hectares, extract titanium	Application under consideration by county officials.
Galole Horticulture	Unknown	5000 hectares, maize	Land being cleared.
Bedford Biofuels Inc.	Canada	70,000 hectares, 45 year lease agreement, jatropha curcas	Plantation to be established on what currently is six group ranches that are unfenced.
G4 Industries	United Kingdom	50,000 hectares, oil seed	Environmental and social impact assessment completed.
	Qatar	40,000 hectares under long-term lease, food crops	Bilateral negotiation underway; details include Qatari investment in £2.4 billion port in Lamu.

Kikuyu at Mokowe in Lamu. Other schemes were established in the 1990s and early 2000s. Members of communities in the delta were to be given priority in the allocation of plots that ranged between 10 and 15 acres in size. However, less than 5 per cent of plots were eventually allocated to local residents, with the rest allocated to government officials and others from outside the delta, including an estimated 500 households who were displaced by the 2008 post-election violence (personal communication, Mzee Ijema, District Peace Committee Chairman). Further, since land was allocated to individuals rather than to families or households, multiple plots were registered to different members of the same family. Until recently, many of these lands were not fenced and/or cultivated, which permitted pastoralists to continue grazing these sites. However, many plot holders are now fencing their land ahead of Kenya's forthcoming land reform process. A local councillor claims that 50 per cent of currently available grazing in the delta is land demarcated for settlement schemes, suggesting the enormous impact on pastoralists once plots have been fenced (personal communication, Councillor Guracho, July 2010).

Orma and Pokomo elites have carved out other large ranches ranging between 40,000 and 150,000 acres. Nyangoro, an 80,000 acre ranch, was established by wealthy Orma herders as a way to protect part of the rangeland from encroachment. While the herders do not hold a title to the ranch, they are recognized as the de facto holders by area residents. These ranches have not been fenced and access is relatively uncontrolled.

However, there are signs that rangelands reserved by elites could be enclosed in the future. The infrastructure for selling livestock continues to improve with saleyards opening in ever smaller and more remote parts of the delta. Livestock auctions are now held twice weekly, once in Garsen and once in Nagele, a newly established saleyard. Expanding market activity is in turn leading to new social organization. Near Nagele, a group of women have formed a livestock trading group to negotiate higher prices for fattened livestock. Other innovation is evident in the use of mobile phones to access reliable market information, as well as in new forms of transport, which is notoriously difficult in the delta; in particular, the expanding use of motorbikes as a form of public transport is doing much to improve the flow of people and small goods alongside the operators of small boats that cross the many inlets and tributaries bissecting the delta.

As markets penetrate ever deeper into the delta, this is giving rise to new forms of pastoralism centred on selling livestock to large traders and buyers for urban abattoirs. The wealthiest pastoralists have purchased lorries to transport livestock to abattoirs in Mombasa and Mariakani, outside of Mombasa. The elite pastoralists who are expanding their involvement in commercialized forms of livestock-keeping require access to high value fodder to fatten animals for sale. Members of the Nagele women's livestock trading group have leased grazing from distant sites as far away as Taita to improve their livestock. One scenario creating tensions within the pastoralist communities of the delta is that elite herders rearing livestock for Kenya's large urban markets may separate themselves from customary systems by enclosing large ranches to produce fodder or by grazing their livestock on the private paddocks that are multiplying on the outskirts of the major towns and centres in the delta and nearby areas. Investment in private water facilities and commercial feed is occurring as access to high value fodder and water is increasingly constrained. The owners of private paddocks are charging between 100 and 200 Kenyan shillings per day to livestock owners and traders for grazing. The value of farm residues has also increased as many herders seek to acquire alternative sources of fodder for fattening livestock for sale or to stave off distress sales of animals. However, it is mainly wealthier herders who are able to pay usage fees to water and feed livestock at privately owned boreholes and paddocks.

Local perceptions of the likely impacts of imminent land deals are mostly negative. Fifty respondents in the delta were asked for their views on the possible positive and negative outcomes of land deals. Sixty-nine per cent report that land deals will reduce available grazing. Other frequently reported impacts include environmental degradation (47 per cent) and conflict due to an influx of pastoralists from neighbouring areas also affected by land grabs (22 per cent). Only six respondents (12 per cent) mention employment as a possible positive outcome of land deals. No other positive impacts were reported by more than one respondent.

Changing livelihoods and responding to expropriation

The changing political economy of the delta is creating widely different options and opportunities for pastoralists to secure better livelihoods. The greater encapsulation of the delta into national and regional economies presents opportunities for wealthier herds to accumulate wealth through commercialized forms of pastoralism. A few elite herders, not more than a few individuals, are cross-breeding livestock, largely to improve milk yields. Yet sustaining improved breeds much less fattening old breeds requires a steady and reliable access to high value fodder and water, with the implication of further fragmentation and new tenure arrangements as elites consolidate their hold of the resource base to support commercially valuable livestock.

However, the wider implications of the changing political economy, including further fragmentation of the delta and greater restrictions on mobility and resource access, are particularly damaging to the majority of pastoralists whose livelihoods depend on the continued ability to move and use pockets of high value resources at key moments in the drought cycle. As the pressure to secure access to valuable land and resources intensifies, some Orma and Wardey have resorted to fencing livestock corridors as a way of maintaining access to particular resources. Although it was intended that livestock corridors would be preserved in areas where settlement schemes were established, corridors were not demarcated on the ground. This was unproblematic for a time since pastoralists continued to enjoy access to much of this area as many plots were not fenced. However, as more plots are fenced, pastoralists have sought to demarcate corridors on the ground, even though in practice it has proved incredibly difficult to locate the corridors since they were not indicated on planning maps.

The establishment of large commercial farms will produce new work opportunities for a few, but at the expense of diminished access to pasture and water. Further opportunities for work, trade, exchange and social assistance are arising through the growth of small-towns and market centres. However, many are unprepared to benefit fully from these new opportunities, having been pushed by wider circumstances into seeking options and opportunities for survival. Still, this does not exclude possible innovation that could support new secure livelihoods off the range.

As mobile livestock-keeping systems are increasingly compromised by restrictions on livestock movements and access to key resources, Orma pastoralists are increasing their involvement in alternative economic activities. Although livestock-keeping remains the most important livelihood activity for most of the inhabitants in the Tana Delta, cultivation has become more important, particularly for poorer pastoralists. There is a tradition in Orma society of women cultivating small plots to grow maize, beans, peas, vegetables, bananas and tobacco, largely for home consumption. However, opportunistic cultivation by women has become a more permanent fixture of Orma livelihoods to compensate for the diminishing returns from livestock-keeping.

The growth of small towns and settlements has created new opportunities for petty trade and casual labour, both of which are becoming more important in the make-up of Orma livelihoods. Casual work opportunities in the past were confined mostly to contract herding but now many youth and poorer herders are engaged in a range of tasks-for-cash in towns. Many seek work opportunities on the new commercial farming schemes yet these are limited. Although poorer pastoralists are seeking casual work and petty trade as alternatives to depleted herds, wealthier herders are constructing new buildings in larger towns such as Witu and Garsen, as well as fast-growing market centres such as Moa, Didewaride and Chalaluma. The main road linking Garsen and Witu has emerged as an important growth corridor in the delta, with many settlements expanding and cropping up as pastoralists from surrounding areas seek to benefit from new opportunities for work, trade and exchange. Orma herders report the greater opportunities to trade and exchange in towns as an important reason why they are keeping more small livestock in their herds, which are also more easily supported under conditions of constrained resource access.

One of the unforeseen consequences of commercialization processes in the delta has been the decreasing availability of casual labour for contract herding, since many youth prefer to move to towns to seek work opportunities. In the past, contract herdsmen were paid in kind – typically livestock. Several households, including wealthier and poorer units alike, would pool their animals for herding. Wealthier herders would usually give livestock from their herds as payment, an accommodation that clearly benefited poorer herders who would otherwise be unable to pay contract herders. However, as the labour market reconfigures itself in response to the growth of small towns and the diversifying economy, there has been a shift in payment toward cash rather than payments in kind. Under current arrangements, poorer pastoralists are expected to contribute to cash payments to hired herdsmen.

As many are unable to do so, this has meant poorer herders have been excluded. Making matters worse is that the age of available labour for herding is decreasing as older boys seek to work in towns and on commercial farms and ranches. However, elders complain that the younger children that generally look after herds now lack the know-how and intuition to look after livestock well.

A notable facet of changing livelihoods in the Tana Delta is the increasingly important role of women in the diversifying economy, a trend seen elsewhere in the region (Hodgson, 2000; Livingstone and Ruhindi, this book). Women are leading many of the newly important livelihood activities as well as innovating in key areas of the economy as the delta opens up to greater outside investment and trade. In Witu, a group of women have sold *labania*, a confectionery made from milk, sugar and spices, in the town's market as well as to travellers. Women living in remote areas have also reaped healthy takings from selling milk in the Garsen and Witu markets. Women have negotiated with motorbike, boat and bus operators to send milk in large jerricans to market with an accompanying note that details the commodities they want in exchange. This trade operates on the basis of trust and has enabled women in distant villages and encampments to add value to livestock products. The women's livestock trading group in Nagele has partnered with the local Lamu County Council to operate the newly created Nagele weekly livestock auction, splitting revenue with the council. Although women are burdened with many of the newly important livelihood activities, they also exert greater control over the use of the income and livelihood generated from these activities.

Conclusion

The future of the Orma pastoralism is entwined in the shifting political economy of the Horn of Africa. Far from existing on 'the margins', pastoralists like the Orma are at the very centre of processes of commercialization and capitalist incorporation that are sweeping the region. A visible feature of market intensification in pastoral areas has been increasing social stratification, with a significant proportion of pastoralist societies unable to adapt to the fragmentation of rangelands and weakening customary social support networks that characterize the penetration of new domestic and foreign capital in drylands.

Recent and proposed land deals are resulting in significant new fragmentation of the Tana Delta. This fragmentation is further diminishing pastoral mobility and access to key resources. Many of the highest-value key resource areas are being excised for commercial agriculture, the extraction of internationally valuable minerals alongside other uses. These processes of incorporation into a wider political economy benefit a minority, pastoral elite that is increasingly engaged in commercialized forms of pastoralism and complementary economic activities. By virtue of their wealth and status, wealthier herders can secure access to alternative sources of fodder and water to fatten animals for sale, and use their wealth to further their livestock specialization while also diversifying into new opportunities that are arising from the growth of small towns and improved connections to regional towns and market centres that is occurring as the region becomes more tightly incorporated into national and regional economies. However, there are bleak prospects for the great majority of herders who are finding it increasingly difficult to access high-value resources.

Until now, pastoralists have been mostly unsuccessful at challenging proposed land deals through the Kenyan courts. Yet new arrangements concerning the administration of land tenure under the new Kenyan constitution might provide different avenues for pastoralists to influence deals. Following the new constitution, a new National Land Commission is being established, which will have oversight responsibilities of land administration and use decisions. Decision-making powers will be decentralized to county authorities. The powers of the Ministry of Lands will be curtailed under these arrangements and the all-powerful position of Commissioner of Lands is being abolished. In theory, the devolution of decision-making powers to counties might strengthen the representation of pastoralists' interests since decisions will be made nearer to the people directly affected by a particular deal. Already, there is quickening land rush as various interest groups seek to grab land ahead of the installation of new decision structures for land administration and use. This could suggest that elites are fearful that grabbing might be made more difficult under incoming structures for land administration and use. However, given that some pastoralist elites are also benefiting from commercialization processes and are necessarily able to circumvent resource constraints by purchasing high value fodder and water from private boreholes, there is no guarantee that pastoralists will be united in their opposition to land deals. The future of pastoralism in the context of land deals remains highly uncertain.

14

SQUEEZED FROM ALL SIDES

Changing resource tenure and
pastoralist innovation on the Laikipia
Plateau, Kenya

John Letai and Jeremy Lind

Introduction

Land and resource grabs existing alongside processes of commercialization in pastoral areas of the Horn raise questions concerning what forms of pastoralism may exist in the future, how pastoralism might exist alongside other land uses including elite livestock specialists who supply larger markets, as well as who stands to benefit from changing resource tenure and associated economic opportunities and who might become newly vulnerable. Because the pastoral margins were for so long regarded as of little economic value to state bureaucratic officials, and there was in turn little investment in connecting these areas to larger markets and services, the dynamics of transition are perhaps most acute in these areas. Yet there are examples of pastoralism in the region, due to their proximity to urban centres and farming and areas of natural beauty that are valued by the state, which have been incorporated into larger economies and have developed alongside other land uses over a longer period of time.

One such area is Laikipia, a plateau stretching west of Mount Kenya that historically was inhabited by a mix of Maa-speaking livestock-keepers and hunter-gatherer groups (the Yaaku), with farming being practised in adjacent strips of land on the slopes of Mount Kenya and the Aberdares Range. The plateau is a mosaic of land uses and competing interests. Pastoralism here has long existed alongside other land uses, including small-holder agriculture, commercial ranching, horti-culture, cash cropping, luxury tourism, and conservation. However, customarily there was considerable crossing of social and ecological borders, with individuals moving between herding, hunting and gathering and cultivation as the conditions for particular activities changed. Such flexibility was helped by exchange relations that bonded groups occupying particular ecological niches. Yet over time this mobility and flexibility has diminished as borders have become more rigid and fixed, with different land uses separated by fences and other administrative barriers.

Today, pastoralists are largely restricted to group ranches, located in the arid northern reaches of the plateau, as well as on patches of rangeland adjacent to large private, commercial ranches, individually titled lands and other protected areas. In addition to physical barriers that exclude pastoralists from these lands and restrict mobility, the resilience of pastoralists in Laikipia is tested by brittle social relations resulting from a long history of tensions around land and access to grazing as well as mistrust between individuals 'belonging' to different ethnic groups defined by their uses of the land. These pressures have grown more extreme in recent years, with a host of new land deals removing even more grazing lands and key resource sites from pastoral use, resulting in ever greater fragmentation of the resource base.

Thus, in important ways, Laikipia presents a scenario of what the future of pastoralism might look like in other pastoral areas that are at the cusp of an intensifying transition to an economy penetrated by various forms of capital and outside interests, and connected to broader national and regional markets. There are important caveats to this, of course, not least the location of Laikipia in the Mount Kenya circuit and its proximity to Nairobi as well as the sheer extent of outside investment in Laikipia.

Using pastoral responses to the severe drought crisis (2008–10) in Laikipia and surrounding areas as an entry to examine patterns of vulnerability and innovation, this chapter explores how the squeeze from a variety of competing land uses, and the tenure patterns associated with changing forms of land expropriation are shaping new forms of pastoralism.

History of land expropriation and land use change

A history of expropriation of land and resources stretching back over one hundred years has shaped the nature of pastoralism in Laikipia. Records from the colonial era indicate that there were innumerable resource use options for livestock keepers on the plateau, which had 'plenty of water, wonderful pasture, little or no big game . . . and therefore fewer tick hosts' (Hughes, 2006, p114). The story of land expropriation in Laikipia begins in 1904–05, when the British forcibly moved certain Maasai sections from grazing grounds around Nakuru and Naivasha in the Rift Valley to the Northern Masai Reserve (what is now Laikipia) and the Southern Masai Reserve, a semi-arid plain lying south of Nairobi that stretches down to the border between Kenya and Tanzania (then German East Africa). The reserves were committed to the Maasai in perpetuity under the terms of a 1904 Maasai Agreement between the British and Maasai elders. In the ensuing years, Maasai herds flourished on the highly productive pastures of Laikipia, with the cattle population trebling between 1904 and 1911 (Hughes, 2006, p36). It was not long after the move that white settlers, who had already been transferred rights to the former Maasai-inhabited rangelands in the central Rift Valley, began to covet the plateau because it was free of East Coast Fever, which was spreading from the south into British East Africa. They sought a disease-free zone to establish dairy and beef ranches. In 1911, the British reneged on the Maasai Agreement and forced the Maasai from the

Northern Reserve to make way for white settlement. Although the second move in 1911 was sanctioned by a second agreement, Maasai contend that their leaders signed under duress. Subsequently, most Maasai were moved over a two year period to the Southern Reserve, which compared to Laikipia was drier, had fewer sources of water and was disease-infested (Hughes, 2006).

Some Maasai did not make the move to the Southern Reserve and remained in Laikipia. Those who stayed behind were predominantly from Mukogodo sections of the Maasai (Herren, 1990b). They were in conflict with other Maasai sections. By affiliating themselves with the Yaaku, who resided primarily in the Mukogodo Forest and were treated more sympathetically by colonial administrators (Carrier, 2011), they were able to create a separate identity and avoid being moved south with other Maasai sections. For a time the Mukogodo Maasai prospered as they were still able to move widely across the plateau. White settlers who were granted land in Laikipia, many of them ex-servicemen from the First World War, did not begin fencing their land until after the Second World War. In the period between the wars, with the livestock population considerably diminished after the Maasai moves to the Southern Reserve between 1911 and 1913, the Maasai sought to take advantage of available grazing and exploit the range of resource use options to expand their herds. This was also a period during which Yaaku also 'became' Maasai by acquiring cattle alongside the small-stock which they had traditionally kept (Cronk, 2004).

In the 1930s colonial officials made their first moves to circumscribe Maasai movements on the plateau. In 1934 a Native Reserve was demarcated in the north-eastern edge of the plateau to cater for the needs of the Maasai who had remained behind. The demarcation of the Mukogodo Reserve resulted in the Maasai losing two-thirds of the land they had utilized in 1920 (Herren, 1990b). In time, the reserve was enclosed with a solid perimeter fence in the south and west with two police posts to separate it from the settler ranching area. The north and east boundary separating the reserve from a government-controlled livestock quarantine block was closely patrolled (Herren, 1990b). By 1950 the boundaries of Mukogodo were tightly controlled, preventing wider pastoral movements across the plateau (Herren, 1991). Even though livestock movements were restricted to within the Native Reserve, the Maasai in Mukogodo were able to recover from a severe drought in 1953, helped by years of favourable rainfall. They also became increasingly incorporated into markets at this time, primarily by selling animals to the African Livestock Marketing Organisation, which later became the Livestock Marketing Division. Although herders seized the opportunity to sell, this came at the expense of investments in traditional safety nets, which operated according to mutual exchange of livestock and other forms of support (Herren, 1991).

When the terms of Kenya's independence were being negotiated during the Lancaster House talks, the Maasai stated their claims to the Laikipia Plateau. However, their calls for these lands to be returned were unheeded. The Mukogodo Reserve was later to be divided into thirteen group ranches to settle pastoralists following the Group Representative Act of 1976, and supported financially by the

World Bank. Other Maasai elites received titles as individuals to establish a further 36 private ranches. Some white settlers opted to leave after independence in 1963, with the purchase of their lands being financed by the British and World Bank funded Settlement Transfer Funds Scheme. Influential figures in the government led by Kenya's first president, Jomo Kenyatta, formed land buying companies to acquire approximately 30 per cent of ranch lands. They established large ranches and farms on these lands, which exist to this day and are one of the hotspots of conflict. Other tracts of former ranch lands were sub-divided for landless Kikuyu from Central Province. However, most of these lands were never settled except for better-watered plots on the southern flank of the plateau. Rather, the title-deed holders used these lands as collateral to access bank credit for investment in land and property elsewhere. Thus, although the Maasai were denied any legal rights to these lands, they continued to use them, and indeed over time they erected settlements and livestock kraals on these lands. Swathes of other land were registered as government land (or outspans), which pastoralists continued to access, as well.

These forms of tenure persisted until the late 1980s. As boundaries became fixed in this period, and the Maasai were excluded from key resource patches lying outside the group ranches, this compromised the functionality of customary forms of pastoralism, which depended on wide movements and access to key resource sites to make productive use of the larger rangeland, in particular the more arid reaches of the plateau where the group ranches were located. The need for flexibility and mobility became more important as pressures on the land within group ranches increased. During this time, Maasai pastoralists began settling on plots held by absentee Kikuyu. With options limited, many began exiting pastoralism and sought work opportunities elsewhere, unable to adapt to the new pressures. Small-stock

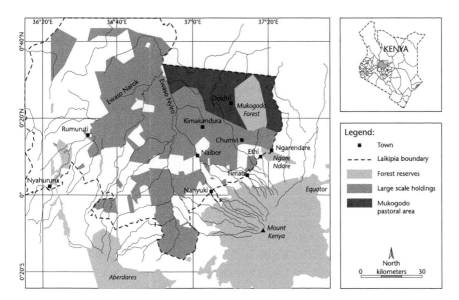

FIGURE 14.1 Land uses on the Laikipia Plateau.

became more important in the make-up of herds, as they have more manageable herding requirements and can be easily converted to cash (Herren, 1991).

These pressures have intensified as a result of more recent expropriations and associated changes in land use. By the early 1990s, beef ranching in Laikipia became unviable following the collapse of the Kenya Meat Commission and export market for live cattle to the Middle East coupled with the rising costs of inputs (Heath, 2001). Commercial ranches destocked to meet recurrent costs before many were pushed to close down. Two ranches in Laikipia were handed over to the Ministry of Lands and Settlement for sub-division and were immediately overrun by Pokot and Samburu herders (Heath, 2001). Several were sold off to wealthy investors from the Middle East, Europe and North America, and they included international conservationists, an arms dealer and an executive for a multi-national corporation based in Europe. Others diversified into a variety of other uses including the conservation of internationally valued wildlife and luxury safari lodges, livestock breeding and genetics, and horticulture to supply vegetables and flowers to European markets. Some still do beef ranching, mostly for high end butchers in Nairobi. However, with some notable exceptions, as discussed below, the Maasai remain excluded from entering most ranches.

Other lands have moved to more exclusionary forms of tenure. Many outspans have been grabbed by senior government officials, politicians (including Maasai) and military officers, removing even more land and key resource sites from pastoral use. There has also been a recent rush to acquire lands that were allocated to Kikuyu small-holders after independence. Brokers have approached the owners of adjacent plots and encouraged them to consolidate their plots into a larger holding for sale. Buyers of these consolidated holdings include wealthy Kenyans, white Zimbabwean farmers, and European diplomats and NGO officials. The new owners of these larger plots have evicted the Maasai squatters who have routinely used the lands over many years, as well as erected fences and employed guards to prevent the passage of herds.

These various converging processes of land and resource expropriation have had a pincer effect on pastoralism on the plateau. More and more land has become off limits to grazing by Maa-speaking pastoralists, who are mostly hemmed in to an area that is approximately 7 per cent of the overall plateau. An accumulation of livestock losses coupled with severe constraints on mobility has resulted in weakened abilities to rebuild and expand herds. An ever greater number of Maasai have left pastoralism. Others have been pushed to extraordinary lengths to support their herds. In 2000, a drought year, some pastoralists invaded the private ranches. Happening at a time when the white-owned farms in Zimbabwe were being invaded by veterans of the bush war against the former white minority government, the ranch invasions by Maasai garnered international attention. Meetings between pastoralist representatives and ranch owners resulted in an agreement to allow 2000 head of breeding livestock to graze inside private ranches for the duration of the drought, mainly belonging to the better-off whose influence gave them access to the negotiations (Heath, 2001). The government also intervened to reduce tensions by permitting pastoralists to access grazing inside the Mount Kenya forest reserve. However, up to 60 per cent of the cattle in some herds died in the forests. Seeing an opportunity to influence more favourable perceptions amongst the Maasai, and reduce pressure on the ranches to open grazing still further, ranch owners purchased relief food, veterinary drugs and pesticides for pastoralists who trekked up the mountain, as well as rehabilitated cattle dips and crushes (Heath, 2001).

The invasions were repeated in 2004, a drought year. The argument of the Maasai activists ran that the 99-year leases under the 1904 Maasai Agreement had expired and that pastoralists were entitled to graze on lands that once belonged to them.[1] In response to the invasions, the provincial security administration ordered the General Services Unit (GSU), a paramilitary wing of the Kenyan military, to forcibly remove Maasai herders that entered ranches. Some Maasai leaders alleged to have incited the invasions were detained.

The onset of severe drought conditions in late 2008 raised fears of further invasions. The drought, referred to as *Olamei Oodo* or 'the Great Drought' by the Maasai, was the worst in living memory, its consequences felt more severely than the 1984 drought that had led many Maasai herders to leave livestock-keeping. An estimated 64 per cent of cattle herds were lost, and 62 per cent of sheep (ILRI, 2010). However, meteorologically, there has been no precipitous decline in rainfall levels in Laikipia and surrounding rangelands in recent years. For example, four of six stations in northern Kenya monitored by the Kenya Meteorological Department reported higher rainfall deficits during droughts in the 1980s and 1990s than in the two years preceding the 2011 food security crisis in northern Kenya.[2] Levels of vulnerability amongst pastoralists are increasing, even to slight variations in the frequency and intensity of rainfall. In Laikipia, changing forms of resource tenure associated with expropriations have created significant vulnerability, but also innovation with new forms of pastoralism arising in response to systemic pressures. Thus, although the situation for many Maasai was perilous at the onset of the severe drought in late 2008, there was no repeat of the invasions seen in 2000 and 2004, as detailed in the following section.

Pastoralist innovations and the 2008–09 drought cycle

> There is a philosophy in Maasai culture that a drought that doesn't spare donkeys will kill people as well.[3]

The early drought (December 2008–February 2009)

The severe drought in 2009 came upon consecutive seasons of poor rainfall in 2008. Rangelands that were accessible to Maasai herders were quickly exhausted after the short rains failed late in 2008. The many small-holder farms cultivated by Maa speakers were barren. Maasai herders recall that beginning in January 2009 they turned to an assortment of customary coping practices to manage the deteriorating situation. Herds were split, keeping milch and weakened stock at homesteads in the group ranches. Calves were slaughtered to reduce the stress on their mothers.

Herders resorted to pruning the branches of trees near to town and along the river flowing downwards from the Mukogodo Forest through the group ranch in order to feed weaker livestock at home and avoid moving them over long distances. Maasai women recalled that the severity of the drought was such that elephants which roam the group ranches were too weak to tear the branches off of trees. Elephants would listen for the sound of trees being cut and would come to browse, making it necessary for someone to keep watch for approaching elephants while someone else cut the branches and fed the livestock.

Herders avoided bleeding healthier grazers as drought conditions intensified and sought to move them more widely to the Ngarendare and Mukogodo Forests as well as southwards towards the Aberdares Range. However, livestock moved to these areas were also exposed to diseases, and there was an increase in small stock diseases such as CCPP (contagious caprine pleuropneumonia), diarrhea and skin diseases. Thus, improved veterinary care and dipping were important to maintain the health of stronger animals. Out of desperation, some cattle were driven surreptitiously into neighbouring commercial ranches, a practice referred to locally as 'night grazing'. Several herders were arrested and arraigned in court, and their livestock were removed to the group ranches.

Others intensified their involvement in a variety of non-livestock tasks, such as burning charcoal and collecting fuelwood for sale, buying chickens and selling eggs, tending bee hives, and seeking casual work on horticulture farms and large ranches. There was also an increase in distress sales as herd owners sought to sell goats in towns to earn income for buying drugs to treat sick livestock and to purchase cereals to feed household members.

Deteriorating conditions and herder-rancher agreements (March–May 2009)

The failure of the long rains that typically arrive in March pushed herders to seek new ways of accessing high value fodder. Drought reserves in the Ngarendare and Mukogodo Forests were depleted by late March, when the rains should have arrived. Although there was light rainfall in the group ranches, and some regeneration of vegetation, this was quickly depleted. In recent years, many Maasai have begun cultivating wheat on individually titled lands, particularly around Ethi, a better-watered area nearer to Mount Kenya, further limiting access to some of the more reliable grazing sites.

As in any drought, wealth was an important determinant of pastoralist responses to scarcity. Better-off herd owners paid a fee to small-holder farmers to graze standing wheat or maize stalks on fields. Some negotiated with the Kenyan Air Force, which has a base west of Nanyuki town, to pay a fee to permit livestock to access pastures within the Air Force compound.

By March, the areas within commercial ranches where pastoralists sought 'night grazing', typically near the ranch perimeter, were also barren. Commercial ranches were of course feeling the impacts of the drought, as well. However, there was limited grazing available in the interior of some ranches. Yet, access to grazing for pastoralists on large ranches is highly sensitive. Maasai pastoralists have entered ranches without seeking the prior consent of ranch owners on many occasions over the years, as explained above. By the beginning of 2009, night grazing was a problem on many ranches. However, there was no repeat of the organized large-scale invasions. Rather, night grazing was practised spontaneously by individual herders seeking to sustain healthier grazers. By February 2009, conditions had deteriorated to a point where pastoralists had to seek access to grazing across borders. Pastoralist elders from Maasai group ranches and settlements approached ranch owners and managers to negotiate terms to open grazing on the ranches. Negotiations took place between elders representing particular group ranches and managers or the owners of particular ranches. The negotiators had to overcome considerable mistrust by both sides and against a backdrop of historical claims to land and recent ranch invasions. Pastoralists considered access to be an entitlement. Ranchers worried that opening access, even on a limited basis, would lead to more permanent claims to land.

Through careful negotiation, elders from group ranches and the managers of large ranches reached agreements permitting pastoralists to graze a limited number of cattle and sheep inside commercial ranches on a controlled basis. Browsers were not allowed into the ranches. Not all commercial ranches agreed to open grazing to pastoralists. Improving relations with neighbouring pastoralist communities and reducing pressure to grant wider access rights were important motivations for commercial ranches to negotiate with elders from Maasai group ranches. The conditions for grazing, restrictions on herding practices, and the number of livestock that were allowed varied. Each group ranch was given a quota and livestock owners decided how to divide the quota amongst the group ranch members. Pastoralists explained that these agreements also helped ranchers. Livestock brought for grazing helped to carry ticks off pasture that was undergrazed. The urine and dung of livestock added nutrients to the soil and the stomping of livestock helped to break open the soil for fresh seeding once the drought was over.

Given the poor conditions in ranches, and the widespread need for fodder, livestock owners had to split their herds, keeping some animals on large ranches, while others were grazed near to homesteads within group ranches and other grazers driven to Mount Kenya and the Aberdares. Small-holders that had standing hay on their plots charged Maasai a fee for grazing, primarily for weak and milking livestock.

Intensifying drought and moving to Mount Kenya (April/May–November 2009)

As drought conditions intensified once the long rains failed in March and April, herders were pushed to extraordinary lengths to sustain herds. The body condition of most livestock was poor. Many were weak and emaciated. Wealthy herders continued to purchase hay as a fallback measure. Yet the cost of fodder spiked. Hay was being transported from as far away as Kitale, a farming area 450km from Laikipia in western Kenya.

A complementary response by pastoralists involved reciprocal agreements that individual herders negotiated with Kikuyu and Meru small-holders living adjacent to the Mount Kenya forest. From April 2009 as drought conditions worsened, pastoralists began driving their herds to Mount Kenya in search of fodder and forage. However, until August 2009, pastoralists were prevented from residing inside the forest, a move intended to conserve the forest vegetation and prevent destructive grazing practices and illegal logging under the cover of darkness. Herders were permitted to graze inside the forest during the day. This made it necessary for herders, many who had travelled long distances, to find locations near the forest to kraal their livestock at night.

Drawing on this earlier experience, livestock-owners negotiated agreements with small-holders living adjacent to the forest to kraal livestock on farms at night and drive their animals into the forest during the day. In previous droughts, some herders had approached small-holder farmers to agree terms to keep their livestock on farms, both to graze dry crops but also to kraal livestock that were grazed inside the forest. These agreements built on the extensive connections between Maa-speaking herders and Meru and Kikuyu small-holders on the west and north side of Mount Kenya. These connections involved boundary-crossing, trade, resource-sharing agreements, and inter-marriage but over time they diminished in importance as administrative and identity boundaries hardened. However, these ties have become more important as access to high value fodder has become more restricted. Individual herders and farmers have slowly resuscitated these ties over the past 15 years, in the process helping to support the exchange of agro-ecological knowledge and expertise in herding and farming alike.

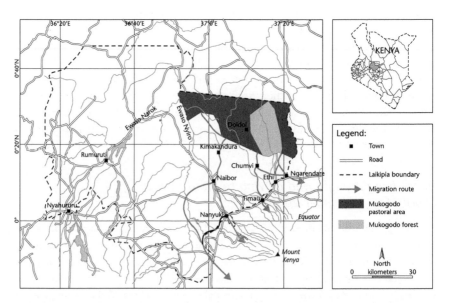

FIGURE 14.2 Livestock movements from group ranches to Mount Kenya in 2009.

Their interactions have not always been peaceful, however. In the lead up to moving livestock up the mountain, elders from group ranches visited farming communities on the mountain in April 2009, concerned to avoid stoking tensions with farmers that erupted in 2006 when pastoralists last came to the mountain. Pastoralist elders met with local administrative officials and farmer leaders to open the way for herd owners to come up the mountain, as they did in large numbers in May and June 2009.

Farmers' concerns were that livestock did not damage the water intake points in the forest and that herders help track stolen animals. The agreements, negotiated between individual herd owners and farmers, were mutually beneficial (see Table 14.1). Pastoralists were able to access a critically important drought reserve. Getting manure was the most important consideration for farmers. Some farmers charged visiting pastoralists an initial one-off fee to graze farm residues, which sustained livestock weakened by drought and trekking over a long distance to reach the forest's edge. Farmers also benefited from buying weak animals from pastoralists. Some herders shared milk with farmers; in return, farmers gave farm produce to herdsmen.

This reciprocity and mutual help between herders and farmers existed in previous crises but never before had agreements been reached so systematically. After the drought, many herders remained in mobile phone contact with farmers. Farmers, reaping a bumper harvest from the good rains in 2010, were sending gifts of maize and other farm produce to herders while herders gifted small-stock to farm owners. Reported incidents of livestock theft on farms also declined, which has contributed greatly to better relations overall between farmers and herders. Pastoralists were hopeful that this bonding would lead to more permanent connectivity in the way of social learning, sharing technology and skills, and strengthening market ties and exchange relations with neighbouring small-holder communities.

TABLE 14.1 Benefits of herder-farmer agreements

Pastoralists	Farmers
• Space for kraaling livestock, which enabled continued access to grazing inside Mt Kenya and Aberdare forests • Acquiring agro-ecological knowledge to begin cultivation • Knowledge and opportunity to purchase small plots near the forest's edge • Lower prices for cereals and vegetables purchased on-farm • Higher price for livestock sold to farmers than prices paid for weak animals at markets in the group ranches, where buyers are mainly butchers from Nanyuki, Timau and Dol Dol	• Fees paid by herders to graze standing and residual crops • Enhanced soil fertility from livestock dung and urine • Small amounts of milk and meat • Purchased weak animals, which they fattened and sold at higher prices • Sold farm produce to herders

Changing forms of pastoralism

The 2008–10 severe drought crisis in Laikipia pushed Maasai pastoralists to the limit. While the crisis spurred greater connectivity and mutual support between pastoralists, ranchers and small-holders, this did not prevent catastrophic livestock losses as herds were weakened by drought and decimated by cold and disease encountered on Mount Kenya. Yet, far from dying out, Maasai pastoralists are continuously adjusting their livelihoods to a changing resource base and shifting political and economic conditions, with the result that new forms of pastoralism arise. Changes are evident in the way that herders are accessing pasture/land, selecting livestock and rebuilding herds, and engaging with markets.

Pasture/land

Restricted access to high value fodder has driven a number of changes in land use and social relations. The most important of these is renewed Maasai efforts to establish better relations with the owners of private ranches as well as small-holder farmers living on the slopes of Mount Kenya, as explained above. Yet these relations are far from secure. Many owners of private ranches remain reluctant to permit pastoralists rights to access grazing, even for limited numbers of livestock on a controlled basis. The background of invasions and tense relations has left some ranchers fearing that pastoralists might use limited access as a bridgehead to establish claims to land. Furthermore, some private ranch owners are struggling financially and are reluctant to provide help to pastoralists when they are seeking to care for their own livestock and wildlife. On the eastern flank of the plateau, representatives from four group ranches and four commercial ranches have come together to discuss what joint management of pasture on adjoining lands under different tenure might look like. The idea is to permit controlled grazing by pastoralists inside private ranches during the rainy season to reduce grazing pressure inside group ranches, which it is hoped would provide greater drought reserves for pastoralists.[4] It remains to be seen whether such cooperation will work in practice, but already group ranch leaders have enforced controls on grazing of certain areas within group ranches during the rains.

Maasai-rancher agreements have already been tested by an influx of pastoralists from neighbouring areas, mostly Pokot and Samburu, who have sought grazing backed by the threat of violence. They are grazing in areas outside of private ranches that are used by the Maasai, which indirectly increases pressure for Maasai to graze inside private commercial ranches. They have also undermined Maasai efforts to establish drought grazing reserves.

Some Maasai and Samburu small-holders living nearer to Mount Kenya have turned their fields over to grass in recent years to produce hay for sale as well as to hire out grazing. In late 2009, herders who could afford to purchase hay from small-holders were able to come off the mountain sooner and so minimize the risk of losing livestock to pneumonia when the rains returned. Better-off Maasai are also investing in land, both plots on the mountain and absentee holdings on the plateau that are coming up for sale.

Livestock selection

Given fluctuating environmental conditions and severe limitations on access to high value fodder, traditional pastoralism based on maximizing herd sizes has been more of an ideal than a practical objective for constituting a herd for most Maasai. An older generation of Maasai livestock owner still prefers traditional cattle breeds that are thought to be more tolerant of drought and resistant to disease. Furthermore, they focus on keeping a larger number of heifers to increase the herd when conditions allow. Most other Maasai have shifted away from a focus on breeding and enlarging the herd. Youth, in particular, have sought to invest in improved breeds, including Dowper sheep, Boran goats and Sahiwal cows, which compared to traditional breeds put on weight more quickly and so can be sold at an earlier point in their development. Marketing, not breeding, is the aim of production. Following the drought crisis of 2009, many Maasai purchased steers from drought-stricken livestock owners from north-eastern Kenya, who had moved toward Mount Kenya and sought to dispose of livestock they were unable to support. Maasai and ranchers alike focused on fattening these weakened steers and selling them as a way of rebuilding. Some Maasai, especially in the drier western flank of the plateau, are adding camels to their herds, and moving into dairying.

Marketing

The shift from a breeding herd to a trading herd is perhaps the biggest shift in Maasai pastoralism (Karwitha, 2009). A young Maasai herder described this change: 'In my generation, the youth no longer focus on rearing animals over a few years and then selling them but rather on value-addition and making quick income.'[5] Explaining how Maasai restocked their herds in 2011 with livestock disposed by herders from Wajir and Moyale in north-eastern Kenya, another young Maasai added, 'The markets are full of female cows but it is the bulls that are being taken. They [Maasai buyers] are wary of staying with a female for a few years and waiting for it to give birth. They know from experience that when the drought hits you are left with only one cow. People are looking for short-term, quick sales.' However, not all Maasai pastoralists are able to establish a toehold in the 'fatten and sell' trade. Mostly, buyers have been individuals with access to alternative income streams and/or credit, or have family members employed outside of the livestock sector. Better-off livestock owners have also participated in the trade, selling a healthy bull to raise money to purchase five or six weakened steers.

Conclusion

Recent crises afflicting Maasai pastoralists are the result of longer-term trends and systemic changes engendering considerable levels of vulnerability. Processes of expropriation stretching back over 100 years have reconfigured the options and opportunities for pursuing traditional forms of pastoralism. Pressure on the land inside group ranches has increased, yet this is an issue that is inseparable from the Maasai being squeezed from all sides. A parallel trend has been the incorporation of pastoralists into markets since the 1950s. Selling livestock has long been a routine way for pastoralists in Laikipia to meet cash needs, which are particularly acute during crises. However, as explained earlier, the flip side of this is that mutual support networks have eroded since livestock have been directed away from customary exchanges to provide animals for sale. New forms of pastoralism are emerging as a result of these converging processes, with many intensifying their involvement in marketing alongside diversifying out of livestock-keeping and some exiting pastoralism altogether.

In other pastoral margins in the Horn of Africa, land and resource grabs and related processes of market incorporation have generated considerable concern over what the future might hold for traditional forms of pastoralism. The food security crisis in the Horn in 2010–11 has renewed debate around the 'viability' of pastoralism, with some development actors suggesting that pastoralism might die out. The problem with this way of framing the debate on pastoralist livelihoods is that it suggests pastoralism is an outdated production system, doomed to collapse under the weight of modern pressures, and that new livelihoods outside of livestock-keeping should be created for pastoralists. However, the experience of herders in places that have been incorporated into wider economies and penetrated by outside capital is that there clearly is a future for pastoralism in the Horn of Africa, albeit a system of production that is very different from customary forms. The experience of the Maasai on Laikipia Plateau is a cautionary tale of the real threats to pastoralism, but also the responsiveness and innovative capacity of herders to formulate new pathways.

Notes

1   This argument is contested though, as a close reading of the Agreement suggests it was not a lease, or time-bound in any way. Authors' communication with Dr Lotte Hughes, November 2011.
2   See www.scidev.net/en/sub-suharan-africa/opinions/better-grazing-practices-hold-key-to-kenyan-droughts.html, accessed 4 November 2011.
3   Focus Group Discussion with youth in Makurian, 9 June 2010.
4   Participant contribution, 'Workshop on land, livestock and the changing political economy of pastoralism in Laikipia and Samburu', 15–16 September 2011, Old House, Nanyuki.
5   Participant contribution at the 'Workshop on land, livestock and the changing political economy of pastoralism in Laikipia and Samburu.'

15

MOBILE PASTORALISM AND LAND GRABBING IN SUDAN

Impacts and responses

Mustafa Babiker

Introduction

The drylands of central Sudan have been the home to various forms of mobile pastoralism for centuries. Mobility is a necessity dictated by the extreme temporal and spatial variability of rainfall in this environment (Abu Sin, 1998). But movements by pastoralists have always been limited by various restrictions including the shortage of labour to move herds, political and ethnic tensions, civil war, demographic pressure leading to more rigid and fixed tenure rights to key resources, and a scarcity of water and grazing along corridors used by herders to move livestock (Ahmed, 2009; Osman, 2009; Calkins, 2009). However, the determinants of pastoral mobility are constantly changing. In recent times, land grabbing for large-scale commercial farming and wildlife conservation has severely constrained pastoral mobility in the central Sudan rangelands. Although there has been a long attrition in pastoralists' access to resources in this region, recent and ongoing land deals involving a variety of foreign investors are particularly threatening to the livelihoods of herders who have been pushed to the edge.

This chapter develops a detailed picture of how land grabbing affects the livelihoods of pastoralists through a case study of herders in Gedaref State, a former rangeland area that was transformed over a long period into a region of large commercial farms. The experience of pastoralists here is a cautionary tale of how sedentarization and the expansion of mechanized farming in drylands, so often presented by policy-makers across East and the Horn of Africa as the pathway to better livelihoods for pastoralists, may actually generate greater vulnerability and poverty while enriching the few well-connected elites whose livelihoods are already secure.

The roots of fragmentation

The vast rangelands of central and eastern Sudan have experienced a remarkable transformation stretching back over 150 years. The roots of this transformation, from a system of mixed land uses that encouraged movement and exchange relations between and amongst livestock keepers, smallholder farmers, and hunters and gatherers into one dominated by mechanized farming for the export of cotton, cereals, oilseed and sugar, was supported by colonial and post-independence regimes acting with domestic and foreign investors (Bernal, 1997). It is estimated that by the early twenty-first century, mechanized farms in Sudan covered an area greater than 10 million ha. (UNEP, 2007).

The conversion of rangelands into mechanized farms in central and eastern Sudan dates to the late 1860s when Sudan was under the rule of the Othman administration (Bernal, 1997). One of the first schemes to be established was in the Baraka and Gash river deltas, the ancestral home of Beja herders, and was for growing cotton. However, the development of commercial farms took off in the early twentieth century. The Sudan Plantations Syndicate, a private British enterprise, established what would become the Gezira scheme in 1911 principally to grow cotton to supply the British textile industry. It steadily expanded and by 1931 its size was estimated to be 450,000 ha. The scheme was nationalized in the 1950s and came under the operation of the Sudan Gezira Board, a government enterprise. In the early 1960s the Manaqil Extension was completed, adding 400,000 ha. to the existing scheme, making Gezira the largest centrally managed irrigation project in the world (Bernal, 1997, p447). Additional governmental and private investments have brought the total area under irrigation to more than 2 million ha.

Over time, the commercial farming sector has drawn substantial private investment to cover an ever-widening area beyond the prime eastern region into the clay zone of central Sudan including Sennar, Blue Nile and White Nile States. In 1968, more than 750,000 ha. were under cultivation in these states of which more than 200,000 ha. constituted unauthorized holdings. By the late 1970s, about 2.2 million ha. was allocated for mechanized farms and an estimated 420,000 ha. was under cultivation on lands that were not officially demarcated for farming. Today, mechanized farming is centred in the eastern region, where 43 per cent of the total land area is taken up by mechanized farms, followed by the central region (32 per cent of land is used for mechanized farming) and Upper Nile State (20 per cent). In recent decades, mechanized farming had been initiated in South Kordofan and South Darfur as well (UNEP, 2007).

There has been renewed interest in large-scale, rain-fed mechanized farming following on the secession of South Sudan and the concomitant loss of oil revenue for the north. A Five Year Plan (2007–11) for agricultural expansion sets an ambitious target for establishing mechanized farms across prime arable lands, through Middle Eastern and Asian capital. A reported 8 million ha. of an estimated 34 million ha. is to come under mechanized cultivation (NCSP, 2007). Details of recent land deals are notoriously difficult to identify yet Sudanese and international

TABLE 15.1 Recent land deals in Sudan

SN	Country	Area (ha.)	Location	Type of contract	Nature contract
1	Syria	30,000	unknown	Gov-to-Gov	50 year free lease
2	China	100,000	Gezira Scheme	Private investors	Unknown
3	South Korea	700,000	unknown	Unknown	Unknown
4	UAE	400,000	unknown	Unknown	Unknown
5	Egypt	400,000	unknown	Unknown	Unknown
6	Saudi Arabia	60,000	Nile State	Private (Al-Rajhi Group)	40 year lease
7	USA	400,000	South Sudan	Jarch Management Group, Ltd	Unspecified lease
8	Morocco	Unknown	White Nile	Private investor	Unknown
9	Jordon	170,000	Nile State	Gov-to-Gov	Unknown
Total	2,260,000				

Source: Durali, 2008; *Sudan Tribune*, 2009; *The Economist*, 2009.

media report that over 2 million ha. of land are 'up for grabs' in ongoing deals involving a range of foreign investors.

The establishment of large mechanized farms in former rangelands has been promoted by official land use policy and planning and accompanying land laws. These favoured the expansion of commercial agriculture in drylands as a vehicle for national economic growth, but at the expense of pastoralists whose movement and access to resources were increasingly constrained (Ahmed, 1987). The 1944 report of the Soil Conservation Committee recommended: 'Where nomadic pastoralists were in direct competition for land with settled cultivators, it should be the policy that the rights of the cultivator be considered as paramount, because his crops yield a bigger return per unit area' (quoted in El-Tayeb, 1985, p35). Such recommendations reflected a bias against pastoralist land uses and rested on unsubstantiated claims that pastoralism was unproductive (Casciarri and Ahmed, 2009; Behnke and Kerven, this book). In turn, this bureaucratic outlook served the political and economic interests of regimes to alienate grazing lands and resources for developing the commercial farming and conservation sectors. The bias against pastoralism is evident even in a recent academic work based as it were on an inverted reading of the history of land grabbing in Sudan: 'Considerable conflict between herding and crop agriculture is reported to exist as a result of *the encroachment of herding on cropland*' (Khan, 2004, p5, emphasis added).

The expansion of commercial farms in central Sudan drylands has been a bridgehead for extending forms of private tenure in pastoralist areas. The 1970 Unregistered Land Act restructured land tenure with complete disregard for the rights of smallholders and pastoralists inhabiting the rangelands (UNDP, 2006). The concept of private tenure that was introduced in drylands through the expansion of commercial farming has altered the way that people relate to land as a resource, with even some pastoral elites seeking to 'grab' and protect vital resources for herds. This has created uncertainty and tension, not only between different land user groups but also within herding societies that are split by differences in wealth and status. The process of individualizing resource rights has meant that the central Sudan rangelands have become increasingly fragmented like elsewhere in the region (Flintan, 2011; Dida, this book; Letai and Lind, this book; Nunow, this book). The fragmentation of rangelands has had severe repercussions for customary patterns of movement and coping, making the impacts of drought and scarcity even greater for herders (Abu Sin, 1998; Babiker, 2007; Osman, 2009).

Land grabbing in Gedaref State

Land use in Gedaref State in central Sudan has undergone a transformation over the past 70 years as grazing lands have been converted into mechanized farms (see Table 15.2). During the colonial period, Gedaref District was divided by an administrative boundary known as *khat el-mara'a* or 'Sanfor' as a namesake of Sandford, a colonial administrator. The boundary separated zones for herding, namely the Butana rangelands, and farming, centring on the clay plain in the then southern Gedaref District. Large-scale mechanized farming was prohibited north of this line and farmers had no legal remedy for crop damage caused by livestock in the Butana rangelands. In return, herders had to stay north of the boundary until the end of the grain harvest, when herders would migrate south and exchange manure for crop residues. On occasion, during droughts these mutually supportive exchanges would come under pressure, when herders would migrate before harvests were completed (Shazali, 1988; Elhadary, 2010).

Land grabbing in Gedaref State began in 1945 when a relatively modest mechanized scheme totalling 5,000 ha. was established in the Gedembeliya area. This and other schemes that were established in the 1940s existed initially to meet the food needs of British army units stationed in eastern Africa. An average of about 6,000 ha. a year was cultivated between 1945 and 1953 under a sharecropping arrangement between the government and farmers to produce sorghum. These estates proved costly and in 1954 the government began encouraging the private sector to take up mechanized farming in the area, a policy that continued after Sudan gained independence in 1956 (Shepherd, 1983).

The area of arable land under cultivation has greatly expanded since then, rising from 168,000 ha. on the eve of independence to 1.3 million ha. in 1990. In 2004, cultivated lands covered an area in excess of 3.4 million ha., of which approximately 44 per cent was holdings of land that were not demarcated for agriculture (El-Faki, 2005). A more recent estimate is that mechanized rain-fed farming in eastern Sudan had expanded to an area of 5.8 million ha. in size (East Sudan Conference, 2009).

TABLE 15.2 Changes in land use in Gedaref State, 1941–2002

Type of Use	Area 1941		Area 2002	
	Km²	%	Km²	%
Mechanized farming	3,150	8.7	26,000	72.2
Forest and rangeland	28,250	78.5	6,700	18.6
Hills and watercourses	3,300	9.2	2,000	5.6
Wasteland (*kerab*)	1,300	3.6	1,300	3.6
Total	36,000	100.0	36,000	100.0

Source: Land Use Map, State Ministry of Finance, Gedaref, 2002.

A smaller area of land in Gedaref is used for irrigated farming. The New Halfa Scheme was established in the 1960s in the Butana rangelands and totalled 210,000 ha. The Rahad Scheme was established in the 1970s covering an area of 126,000 ha. of land that was formerly used for grazing. In New Halfa, tenancies were granted to pastoralists as compensation and as part of a policy to turn herders into full-time farmers. Out of a total of 22,367 tenancies 29 per cent were allocated for the resettlement of Nubians, with the remaining 71 per cent distributed to other pastoralist groups. However, the majority of the pastoral tenants did not give up herding as planners envisaged. Rather, most combined some type of livestock-keeping with cultivation of irrigated fields (cf. Hoyle, 1977; Salem-Murdock, 1989; Sörbö, 1991).

Impacts of land grabbing on pastoralism

Many large farms in Gedaref were established on lands that were not designated for a particular use, let alone for farming. Many such 'undemarcated' lands were actually rangelands that were considered to be uninhabited even though they were vitally important to pastoralists for managing routine drought cycles and more severe crises. A worsening scarcity of land available in the southern agricultural zone has meant that large mechanized farms have been established in the Butana rangelands in recent decades (Shazali, 1988; Babiker and Abdel Gadir, 1999; Beshir *et al.*, 2005). The expansion of large farms in the grazing zone lying north of the colonial-era *khat el-mara'a* has continued apace even though land use plans have not designated such lands for cultivation and a de facto commitment by the regional government to improve protection of pastoralists' access to resources. Unsurprisingly, relations are antagonistic between herders, the operators of new schemes and other large farmers. The quality of existing rangelands has declined as herders are squeezed onto an ever-decreasing rangeland area, and typically onto lands that are the furthest from water sources. Overgrazing has become a problem along livestock corridors, which have decreased today to anywhere between 150 and 300 metres in width (Abbo, 2005) compared to 2 and 4 miles during the colonial period (El-Hassan, 1981). Opponents of pastoralism have seized on this to peddle tired arguments that customary herding practices are inherently destructive even though the problem has come about through poor planning and inadequate protection of resource access for herders (Shazali, 1988).

To add to the predicament of pastoralists, the need for fodder has meant that the value of dry crop residues has increased greatly, meaning that poorer herders find it difficult to access fields they were accustomed to using. In 2005, a herder might pay the equivalent of US$4,000 or three or four camels to keep 100 camels on a sorghum field between January and July during the dry season (Babiker, 2007). The squeeze on resources has meant that livestock intrusions onto sorghum farms have become a perennial concern as livestock are moved along corridors adjoining farms to drought grazing reserves. Considerable labour is required to keep camels away from the fields. The situation is exacerbated by the unpredictability of areas where sorghum is planted. In some years, grazing areas have been entirely encircled by areas under cultivation. Punishments and fines levied against herders for livestock damaging crops are harsh, irrespective of the circumstances that led to a particular incident of crop destruction.

Moreover, some scheme operators are denying pastoralists entry to their lands out of fear that livestock will inadvertently seed noxious weeds. Some scheme operators have avoided digging *hafirs* (artificial pools) and burning grass out of fear that this may entice herders to bring livestock.

The necessity to access high value fodder dictates that pastoralists migrate southwards sooner in the drought cycle as many key resource areas have been grabbed to establish mechanized farms and protected areas. Dinder National Park, a 1 million hectare protected area, was previously a dry season grazing area used by pastoralists. Annually, 900,000 cattle, 2,000,000 sheep, and 500,000 camels enter the park between January and July even though such access is officially prohibited (Scholte and Babiker, 2005).

The massive expansion of mechanized agriculture in the farming zone has squeezed smallholder farmers as well. There is a history of smallholder agriculture in the area. Customarily, smallholders practised a form of rotational cultivation known locally as *hariq* that allowed land to recover and enabled herders to access resources in years when fields were left in fallow. While many policies emphasize the presumed inherent destructiveness of pastoralist land uses, mechanized farming has entailed deforestation contributing to soil erosion as well as the loss of rotational and grazing practices that had enriched soil fertility and contributed to higher productivity (El-Tayeb and Lewandowski, 1983; El-Tayeb, 1985; UNEP, 2007).

Official and popular responses

Official policy resulting in the alienation of lands and resources integral to the productivity and sustainability of mobile pastoralism in the central Sudan rangelands has led to displacement and, increasingly, violent conflict. Except for recognizable and socially legitimated 'tribal usufruct rights' to land held by the state, both colonial and postcolonial land policies and laws were silent on the rights of pastoralists to access and use land and resources (UNDP, 2006). Nevertheless, the rights of pastoralists were catered for by other means, notably through local-level legislation in the form of Local Orders, strict enforcement of 'grazing lines', and manipulation of water policy and administrative measures (Delmet, 2005). Colonial legislation on Native Administration, moreover, instituted enforcement mechanisms to safeguard pastoral resource rights. Yet these arrangements proved weak and ineffective to guaranteeing the rights of pastoralists to resources, particularly land.

The categorical classification of the rangelands as 'government owned' though 'subject to usufruct rights' has endowed the state with the legal weapon to withdraw usufruct rights in order to introduce other forms of land use, mostly at the expense of pastoral dry season grazing grounds (UNDP, 2006). The precedent in settling land use disputes has time and again gone against the interests of pastoralists. Many disputes have concerned 'undemarcated lands', which have been claimed for commercial farming.

The failure of the pastoralists to defend their land tenure rights is a factor of their political marginalization and the hijacking of their representative institutions by livestock traders (Shazali and Abdel-Ghaffar, 1999). Large livestock traders affiliated to the ruling National Congress Party dominate pastoral unions in many states, as well as at the national level. These same traders also have a stake in mechanized farming, so they do not necessarily represent the interests of poorer and more subsistence-oriented pastoralists. Proposals to establish grazing lines for the northern limits of mechanized farming, the demarcation of pastoral migration routes, and the allocation of exclusive dry season grazing grounds have been aborted by more powerful commercial farming interests that dominate the legislative institutions at the state and federal levels (Scholte and Babiker, 2005). The Farmers Union is powerful in Gedaref State. Not only is the State Legislative Assembly dominated by commercial farming interests, the president of the Sudanese Farmers' Union is also the *Wali* [governor] of Gedaref State. The predominance of commercial farming interests in state politics has meant that measures intended to redress the resource rights of pastoralists have not been implemented. Key among these is a Federal Directive (1992) that sought to regulate land use in the southern part of Gedaref State to protect the rights of pastoralists to access dry season grazing grounds. This followed a study and land use plan developed by technical departments in the regional government to designate specific areas as dry season grazing reserves for pastoralists. However, to date, the political establishment has thwarted any attempt to implement the land use plans.

The Farmers Union has also sought to sabotage efforts to demarcate livestock corridors, a process begun by the state government. However, pastoralist leaders have complained that the corridors are too narrow and warned that conflict is likely to flare as livestock stray into fields adjacent to corridors. Planners tend to view the corridors as routes for transporting livestock rather than as a space in which pastoralists on the move must also rest, cook, eat, pray and gather for cultural and family festivities. Yet, these corridors are centuries old and there is a tradition of herders developing mutually beneficial exchange ties with sedentary farmers living along them.

Advocates for pastoralists are currently using the constitutional reform process in north Sudan to promote pastoralists' access to resources. While there is no explicit mention of pastoral land rights in the Interim National Constitution, groups campaigning for land tenure reform have turned to Article 186 (3) of the Interim Constitution which states: 'All levels of government shall institute a process to progressively develop and amend relevant laws to incorporate customary laws, practices, local heritage and international trends and practices.' However, given the reluctance of the ruling National Congress Party to translate the spirit of the Interim National Constitution into effective legislation, prospects are bleak for meaningful reform that might improve pastoralists' access to resources, which is essential for guaranteeing better livelihoods for pastoralists in the future.

Conclusion

Productive livelihoods for pastoralists in drylands such as those of central Sudan depend on clear and enforceable rights to key resources and the ability to move between these areas. Both of these fundamentals have been undermined through a long transition in land use in rangelands, from a mixed system including mobile livestock-keeping to a system dominated by commercial farming interests. While new forms of mobility are emerging across the region, as 'pure' mobility in the customary sense is no longer feasible in most places (see Oba, this book), many of these depend on the relative wealth and/or status of particular herd owners. Thus, social differentiation is indispensible to understand the predicament of herders in fragmented rangelands like Gedaref, where a majority of herders are vulnerable precisely because their poverty and weak political status mean they lack the options and opportunities to negotiate barriers to mobility and resource access.

Contemporary debates on land grabbing draw attention to the continuing attrition in pastoralists' access to key resources including land. Researchers and advocates of pastoralist rights across the region are warning of the consequences of recent and proposed land deals for pastoralists in places like the Tana Delta region of Kenya (Nunow, this book) and the Omo River delta in south-eastern Ethiopia, where the penetration of capital is relatively recent.[1] Yet the shift in the use of rangelands to commercial farming has been happening for over a century in central Sudan; hence, its importance to understand possible livelihood trajectories for pastoralists in other parts of the East and the Horn of Africa who are now confronted with similar dynamics of capital penetration and land grabbing.

Lacking adequate protections and safeguards for pastoralists to move and access high value fodder and water, the future of pastoralism in a context of intensifying commercialization and competing land use is one of uncertainty and conflict. The dynamics of changing land use in Sudan overlay complex and explosive political and social divisions. The contracting resource base for mobile pastoralists has already contributed to a reported increase in incidents of banditry, which has become a survival strategy for impoverished herders. More worrying are national issues concerning the unresolved border with the new state of South Sudan, the resumption of hostilities in Abyei and South Kordofan, and rising tension in the Blue Nile. These conflicts will compound the situation of pastoralists in the north by preventing their access to summer grazing sites in South Sudan. The conflict in Darfur may be a harbinger of the future in central and eastern Sudan, should current restrictions on pastoralists and related tensions deteriorate further still.

Note

1   'Southern Ethiopia: A debate on the dams controversy', Royal African Society event, Oxford, 11 October 2010, www.royalafricansociety.org/country-profiles/683.html? task=view, accessed 22 November 2011.

16

THE NEED TO STRENGTHEN LAND LAWS IN ETHIOPIA TO PROTECT PASTORAL RIGHTS

Abebe Mulatu and Solomon Bekure

Introduction

Historically, land tenure policy and legal frameworks in Ethiopia have been silent on the rights of pastoralists to access key resources and to move freely between these in seasons of need. Indeed, the omission of pastoral rights from land tenure regimes is a manifestation of a development paradigm that favours sedentary agriculture over mobile pastoralism and encourages excising high value resources in pastoral areas for other uses, predominantly the expansion of plantation agriculture (e.g. Babiker, this book; Galaty, this book; Behnke and Kerven, this book). This paradigm has had a remarkable persistence over time in spite of radical political change. Successive regimes in Ethiopia have expropriated high-value key resource areas within pastoral rangelands to establish large plantations. As explained elsewhere in this book (Benhke and Kerven), arguments that mobile livestock-keeping is unproductive and increasingly unviable due to presumed changes in rainfall patterns have provided the needed logic for different regimes to justify resource expropriation in the pastoral lowlands of Ethiopia. This expropriation has happened with no regard for the need for pastoral mobility and access to pockets of key resources that are disproportionately important to the sustainability of mixed-species herds. Although there is little factual evidence that pastoralism is less productive, the removal of key resources from pastoralist systems and greater restrictions on mobility have been particularly damaging to pastoral productivity, especially herding units that lack the relative wealth and status that is necessary to manage greater restrictions on key resource access.

The need to find ways of protecting pastoral land rights is more pressing in the current context of large acquisition of land for commercial farming, involving a variety of domestic and foreign investors in Ethiopia. While it has long been recognized that there is a need to enshrine enforceable protections of pastoral rights in law, there has been relatively little effort to do so in Ethiopia or elsewhere in the

Horn of Africa. In Ethiopia, the existing legal framework for land tenure, established under the Federal Rural Land Administration and Use Proclamation No. 456 (2005a), contains no specific provisions pertaining to pastoral lands. However, the constitution of Ethiopia that was enacted after the current ruling Ethiopian People Revolutionary Democratic Front (EPRDF) came to power in 1991 confers powers to regional states to enact their own laws within a federal administrative system. It is in this context that in recent years regional states with large pastoralist populations have begun formulating a legal and regulatory framework for land administration and use. While Somali Regional State is at an early stage in drafting its land policy, the Afar Regional State has progressed much further. It issued its land administration and use policy in 2008 and enacted a proclamation in 2009 (Afar Regional State, 2008, 2009). The cabinet of the regional government approved a set of regulations to implement the proclamation in 2011 (Afar Regional State, 2011a, b). This chapter critically assesses these recent efforts and whether they indicate a promising pathway to better protect pastoral land rights.

Pastoral land rights in policy and law

Under successive regimes in Ethiopia, government policy and statutory law have been ineffective at protecting the rights of pastoralists to land and other key resources. The failure of the state to protect pastoral land rights is a reflection of its inherent bias against mobile livestock-keeping. Officials in different governments have held similar attitudes, that pastoralism is inherently backward and unsustainable and that pastoralists should be settled, ostensibly so that they may pursue more secure alternatives to mobile livestock-keeping. Unlike the Imperial regime, the military Derg regime recognized the land rights of pastoralists while the ruling EPRDF government introduced better constitutional and legal protections for pastoralists. Yet, the fundamental aims of state policy to sedentarize pastoralists remain unchanged.

The Imperial regime under Emperor Haile Selassie considered communal lands to be property of the state. According to the Constitution of Ethiopia (1955) that came into effect under the Imperial regime:

> all property not held and possessed in the name of any person, natural or judicial, including all land in escheat . . . as well as all products of the sub-soil, all forests and all grazing lands, water-courses, lakes and territorial waters, are State Domain.
>
> *(Imperial Ethiopian Government, 1955, Article 131)*

There was no explicit recognition of pastoral rights to access and use rangelands. The lack of protections was evident in early expropriation processes under the Imperial regime whereby commercial farms and protected areas for wildlife were established on some of the most valuable lands in the Awash River valley (see Behnke and Kerven, this book). Afar and Kereyu pastoralists who customarily used these areas were not compensated. The Second Five Year Development Plan (1968) initiated a policy of pushing pastoralists into sedentary agriculture, with many Afar herders settled on schemes in the Awash valley. Still, while the regime expropriated pastoral key resources to develop a commercial agriculture sector and resettle herders, it did not seek to intervene in customary management of rangelands, which was left to chiefs and clan leaders who also acted as de facto administrators for the regime in administering justice and collecting taxes.

Following the fall of the Emperor in 1974, the Derg regime nationalized all lands through the Rural Lands Nationalization Proclamation No. 31/1975 (PMAC, 1975). Pastoral land rights were recognized under Article 24 of the proclamation: 'nomadic people shall have the possessory rights over the lands they customarily use for grazing or other purposes related to agriculture'. However, Article 25 stripped powers from chiefs and clan leaders in administration, jurisprudence, the collection of taxes and management of grazing lands. Instead, pastoralists were asked to form associations with chairpersons and executive committees. Under Article 10, associations were granted powers to 'induce the nomads to cooperate in the use of grazing and water rights; and to carry out the functions of applying land use directives of the government; administer and conserve public property; establish judicial tribunals; etc. within their locality'. Even though pastoral land rights were recognized, ostensibly, under the Rural Lands Nationalization Proclamation, the Derg regime expropriated rangelands to expand state-owned commercial farms and national parks without compensating pastoralists. The Derg continued a policy started under the Imperial regime of seeking to sedentarize pastoralists on several irrigation schemes, for instance, near Gode in Somali Region and Alwero in Gambela were established to implement this policy.

Under the regime of the ruling EPRDF, whose forces helped topple the Derg in 1990, there has been greater policy and legal recognition of pastoral land rights. Article 40(5) of the 1994 constitution of Ethiopia guarantees pastoralists cannot be displaced from their own lands. However, this protection has not been translated into federal law. Tellingly, the Federal Lands Expropriation and Compensation Proclamation No. 455/2005 and the implementing Regulation No. 137/2007 do not provide for compensation in situations where communal lands have been expropriated. Further, federal development policy remains inherently biased against pastoralism. Both the five-year Plan for Accelerated and Sustained Development to End Poverty (FDRE, 2005b) and the preceding Poverty Reduction Strategy Paper (FDRE, 2003) promote settled agriculture as an alternative livelihood for pastoralists. Both policies are silent on pastoral land tenure or other ameliorative measures to improve access to high value fodder and water. The draft Growth and Transformation Program (2011–15) seeks domestic and foreign investment to expand cultivated areas in lowlands to settle pastoralists,

> agricultural development will be undertaken by private investors in lowland areas where abundant extensive land exists. Assessment will be made to identify suitable land that will be listed in an organized land bank; and promoting such lands for investment by facilitating for local and external investors to develop it using the lease system.
>
> *(FDRE, 2010, pp25–26)*

The constitution also devolves administration, law making, and judicial powers to regional states under a federal system of government. This includes powers to formulate laws concerning land use and administration, albeit in accordance with federal law. In theory, this should create opportunities for pastoralists' interests to be considered in decision-making since pastoralists are represented on regional councils. However, the Federal Land Administration and Use Proclamation No. 456/2005 that empowers regional states to enact their own land laws has no provisions concerning the tenure and administration of pastoral lands. Far from providing a legal basis to strengthen the tenure rights of pastoralists, it gives regional and local government considerable leeway to expropriate communal rangelands for other uses. Many states are lagging in developing clear policies and provisions for protecting pastoral land tenure. As detailed below, with the exception of Afar Regional State, which has developed a policy and legal provisions concerning the administration of pastoral rangelands, other states with significant pastoral populations have yet to formulate laws concerning access rights and administration of rangelands, though a consultation process is underway in Somali Regional State to solicit views on a draft land administration and use policy. Moreover, there are no provisions to safeguard pastoral land tenure in the state constitutions of Afar and Somali Regional States, whose populations are from predominantly pastoralist and agro-pastoralist backgrounds, or in Oromia and Southern Nations, Nationalities and Peoples Regional States, which both have sizable pastoralist and agro-pastoralist populations.

Developing law for pastoral land tenure: experiences in Afar Regional State

Officials in Afar Regional State initiated a process to formulate a policy and administrative land tenure framework in 2006. The Regional State Council approved a land policy in June 2008, after which time the regional Pastoral, Agriculture and Rural Development Bureau began work to draft the Land Administration and Use Proclamation No. 49. It was enacted in 2009.

Officially, the land policy seeks to ensure secure land use rights and specify obligations of pastoralists, agro-pastoralists, investors and other users to prevent and reduce land-related conflicts, and ensure sustainable land uses through public participation. Yet, on closer inspection the policy fails to provide tenure security to pastoralists. It asserts that all lands are state-owned and that the government reserves the powers to transfer rights to these lands to private investors, or to redistribute communal lands to individuals for resettlement. Further, it proposes to survey rangelands to identify further areas suitable for cultivation and to allocate these to those wishing to practice settled agriculture. More concerning is that the policy contains no provisions to safeguard pastoral mobility or to ensure access to dry season grazing and watering sites. As such, the Afar land policy affirms past government practice and does little to safeguard pastoral mobility.

The Afar Regional State Land Administration Proclamation No. 49/2009 that was drafted in consultation with representatives from different land user groups, clan and women's leaders and members of *woreda* (district) and regional councils addresses some of these limitations. The proclamation provides that 'grazing lands that have been customarily used by pastoralists shall be identified and delimited' [Article 5(3)] and that 'communal pastoral lands used communally by pastoralists shall not be transferred into private holdings' [Article 5(8)]. Article 5(9) further states 'communal lands that are communally used by pastoralists for grazing and social purposes shall not be given/leased out to investors'. Crucially, it includes a proviso that 'this, however, shall not affect the power of the government, as owner of all lands, to transfer communal lands into private holdings as deemed necessary and in consultation and in agreement with pastoralists'. While it is encouraging that the proclamation acknowledges the principle of consultation, there is no guarantee that consultations could challenge state plans to expropriate certain lands for development. Further, the proclamation leaves open the possibility for unchecked bureaucratic discretion, by not specifying parameters to determine that pastoralists are in agreement with proposed plans. Considering the background and history of land expropriation in pastoral areas for 'development', it is possible, if not likely, that proposed expropriations would go forth irrespective of consultations and the interests of pastoralists to protect mobility and access to high value fodder and water.

To establish the holding rights of pastoralists over their communal lands, Article 6(1) of the Proclamation proposes to survey and register all clan lands and to issue certificates of holdings in the name of the clan using particular communal lands, which would be deposited with a clan leader or *kebele* (sub-district) chairperson acting as a community representative. However, plans to register pastoral lands on the basis of clan territories have raised fears that conflict might ensue over the location of boundaries delimiting lands belonging to different clans, since the customary clan boundaries were abolished during the Derg regime. It is also unclear whether pastoralists belonging to a particular clan would be able to freely move with their livestock into a neighbouring area, or whether the establishment of clearer land rights on the basis of clan affiliation might lead to more rigid and fixed boundaries. Leaving aside these concerns, it is as yet unclear whether the certification of pastoral lands will be sufficient to protect the full set of resources that herders require to sustain herds, since both regional and federal administrative officials retain powers to expropriate high value resources for other uses.

Other provisions in the proclamation indicate the intention of the state to shift some pastoral lands to other uses. It guarantees individuals over 18 free access to land for farming. Pastoralists who choose to farm may also enter into planned government resettlement programmes [Article 5(6)]. Yet there are currently very few resettlement areas for new farmers although the federal government, in consultation with the Afar regional government, has identified several hundred sites for potential resettlement. In consultations organized by the task force that drafted the land proclamation, clan representatives vehemently opposed any lands in their area designated for farming being allocated to members of other clans. This holds in particular for pastoralists from areas where there is land suitable for cultivation, such as Assaita, Amibara and Gewane. Many pure pastoralists were against settlement and removing land and resources from mobile livestock-keeping, even when compensation is paid. Pure pastoralists from the northern and north-western reaches of Afar, including Awra and Gulina, indicated difficulty accessing high value fodder during drought years and asked that the law should make provisions to enable them to access land for farming.

The proclamation recognizes and seeks to empower customary institutions to manage natural resources and handle land disputes: '[l]and disputes arising between pastoralists shall be settled under the customary dispute settlement system' [Article 7(1)]. The proclamation requires the regional government to assist customary institutions to settle disputes and to facilitate execution of their judgments [Article 7(2)]. A party that is aggrieved by a decision reached by a customary authority may appeal to the *woreda* court, then to the zonal court and all the way up to the Supreme Court [Article 7(3-6)]. It is presumably too simplistic to allocate appellate jurisdiction to the regular courts in all types of disputes that arise in pastoral areas. Disputes in pastoral areas may generally arise among individuals of a clan or sub-clan, between individuals of different clans or sub-clans that may have the effect of involving the clans or sub-clans of the disputants, or between two or more clans or sub-clans such as disputes over clan borders that involve all clan members. Customary institutions have elaborate laws and procedures to handle these various types of disputes.

However, revising decisions arrived on customary substantive and procedural laws by appeal to formal courts that apply statutory laws will be challenging. First, the customary law and procedures applied to a case, and the government law to be applied to the same case on appeal, could be different. Second, statutory law has precedence over customary law, which will have a bearing on courts when adjudicating appellate cases arising from customary institutions. Third, judges in the formal courts may lack the knowledge and understanding of customary law even in cases where customary law is not contradicting statutory law and is applicable to the case on appeal. Furthermore, the recognition given to the customary land dispute institutions should be clearly elaborated. The proclamation is unclear whether the customary dispute settlement institution envisaged under the proclamation is autonomous and whether it would be governed by authorities recognized under customary law. It is also unclear what the role of the appellate customary court vis-à-vis the formal courts would be.

The regional government has yet to clarify the type and level of financial, legal and technical assistance that will be made available to customary authorities for settling disputes. There is a need to determine the type and level of assistance that customary authorities require, after which time new legislation or amendatory laws will need to be enacted by the regional government to institutionalize the type and amount of assistance. For example, the laws allocating budgetary responsibility or jurisdiction, or laws that empower customary authorities to request police assistance in proceedings or to execute judgments will need to be made or amended.

It is uncertain that customary institutions are equipped to handle disputes involving individuals engaged in economic activities outside of livestock-keeping. Since individuals, and not clans or sub-clans, are engaged in such economic activities, they are beyond the control of traditional authorities. Customary institutions are incapable of administering private property relations. Furthermore, customary authorities themselves have been implicated in the capture of high value lands. In 1991, after the downfall of the military government and seizure of power by the EPRDF, the Transitional Government of Ethiopia decided to return, on the insistence of the Afar regional government, pastoral lands that were taken for agricultural development. More than 6,500 hectares of land that were under the Middle Awash Agricultural Development Enterprise, a state farm, were returned to a clan (Hundie and Padmanabhan, 2008). However, influential clan members appropriated large sections of the land for their individual benefit. Parts of the remaining land were rented out by the clan leaders to investors in the name of the clan but the rents were captured by the clan leaders and not shared with other clan members equitably.

This situation has created numerous problems. First, adjacent clans are trapped in border conflict in order to control larger lands to be leased out. Many allege that clan border conflicts are instigated by clan leaders because they are the beneficiaries of leasing out lands to investors. Second, since individuals are not sharing the benefits of rents received from lands leased to outside investors, other clan members have tended to be hostile to investment, with some resorting to destroying crops on leased lands. Third, there are different views within clans as to how to use high value lands. Consultations organized by the task force that drafted the proclamation found that most clan members who have not benefited from existing leasing arrangements support the partition of clan land equally to all clan members. Unsurprisingly, those who currently hold large areas of communal land and receive income from land leased to investors object to any partition that might include lands they currently hold. Clan leaders oppose the idea of further partitioning. They also object to using the proceeds from current leasing arrangements for community development projects, such as constructing classrooms or health clinics. This experience shows the incapacity of traditional leaders to handle disputes involving a range of interested parties, some of whom have considerable wealth and stand to lose enormously from any planned repartition of communal pastoral lands. Such conflicts seem to emanate from the lack of clear federal and regional state policies on how high value communal lands should be administered for the benefit of the whole community.

Administrative capacities to implement the Afar land law are weak, which will also complicate effective regulation and enforcement of the provisions in the proclamation. Regional authorities established an Environmental Protection, Land Administration and Use Agency, which is mandated to administer all rural lands and implement provisions in the lands proclamation. The constitution of Afar Regional State establishes *woreda* and *kebele* administrations that have the power to administer and implement government plans and programmes as well as the power to manage and administer natural resources within their respective jurisdictions, displacing the customary pastoral land administration system (Afar Regional State, 2002, Article

72). However, the *woreda* and *kebele* administrations are weak and lack capacity to effectively undertake the functions that used to be performed by the customary administration, especially the management of natural resources. This has contributed to problems of resource depletion, enclosure of communal rangelands, and other mismanagement of natural resources. The constitutions have also established formal court systems and *kebele* social courts.

Conclusion

Protecting the dry season grazing areas and allowing access corridors to these areas is necessary to sustain the productivity of mobile pastoralist systems. However, pastoral land rights have been threatened since the 1950s and 1960s when high-value resource areas within rangelands were excised by the state to introduce and expand plantation agriculture. Buoyed by the absence of any policy or legal protections of pastoralists' access to key resources, large acquisitions of land in pastoral areas for commercial farming and wildlife protection have continued unabated under successive political regimes. The Imperial and Derg regimes initiated settlement programmes and rendered technical and financial assistance to pastoralists who were directly affected by government land acquisitions, believing that the socio-economic development of pastoralists lies in their becoming full-time farmers or labourers. While the 1994 constitution of Ethiopia includes a provision guaranteeing that pastoralists are not displaced from rangelands, other provisions in existing federal policy and law reaffirm the powers of the state to expropriate land in pastoral areas for development.

In the absence of clear federal policies and provisions in law to protect pastoralists' access to land and key resources, regional states led by Afar are using powers conferred under the Ethiopian constitution to introduce their own legal provisions and regulations to redress insecure pastoral land rights. Other states with large pastoral populations including Somali and Oromiya intend to formulate their own laws and accompanying regulations concerning the rights of pastoralists to access rangelands and key resource areas within these. The Afar experience is thus significant as it is likely to inform processes underway elsewhere in the Ethiopian lowlands.

Like the national constitution, the Afar land proclamation guarantees the rights of pastoralists not to be displaced. It goes further in seeking the protection of rangelands from being further parceled into privately held areas, in part by dividing rangelands into units corresponding to clan territories and issuing holding certificates to clan representatives. Much will be determined by the process for deciding boundaries between different clan-held rangelands and whether high-value riverine resources are included in these. This process is likely to be fraught as clans and different factions within these seek the best outcome.

Still, in spite of the spirit of the proclamation to introduce legal and regulatory protected access to key resources for pastoralists, it falls short of doing so by reaffirming the powers of the state to expropriate such resources for agriculture and other development. Further, it does not specify guidelines, nor have other regulations been enacted, to guide how consultations with pastoralists around proposed expropriations would be undertaken or the criteria to be used to judge that members of a clan agree with state plans for compensation. Given the establishment of formal administrative structures that displace the traditional governance structure and the history and background of state expropriation of key resources in pastoral areas for agricultural development without adequately compensating herders, as well as existing plans to expand the area under irrigation in the Awash river valley (Behnke and Kerven, this book), the proclamation will fail to protect pastoral land rights unless laws that allocate powers and duties in resource management and dispute resolution to the traditional institutions are in place and implemented.

PART IV

Alternative livelihoods

17

SEEKING ALTERNATIVE LIVELIHOODS IN PASTORAL AREAS

Elliot Fratkin

Introduction

The seeking of alternative livelihoods by former pastoralists is not a new phenomenon in Africa, particularly in times of drought and conflict (Johnson and Anderson, 1988). But the settling of former pastoralists has increased dramatically in the past half century, driven by stock loss and impoverishment due to drought, resource competition and population pressure (Hogg, 1986; Fratkin, 1992; Scoones, 1995a; Desta and Coppock, 2004; McCabe, 2003), and increasingly to escape war and violent conflict (Goldsmith, this book; Jok and Hutchinson, 1999; Randall, 2005). While exogenous factors have 'pushed' former pastoralists into settling and seeking alternative livelihoods, many have also been 'pulled' by the benefits of sedentary life, including food security, physical safety, access to health care and formal education and new economic opportunities. Former pastoralists have settled in rural, urban or peri-urban settings, either adapting their livestock based economy to settled agro-pastoral life, or abandoning the pastoral economy as they seek new livelihoods as farmers or town dwellers engaged in trade, wage labour and craft production (McPeak *et al.*, 2011). Multiple future pathways exist for pastoralists today, with difficult choices and trade-offs involved.

The settling of former pastoralists entails both costs and benefits. Several studies point to increased impoverishment and destitution of pastoralists who settle (Adano and Witsenberg, 2005; Fratkin, 1992; Hogg, 1986; Little, 1985b; McCabe *et al.*, 2010) which may particularly affect the well-being of women and children in terms of poorer nutrition and greater exposure to infectious diseases (Galvin *et al.*, 1994; Sheik-Mohamed and Velema, 1999; Talle, 1999; Fratkin and Roth, 2005). However, there are specific benefits in leaving the pastoral economy. For production, these include increased marketing opportunities for livestock, livestock products or agricultural produce, even in areas with poor infrastructure or conflict

(Ensminger, 1992; Little, 1996; McPeak *et al.*, 2011; Sato, 1997; Zaal and Dietz, 1999). These new opportunities have also benefited pastoralist women who are able to sell dairy and horticultural products, including vegetables, tobacco and *khat* (Fratkin and Smith, 1995, Little, 1994; Smith, 1999; Waters-Bayer, 1988).

What then is a 'sustainable livelihood' (cf. WCED, 1987; Scoones, 1998, 2007; Chambers and Conway, 1992) in a pastoral area? What alternative pathways are available, when 'traditional' nomadic pastoralism is challenged? The concept of alternative livelihoods appeared in particular regard to former pastoralists in Africa's arid lands who were driven out of the pastoral economy by famine, poverty, and political insecurity (Hogg, 1992; Scoones, 1995a; Brockington, 2001; Desta and Coppock, 2004; Little *et al.*, 2001), but, as already noted, alternative pathways may also be positive choices, not always resulting in a complete 'exit' from pastoralism.

Factors leading to alternative livelihoods

What is driving the process of diversification in pastoral livelihoods? Several factors play a role, including drought and famine, population growth, loss of common property resources, commoditization of the economy, sedentarization and urban migration and political turmoil and conflict.

Kenya, Tanzania and Uganda continue to have among the world's highest population growth rates (2.6 per cent, 2.9 per cent and 3.1 per cent annual increases respectively in 2010); although this growth rate is declining with drops in total fertility rates (World Bank Development Indicators, 2011). Specific growth rates in pastoral areas are not typically known, although several studies report lower fertility rates among pastoralists (Leslie and Fry, 1989; Roth, 1994; Randall, 1996). Rapid population growth has affected rural and urban areas alike, where farmers increasingly move onto less productive lands to raise their crops and families, restricting the rangeland necessary to sustain pastoral livelihoods (Homewood *et al.*, 2009). Furthermore, pastoralists have increased farm cultivation, leading to a loss of pasture and water resources for pastoral production, as among the Tanzanian Maasai (McCabe *et al.*, 2010).

The settling of former pastoralists has contributed dramatically to the growth of towns in arid regions of Africa. The town of Garissa in north-east Kenya, for example, grew from several thousand to 100,000 in 25 years, making it the largest commercial town between Nairobi and Mogadishu (Republic of Kenya, 2005). But Garissa town itself was dwarfed by the neighbouring United Nations High Commission for Refugees (UNHCR) camp of Dadaab which swelled to 470,000 refugees in August 2011 as many pastoralists sought relief from drought and famine in Somalia. Indeed, the United Nations Population Fund (UNFPA) estimated 12.5 million people in north-east Africa, many from pastoralist backgrounds, were made destitute by drought during this period, leading to greater migration and seeking alternatives to pastoral economies (UNFPA, 2011).

Drought has occurred with greater frequency in the second half of the twentieth century compared to the first (Toulmin, 2009; Ericksen *et al.*, this book). Pastoralists have historically adapted to conditions of drought or low and erratic rainfall by physical mobility, dispersion of their herds and people and seeking different food sources through fishing, hunting, gathering and agriculture (Scoones, 1995a; Homewood, 2008). In the late twentieth century, pastoralists added new mechanisms to cope with drought and famine including migration for wage labour in rural and urban employment (Abdelkarim, 1986; Salih, 1995; Hampshire, 2006; May and McCabe, 2004), the adoption of agriculture (McCabe, 2003; McCabe *et al.*, 2010; Sandford, this book) and, less productively, migration to famine relief centres (Hogg, 1986; Rutledge and Roble, 2010).

Another force of change affecting pastoralists has been the loss of communal land rights and the increasing promotion of private titling and individuation of the rangeland, something that has occurred throughout the continent but most particularly in east and north-eastern Africa (Ensminger and Rutten, 1991; Galaty, 1992). Since independence, Kenya has moved away from recognizing communal land tenure in favour of individual tenure rights, as have other African countries living in the neoliberal framework of World Bank and bilateral loans.

Some pastoralists have shifted their economic activity from subsistence to commercial production. Both the demands and opportunities for market sales of livestock in northern Kenya have increased substantially in the past 25 years, as have opportunities for wage labour (McPeak and Little, 2005; see Mahmoud, this book). However, increased commoditization of the livestock economy has benefited those with large livestock herds, allowing them to remain in the pastoral economy, while those without sufficient herds often migrate out of the pastoral economy and seek jobs in towns or livelihood on farms (Fratkin and Roth, 1990; see Catley and Aklilu, this book).

Although not experiencing the civil wars of neighbouring Sudan, Ethiopia, Uganda and Somalia, Kenya has seen its share of violence, mainly from banditry and inter-ethnic livestock raiding in areas not well policed (Fleisher, 2000; Mkutu, 2008; Goldsmith, this book). As reported in other areas of Africa, political conflict and violence has negative effects including economic disruption, displacement and moves to refugee centres as both internally displaced and internationally displaced persons (Rutledge and Roble, 2010; UNFPA, 2011).

These diverse drivers are shifting the composition and location of pastoral livelihoods. Many alternative livelihoods involve a process of sedentarization, the subject of the next section.

Settling down

Sedentarization is the process of individuals, households or entire communities of formerly nomadic populations, settling into non-mobile and permanent communities seeking alternative livelihoods (Little *et al.*, 2001; McPeak *et al.*, 2011). Yet sedentism is neither a recent event nor a unidirectional process, and has occurred in many regions of the world at different points in history. Policies encouraging sedentarization have long been part of state efforts in pastoral areas, as part of economic policies of incorporation, political attempts at pacification and control, and as part of a narrative of 'modernization' and 'civilization' (Hodgson, 2001).

Pastoralists have long depended on symbiotic ties of trade and production with agricultural communities and mercantile towns, as among Fulani in Sahelian West Africa who traded livestock, leather and meat for grains, metal work and other commodities (Stenning, 1959; Waters-Bayer and Bayer, 1994; Moritz, 2006). In East Africa, pastoralists historically obtained necessary grains by trading regularly with agricultural neighbours, e.g. Maasai with Kikuyu in the nineteenth century (Waller, 1988), or they took up agriculture themselves, as did the Il Chamus (Little, 1992) and Arusha or 'agricultural' Maasai (Spear, 1997). In the twentieth century, many Maasai settled near roads for access to cattle markets, while in northern Kenya, Boran and Samburu cattle herders provided beef and milk to both colonial administrators and growing towns (Adano and Witsenburg, 2005). Maize cultivation is becoming increasingly important for Maasai pastoralists living in southern Kenya and northern Tanzania (McCabe et al., 2010). In addition to cultivation, pastoralists have also settled near urban areas to market milk, meat and livestock (Little, 1994; Salih, 1995).

As discussed, diversification is an essential component of pastoral livelihoods to cope with varying and unpredictable resources. Pastoralists practise multi-species herding, enabling them to utilize different herding environments (Fratkin, 2004; McCabe, 2004; Oba, this book). Similarly, living in towns or farms offers alternative livelihoods where one can take up, permanently or temporarily, farming, wage labour or entrepreneurial activities including shop keeping, livestock marketing, charcoal or beer production and so on. Former pastoralists living in towns or farms often own livestock which are herded by kinsmen or friends in the pastoral economy, or divide up their households with some members farming and others herding as among Il Chamus (Little, 1992), Datoga (Sieff, 1997), Fulani (Hampshire, 2006; Swift, 1986; Turner, 1999) and other agro-pastoral regimes in Sahelian Africa (Mace, 1993). Grain for livestock exchange or herding labour is maintained by social ties and ritual life (marriages, age-set rites) and serves to keep the pastoral and agricultural/town communities integrated (Little, 1983). Sedentarization therefore is a process that operates along a continuum from highly mobile pastoral households to permanently settled households, of which individuals may move from one domain to the other (Spencer, 1998).

Despite ties to the pastoral communities, settled townspeople and farmers often undergo dramatic changes in customs and relationships, including a departure from communal and kin-based relations in the pastoral communities to individualized identities in the towns and farms. For settled Rendille in the farming community of Songa in Marsabit District, Kenya, former age and gender roles transformed as young men marry earlier and young women, if educated, later, while the authority of male elders over young men is declining (Smith, 1999). In addition, there has been a decline in the 'moral economy' of redistribution (Scott, 1976), where women living on isolated farming plots at Songa no longer share food with others as they did in the pastoral setting (Fujita et al., 2004).

Alternative livelihoods in northern Kenya

Marsabit District in northern Kenya is home to 100,000 people, the majority being from pastoralist backgrounds including Gabra, Boran, Rendille, Samburu and Ariaal (mixed Samburu/Rendille) communities. Beginning with the extensive droughts of the early 1970s, one-third of the district's nomadic households have settled in small towns or famine relief centres to pursue non-pastoral livelihoods (Fratkin and Roth, 2005; McPeak *et al.*, 2011). Alternative livelihoods include:

- marketing – livestock, dairy, hides, cultivated crops;
- entrepreneurship – businesses, shops, building and construction, truck transportation;
- wage labour – construction, driving, restaurants and shops, domestic work;
- petty commodity trade – tobacco, *khat*, charcoal, firewood, beer-brewing (particularly by women); and
- salaried employment in schools, administration, health, police and army, game scouts.

Where the sale of livestock and employment in construction and transportation have typically been the domain of men, women have earned more marginal livelihoods selling milk and/or cultivated crops including garden vegetables, tobacco, and *khat* (the stimulant *Catha edulis*) (Fratkin and Smith, 1995; Smith, 1999), or at lower rungs of the economic ladder, collecting and selling firewood, making charcoal, beer brewing, and for some, prostitution, increasing their exposure to HIV/AIDS and other sexually transmitted diseases (Talle, 1988; Klepp *et al.*, 1995; Roth *et al.*, 2009). Education has played an increasingly important role in livelihood diversification, particularly as access to obtaining professional employment in hospitals and health clinics, government offices, military and police and employment in non-governmental organizations (Siele *et al.*, this book).

Three recent research projects have investigated outcomes of alternative livelihood strategies in Marsabit District: the PARIMA project in Kenya and Ethiopia (McPeak *et al.*, 2011), Adano and Witsenburg's (2004) study of Marsabit town and Fratkin and Roth's (2005) study of health and nutritional changes among mobile and sedentary Ariaal and Rendille communities.

The PARIMA project (Pastoral Risk Management Project of the Global Livestock Collaborative Research and Support Program) was a multi-ethnic study of economic diversification in northern Kenya and southern Ethiopia between 1997–2007, funded mainly by USAID (e.g. Little *et al.*, 2001; McPeak and Barrett, 2001). One subset of this study in northern Kenya drew on data from 180 households in six pastoral, agro-pastoral and agricultural communities (thirty households each) among Ariaal, Boran, Gabra, Il Chamus, Rendille and Samburu communities (McPeak and Little, 2005). Drawing a composite of income generating strategies, they found a distribution of activities as shown in Table 17.1.

TABLE 17.1 Income generation sources among Northern Kenyan pastoralist households (after McPeak and Little, 2005, p95)

Livestock sales	34%
Salary	18%
Trading revenue	16%
Wage labour	10%
Milk sales	8%
Hides and skin	5%
Fuelwood/charcoal sales	5%
Cultivation	2%
Craft sales	1%
Water sales	1%

McPeak and Little drew several conclusions from this study:

- Over half (53 per cent) of the total income reported came from sources other than livestock or livestock product sales.
- Households with better access to markets and infrastructure have higher and more diversified incomes.
- Larger herds are concentrated in drier areas, and where herders derive a higher share of their income from livestock and livestock production. They also have more milk available for home consumption.
- Those herders who are more mobile suffer lower losses during drought. Those households with larger herds before the drought have larger herds after the drought, showing that herd accumulation at the household level provides a self-insurance role.
- Areas with a higher share of income from non-pastoral sources have higher welfare in terms of higher income, higher expenditures and lower variability in the measure of milk value plus expenditure. In some cases they are more food secure because they could convert wages into food purchases.
- Formal education plays an important role in the way households earn their income and cope with food insecurity. Areas where household members have spent more time in formal education get a higher proportion of their income from non-pastoral sources and have higher incomes and expenditure levels. Investment in formal education for children in order to obtain salaried jobs is one of the most significant diversification strategies employed by these households (McPeak and Little, 2005, p96).

A second research project was carried out by Wario Roba Adano and Karen Witsenburg on pastoral sedentarization and livelihoods on Marsabit mountain in Kenya (Adano and Witsenberg, 2004). This area has attracted 30,000 settlers in the past 40 years, mainly impoverished Rendille and Boran who settled on church-initiated agricultural schemes and engaged in cultivation and agro-pastoralism. This study surveyed 287 households and found:

- 80 per cent of the households owned less than eight total livestock units (TLUs) per household, which amounted to only 16 per cent of total TLUs on the mountain.
- Income from arable farming was meagre, and households relied on market sales of female grown vegetables including kale, tomatoes and *khat*.
- While households produced an average of 1000kg maize annually, less than 20 per cent of households were self-sufficient in grain (at 253kg/person/year).
- Only three per cent of households earned more than US$1 per person per day.
- Nevertheless, 80 per cent of households surveyed said they would *not* return to a pastoral lifestyle if they had the chance. Their reasoning was that a pastoral lifestyle was too onerous and risky.

As with McPeak and Little's study, Adano and Witsenberg found a strong correlation between household income, children's education and livestock wealth (Adano and Witsenberg, 2005).

A third study on pastoral sedentarization by Fratkin and Roth (2005) focused on health and nutritional outcomes of settling down. This study compared five Ariaal and Rendille communities over a three year period which included both a drought year (1996) and a normal year (1995). The five communities depended on different livelihood strategies including fully nomadic pastoralists (Lewogoso), agro-pastoralists relying on dry land maize production and cattle raising (Karare), irrigated agriculture (Songa), a small town community (Ngrunit) and a famine-relief based town (Korr). Measurements of child malnutrition revealed large differences in the growth patterns of children, where settled children in all communities showed three times the level of stunting (measured by height by age) and wasting (measured by weight by age) than the nomadic Lewogoso community. Figures 17.1 and 17.2 show the percentage of children under six years old who displayed wasting or stunting, measured as two standard deviations below the accepted mean of weight by age and height by age (measured in z-scores).

Children in settled communities suffered both short-term malnutrition (which results in wasting) and long-term malnutrition (which results in stunting). These differences were attributed to protein deficiencies brought about by a greatly reduced access to milk and a higher reliance on grains in all settled communities. Nomadic Lewogoso children were able to consume up to three times the average number of cups of milk reported in the four sedentary communities (Fratkin *et al.*, 2004, p548).

Although both settled and nomadic communities in the lowlands had high levels of malaria, settled children showed a greater incidence of diarrhoeal and respiratory illnesses (Nathan *et al.*, 2005). Nevertheless, the greater access to clinics and health services reduced mortality of individuals in the settled communities, and compensated, to a degree, for the health costs. In terms of nutritional outcomes (and their importance in child health), the authors recommended that policy-makers increase protein sources to settled communities, including raising dairy animals and growing

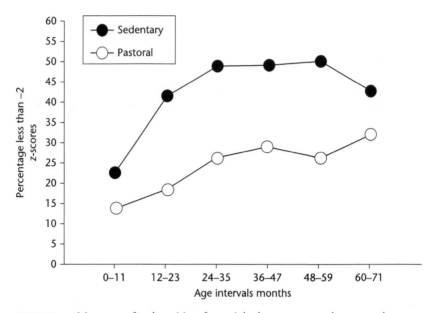

FIGURE 17.1 Measures of malnutrition for weight-by-age, pastoral versus sedentary samples, wasting defined as below −2 z-scores (Fratkin *et al.*, 2004, p548).

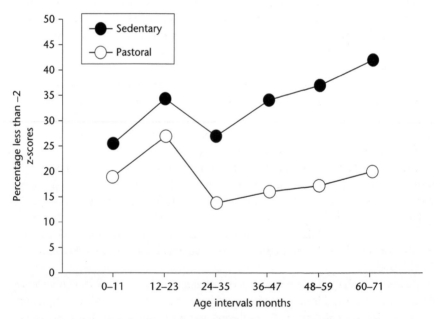

FIGURE 17.2 Measures of malnutrition for height-by-age, pastoral versus sedentary samples, stunting defined as below −2 z-scores (Fratkin *et al.*, 2004, p548).

protein rich crops (e.g. beans); and provide greater health care including vaccinations and marketing services to the nomadic communities (Fratkin *et al.*, 2004).

Conclusion

The seeking of alternative livelihoods in agriculture, commerce and wage labour by former pastoralists has increased steadily with declines in the sustainability of pastoral livelihoods, which are jeopardized by stock loss brought about by drought, resource competition and conflict. Living at the margins has meant seeking out alternatives. Sedentarization and alternative livelihood pathways confer both benefits and costs to former pastoralists. The benefits are clearly: increased access to public education, food security, health facilities, larger markets, police security and increasing female involvement and decision making in commerce. The downsides of leaving the pastoral economy include negative impacts on health and nutrition of children, and loss of kinship networks and supportive communities during periods of drought and risk. Seeking alternative livelihoods is a necessity for many impoverished pastoralists who, although they continue to face poverty in settled communities, still prefer the security of settled life to the vagaries and hardships of nomadic pastoralism. Although opportunities in farming or wage labour may be few, this is compensated for by greater access to food security, health care, education and physical security, which increase the chances of long-term survival and sustainability.

18

REACHING PASTORALISTS WITH FORMAL EDUCATION

A distance-learning strategy for Kenya

David Siele, Jeremy Swift and Saverio Krätli[1]

Introduction

Demand for education among pastoralists, including children actively involved in production, is rapidly increasing. Education is seen by impoverished households as a pathway out of poverty, and by the households actively involved in pastoral production as a way to support their production system in an increasingly globalized world.

However, education systems are failing to respond to this shift in demand, and remain oriented towards 'educating pastoral children out of pastoralism'. Education programmes for pastoralists tend to be an extension of those designed for sedentary people, and are based on a simple adaptation of sedentary models to some aspects of nomadic life. This approach has a poor record worldwide (Krätli, 2001; Carr-Hill and Peart, 2005; Dyer, 2006; Krätli with Dyer, 2006). The model used is that of a teacher in front of a class; a model that effectively excludes the children directly involved in pastoral production. Where pastoral families adapt to this limited service, it is normally by 'giving' some children to formal education and keeping others to run the family business of livestock production. In this way, productive households have to make a damaging trade-off between gaining access to formal education (through a school system that diverts children away from the pastoral economy) and maintaining the family business (through the specialist work and learning that takes place within the household and camp). Such learning is essential if the child is to acquire the knowledge about and membership of the complex social networks of pastoral life, which is a condition of success as an adult producer.

Educational delivery systems tried so far – boarding schools, mobile schools, special uses of sedentary schools – have not successfully resolved this trade-off. Experiments are currently under way in Kenya to develop a distance learning system (using a combination of radio programmes, mobile tutors and audio/print materials), aimed at broadcasting a full primary curriculum including literacy to individual children and their families directly at the camps. The aim is to enable children to acquire a formal education and thus to become more effective producers, as well as to compete with other Kenyan children – if necessary in the world outside pastoralism.

Reaching the hardest-to-reach with formal education

Pastoralists are demanding education across East Africa and the Horn. This is not only among those who have been impoverished and sedentarized, but also among households actively involved in production that manage huge dryland areas and supply most of the domestic and export livestock market in their countries. Demand for education comes from several sources: education is seen as a way of supporting the production system, as a way out of poverty, as a way to reduce conflict, as a source of economic diversification, as an insurance against drought and, in the longer run, as an adaptation to climate change. In this way, education is a critical foundation for future pathways.

About one million children are out of school in Kenya. Almost all of these are either in the slums or in the arid and semi-arid areas, which are predominantly occupied by pastoralists. The absence of schooling affects girls in particular. National net enrolment rate at primary level in Kenya in 2009 was 94.5 per cent for boys and 90 per cent for girls. Yet, in Wajir district, which is predominantly pastoral, it was 31 per cent for boys and 20 per cent for girls (MOESTK, 2009).

African pastoralists are increasingly exposed to globalization and world economic trends. New technologies are becoming available. Rapid urbanization, accompanied by increasing demand from urban populations for milk and meat, is changing the economic geography of the dryland areas. If pastoralists can adapt their production system to this new challenge – and everything we know about pastoralists suggests they will adapt if the legal and economic framework within which they operate is supportive – the future of pastoralism is brighter than many people suggest. A crucial part of this adaptation lies in the education system, and in the ability of the education system provided by the government to adapt to these new challenges.

But education services for pastoralists are failing to respond to the demand (UNESCO, 2009, 2010), and are still generally oriented towards educating pastoral children for skills and careers that are not part of the pastoral economy. While there is an important need to equip those who leave pastoralism to find employment in the wider economy, there is an equally urgent need for those children who are active pastoralists, and will be responsible for tomorrow's animal production in the drylands, to have access to the same education as others. In both cases the aim must be to provide a level playing field for pastoralists in economic development.

Services operate on the assumption that educational provision must involve standard classrooms and teachers. However, mobile pastoralist families find it exceptionally difficult to take advantage of an educational service locked into the classroom model. Those households that want to secure access to education, for at least some of their children, have to adjust to the service and face unfavourable trade-offs. By releasing some children to school, households typically compromise on productivity by weakening both the pastoral production team, and the quality of strategic mobility. Therefore the dominant strategy of formal educational provision routinely (if unintentionally) selects a predictable and identifiable proportion of pastoral children: those actively involved in production. This has far-reaching economic and political consequences.

This chapter presents the strategy recently adopted by the Kenyan government to avoid these dangers. The strategy, the result of a partnership between the Ministry of State for the Development of Northern Kenya and Other Arid Lands and the Ministry of Education, working with the Education for Nomads group of researchers, is based on a comprehensive review of the options and possibilities for nomadic education in Kenya and elsewhere and of experiments within Kenya itself.[2]

Nomadic education in Kenya

Kenya, like other countries with significant pastoral populations, faces a problem of poor attendance and graduation rates of nomadic children in school. The issue is not that pastoralists refuse a modern system of learning. Rather it is the result of the damaging trade-off that parents and children have to make between children acquiring formal schooling and the fundamental, informal education that takes place within the household and the camp about their own cultural, social and economic world. Such learning, embedded in the networks of pastoral life, is crucial to a child's development. To be a successful economic operator in a pastoral economy requires among other attributes: a detailed knowledge of the technical aspects of livestock husbandry – for example a sophisticated knowledge of grasses, shrubs and animals, and membership of social networks which enable the capture of economies of scale in production and provide the basis of risk management. These are all a critical part of education but are not taught in school.

Current educational practice confronts pastoralists with an unfavourable choice between these two types of learning: formal schooling within the national system or informal education in the camps. Formal schooling is useful for many purposes, but separates children in school from their family, their wider social environment and their cultural background, and is acquired at the cost of the informal learning acquired in households and camps. Children who stay in the camps acquire these social and economic skills, but do not acquire formal learning. Crucial challenges in the provision of education to pastoralists follow from resistance to this forced separation more than from a refusal of formal education itself (Krätli and Dyer, 2009). Indeed, pastoralists no longer resist the idea of formal education, as they commonly did 20 years ago. Children and adults now fully understand the importance of education and are enthusiastic about learning (Birch *et al.*, 2010).

Kenya's experience

Kenya Vision 2030 and the national policy framework on education set out an ambitious goal: education for all by 2015 (MOESTK, 2005, 2007). Although pastoralists are scarcely mentioned in the strategy, this target applies to them as to others. This is not a trivial objective. It is estimated that some 300,000 pastoral children are currently out of school in North East Province alone.

The aim of the strategy adopted in 2010 by the Kenya government is to recognize the unique nature of nomad education and to propose ways of reconciling the fundamental choices children face (MDNKOAL, 2010a, b). The problem is clearly recognized by the Kenya government and by international agencies working in this field. 'Education for all is more likely to be achieved if boys and girls are not forced to choose between herding and schooling', writes UNICEF (2007, p6). The Kenyan Ministry of Education's nomadic education policy framework states: 'nomadic pastoralists require flexible education delivery modes that take into account their children's work at home' (MOESTK, 2010, paras 1.1.7). The strategy addresses the fundamental challenge identified above: to extend good quality formal education to all children living within nomadic livelihood systems or directly involved in pastoral production, without undermining the children's economic and social position in those livelihood systems.

According to the national policy framework, every child is entitled to free quality basic education. The policy framework outlines the main actions needed to achieve this. It supports setting up a variety of local alternatives to formal schooling, adapted to the local ecology. New technologies will be welcomed. It agrees that it is essential to create a relationship between non-formal and formal education systems, so pupils can move between the two. Timetabling and children's movements should reflect pastoral reality and remain flexible (MOESTK, 2010).

In Kenya, nomadic pastoralists are a majority or significant minority in all arid and semi-arid lands (ASAL) districts, and they occupy a large part of the national territory. There are eight main pastoralist language groups and the first language of around 2.1 million people belongs to one of these groups (Lewis, 2009). Kenya has for some years experimented with different educational delivery systems to reach the children in these nomadic groups. These lessons of these experiments provide important information for the design of a new strategy.

Boarding schools are an option for a small minority of nomadic children. Some active pastoralists prefer boarding schools if they are in a position to leave their children in school. Girls-only boarding schools have increased the enrolment of girls in their catchment areas. On the other hand boarding schools still require the separation of children in education from the rest of the family and thus cannot serve children who work in the household. They are also not appropriate for children under the age of ten. Boarding schools are effective in socializing nomadic children away from their own communities, something pastoral parents fear.

Around 50 pilot mobile schools are now in operation in six arid districts.[3] Teachers are attached to a nomadic family or group of families. Often adults as well as children attend the schools. After three years in the mobile school children are supposed to enrol in conventional boarding schools (MOESTK, 2008c). The advantage of mobile schools is that children do not have to leave home, and can continue their household work. The disadvantage is that mobile schools are difficult to staff, manage and monitor. Households can scatter at any time, causing children to move in and out of the system with negative consequences for a classroom-model of teaching based on continuity of attendance. In practice, most mobile schools do not serve the more mobile households.

Alternative Basic Education for Turkana (ABET) has set up learning centres at semi-permanent villages near important roads. In Samburu district, shepherd schools (*lchekuti*) are evening classes in conventional schools for village children who spend the day herding. Mainly girls attend (MOESTK, 2008c). In Marsabit, the shepherd schools are evening classes in mobile schools.

Boarding and mobile schools, and the use of fixed schools for classes, have not provided the desired outcome. Despite substantial investment in infrastructure and teachers only about a third of pastoral boys are enrolled in pastoral districts, and gross enrolment figures are halved for girls (MOESTK, 2008a). Schooling options which require a teacher in front of a class can only cater for a proportion of the children in pastoral households, typically those not directly involved in production. When conceived as mere variations on this model, even state-supported and well-funded alternative basic education programmes such as Alternative Basic Education for Karamoja (ABEK) in Uganda, have found it extremely challenging to deliver on their promises to reach pastoralists (Krätli, 2009). But the failure of conventional models to deliver education to pastoralists is only part of the problem. A larger and more complex problem is the nature of the education on offer itself.

For nomads principally involved in animal production in the drylands, formal school-based education has three serious consequences (Krätli and Dyer, 2009, p13):

- The household has to be split in a way that makes school attendance easier; this may make running a pastoral enterprise more difficult.
- Herd management and livestock mobility patterns have to be modified in ways that reduce their productivity and the reliability of the production system.
- Some, but not all, the children in the family will be enrolled in school, creating at an early age a separation between educated children whose best hope in life is outside the pastoral system (and who indeed often lack the skills necessary to be effective producers in a pastoral economy), and other children whose skill is in animal production and have little experience of the world outside pastoralism.

There is thus incompatibility between most models of classroom schooling and socialization into nomadic society and culture. This is compounded by material shortcomings in pastoral schools themselves: especially a shortage of qualified teachers from pastoral communities, with the necessary command of local language and understanding of pastoral livelihoods, as well as a lack of appropriate teaching and learning materials. There is also little monitoring or evaluation.

Distance learning as an alternative?

A distance learning approach provides ways to by-pass many of these problems, with a significant proportion of the teaching conducted without face-to-face contact through a technical medium (for a long time books, now also radio). By operating outside the classroom model, this approach can be more flexible and better able to adapt to changing circumstances, while maintaining standards as high as those in a conventional school system. The content can be better adapted to the significant differences in livelihood between urban and settled farming areas on the one hand, and the arid and semi-arid pastoral areas on the other.

A distance learning system designed for nomadic education in Kenya would integrate innovative uses of radio – and potentially in the future other mobile technologies – with the relevant parts of the existing school system and a new distance learning system within the new framework put in place by the Ministry of Education and the Ministry of Northern Kenya jointly through the proposed new National Commission on Nomadic Education in Kenya (NACONEK). Currently the approach uses the Kenya Broadcasting Corporation (KBC) system, with near-universal national coverage, alongside community radio, with uneven but wide-spread coverage. In the future, the satellite network may become important, as may the cell phone network.

KBC has substantial experience in distance education by radio. KBC has both technical and methodological capacity, including broadcasting in most of the local languages. However KBC does not have experience of the sort of programme proposed in the current strategy, which depends on broadcasting to individual students without an intermediary. A community radio approach would require one station per district (with repeaters if necessary). In the longer term, the migration to digital broadcasting will make available a large number of new channels and frequency scarcity will no longer be a problem. In all cases, the frequency modulated (FM) spectrum is currently almost completely unused throughout the dryland areas of Kenya. The local nature of these radio stations will allow for easy access by students and make it relatively easy for a distance learning team to visit students in order to record materials for community broadcasts.

Hitherto, distance learning has generally used a classroom model of teaching, with group listening and a teacher operating the audio device (radio, CD player or tape recorder). Providing a sustainable educational service to nomadic children will require the capacity to reach students individually and independently of one another. Students – mainly children and adults in non-literate pastoral households – will have direct access to the audio units of the distance learning programme, together with printed materials and tutoring from visiting teachers. They will need to access the right frequency, listen to the full range of distance learning broadcasting and play back individual audio units at will. The programme requires low-cost devices with a playback function, easy to use and to power, and capable of storing and retrieving audio units.

In a distance learning system for nomads, communication between the field components of the programme, as well as with monitoring and evaluation and coordination and management staff, is essential. Visiting teachers must maintain regular communication with the radio station and with the supervising body, as well as with individual students. Cell phones could meet this need in part. As network coverage and cell-phone usage expand in the north, cell phones could play a more direct role in education provision.

At enrolment, students and adult members of their household are invited to attend a one week intensive induction course, held in a boarding school or place with boarding facilities, or even at large gatherings directly in the bush. During this course, students meet their tutors and are introduced to the programme: they learn how to use the receiving/playback device, how to communicate with the tutors and how to use the progressive testing system with periodical exams. The timing of induction courses is decided in the light of seasonal demands for children's pastoral work-load. Each student is given a receiving/playback device loaded with the first memory card. Subject modules are in the local language for the first two to three years of the curriculum. The structure of the programme will however allow a module of spoken English designed for non-literate students.

A National Commission on Nomadic Education in Kenya (NACONEK) is being created. Its purpose will be to formulate policies and guidelines, to mobilize funds, to create mechanisms to coordinate and evaluate the activities of agencies in the field of education, to ensure that nomadic education reaches across district boundaries, to establish linkages with other ministries, to establish standards and skills to be attained in nomadic schools, to prepare statistics and to channel external funds to nomadic schools (MOESTK, 2008b; cf. MOESTK, 2010).

Teachers destined for jobs in the pastoral drylands will receive additional training covering local livelihoods, especially pastoralism and the practical problems of living in the drylands. Teachers will be selected who speak the same local language as their pupils; where possible they should come from a pastoral background. A distance learning education system does not mean that pastoralists should be provided with a second-class education or one substantially different from that available in the rest of Kenya. On the contrary, the system should equip nomadic children to compete with children from elsewhere in Kenya throughout the school system and later in life. Kenya has a national syllabus for primary education, which the Kenya Institute of Education (KIE) is mandated to develop (Kenya Institute of Education, 2002). Nomad children in Kenya are subject to the Kenya National Exams Council independent exams system based on standards set by KIE. Children at primary level will be aiming at the Kenya Certificate of Primary Education (KCPE), as a marker of their initial achievement and as the condition of access to secondary education. The uncertainties of pastoral life require that the educational system should be flexible. The students must be given the possibility to stop at any time without losing out on their achievements up to that point, and the possibility to pick up from where they left off if they have the opportunity to go back into education. The distance-learning programme has started to work with KIE in analysing the existing national syllabus and in developing a programme based on the national curriculum and leading to the KCPE. This will lead to setting up a joint curriculum development team to research and where necessary adapt curricula to be used in radio broadcasts for nomadic education programmes.

Literacy is currently taught as a part of the primary curriculum. The distance learning programme will experiment with intensive teaching of basic literacy and numeracy in local languages, for both children and adults, through radio broadcasting in combination with printed materials. Mobile teachers are to provide support for these intensive courses, particularly in the initial phase, but the aim should be to make literacy courses stand on their own in the future, once a critical mass of printed materials has been distributed across the communities and a critical number of people have become literate and can therefore provide help within the family.

Newly literate adults and children need relevant and good quality printed materials, in addition to the foundation materials in support to the radio programmes, to be easily available. In the past, teaching materials for pastoralists have at times been inaccurate, out of date, and sometimes demeaning to the pastoralists. Learning materials for the distance learning system will be both audio and printed.

Work on the new system in Kenya is under way. Scenario planning exercises have been carried out in Maasailand to identify hopes and fears of pastoral families about education. A steering committee which brings together the main actors – KIE, Kenya National Examinations Council (KNEC), Ministry of Education, Ministry for the Development of Northern Kenya and Other Arid Lands, the universities and the Teachers Service Commission (TSC) – is being set up so all the key actors are on board.

The new system requires a revolution not only in delivery, but also in educational culture and attitudes. Nomadic schooling has worked well where the local administrative culture was sympathetic to and supportive of pastoralism as a livelihood system e.g. in Mongolia and Iran (Demberel and Penn, 2006; Steiner-Khamsi and Stolpe, 2005; Krätli, 2001; Shahshahani, 1995; Barker, 1981; Varlet and Massoumian, 1975; Hendershot, 1965), and has not worked well where it was not sympathetic and supportive (everywhere else). It is essential therefore that the entire educational system is well informed and sympathetic to nomadic livelihood systems and pastoral societies. Distance learning radio programmes must help do this, encouraging a dialogue around radio broadcasts, with phone-ins, 'question times' and debates. Parental links to the education process and their participation in management decisions are essential.

For many years, policies aiming at enhancing the availability and quality of school-based education in pastoral areas have not succeeded. Education has not been provided for all – even most – children in mobile pastoralist households. It is critical to recognize at this juncture that continuing with a strategy that can at best be only partially effective will inevitably endanger the national commitment to 'education for all'. It will also prevent Kenya from ensuring the fundamental human right to education of pastoral children

Conclusions

Much of the evidence shows that the dominance of the school-based system itself has been responsible for the historically poor record of ensuring that pastoralists can access good quality education. Both the structure and the culture of the school-based system have so far offered education as an alternative to pastoralism and have been locked into the 'classroom' model of teaching. For children in pastoralism, school-based provision raises an unnecessary barrier to learning.

The message coming loud and clear from pastoralists themselves is a demand for a formal education – in the sense of equal status with school education – capable of complementing pastoralism, adding further opportunities to the pastoral livelihood, rather than trying to replace it altogether or undermining it by virtue of its fundamental requirements. At the moment there is no service supply to match this kind of demand.

This needs to change. Effective strategies for educational inclusion require better informed understanding of the role mobility plays in pastoral production. This must mean escaping the unfavourable trade-offs pastoralists experience when, in seeking to acquire 'modern' education, their only option is a school-based model of provision that enforces compromises with pastoral production and closes livelihood opportunities within pastoralism. Such an approach limits future pathways, rather than opening them up.

Blaming pastoralists for their low enrolment in schools has distracted policy-makers from realizing that it is the system of educational provision that is, by its very nature, excluding the would-be students within the pastoral system. Plans for the inclusion of pastoralists, rooted in a conceptual misunderstanding of pastoralism and tacked onto the classroom model of teaching, have largely led to failure. The challenge of providing education to mobile pastoralists requires some radical innovation. With new technologies expanding their reach and with reducing costs, the potential for adapting educational systems to the needs of mobile populations expands. Certainly, if the grand policy ambitions and pledges are to be met, new ways of responding to the demand for education among pastoral people are required. The experiments in Kenya will hopefully show the way for other areas across Africa.

Notes

1   David Siele is the Director of Human Capital Development in the Ministry for Northern Kenya and Other Arid Lands, responsible among other things for the development of a new education strategy for pastoralists. Jeremy Swift and Saverio Krätli were the principal authors of the distance learning strategy commissioned by this Ministry and adopted by the government of Kenya in 2010 (MDNKOAL, 2010a).

2   The following is a synthesis of the official strategy contained in: MDNKOAL (2010a) *Getting to the Hardest to Reach: A strategy to provide education to nomadic communities in Kenya through distance learning*, Minister of State for Development of Northern Kenya and Other Arid Lands (Office of the Prime Minister) and Education for Nomads programme, Nairobi. http://pubs.iied.org/G02742.html, accessed 20 November 2011.

3   Wajir, Garissa, Moyale, Ijara, Turkana and Samburu.

19

SOCIAL PROTECTION FOR PASTORALISTS[1]

Stephen Devereux[2] and Karen Tibbo[3]

Introduction

Social protection is a relatively new addition to the development policy agenda, and its application to pastoral contexts is even more recent because, as with many other policy initiatives, it reached pastoralist communities later than elsewhere. The rapid evolution of the social protection agenda in recent years has tended to focus on food-insecure farmers, or on categorical 'vulnerable groups' such as older persons and people with disabilities. Pastoralist exclusion from social protection programmes is related to their broader social, economic and political marginalization. But this neglect does not mean that social protection is not needed in pastoral areas, nor that pastoralists have not received social assistance and 'safety net' support in the past. In fact there is a rich history of experience to draw on, because a range of mechanisms have been introduced to protect pastoral livelihoods against shocks and stresses over several decades – long before social protection was conceived. In fact, the sophisti-cated range of risk management mechanisms designed and deployed to address pastoralist vulnerabilities offers useful lessons to social protection thinking and practice in other contexts, where 'social insurance' mechanisms remain under-developed to date.

There are at least two reasons why people living in pastoral areas need specifically designed social protection. First, pastoralists face very different vulnerabilities to farmers and other 'vulnerable groups'. Second, many different types of people live in pastoral areas – including different types of pastoralists, but also people who are not pastoralists – yet social protection instruments are rarely adapted to these different livelihood systems. With this in mind, this chapter has three objectives. First, we discuss the risks and vulnerabilities faced by people living in pastoral areas. Second, we critically review the evolution of social protection interventions for pastoralists, from food aid to 'drought cycle management' to 'index-based livestock insurance'. Third, in the context of the 2011 famine in pastoral areas of the Horn of Africa, we argue for stronger integration between social protection, risk management and emergency programming – hardly a new call, but one that the social protection agenda plus telecommunications technology make more feasible than ever before.

Pastoral vulnerability

Pastoralists in Africa are politically, economically and socially marginalized, confined to the arid and semi-arid borderlands of their countries where central government exerts little influence and the delivery of public services – including social protection – is weak or non-existent. Marginalization and isolation from government services compound the vulnerability of pastoralists to natural disasters or even moderate perturbations in weather, as well as to conflicts over assets (especially livestock) and access to resources (water and grazing). The paradox is that people who arguably need social protection most (in the form of regular provision of social assistance and access to social insurance) often get the least, until disaster strikes, when standard humanitarian relief responses – food aid, water tankers, destocking programmes – expose the failure or absence of interventions to build resilience and insure against livelihood shocks in the periods between disaster events. Social protection in a pastoral context must extend its remit beyond emergency relief, to include insurance mechanisms, perhaps even conflict resolution.

Understanding differentiation within pastoral communities is crucial to delivering better designed and more effective policies and programmes. This requires a disaggregated analysis of the complex nature of vulnerability in each specific pastoral context, recognizing the several distinct but often interconnected livelihood systems that are pursued by people living in pastoral areas, and adapting and targeting policy interventions to the specific needs of different categories of people – while recognizing also that many people will be moving between livelihood systems at any point in time.

Differentiated vulnerabilities

> Concepts of vulnerability and risk in pastoral areas are not well captured or understood by policy makers.
>
> *(Aklilu and Catley, 2009, p4)*

Until the 1980s, pastoral ecosystems were believed to be 'potentially equilibrial grazing systems' that become destabilized by overstocking and overgrazing. But emerging thinking on 'disequilibrium dynamics' recognized that this analysis does not apply in many arid and semi-arid areas. 'Rather, ecosystem dynamics are dominated by the stochastic perturbations of multi-year droughts' (Ellis and Swift, 1988, p457). Pastoralists survive in these difficult conditions by attempting to stabilize their livelihoods against inevitable but unpredictable environmental shocks and stresses. One strategy is to maximize natural reproduction of herds and flocks, in the expectation that many animals will be lost when drought strikes. So periods of livestock accumulation through reproduction are followed by decimation of herds and flocks during droughts (or epidemics, or livestock raiding), which are followed by periods of post-shock rebuilding of animal numbers. This 'boom and bust' cycle means that it makes little sense to calculate 'average herd sizes' or to plan 'linear growth trajectories' for pastoralist livelihoods.

These cycles are longer and more unpredictable than regular seasonality, so cycles and seasons overlap and interact in complex ways in pastoral ecosystems. Agricultural seasonality is relatively regular and predictable, but the 'boom and bust' cycle is unpredictable in its occurrence, timing and magnitude. Farmers and pastoralists have developed 'seasonal coping strategies' against regular seasonality, but droughts and other threats to crops and livestock are potentially lethal, in the absence of social protection, because farmers and pastoralists are inadequately insured against them. Ellis and Swift (1988) argue that pastoralist livelihood strategies are well adapted to dry seasons and single-year droughts, but are highly vulnerable to multi-year droughts, which can reduce herds and flocks below minimum thresholds of viability.

Weather-related vulnerability is also increasing because of climate change, which makes the natural environment on which livestock depend for their survival more variable, unstable and unpredictable (see Ericksen *et al.*, this book). Climate change is not necessarily reducing total precipitation in pastoral areas (climate forecasting models are unclear on this) but rainfall is becoming more variable and unpredictable, and extreme weather events are projected to increase in their incidence and intensity (HPG, 2009c). In the Horn of Africa, three severe droughts occurred in the first decade of the new millennium – in 2000, 2005 and 2009–11 – resulting in tens of thousands of deaths in Somali Region, Ethiopia in 2000, and in neighbouring southern Somalia in 2011. This represents a tragic failure of humanitarian response during crisis periods, but it also reflects an inexcusable failure to install effective social protection mechanisms in the recovery periods between droughts.

Although drought is a perennial risk to pastoralist livelihoods, an emerging concern is securing access to high value fodder and other resources to support herds, in areas where rangelands are becoming increasingly fragmented due to the capture of key resource sites. Conflicts over livestock and access to water or grazing are often a consequence of resource scarcity. Hendrickson *et al.* (1998, p185) argue that responses to food insecurity in Turkana district in Kenya 'have largely been drought-driven, for example, food assistance and livestock restocking programmes . . . The role of armed conflict in the form of raiding has been overlooked'. Paradoxically, in pastoral communities greater wealth can also signify greater vulnerability. Owning more livestock means having more to lose to drought or disease, while livestock owners with large herds are often targeted during livestock raids or wars (Deng, 2007). Effective responses to livestock raiding are very different to responses to drought, but mechanisms like conflict resolution fall outside even broad, 'transformative' definitions of social protection.

Apart from production-related risks such as drought, conflict and livestock disease, pastoralists also face market-related risks. The impoverishing effects of declining livestock–grain price ratios in times of stress are well known – Swift (1989) argued that a falling trend in the 'pastoral terms of trade' could be a trigger for timely safety net interventions.[4] Risks in relation to the new marketing and trade dynamics in many pastoral areas are less well understood. The creation of a relatively elite commercial class within pastoral societies is changing the nature of vulnerability in pastoral areas, which are increasingly connected to national and regional markets.

The implications of this rapid process of socio-economic differentiation are evident in the erosion of customary safety nets, as Letai and Lind (this book) explain in the case of the Laikipia Maasai. Nunow (this book) similarly describes the loss of cooperative herding arrangements in Kenya's Tana Delta. In the past, wealthier and poorer herders would combine their herds and hire a shepherd to move their livestock to distant grazing, compensating the shepherd in kind with an animal belonging to a better-off herder. But wealthier herders are now backing out of such arrangements and paying hired shepherds in cash to move their own livestock that is being reared for the market. Poorer herders are losing out, unable to afford to pay cash to hire shepherds and facing shrinking social networks.

'Disequilibrium dynamics', climate change, livestock-raiding and socio-economic differentiation all challenge conventional thinking on appropriate responses. Which social protection instruments should be introduced to pastoralist livelihood systems characterized by 'boom and bust' cycles, both increasingly unpredictable in their occurrence, timing and magnitude, and making it increasingly difficult for smaller herders to maintain viable herds?

Differentiated livelihoods

> Pastoralists are too often treated as a homogeneous aggregation of people and places. Our analyses reveal striking heterogeneity . . . This finer-grained analysis is important to targeting policy and project interventions.
>
> *(McPeak* et al.*, 2011, p7)*

Different modes of pastoralism, characterized by degree of mobility of livestock and herders, require different social protection interventions. Apart from nomadic herders, transhumant pastoralists and agropastoralists (Blench, 2001), in most pastoral areas there are also ex-pastoralists, traders, sedentary farmers, and urban residents. Van den Boogaard (2006, p3) argues that it is essential to distinguish between the various groups living in pastoral areas when designing and targeting interventions, 'but in practice the distinction is not often made'.

HPG (2009a) points out that urban populations in the arid and semi-arid areas of the Horn of Africa are growing faster than rural populations, but that governments and agencies are not adapting their policies to this reality. Many of these urban residents are former pastoralists who have lost all their livestock and are now destitute, struggling to make a living in informal income-generating activities, given the limited opportunities for viable non-livestock related employment in pastoral areas (Aklilu and Catley, 2009, p4). A survey in Somali Region, Ethiopia enumerated over 60 livelihood activities apart from livestock rearing, but the most 'popular' of these – firewood collection, charcoal burning and weaving baskets or mats – all generated very low incomes (Devereux, 2006). The majority of relief, rehabilitation and development interventions in these areas are targeting former pastoralists, but often with the aim of returning these households to pastoralism – which may be inappropriate and impractical – rather than integrating them into the urban economy.

Apart from this 'horizontal differentiation', there is evidence of increasing 'vertical differentiation' between pastoralist households in the Horn of Africa, with wealthier households accumulating larger herds but middle-income households losing animals and many poorer households dropping out of pastoralism altogether (Catley and Aklilu, this book). Inequality within pastoral areas is higher than in farming communities, mainly because livestock (especially camels and cattle) are valuable assets, so livestock owners appear wealthier than ex-pastoralists by orders of magnitude. Devereux (2006, p76) estimated a very high Gini coefficient (a measure of inequality between 0 and 1) for surveyed communities in Somali Region of 0.74.

Inequality occurs not just among but also within households. Gendered inequalities result in lower life expectancy and higher child mortality rates for females than males in many pastoralist societies. Male bias is revealed in a preference for sons rather than daughters, and in males being favoured in the intra-household allocation of food as well as access to health and education services (Devereux, 2010). There are also significant numbers of female-headed households in pastoral areas, especially *de facto* female heads in settlements where people have dropped out of mobile pastoralism or where men are moving with animals, leaving semi-sedentarized women, children and older people behind. Social protection and other interventions should redress these patriarchal imbalances by targeting resources at girls, women and female-headed households.

Social protection responses

Social protection has been defined as 'all public and private initiatives that provide income or consumption transfers to the poor, protect the vulnerable against livelihood risks, and enhance the social status and rights of the marginalized; with the overall objective of reducing the economic and social vulnerability of poor, vulnerable and marginalized groups' (Devereux and Sabates-Wheeler, 2004, p9). This definition generates three intervention categories: social assistance, social insurance, and social equity. A fourth category often added is livelihood promotion, describing mechanisms that simultaneously deliver social assistance and support income generation.

Given the range of interventions that have been used to achieve social protection objectives in pastoral communities in the past, one purpose of this paper is to propose a classification of these instruments in terms of social protection categories. The indicative (rather than exhaustive) list in Table 19.1 differentiates 'traditional' interventions from 'new' social protection mechanisms – an artificial distinction, but one that highlights both the wealth of historical experience to draw on and the innovative thinking that the social protection agenda brings to the table. By contrasting 'traditional' with 'innovative' mechanisms, we are not implying that the new should displace the old, rather that they complement and add value to each other. Many risk management and service delivery mechanisms that were devised in the 1970s or earlier remain relevant today, while some that have disappeared from the policy agenda could usefully be revived.

Social assistance

A fundamental principle of social protection is to ensure that essential assistance – whether in the form of food or cash – is delivered to all people who need it, when they need it. Regular transfers such as cash transfers or food packages are required for chronically poor people in pastoral areas, as elsewhere, while temporary transfers must be mobilized promptly when lives and livelihoods are threatened. Especially in pastoral areas, where conditions vary dramatically over short periods of time, institutionalized contingency planning is essential. In Ethiopia, the Productive Safety Net Programme (PSNP) holds 20 per cent of its budget at district level as a contingency fund. In 2008 when the *belg* rains failed this fund was released to extend the period of transfer payments from six to nine months and to register additional drought-affected beneficiaries – an innovative but rare example of social protection and emergency programming working synergistically rather than in separate silos.

Food aid or cash transfers?

Cash injections provide more and wider impact levels compared to food transfers.

(Van den Boogaard, 2006, p3)

TABLE 19.1 Classifying social protection interventions for pastoral areas

Social protection categories		'Traditional' pastoralist interventions	'New' social protection mechanisms
Provision	Social assistance	Food aid	Cash transfers
Prevention	Social insurance/ risk management	Livestock destocking/ restocking Drought cycle management	Index-Based Livestock Insurance (IBLI)
Promotion	Livelihood support	Public works projects	Employment guarantees
Transformation	Social equity	Participatory approaches	Voice and empowerment

Food aid has been the standard response to food insecurity in pastoral areas for decades, but the new social protection agenda argues strongly for cash transfers rather than food aid, on the grounds that cash gives more choice, stimulates local markets and incentivizes local farmers to produce food. The case might seem to be stronger in pastoral areas, where livestock owners routinely engage in selling animals and animal products to buy grain and other goods and services in local markets. But the arguments for and against food aid and cash transfers are complex and context-specific, and some of these issues are briefly reviewed below.

Food aid is an appropriate response to household food insecurity in contexts where food supplies are constrained and markets are weak and unresponsive to cash transfers. This is the case in parts of northern Kenya, where De Matteis (2006, p4) argues for food rather than cash transfers, based on his analysis of markets in Turkana district: 'The gap between food requirements and supply is reflected in high prices . . . The high prices prevalent in the district make a commodity-based strategy more cost-efficient than a cash-based one.'

But food aid has proved an ineffective intervention in many pastoral contexts. McPeak *et al.* (2011, pp96–97) found that 'Food aid provides a relatively small contribution to total income' in northern Kenya, and its distribution is often badly targeted and badly timed. 'Food aid was not received when income was lowest and need was greatest, and the maximum value of food aid is observed after the recovery in other income had begun.' Pantuliano and Wekesa (2008, p14) found that food aid was not a preferred drought response by pastoralists in Ethiopia, who favoured 'cereal price stabilization through cereal banks, even on a commercial basis', also commercial destocking and supplementary feeding for livestock. Beneficiary preferences are rarely considered in the design of social protection programmes. 'Food aid has been provided without regard for its appropriateness or whether its beneficiaries wanted it' (HPG, 2009b, p3). Evidence for this comes from the high volumes of food aid that are sold by pastoralists in local markets, either for preferred foods or to meet non-food needs.

On the other hand, cash transfers are vulnerable to price rises that undermine their purchasing power and fail to deliver the intended quantity of food to beneficiaries. Injecting cash transfers into areas where markets are thin might simply drive up prices, rather than provoking a supply response. Alternatively, independent movements in prices, such as seasonality or inflation, also reduce the real value of cash. On both Ethiopia's PSNP and Kenya's Hunger Safety Net Programme (HSNP), the purchasing power of cash transfers collapsed to less than half of their initial value because of rapid price inflation in 2007–08. In Ethiopia this prompted a substantial shift in beneficiary preferences away from cash and towards food transfers (Sabates-Wheeler and Devereux, 2010). Nonetheless, it is our view that this was primarily a consequence of the 'global food price crisis', rather than a rejection of cash transfers in principle, and that well designed and index-linked cash transfer programmes should generally be preferred as a long-term alternative to food aid.

Innovative delivery mechanisms

New telecommunications technology allows for innovation in social protection delivery mechanisms, and this potential is being explored in both pastoral and non-pastoral contexts. In Kenya, a mobile phone company has developed an SMS-based way of uploading cash and sending it to any person in range of the network, who is notified on their phone and then downloads this cash from an airtime retailer (Devereux and Vincent, 2010). This technology can be used to deliver cash transfers to social protection beneficiaries, and being a 'push' rather than 'pull' mechanism – i.e. it does not require beneficiaries to report to a designated pay-point on a specific day – this is especially well adapted to mobile pastoralist populations.

Also in Kenya, the Hunger Safety Net Programme is an innovative cash transfer programme that targets 300,000 poor and vulnerable individuals in the pastoral northern districts. Cash is delivered to registered households through a smartcard, which has a microchip that stores information about the card owner and a nominated representative, as well as details of previous transactions and the balance remaining on the card. Numerous requests have been made by aid agencies to the HSNP Secretariat to use the smartcard to deliver other kinds of support. During the 2010–11 drought, for instance, it became apparent that the quickest way to deliver relief would be through such a card. However, the drought-affected population comprised a much larger group than HSNP beneficiaries, so one proposal under consideration, as of late 2011, is to give a smartcard to all residents of Kenya's arid northern districts. This would have several potential benefits.

First, issuing smartcards to everyone in the project area would provide an opportunity for data capture of key household characteristics. Given that many projects are currently planned and implemented in the absence of data, such a database would be invaluable in the development of more appropriate and better targeted responses. However, care would be needed to protect the integrity of this database and ensure that it never faces any risk of political or commercial manipulation.[5] These data could feed into a single registry (which is also under discussion in Kenya). Single registries generate well-documented efficiencies in terms of allocation of public resources, reduced 'double-dipping' and better coordination.

Second, linking emergency relief to longer-term development programmes has never been straightforward, because of institutional constraints: perverse incentives, unaligned systems, weak coordination. However, smartcards open up possibilities for delivering commodities in a more timely and responsive manner – rapid enabling and disenabling of specific entitlements on the card – as well as scaling levels of entitlement to cash or food up and down, during and after emergencies. Provided they are regularly updated, a social protection database and a single registry should ensure more accurate targeting of the 'right' people at the right time with the appropriate levels of social assistance. Moreover, smartcards can be used to deliver access to a variety of other publicly financed programmes, such as animal health services, livestock insurance, microfinance, maternal healthcare and education.

Finally, smartcards can avoid the problem of inflexibility that is associated with conventional 'pull' delivery mechanisms, such as food aid and cash transfers that can only be collected from designated local pay-points on specific dates. Like SMS transfers, loading cash or other benefits onto smartcards that can be redeemed at a range of shops or ATMs (or clinics in the case of subsidized healthcare, and so on) are better attuned to pastoralist lifestyles. Especially during difficult times, mobility is fundamental to pastoralist survival, so social protection should support mobility rather than trapping people in the epicentre of a crisis waiting for aid to be delivered. Delivering transfers through mobile phones or smartcards extends the points of payments beyond the rangelands, to include towns and cities where stressed herders are likely to move to in search of work, and gives recipients choice over when and where to collect their transfers.

Social insurance

After social assistance, the second pillar of social protection programming is social insurance, which in the context of pastoralism implies a focus on risk management strategies. Many familiar interventions fall under this category, including livestock destocking and restocking, and drought risk management. This section also discusses an innovative approach to insuring livestock against drought: Index-Based Livestock Insurance (IBLI).

Livestock destocking and restocking

The extensive livestock losses that occur during droughts in the Horn of Africa can amount to tens of millions of dollars and irreparably disrupt the livelihoods of thousands of pastoralists, causing them to 'drop out' of pastoralism. Restocking and destocking programmes have long been important forms of support provided to pastoralists, in an attempt to contain livestock losses and preserve their livelihoods after the drought. Following severe droughts in the 1960s and 1970s, when vast numbers of livestock were lost (up to 90 per cent in some years), the discourse centred around alternative livelihoods to nomadism, due to the perceived 'over-population' of the range. The debate about whether the rangelands are overstocked persists, but in the 1980s, proponents keen to support the preservation of nomadic pastoralism proposed restocking as a better solution than non-livestock-based alternatives, such as irrigation for farming or agro-pastoralism (Hogg, 1985).

These days mostly NGOs are active in restocking, which means that projects are usually small-scale and often the replacement stock provided are fewer than are required for a viable herd. Heffernan and Rushton (1999) outline the pros and cons of restocking and conclude that while rebuilding the herds of destitute pastoralists can be a pathway to successful rehabilitation, many aspects remain unproven and controversial. Despite the majority opinion broadly in favour of restocking, it seems that the impacts are not always as positive or as sustainable as the literature suggests.

Destocking is an attempt to minimize stock losses during droughts by purchasing animals before they die from lack of food and water, or are sold at 'distress' prices. Destocking usually involves paying livestock keepers for animals at risk, which are then slaughtered and the meat distributed to local households. The key to effective destocking is timing; significant organization and management are required to ensure that the value of stock is maintained to the point of slaughter. Aklilu and Wekesa (2002) describe a successful destocking intervention in northern Kenya during the 1999–2001 drought. Around US$2 million worth of livestock were saved, although US$80 million worth of stock were lost. The early warning system had provided timely information to decision-makers, but a sufficiently timely response was not triggered. Again, during the 2008–09 drought in Kenya, truckloads of dead and dying heads of livestock were common (ILRI, 2011a). In fact, the government contributed to losses by failing to provide water at livestock collection points.

Drought risk management

For decades, responses to the significant food insecurity that arises from droughts in pastoral areas have been dominated by costly, unpredictable and often inadequate investments in humanitarian assistance. Such assistance, while vital for saving lives, has been ineffective in terms of lifting people out of repeated exposure to risk and vulnerability, and has probably undermined resilience (DFID, 2004).

Disasters can be prevented, or their impacts substantially mitigated, through effective risk reduction measures. Tools are available that help to plan and operationalize appropriate interventions at sequential stages during an unfolding disaster event. The Drought Cycle Management (DCM) approach was developed during the 1980s, following the realization that, far from being unusual, droughts are regular and recurrent in the Horn of Africa, and should be anticipated and managed (Pavanello, 2009). The DCM model identifies a four-phase drought cycle – normal, alert, emergency and recovery – and proposes appropriate activities for each phase: preparedness, mitigation, relief assistance and reconstruction, respectively (Pantuliano and Wekesa, 2008). Van den Boogaard (2006, p3) argues for a differentiated package of targeted interventions, each 'linked to a specific need that exists during the particular period of the drought cycle'. But DCM is not just a toolkit of 'off the shelf' interventions; it also offers an institutional context from which these activities can effectively emerge. The key to effective DCM is coordination structures reaching from local to national level (and back again), which can support an early warning and information system linked to appropriate responses.

Despite significant efforts, institutionalization of DCM has been challenging and has largely failed. The main weakness of DCM has been in linking early warning system (EWS) alerts to the funding and implementation of contingency plans. In practice, DCM has been implemented in a piecemeal way, often by NGOs attempting to mitigate drought impacts, with weak coordination at local and national levels. Lack of sufficient funds that can be released in a timely manner have led to the emphasis on humanitarian assistance, which should be, according to the DCM model, a last resort mitigation or relief provision (Swift *et al.*, 2002).

Notwithstanding these challenges, the objective of linking different but overlapping policy instruments is sound. Social protection should be adapted to where pastoralists are in the drought cycle: the focus of interventions is typically on drought and post-drought recovery periods, but more attention should be paid to the 'whole inter-drought cycle' (Ahmed *et al.*, 2002, vii). This implies supporting positive coping strategies during droughts and building resilience in post-drought recovery periods.

In the past there has been an absence of alternatives to year-on-year food aid. However, the range of available instruments is increasing. The existence of National Contingency Funds in social protection programmes in both Ethiopia and Kenya means that there is now capacity to apply a more integrated approach to risk management that is flexible, scalable, timely and addresses the underlying causes of vulnerability (Pantuliano and Pavanello, 2009). These Funds should be linked to both the implementation of longer-term cash transfer programmes as well as to emergency relief.

Innovative approaches to livestock insurance

During the 2009–2011 drought in the Horn of Africa, several hundred pastoralists who participated in an Index-Based Livestock Insurance (IBLI) scheme in northern Kenya received cash payments, when satellite images revealed that grazing conditions had deteriorated to the extent that more than 15 per cent of livestock were predicted to die. These payouts provided partial rather than full compensation, only covering projected livestock losses above 15 per cent, so in areas where a fatality rate of one-third was expected the payment covered 18 per cent rather than 33 per cent of lost livestock value – enough to replace half the animals that died. A major advantage of the IBLI approach is that actual livestock deaths for each client do not need to be known, and the evidence from Kenya is that predicted and actual livestock deaths do track each other closely (ILRI, 2011b).

This is a pilot project, and like other weather-indexed insurance schemes it has yet to prove its commercial viability in contexts of high risk and extreme poverty, where market-determined premiums are high and ability to pay is low.[6] Discount vouchers were made available in Kenya to encourage uptake and to extend coverage to poorer herders; however, it seems likely that wealthier herders, with more income and more to lose, were quicker to sign up. Nonetheless, as a subsidized social protection intervention, IBLI schemes can play a significant role in securing the viability of pastoralism as a livelihood, at a time of rising uncertainty over the implications of climate change for weather patterns in arid and semi-arid environments.

Livelihood promotion

Social protection should aim not only to protect lives today, but also to build resilience and secure livelihoods for the future. Pavanello (2009, p24) argues against food aid and in favour of 'livelihoods interventions [to] save lives and livelihoods', which implies protecting livestock as well as human well-being, because pastoralist survival depends on having large enough herds to survive shocks. Similarly, Aklilu and Catley (2009, p4) argue that a 'poverty-focused approach in pastoralist areas would explicitly recognize and support a strategy of herd growth for poorer households'. This strategy complements but falls outside the mandate of social protection. A more conventional social protection mechanism that aims to promote livelihoods is public works programmes, which transfer food or cash to poor participants while also trying to create useful infrastructure that can generate economic value.

From workfare to the right to work

Public works have always been controversial. They are often associated with pointless and unproductive 'make work' (much infrastructure constructed on public works is low quality, rarely maintained and deteriorates rapidly) (McCord, 2005), workers are underpaid (in order to 'self-target' the poorest, wages must be set below market rates), it requires people who are weak and undernourished (including women, older people and sometimes children) to perform heavy manual labour, and payment is typically in food rations (which is often considered demeaning) rather than cash wages.

The World Food Programme (WFP) has been operating recurrent Emergency Operations (EMOPs) in pastoral areas of northern Kenya since 2000. Although some food aid is distributed freely, a large proportion is allocated as food-for-work. WFP's justification for making people work is 'a fear about creating dependency' (WFP, 2009a), but this seems misplaced given that the acute malnutrition rate in this population consistently averages 30 per cent. Harvey and Lind (2005) undertook an analysis of 'dependency' in Ethiopia and Kenya and concluded that vaguely formulated concerns about dependency should not be a good enough basis for humanitarian programming. The larger problem is the poor design of public works programmes, resulting in poorly maintained assets that are not valued by the community. The case for providing more appropriate forms of assistance becomes even more convincing given that food-for-work participants in Kenya (60 per cent of whom were women) were carrying out labour-intensive activities such as soil excavation with their bare hands, due to insufficient provision of tools (WFP, 2009a). The review of WFP's EMOP concluded that public works should not have been included in an emergency of that nature. However, Food for Assets (similar in practice to food-for-work) is a major part of WFP's Protracted Relief and Recovery Operation (PRRO) (2009–12) (WFP, 2009b), implemented during one of the most severe droughts of recent years.

Recent innovations in public works are challenging some of these negative perceptions and dubious practices. Payment is increasingly made in the form of 'cash-for-work' rather than 'food-for-work'. More attention is being paid to participatory selection of useful projects that create productive assets (such as irrigation canals for farming) and to ensuring that these assets are sustainable, i.e. of adequate quality and well maintained. These 'principles' were reflected in a proposal to extend labour-based public works on Ethiopia's Productive Safety Net Programme to pastoral areas:

• 'Projects will be identified in a participatory way and answer to the needs of the people that work on them;
• Projects are not simply "make work" but are soundly constructed and constitute genuine contributions to local infrastructure;
• Projects are environmentally sustainable and social or economic mechanisms have been identified for their maintenance'

(Behnke et al., *2007a, viii)*

Most importantly from a social protection perspective, introducing a 'right to work' transforms public works from discretionary and supply-driven projects to a demand-driven 'last resort' source of work and income. India's Mahatma Gandhi National Rural Employment Guarantee Act (MGNREGA) gives every rural household the right to demand up to 100 days of employment every year from their local administration, at the minimum wage. The employment guarantee idea has been adopted by several countries in Asia, and a version is being piloted in South Africa as the Community Works Programme. But would an employment guarantee scheme be feasible in pastoral areas? One challenge is to find enough useful work to meet any level of demand (in India, if suitable work cannot be found within a reasonable time and distance, applicants must be paid anyway).

Pastoral areas might not face the same level of need for rural feeder roads and irrigation canals as farming communities, but they do face severe infrastructure deficits in other arenas. In one district of Somali Region, Ethiopia, local people were so tired of being told by government that pastoralists don't value education and are too mobile to be reached with education services that they took matters into their own hands, and built a primary school with their (unpaid) labour, buying materials with cash they raised themselves (Devereux, 2006, p157). Schools, clinics and water-points are among many kinds of community infrastructure projects that public works in pastoral areas could deliver.

Social equity

A fundamental reason for the vulnerability of pastoralists is their political marginalization and exclusion from decision-making processes and institutions of power. As a result, social protection is often required to deal with the consequences of this marginalization and exclusion. For instance, people might need food aid because a decision to dam a river that had been used for watering animals forces local herders to sell their livestock and lose their livelihoods. A 'transformative' approach to social protection recognizes that tackling the root causes of vulnerability – which are very often political – is more effective than continual transfers of food, cash or assets. So strategies of empowerment and giving pastoralists voice must be an essential component of a comprehensive social protection strategy that aims to reduce and not just manage vulnerability.

Participatory approaches to development recognize the need for poor people to be actively engaged in decisions that affect their lives. Governments and agencies have made many efforts over the years to consult with pastoralists, either by liaising with traditional political institutions in pastoral communities or by setting up committees or forums. But these mechanisms are often ineffective and interact uneasily with the formal political structures that exercise real power over people's lives. Participation is not enough unless it gives pastoralists voice and leads to their empowerment. A fundamental shift in power relations is needed to build trust and strengthen the social contract between the state and groups of citizens who continue to feel inadequately represented, or even disenfranchised.

There is some evidence that social protection programmes can help to redress the balance of power between the state and pastoral citizens, at least at the margins. Despite being simply a cash transfer programme, certain design features of the Hunger Safety Net Programme (HSNP) in northern Kenya can be described as empowering. The HSNP required beneficiaries to acquire their national identity cards, and established local 'Rights Committees' as a grievance procedure, allowing people who felt unfairly excluded to register complaints, for instance. Research conducted by HelpAge International (2011) recorded unintended positive spillover effects around citizen participation and engagement with local authorities, that were attributed to civil rights education provided by Rights Committees.

Other democratic mechanisms could also be introduced to hold local authorities and programme administrators to account, such as 'social audits' which are popular in India. Such relatively minor innovations can go a long way towards building citizen participation and ownership of policies and programmes from below, reversing the disempowering delivery of services from the top down, entirely at the discretion of governments and donor agencies.

Given the democratic deficits in pastoralist communities and the inequalities and discrimination that occur along several axes – between herders and farmers, between clans, between men and women – this is an area where innovative thinking is urgently needed. Broader concepts of social protection can certainly contribute, for instance by promoting a rights-based approach and by targeting social protection policies at sub-groups that currently face systematic discrimination and exclusion, such as women and girls.

Conclusion

Livelihoods and vulnerabilities in pastoral areas are complex, diverse and subject to rapid and often dramatic change. But limited knowledge – about the range of livelihoods being pursued and the extent of differentiation within livelihood systems and transitions occurring between livelihood systems – leads to important policy decisions being based on unfounded assumptions or outdated information. The unprecedented rate of displacement of African pastoralists into agro-pastoralism, sedentarized farming, or informal work on urban peripheries requires a range of social protection mechanisms and complementary interventions, to support people in negotiating these challenging transitions.

In a context of increasingly unpredictable weather, 'drought cycle management' offers a useful conceptual framework, enabling social protection responses to be calibrated according to where pastoralists are in the drought cycle. But drought is not the only risk that pastoralists face, for which social protection is required. The challenge now is to link various uncoordinated policies, projects and programmes that are currently running in parallel. National contingency funds for pastoralist risk management need to be integrated into ongoing, regular social protection programmes, as well as into emergency relief. Technological advances provide opportunities for coordination. Computer-based management information systems enable the flow and management of information between communities, administrators and policy-makers to facilitate more effective programme management and monitoring (Chirchir and Kidd, 2011). 'Single registry' systems offer a centralized and integrated database, which enables oversight and harmonization of multiple programmes. Finally, mobile phones and smartcards allow for the prompt and flexible delivery of regular social protection and access to social services, as well as more effective humanitarian responses that can be scaled up and down as circumstances require.

A better understanding of pastoralist vulnerability and risk should enable policy-makers to make better-informed decisions around social protection that go beyond safety nets and humanitarian relief. The generic threats faced by livestock-based livelihood systems are unpredictability and instability, while the keys to survival in dryland environments are mobility and adaptability. Pastoral livelihoods are more vulnerable when physical, economic and social mobility are constrained. Social protection and other interventions should not regulate and control pastoralists, but should seek to expand their options and flexibility. This has implications at the conceptual level, for more effective management of drought and other risks, and at the technical level – it motivates, for instance, introducing electronic delivery mechanisms as soon as these are feasible. In the context of the 2011 famine in the Horn of Africa, better integration of social protection and emergency programming for pastoralists also has implications, at the political level, for social justice.

Notes

1   The authors thank Andy Catley, Jeremy Lind and Ian Scoones for their insightful comments on earlier drafts.
2   Centre for Social Protection, Institute of Development Studies, Brighton, UK.
3   Former Kenya-based Coordinator of the impact evaluation of the Hunger Safety Net Programme (HSNP).
4   Pastoralists depend on markets for livestock sales and grain purchases. During a drought, livestock value falls due to deteriorating quality and excess supply on the market. At the same time, grain prices may rise due to drought-triggered crop failure, and the resulting decline in the livestock-grain price ratio has been monitored as an indicator of stress in pastoral economies since the 1980s.

5   Clearly, the practicalities of implementing such a smartcard solution will vary from place to place, and controls to prevent corrupt practices would have to be in place.
6   Although implemented by commercial firms (Equity Bank and UAP Insurance in Kenya), it was devised by researchers (from the International Livestock Research Institute (ILRI), Cornell University and the University of California at Davis) and funded by international donor agencies (including USAID, the European Union, the British Government, World Bank, the Microinsurance Facility and the Global Index Insurance Facility).

20

WOMEN AND ECONOMIC DIVERSIFICATION IN PASTORALIST SOCIETIES

A regional perspective

John Livingstone and Everse Ruhindi

Introduction

Pastoralist societies across the Horn and East Africa are undergoing rapid social and economic change. Multiplying restrictions on access to land and resources have forced many to drop out of pastoralism and it is increasingly apparent that customary livestock-keeping systems cannot any longer provide livelihoods for a majority of people residing in pastoral areas. Yet, a 'modern' form of pastoralism is emerging that is more commercially oriented and connected in numerous ways with diverse land uses and complementary economic activities. Pastoral women, who traditionally have been at the forefront of experimenting and starting new livelihood activities, are taking advantage of new economic opportunities, particularly those associated with the growth of small towns and trading centres. Transition in pastoral areas, characterized by commercialization, small town growth and intensified diversification, has brought expanded choice and opportunities for women to improve their position, incomes and living standards (Smith, 1998). However, for many women, transition in pastoral economies has entailed pressure to take on new, and often onerous, responsibilities as (socially subordinate) breadwinners. Although diversification trends are potentially empowering of women, there are many constraints and risks, not least men becoming engaged in and seeking control of profitable new activities that women pioneer, the remoteness of small pastoral towns from larger markets and economic centres, and a dearth of training and skills needed to add value to products.

At the same time, social stratification is a defining feature of modern pastoralist societies. Politically influential elites are investing in intensified livestock production as well as increasingly sophisticated processing activities. Contrary to received wisdom, a small number of women entrepreneurs are amongst those joining the ranks of these elites. These are women engaged in small-scale enterprises, often packing pastoral-area products, milk, yoghurt, aloe and honey for sale in urban supermarkets or for sale to hotels and better-off households in the booming pastoral-area towns. Women entrepreneurs have the potential to become significant providers of employment for women and others in the pastoral areas, just as elite pastoralists and ranchers employ youth to herd.

This chapter assesses diversification trends in pastoralist areas and their impacts on women, drawing on examples from Uganda, Somaliland and elsewhere in the region.[1] Although there is intensifying diversification in all three countries, the social and economic settings as well as the pace and nature of change vary across these contexts.

Diversification, sedentarization and women's economic activity

Trends towards more diversified economies and new social arrangements are complex, often messy, with a mix of push and pull factors. While greater restrictions on access to high value fodder and the loss of livestock have pushed many pastoralists to seek alternative economic activities, others have been pulled to growing small towns to find work, access relief assistance and other services provided by states and other non-governmental actors. The traditional social organization of pastoralist societies – of entire family units splitting and moving with herds across the rangeland – is increasingly rare. Even in traditional systems, it was common for women, children and the infirm to remain in an encampment for longer periods and to move less frequently. Although the location separation of members of pastoral households was commonplace in the past, the nature of such separation has changed greatly, with different individuals split between herding livestock, staying in towns or on irrigated plots, or migrating further afield for work, employment and education.

Thus, there are very complex and contradictory factors driving sedentarization and diversification in pastoral areas. They include destitution as well as wealth, and the search for crisis survival options as well as opportunities to invest and accumulate. 'Immiserizing sedentarization' involves lower living standards and levels of well-being for underemployed pastoral 'drop-outs' who are driven to settle in towns and smaller centres (see Fratkin, this book). But, there is a 'diversity of diversification' and we should be careful to distinguish between sedentarization driven by a lack of other options and settling as an adaptive response to dynamic change (Morton and Meadows, 2001). The growth of small towns and trading centres is a response to and brings new opportunities for work and wealth accumulation. To varying degrees, pastoralist societies are becoming more integrated, socially and into national and regional economies. The pastoralist elite sell livestock in domestic-urban and regional markets (see Catley and Aklilu; Mahmoud, this book). While many women are now breadwinners for households that have lost their pastoral livelihoods, more settled lives offer women new possibilities for social and economic advancement. Pastoralist women are responding to new opportunities wherever they can – setting up new income-generating activities and businesses, particularly around providing services to growing town populations, as detailed below.

One might view these trends as an inevitable consequence of processes of commercialization and economic transition in pastoral areas, with people moving off the range and into towns, where greater specialization and human capital accompany higher living standards. However, rather than signalling the end of pastoralism, as some observers suggest, sedentarization trends point to changing forms of pastoralism and, therein, new social organization, production aims and patterns of investment and accumulation as pastoralists move further away from customary systems. Indeed, many who settle in towns keep a hand in livestock-keeping by hiring labour to move animals, keeping a small number of livestock near to towns, or undertaking activities that add value to livestock products. Far from dying out, sedentarization in part reflects the increasing wealth of livestock-keepers who specialize in supplying livestock markets while investing in off-range enterprises, as well as the efforts of poorer herders to continue rearing a residual herd alongside complementary activities that enable them to invest in and maintain the health of these animals. As explained in the Introduction of this book, one can foresee multiple pathways for pastoralists in the future, including intensified livestock specialization and commercialization, value-added diversification, practising traditional livestock-keeping, or exiting into alternative livelihoods. Towns are clearly important to at least three of these scenarios, and so too is the entrepreneurialism and hard work of women.

The changing economic life of pastoral women

Women are undertaking a widening range of enterprises, taking advantage of new opportunities to provide services and access markets at roadsides and in small towns and trading centres (see also examples in Nunow, this book). Alongside longstanding activities such as marketing small-stock, and selling charcoal and fuelwood to town dwellers, women are expanding their involvement in milk processing (cheese and yoghurt), juice-making, dressmaking, and trading in produce – notably storing, buying and selling grains and grain milling.

Services provided by women run the gamut, encompassing fetching water for a fee; doing laundry and cleaning for better-off town dwellers; running retail shops, teashops (common in Somaliland) and beer 'joints' (common in Uganda); hairdressing and beauty salons; catering services for weddings and social events (with an increasing degree of sophistication and large fees for major events, covering wedding attire and photography); operating hotels, lodges, bakeries, restaurants, video-shacks and bars with satellite television; recharging mobile phones with solar panels and car batteries; selling human and veterinary drugs; and providing teaching and training.

In major pastoral-area towns, new public and private educational and training institutions provide opportunities for women to set up businesses supplying food and snacks to students. A range of businesses have sprung up around these institutions, even pool (billiards) 'joints'. Public investments in schools, hospitals and clinics not only provide employment for women but also stimulate local entrepreneurial activity. Local women compete for tenders to supply uniforms and meals, and women, as entrepreneurs and as employees, are well represented in this new service sector.

Interesting new opportunities are emerging: from secretarial bureaus serving illiterate businesspeople to photography, art and design for advertising and signpost-making. Pastoral-area towns are developing a fuller range of modern enterprises and women find employment even in male-dominated enterprises, as support and sales staff.

Some women are establishing larger enterprises, as well. In Somaliland, Shukri Ahmed, a woman entrepreneur and activist, co-founded Asli Mills, a company that processes agro-pastoral products, and secured a contract to supply the Body Shop with aloe sourced from pastoral women. The company also trained pastoral women to produce, package and market honey to be sold in Hargeisa. Pastoralist women can themselves take up processing activities, as the Nyakahita Women's Group has done in Uganda, packaging ghee for urban supermarkets. A number of larger commercial enterprises, of varying scale, serve urban, regional and, in some cases, international markets, sourcing products from pastoral communities, and providing incomes and employment for women. These include large milk processors, such as Alpha in Uganda and Brookside in Kenya.

Some women have profited immensely from the regional qat trade, as well. The qat business largely provides retailing jobs for women and two of the biggest qat traders are women of pastoral origin – one owns a hotel in Jijiga and an aeroplane, another is building a shopping mall on the outskirts of Hargeisa.

Not all of the new economic activity is entirely benign. Some activities, like the region-wide charcoal burning business, have undesirable social or environmental consequences. In Karamoja, increased women's incomes from beer brewing are associated with the growing social problem of alcoholism (Chronic Poverty Research Centre, 2008). In Somaliland, heavy male use of the mild narcotic qat displaces other domestic spending (Milanovic, 2008).

Women, economic diversification and social change

Economic diversification in pastoral communities entails significant changes in gender relations. Control of livestock assets was the (economic) basis of patriarchy within pastoralist societies. The widespread loss of livestock and grazing land has significantly disempowered men, leaving women to take up many of the newly important non-livestock activities and tasks-for-cash (Buchanan-Smith and Lind, 2005). Given the extreme pressure on pastoral households struggling to adapt to economic transition and expanding impediments on their capabilities to move and access key resource sites, a common strategy is for different members of a household to pursue their own individual strategies to survive. With important exceptions and variations across different pastoral societies, individuals have tended to exert greater control over the income and livelihood they generate from these activities (Flintan, 2010). Yet these dynamics can be disempowering for women if they involve addi-tional burdens but without any change in social status, and if women are simply forced to take up menial or low-return activities in order to provide for their families when devastating losses have ended their husbands' pastoral livelihoods (Joekes and Pointing, 1991; Kipuri and Ridgewell, 2008). Flintan (2008) notes that in many cases women enjoyed a measure of power and influence in traditional society and may lose this when communities are forced to sedentarize. Diversification trends are not uniform – it is important to assess individual contexts carefully.

Women's increased economic independence is supported by and in turn promotes accompanying changes in social attitudes. Shifts in social norms and attitudes are happening, though in an uneven way. Women are, generally, the household resource managers, and their increased economic activity outside the household is adding to their authority. A common presumption is that pastoralist women are disempowered compared to women in agrarian and urban settings. Indeed, there are stark gender disparities in literacy rates, maternal mortality rates and other key well-being indicators. However, a growing body of works promotes a nuanced perspective, acknowledging the very important role of women in pastoralist livelihoods and societies, and the multiple subtle ways in which women do exercise power (Hodgson, 2000; Flintan, 2008, 2010). In Somali society, women largely control incomes earned from their own activities in accordance with Islamic prescriptions and customs. Somaliland's pastoralist women do not participate in public discussions, but are far from submissive. Increased autonomy has been accompanied by increased responsibility, but also a new vision of a freer, better life that many pastoralist women find attractive.

The legal, economic and governance aspects of women's empowerment are interrelated and mutually reinforcing.[2] Women's rights to own property and land must be reinforced if they are to become effective economic actors (Adoko and Levine, 2007). Formal and customary laws need to be reconciled in ways that establish women's equality before the law. Legal empowerment underpins economic empowerment, which involves expanded access to capital, education and training, business-related information and business networks. Women as economic actors also need to participate more effectively in the public and political arena, given the various ways in which politics and economics interact (Duflo, 2005). Education enhances rural productivity in direct ways and by enabling the use of new technology and information (Lockheed et al., 1980). Access to information enables individuals to seek and discover improved techniques and allows informed choice. Without independent incomes, women are powerless and cannot make their own choices. However, these elements are not always necessary and not always sufficient for women to become successful entrepreneurs, or to be empowered. Across the region, we observe successful entrepreneurs who are illiterate, as well as empowered and assertive women in traditional societies. Yet, without these basic elements, a broad expansion and dynamic development of women's economic activity might not be possible.

Women feel empowered and freer than in previous generations. Women's empowerment is, in essence, the expansion of choice, not only of their options and opportunities, but also their capabilities to make choices that accord with their own priorities and well-being. The objective of empowering women requires working on the relations between and amongst women as well as with men; it is equally important to address the situation of men – such as the disempowering effects of economic transition on men and their responses to these – in efforts to strengthen the position of women. The following section digs deeper on two aspects of economic change that portend potential improvements in the well-being of pastoral women.

Classroom, teacher and mobile phone: improving prospects for pastoral women's empowerment

Improved access to formal education and new technologies is a defining feature of economic transition in pastoral areas of the Horn and East Africa. In the long term, education is fundamental to women's economic empowerment. However, access to formal education is constrained in many pastoral areas, as Siele *et al.* explain in this book. Reasons for the poor provision of formal schooling in pastoral areas include:

- the high costs per head of providing schooling in remote, sparsely populated areas;
- socio-cultural and political marginalization of pastoral societies in many countries;
- seasonal mobility;
- the importance of children's labour in herding, fetching water and firewood;
- the difficulty of attracting teachers to pastoral areas;
- low demand for schooling amongst parents, with girls' schooling seen as a threat to tradition.

Primary and secondary school enrollment and achievement are still much lower than in other communities, but more pastoralist girls are going to school than ever before. Here again, social and economic change is bringing new opportunities. Bahima pastoralists in Uganda have undergone a generational shift. Until recently, approximately 80 per cent of women were illiterate and most girls were married in their teens. However, literacy levels have improved dramatically. Although reliable statistics are hard to come by, an estimated 80 per cent of Bahima women are literate. Educated girls are also seizing the opportunity to move out to seek further education and work elsewhere. In the Kanyanyeru Resettlement Scheme, by Lake Mburo National Park, older and ageing women predominate – their educated daughters have moved up and out, many to nearby Mbarara, a bustling regional centre that is home to a variety of educational and training institutions.

There is increasing demand for education, as parents see that pastoralism can no longer provide livelihoods for all. Pastoral households face a new set of incentives as expanded economic opportunity increases the returns to education. In Somaliland, pastoral households receive remittances from daughters who have found their way to industrialized countries. Anecdotal evidence suggests that diaspora daughters send more money home, more reliably, than do sons. Pastoralists increasingly see the benefits of pursuing a mixed strategy, investing in formal schooling for some children, while bringing up others to help with livestock-keeping and other complementary activities.

Local entrepreneurs, many of them women, are responding to this increased demand for education. In Somaliland, where state provision of education is limited, and in Uganda, many schools and training institutions are operated by private providers. In Erigaavo and Burao towns in Somaliland, which are typical in hosting a large number of pastoral 'drop-outs', street signs advertise a variety of private education and training establishments, often in one or two-room outfits set up by local entrepreneurs. The growth of pastoral-area towns and trading centres and the trend towards living in and around settlements also make it easier to provide schooling, as well as training, just as demand and willingness to pay are increasing for both.

The Internet, mobile phones and satellite television are making pastoral-area postings more attractive, or less unattractive, to teachers and health workers alike. Moreover, with such facilities, local people who acquire qualifications are less likely to move out and away. Few well-qualified workers will be easily induced away from the pull of urban centres of social interaction, but the less well-qualified may find a pastoral posting to be a useful stepping stone. A Danish programme for Burao Hospital provides Internet support for doctors and nurses – 'tele-medicine' is likely to expand in the future, and a similar approach could greatly enhance the quality of education available in rural and pastoral areas.

Greater access to information is changing attitudes and aspirations in profound ways. Satellite television is also reaching trading centres and towns, with dishes visible on shacks across pastoral Uganda, Ethiopia, Somaliland and Kenya. Particularly in Uganda, radios and satellite television are more accessible. Ownership of radios is often low among pastoral women, but access, through relatives and friends, is much wider than ownership. Television and radio have given pastoral women a picture of how women live in other (modern) societies and a confidence in their own future (Devereux, 2006). Access to the Internet is limited in many areas but coverage is beginning to expand, especially in larger towns such as Burao in Somaliland, and Mbarara, Masaka and Moroto in Uganda. Access to the Internet will draw pastoral-area towns into wider business and information networks. The spread of Internet-phone services and the convergence of Internet, audio, television and phone services in coming years are likely to deepen the social and business impacts.

There has been a slow, uneven, but steady extension of mobile phone networks to cover large swathes of pastoral East Africa. Pastoralists have enthusiastically taken up services that enable them to stay in touch with urban relatives; to seek help in health emergencies; to enquire about the availability of pasture and water in different areas and plan seasonal movements (in Somaliland, the traditional function of the 'Sahan' or scout); to quickly ascertain prices in district and more distant market centres (strengthening their hand vis-à-vis middlemen) and, in recent years, to access banking services.

Mobile phone banking is well-suited to remote pastoral areas with dispersed populations, where the cost of establishing branch networks is prohibitive for banks and the costs of travelling to distant bank branches are a major deterrent for potential customers. For pastoralist women, facing restrictions on mobility, mobile money services are particularly attractive. In Somaliland, phone networks have only recently been extended to pastoral areas, but pastoralist women are already making use of Telesom's 'Zaad Services' for payments and savings (up to a limit of several thousand dollars). In El Afwein village, on Somaliland's vast pastoral plains, women engaged in horticulture use their mobile phones to obtain market information in Bosasso, to negotiate prices with truckers, find buyers for their products, and receive payments. Similar services exist in Somalia and Somali-speaking Djibouti, and in northern Kenya. In Uganda, with increased competition between several providers, the use of phone payments systems is widening.

Here, it is crucial as to whether and to what degree the policy environment is business-friendly. While economic growth has facilitated change in pastoral areas, bad policy limits the possibilities of leveraging existing growth and trade in these areas, much of which has been generated in the absence of supportive policy or a capable state that can enable greater investment. Weak government in Somaliland has allowed a rapid expansion of services by multiple (largely Somali) private sector providers, while elsewhere (in Kassala and Ethiopia) government has blocked potential private investment, impeding expansion. Kenya's M-PESA mobile money service, established by Safaricom and Vodaphone, with support from Britain's DFID, has wide coverage and a large volume of transactions. Across the region, few countries have established policy frameworks that are genuinely 'business-friendly', and many severely restrict regional trade, with heavy tariffs and other restrictions. A 'harmonization' agenda can help to establish a regional regulatory framework for livestock products and the cross-border movements of people and livestock, but pastoralists often occupy insecure border regions, where governments are especially eager to control activity.

Conclusions

East African pastoralism is adapting to the loss of traditional grazing lands, expanding and deepening connections to national and regional markets, and the growth of small-towns where the wealthy and poor alike are settling. Households are adopting a mixed strategy, keeping one foot in a modernizing pastoralism, while planting the other firmly in the expanding urban environment of pastoral-area trading centres and towns. Pastoral women, far from being powerless observers and victims of economic transformations, are in many areas important innovators and instigators of change. While pastoral women have been pushed to carry the burden of newly important economic activities to make up for the loss of income/livelihood from livestock-keeping, increasingly they exercise a greater say over livelihoods and how the income from these activities is to be used. Small town growth has brought an expansion of choice and the opportunity to develop alternative livelihoods for women, as well. New educational and training opportunities, and new technology, hold great promise for empowering pastoralist women still further.

There are many constraints on promoting more productive and broadly beneficial economic and livelihood diversification in pastoral areas. They include remoteness and low population densities, which raise the per capita costs of almost all economic activity and organization; poor transport and telecommunications infrastructure; lack of or irregular connections to national power grids; irregular and seasonal incomes, making it difficult to meet the conditions of bank loans; low cash incomes and thin local markets; and policy frameworks that fail to understand and even undermine innovative pastoral responses to change. The impacts of these constraints can be different for women and men. For example, where trunk and rural feeder roads exist, women's access to public and private vehicles is sometimes restricted, for socio-cultural reasons, limiting their trade and marketing activities. Furthermore, policies to promote 'development' or 'modernization' in pastoral areas might inadvertently invest greater control of productive assets in men as 'household heads', bypassing women who through tradition and tact have otherwise found ways to elevate their status.

Pastoral systems are in flux, but the impacts of ongoing transformations are uncertain. The political economy of pastoralism is shifting and some are clearly benefiting from the greater options and opportunities to diversify and accumulate wealth, especially wealthier pastoralists who invest in water points and sophisticated management and veterinary care to meet regional and international standards, and who supply urban and export markets (Catley and Aklilu, this book). Wealthy woman entrepreneurs are emerging in many pastoral towns. However, pronounced social stratification is an important feature of the emerging new pastoralism, and many are falling behind. As in so many transitions before, it is women who are carrying the additional burden of heightened vulnerability but also pioneering pathways to stronger livelihoods.

Notes

1   This chapter is based on the authors' experience working with PENHA, a pastoralism-centred NGO, under a three-year women's economic empowerment programme covering Somaliland, Sudan and Uganda as part of Danida's 'Women In Africa' programme. We drew on the following literature for our analysis: Flintan (2007), GSM Association (2008), Lochhead and Musoke (2010), SCUK (2005), Tooley et al. (2008), and William and Tavneet (2011).

2   The World Bank's *Engendering Development* report (2001) and its subsequent *Gender Equality as Smart Economics* (2006) work provide solid analytical foundations here.

PART V

Endpiece

21

REFLECTIONS ON THE FUTURE OF PASTORALISM IN THE HORN OF AFRICA

Peter D. Little

Introduction

It is a privilege to have been asked to write this 'end piece' as the final chapter of this important volume and to have participated in the Addis Ababa conference on the 'future of pastoralism in Africa' in March 2011 that contributed to it. As a participant at an earlier conference 30 years before on the 'future of pastoralism' held in Nairobi, Kenya in August 1980 (Galaty *et al.*, 1981), I am struck by how many of the cautionary trends that were described – even hypothesized – at the earlier meeting and in publications throughout the 1980s are reflected in this book, but in amplified form and across much larger areas of the Horn.

These processes include inequality and poverty ('stocklessness'), political marginalization, increased conflict, absentee herd ownership and hired herders, economic diversification, private enclosures, growing commercial livestock markets, and so on. There, of course, are obvious and significant differences with the earlier work that are reflected in this book. Most important is the welcome presence of researchers/authors from the region, including several from pastoralist communities; the very different nature of pastoralist conflict, with its geo-political content and modern weaponry; and studies of market-based relations and new niche markets that traverse large areas of the Horn, even those that were considered relatively isolated in the 1980s.

What matters?

The remainder of this chapter discusses six related themes that should matter for the future of pastoralism in the Horn of Africa. Although they are not dealt with as separate issues, equity and gender are cross-cutting topics that traverse each theme and will be critical for understanding pastoralism in the future. The chapter concludes with an optimistic but different scenario of what pastoralism in the region might look like in the next 20 years.

Narratives and language

Perhaps no other livelihood system has suffered more from biased language and narratives than pastoralism. Some of the worst misperceptions equate pastoralism with poverty, violence, illegal trade, economic inefficiency, ineffective tenure systems, environmental degradation, hunger and food aid dependency, and/or 'vacant' wastelands. These discourses have important political, policy, and practical implications and, as this book has shown, can be invoked to justify particular actions by the state. These directives include the sedentarization of pastoralists in settlements, the allocation of pastoralist lands to investors and conservation groups, and/or the imposition of land titling programmes for both pastoralists and non-pastoralists. In the past, one might attribute these misinformed narratives, policies, and programmes to ignorance on the part of governments. However, the massive amounts of money, powerful interests, and personal benefits ('rents') currently associated with some of these actions, such as the leasing or sale of pastoral lands, point to more sinister motivations on the part of state officials. Hidden in these narratives also are political agendas that perceive mobile pastoralism as a security and political threat to the state and, therefore, in need of controlling or eliminating. In sum, the continued existence of powerful and harmful narratives about pastoralism requires persistent efforts to counter them, such as the recent work on economic contributions of pastoralism that Behnke and Muthami (2011) and Behnke and Kerven (this book) have pursued.

Politics

The Horn of Africa region has experienced many political changes during the past 20 years, including increased political and administrative decentralization and multi-party politics (democracy), but not all of these transitions have had the positive impacts on rural communities, including herders, that had been anticipated. Despite recent changes most pastoral communities still have little national and regional power. The persistence of many anti-pastoralist narratives discussed above reflects the lack of political power by pastoral communities. As this book has demonstrated, political decentralization unfortunately also has been associated with minimal devolution of power from the centre to pastoralist leaders and communities (the cases of the Sudan and Ethiopia), or with elite capture and corruption by local leaders resulting in inequitable distributions of resources, especially for poor pastoralists (the cases of Kenya and Tanzania). Moreover, the formation of pastoral parliamentary groups at national levels has not usually translated into better policies and programmes for pastoralists, which raises the important question of what political level should researchers, practitioners, and pastoralist leaders concentrate their efforts. Should the main focus be on educating and training local leaders and building capacities of local institutions and communities, or attempting to build national coalitions and influence national policies and budget decisions? National political processes will continue to matter for pastoralists in the region and efforts by pastoral communities and activists to influence these should continue. However, at the same time training and research on effective models for empowering pastoralists at different levels of the state, including at community and district levels, also should be pursued.

Population

To avoid the Malthusian label, or simply out of ignorance, many social scientists have neglected the important implications of demographic trends in pastoral areas. Although mobile pastoralism requires extensive land areas and relatively low human population densities to operate, population growth in pastoral towns and settlements encroaches on rangelands and constrains mobility. In fact, some of the fastest growing towns in Kenya are in pastoral districts. This phenomenon has reduced available grazing lands, thereby increasing population densities for pastoralist communities. In most pastoral districts in Kenya and elsewhere in the Horn, human populations have more than doubled during the past 20 years, without equivalent increases in livestock numbers or territory. On a regional level, the growth of ex- or non-pastoralist communities in the Horn is increasing considerably faster than populations of pastoralists themselves. In their study of six pastoralist communities in northern Kenya and five in southern Ethiopia, McPeak et al. (2011) found that non- or ex-pastoralists and 'pastoralists exiting pastoralism' outnumbered active pastoralists – those who mainly focused on livestock rearing – both in the aggregate and on a site-specific basis in a majority of the 11 sites.

What are the implications of these trends? First, if the number of non- or ex-pastoralists will soon exceed active pastoralists in the rangelands, political decentralization and development investments may be even more skewed toward non-pastoralists and their priorities. Second, the capacity for pastoralism to absorb additional people (and labour) is limited relative to other production systems (for example, irrigated agriculture), which suggests that the trend of unviable pastoralists (i.e., those with low-levels of livestock) moving into local towns is likely to continue, or even accelerate in the future. Comparative demographic research is needed to identify and compare fertility and population growth rates among pastoralist and settled populations in rangelands, building on earlier demographic work in the region (Roth 1994; Fratkin and Roth 2005) and elsewhere in Africa (Hill, 1985). Finally, with high population growth the importance of rural–urban linkages in pastoral areas, a topic that remains poorly understood in the Horn, is likely to grow in importance and significantly influence the future viability of pastoralism. Town-based economic and social ties, in terms of provision of local markets and services, will be increasingly critical for pastoralists and their livelihoods and can help to sustain productive pastoral systems. Vibrant local towns, with strong and beneficial linkages to surrounding pastoral hinterlands, are more likely to retain economic value and multipliers associated with pastoralism in local areas, than are stagnant towns. Regrettably, most of the value-added from livestock trade and other activities (e.g., tourism) currently is lost from the rangelands to outside regions and cities.

Education

Access to formal education increasingly will be an important asset for pastoralist communities, notwithstanding potential labour problems and deficiencies in current education delivery models highlighted by Siele *et al.* (this book). Local demand for education is consistently high among pastoralists, a pattern that was not the case even 10–15 years ago, and it strongly affects access to employment (see section on diversification below) and national political processes. During droughts it has been documented how educated pastoralists with urban-based employment are able to help their families purchase foods and, thus, avoid the worst effects of disasters (Little *et al.*, 2009). Present rates of educational achievement in pastoral areas, however, are appallingly low relative to non-pastoral locations throughout the Horn of Africa, especially in Somalia and parts of Sudan and Ethiopia. Access to education among females, particularly at secondary and post-secondary levels, is even lower than the general population, which raises an added and especially important concern for the future. Better jobs for women through education, should translate into higher household incomes and improved nutrition and health for children.

Evidence shows that even attending primary school through Grade 4, where basic literacy and knowledge of mathematics often are learned, can have very positive social and economic implications (Gebre-Egziabher and Demeke, 2004). For higher-paying positions and meaningful political participation, secondary and even post-secondary education usually is required. The need for additional education will only grow in the future, especially as regional demand for skilled labour increases.

Diversification

There is little question that pastoralists will continue to diversify their incomes and assets as buffers against risk (especially drought-related), forms of investment, and means to supplement or replace livestock-based incomes. As towns and new markets grow and technologies change, the nature of diversification in pastoral areas, as well as its linkages to pastoral production will increase in complexity. Elsewhere I have tried to disaggregate what is meant by pastoralist economic diversification by distinguishing between survival-type (e.g., casual unskilled labour and petty trade) and accumulation-type (e.g., retail business and real estate investments) diversification, and between diversification strategies that are supportive of pastoralism (e.g., milk and hides and skin trade) and those that are competitive or even harmful to pastoralism (e.g., charcoal making and firewood sales) (Little *et al.*, 2001 and 2009; also see Fratkin and Livingstone and Ruhindi, this book). Presently, most forms of diversification are pursued out of desperation and are survival-based, although wealthier herders increasingly pursue non-pastoral investments and activities with the goal of supporting not replacing or exiting from pastoralism.

The growth in small towns and the importance of education discussed above suggest new opportunities for diversification, both for unskilled and skilled labour, trade, and business investments. The widespread proliferation of pastoralist NGOs based in towns, with their positive contributions to waged employment, is another important form of livelihood diversification in rangelands (Hodgson, 2011). The leaders of these groups usually require formal education and many have reaped considerable benefits for themselves, but their organizations also provide jobs for many individuals. We also are likely to see labour migration from pastoral areas and remittance-base incomes continue to grow, and increasingly they will assist households to remain in pastoralism as families use remittances to purchase foods, livestock, and livestock inputs. On the other hand, for the poor who have exited or who are exiting pastoralism due to drought or other hardships, alternative livelihoods should be sought and external assistance may be required.

Agriculture increasingly is advocated as a key alternative for the poor and a supplement to pastoralism for better-off households, but it raises certain challenges. Most important is that rain-fed and irrigated agriculture is not feasible in many dry rangelands. Although the chapter by Sandford in this book enthusiastically advocates for large-scale irrigation as an alternative to pastoralism in riverine areas, its high costs, competition with pastoralism for riverine grazing and water, and public health impacts warrant caution against it as a panacea for employment and food problems among ex-pastoralists. By contrast, as Sandford notes, small-scale irrigation and recession cultivation always have been important livelihoods for pastoralists and ex-pastoralists and this trend will become even more important in the future. Overall, cultivation by herders and others in suitable environments will grow even more in the next 20 years than current trends. For development practitioners, an important challenge will be to devise policies and programmes that assist ex-pastoralists and the poor without constraining those who still rely on livestock production.

Ecology

It has been more than 20 years since range ecology research fueled the equilibrium versus disequilibrium debates about dryland ecosystems (see Ellis and Swift, 1988; Behnke *et al.*, 1993; Oba, this book). Most of this earlier work was conducted under very different circumstances than contemporary pastoralism, where large-scale loss of land and other key resources, decrease mobility, and widespread changes in land use now are norms not exceptions. At a time when so many of these current trends have fundamental impacts on ecology and landscapes, relevant ecological research is on the decline especially when compared to the 1980s and 1990s. These concerns are not just academic, but have considerable practical implications. For instance, large-scale loss of pasture and land use changes amplify the negative effects of drought, whose present impacts relate as much to shortages of pasture, bush encroachment, and land use changes as they do to climate.

With reduced lands, especially those that support perennial grasses, and restricted mobility, herders are keeping hardier, browse-dependent goats and camels, as well innovating in other ways. For instance, as a number of chapters in the book show, herders are enclosing large areas for their own private use and for protection against competing land claims, while others are purchasing fodder and supplemental feeds to compensate for decreased pastures. Moreover, better-off herders have innovated by hiring water trucks and trucking fodder and animals during periods of shortage, all strategies that further aggravate local wealth differences (see Tache and Catley and Aklilu, this book). Finally, the growth in livestock trade, especially the high-value export trade focused on male cattle ages 4–7 years, creates further pressures on rangelands as large herders and traders enclose communal lands, either illegally or legally, to fatten and graze their trade animals. This fragmentation of rangelands in the Horn is likely to grow and continue to transform landscapes, ecologies, and herd management practices.

A viable pastoralism?

Despite its many challenges, mobile pastoralism will continue in low-rainfall rangelands throughout the Horn for the simple reason that a more viable, alternative land use system for these areas has not been found. This is the reality, but the nature of pastoralism in 2030 will be very different than today in 2012. It will remain the economic foundation of these areas, although pastoralism will not be practised by the majority. The 'livestock revolution' that had been predicted for the livestock sector will continue as urban markets in the Horn and in other parts of Africa will create even more demand for livestock and livestock products, which along with export trade to the Middle East and Asia will further solidify the economic significance of pastoralism. An optimistic scenario for the future would highlight a diversified regional economy with ex-pastoralists investing in local fodder farms, urban-based market and input services that serve the livestock sector, educating their children, and engaging in small-scale trading and other self-employed enterprises (see Chapter 1). Many also would work for livestock producers as hired herders. Fattening operations for export animals and meat-processing plants hopefully would locate nearer to pastoral production areas, thereby generating additional employment for local non-pastoralists. A strong livestock sector, in turn, would generate incomes and economic multipliers for a large segment of the non-pastoral sector and create demand for a range of town-based products and services. In this scenario, the normal occurrence of drought would no longer result in widespread food shortages and hunger as markets would function effectively and local incomes would be sufficient to purchase needed foods.

For those who continue to practise pastoralism, fixed-base settlements and mobile herd camps of hired and family herders would be the norm. Trucking of animals, fodder, and water for better-off herders will widely be practised by 2030, but animals would continue to move according to spatial differences in amounts of rainfall and vegetation. Telecommunications and Internet services would be extensively utilized to facilitate marketing and herd movement decisions, as well as access to climate-related information. At base settlements or in boarding schools outside the area pastoralists would educate their children and each household would have one or more educated children employed for wages. Ideally, the economic and environmental benefits of pastoralism would be sufficient to convince governments, as well as the development agencies that support them, to implement policies that protect pastoralist access to key grazing and water resources, even while investing in crop agriculture and other activities. Improved delivery systems for veterinary services and fodder, as well as better market information and performance, would be the norm and dampen the boom/bust effects of pastoralism and drought-induced losses.

In closing, the future scenario presented above clearly is preferable for pastoralists, non-pastoralists, and governments, than the current picture of heightened poverty, food insecurity, and land grabs. Political and other challenges stand in the way of achieving this sustainable vision of pastoralism, but by not addressing these challenges the social, ecological, and economic losses for the Horn and its populations will be enormous.

REFERENCES

Abbink, J. (1997) 'The shrinking cultural and political space of East African pastoral societies', *Nordic Journal of African Studies*, vol 6, no 1, pp1–15.

Abbink, J. (2006) 'Discomfiture of democracy? The 2005 election crisis in Ethiopia and its aftermath', *African Affairs*, vol 105, no 409, pp173–199.

Abbo, H. (2005) *Suggestions on the Grazing Line and Pastoral Migration Routes*, Gedaref State Pastoralists Union, Gedaref [in Arabic].

Abdelkarim, A. (1986) 'Wage labourers in the fragmented labour market of the Gezira, Sudan', *Africa*, vol 56, no 1, pp54–70.

Abdullahi, A.M. (1993) 'Economic evaluation of pastoral production systems in Africa: An analysis of pastoral farming households in Central Somalia', in M.P.O. Baumann, J. Janzen and H.J. Schwartz (eds) *Pastoral Production in Central Somalia*, Deutsche Gessellschaft fur Technische Zusammenarbeit (GTZ) GmbH, Eschborn, pp129–148.

Abdulsamad, F. (2011) 'Somali investment in Kenya', Chatham House Africa Programme Briefing Paper, The Royal Institute of International Affairs.

Abdurahman, O.S. and Bornstein, S. (1991) 'Diseases of camels (*Camelus dromedarius*) in Somalia and prospects for better health,' *Nomadic Peoples*, vol 29, pp104–112.

Abebe, D., Cullis, A., Catley, A., Aklilu, Y., Mekonnen, G. and Ghebrechirstos, Y. (2008) 'Livelihoods impact and benefit–cost estimation of a commercial de-stocking relief intervention in Moyale district, southern Ethiopia', *Disasters*, vol 32, no 2, pp167–189.

Abebe, M.H., Oba, G., Angassa, A. and Weladji, R.B. (2006) 'The role of area enclosures and fallow age in the restoration of plant diversity in northern Ethiopia', *African Journal of Ecology*, vol 44, pp507–514.

Abel, N.O.J. (1993) 'Reducing cattle numbers of southern African communal range: Is it worth it?', in R.H. Behnke, I. Scoones and C. Kerven (eds) *Range Ecology at Disequilibrium: New Models of Natural Variability and Pastoral Adaptation in African Savannas*, Overseas Development Institute, London.

Abel, N.O.J. (1997) 'Mis-measurement of the productivity and sustainability of African communal rangelands: A case study and some principles from Botswana', *Ecological Economics*, vol 23, no 2, pp113–133.

Abu Sin, M. (1998) 'Sudan', in C.R. Lane (ed.) *Custodians of the Commons: Pastoral Land Tenure in East and West Africa*, Earthscan, London, pp120–149.

Abule, A., Snyman, H.A. and Smit, G.N. (2005) 'Comparisons of pastoralists' perceptions about rangeland resource utilisation in the Middle Awash Valley of Ethiopia', *Journal of Environmental Management*, vol 75, no 1, pp21–35.

ACDI-VOCA (2006) *Pastoralist Livelihoods Initiative Livestock Marketing Project: Second Quarter Report* (January–March 2006), submitted to USAID Ethiopia.

Adams, W.M. (1992) *Wasting the Rain: Rivers, People and Planning in Africa*, Earthscan, London.

Adams, W.M. and Anderson, D.M. (1988) 'Irrigation before development: Indigenous and induced change in agricultural water management in East Africa', *African Affairs*, vol 87, no 34, pp519–535.

Adano, W.R. and Witsenburg, K. (2004) 'Surviving pastoral decline: Pastoral sedentarization, natural resource management, and livelihood diversification in Marsabit District, Northern Kenya', Ph.D. thesis, Department of Geography, University of Amsterdam.

Adano, W.R. and Witsenburg, K. (2005) 'Once nomads settle: Assessing the process, motives and welfare changes of settlements on Mount Marsabit', in E. Fratkin and E.A. Roth (eds) *As Pastoralists Settle*, Springer Publishing Company, New York.

Admassu, B. (2002) 'Primary animal healthcare in Ethiopia: The experience so far', in K. Sones and A. Catley (eds) *Primary Animal Healthcare in the 21st Century: Shaping the Rules, Policies and Institutions*, proceedings of an international conference held in Mombasa, Kenya, 15–18 October 2002, Mombasa, Interafrican Bureau for Animal Resources, Nairobi.

Adoko, J. and Levine, S. (2007) *Land Transactions in Land Under Customary Tenure in Teso: Customary Land Law and Vulnerability of Land Rights in Eastern Uganda*, Land and Equity Movement in Uganda, Kampala.

Adriansen, H. 2006. 'Continuity and change in pastoral livelihoods of Senegalese Fulani', *Agriculture and Human Values*, vol 23, no 2, pp215–229.

Afar Regional State (2002) *Revised Constitution of Afar Regional State*, Semera.

Afar Regional State (2008) *The Afar Regional State Pastoral Lands Administration and Use Policy*, Semara.

Afar Regional State (2009) *Dinkara, the Afar Regional State Pastoral Lands Administration and Use Proclamation*, Semara.

Afar Regional State (2011a) *Dinkara, the Afar Regional State Pastoral Lands Administration and Use Regulation*, Semara.

Afar Regional State (2011b) *Dinkara, the Afar Regional State Environmental Protection, Land Administration and Use Proclamation*, Semera.

African Development Bank (2010) *Eastern Africa: Regional Integration Strategy Paper, 2011–2015*, East Africa Regional Department, Addis Ababa, September 2011.

African Union (2010) *Policy Framework for Pastoralism in Africa*, Department for Rural Economy and Agriculture, Africa Union, Addis Ababa.

Ahmed, A.G.M. (1987) 'National ambivalence and external hegemony: The negligence of pastoral nomads in the Sudan', in M.A. Mohamed Salih (ed) *Agrarian Change in Central Rainlands, Sudan: A Socio-Economic Analysis*, Nordiska Afrikainstitutet, Uppsala, pp129–148.

Ahmed, A.G.M. (2001) 'Livelihood and resource competition, Sudan', in M.A. Salih, T. Dietz and A.G.M. Ahmed (eds) *African Pastoralism: Conflict, Institutions and Government*, Pluto Press, in association with OSSREA, London.

Ahmed, A.G.M. (2009) 'Transforming pastoralism: A case study of the Rufa'a Al-Hoi ethnic group in the Blue Nile state of Sudan', *Nomadic Peoples*, vol 13, no 1, pp113–133.

Ahmed, A., Azeze, A., Babiker, M. and Tsegaye, D. (2002) 'Post-drought recovery strategies among the pastoral households in the Horn of Africa: A review', Development Research Report Series no. 3, OSSREA, Addis Ababa.

Ahmed, S. (1999) 'Islam and development: Opportunities and constraints for Somali women', *Gender and Development*, vol 7, no 1, pp69–72.

Aklilu, Y. (2002) *An Audit of the Livestock Marketing Status in Kenya, Ethiopia and Sudan*, African Union/Interafrican Bureau for Animal Resources, Nairobi.

Aklilu, Y. (2004) *Initial Assessment of the Dairy Marketing Groups in Marsabit, Kenya*, Feinstein International Center, Tufts University, Medford.

Aklilu, Y. and Catley, A. (2009) 'Livestock exports from pastoralist areas: An analysis of benefits by pastoral wealth group', a report for the IGAD/FAO Livestock Policy Initiative, Feinstein International Centre, Tufts University, Addis Ababa, https://wikis. uit.tufts.edu/confluence/display/FIC/Livestock+Exports+from+the+Horn+of+Africa, accessed 7 December 2011.

Aklilu, Y. and Catley, A. (2010) *Mind the Gap: Commercialization, Livelihoods and Wealth Disparity in Pastoralist Areas of Ethiopia*, Feinstein International Centre, Tufts University, Addis Ababa, https://wikis.uit.tufts.edu/confluence/download/attachments/42668652/ mind-the-gap.pdf?version=1&modificationDate=1299863254000, accessed 18 November 2011.

Aklilu, Y. and Catley, A. (2011) *Shifting Sands: The Commercialization of Camels in Mid-altitude Ethiopia and Beyond*, Feinstein International Center, Tufts University, Addis Ababa.

Aklilu, Y. and Wekesa, M. (2002) 'Drought, livestock and livelihoods: Lessons from the 1999–2001 emergency response in the pastoral sector in Kenya', HPN Network Paper, ODI, London.

Al-Najim, M.N. (1991) 'Changes in the species composition of pastoral herds in the Bay Region of Somalia,' Pastoral Development Network Paper 31b, Overseas Development Institute, London.

ALRMP (Arid Lands Resource Management Project) (2001) *Food Security Assessment of Mandera Pastoralists with Comparison to Riverine Populations*, Mandera Assessment Report, www. feg-consulting.com/resource/reports/manderaKenya2001.pdf, accessed 28 November 2011.

Amani Papers (2010) 'Conflict dynamics in Isiolo, Samburu East, and Marsabit South Districts of Kenya', *Amani Papers*, vol 1 no 3, UNDP Kenya.

Ame, A. (2002) 'The paradox of sharecropping in the Middle Awash Valley of Ethiopia', paper submitted to the 12th International Annual Conference on the Ethiopian Economy.

Amede, T., Descheemaeker, K., Mapedza, E., Peden, D., van Breugel, P., Awulachew, S. and Haileslassie, A. (2011) 'Livestock-water productivity in the Nile Basin: Solutions for emerging challenges' in A. Melesse (ed.) *Nile River Basin: Hydrology, Climate and Water Use*, Springer, Dordrecht.

Anderson, D.M. (1999) 'Rehabilitation, resettlement and restocking: Ideology and practice in pastoralist development', in D.M. Anderson and V. Broch-Due *The Poor Are Not Us: Poverty and Pastoralism in Eastern Africa*, James Currey Publishers, Oxford, Ohio University Press, Athens, OH, pp240–256.

Anderson, D.M. and Broch-Due, V. (1999) *The Poor Are Not Us: Poverty and Pastoralism in Eastern Africa*, James Currey Publishers, Oxford, Ohio University Press, Athens, OH.

Anderson D.M. and Johnson, D. (eds) (1988) *The Ecology of Survival: Case Studies from Northeast African History*, Lester Crook Academic Publishing, London.

Anderson, J. and O'Dowd, L. (1999) 'Borders, border region and territoriality: Contradictory meanings, changing significance', *Regional Studies*, vol 33, no 7, pp593–604.

Anderson, P.M.L. and Hoffman, M.T. (2011) 'Grazing response in the vegetation communities of the Kamiesberg, South Africa: Adopting a plant functional type approach', *Journal of Arid Environments*, vol 75, no 3, pp255–264.

Angassa, A. and Oba, G. (2007) 'Relating long term rainfall variability to cattle population dynamics in communal rangelands and a government ranch in southern Ethiopia', *Agricultural Systems*, vol 94, no 3, pp715–725.

Angassa, A. and Oba, G. (2008) 'Herder perceptions on impacts of range enclosures, crop farming, fire ban and bush encroachment on the rangelands of Borana, Southern Ethiopia', *Human Ecology*, vol 36, no 2, pp201–215.

Anon. (2009) 'Policy brief: Climate-related vulnerability and adaptive-capacity in Ethiopia's Borana and Somali communities', CARE International and Save the Children UK, www.iisd.org/publications/pub.aspx?pno=1240, accessed 18 November 2011.

Anon. (2010) *Pastoralism Demographics, Settlement and Service Provision in the Horn and East Africa: Transformation and Opportunity*, Humanitarian Policy Group, Overseas Development Institute, London, www.odi.org.uk/resources/download/3301.pdf, accessed 7 December 2011.

Appadurai, A. (2003) 'Sovereignty without territoriality: Notes for a post-national geography', in S. Low and D. Zuniga (eds) *The Anthropology of Space and Place: Locating Culture*, Blackwell, Malden, MA, pp337–349.

Armbrust, W. (2011) 'The revolution against neoliberalism', *Jaddaliya*, 13 March, www.jadaliyya.com/pages/index/717/the-revolution-against-neoliberalism-, accessed 23 November 2011.

Asefa, D.T., Oba, G., Weladji, R.B. and Colman, J.E. (2003) 'An assessment of restoration of biodiversity in degraded high mountain grazing lands in Northern Ethiopia', *Land Degradation and Development*, vol 14, pp25–38.

Asfaw, A. (2011) 'Agriculture ministry's promise of more despite shortcomings: Ministry leases reclaimed land to investors; secures fertilizer; expand horticulture, fruits, vegetables', *Fortune*, vol 11, no 568, p30.

Asiwaju, A.I. and Nugent, P. (1996) 'Introduction: The paradox of African boundaries', in A.I. Asiwaju and P. Nugent (eds) *African Boundaries: Barriers, Conduits and Opportunities*, Pinter, London, pp1–17.

Asner, G.P., Elmore, A.J., Olander, L.P., Martin, R.E., Harris, A.T. (2004) 'Grazing systems, ecosystem responses, and global change', *Annual Review of Environment and Resources*, vol 29, pp261–299.

Awulachew, S.B., Yilma, A.D., Loulseged, M., Loiskandl, W., Ayana, M. and Alamirew, T. (2007) *Water Resources and Irrigation Development in Ethiopia*, International Water Management Institute, Working Paper 123, Colombo, Sri Lanka.

Ayele, Gebre-Mariam (2005) *The Critical Issue of Land Ownership: Violent Conflict Between Abdalla Tolomogge and Awlihan in Godey Zone, Somali Region of Ethiopia*, Working Paper 2, Swiss National Centre of Competence in Research (NCCR) Bern: NCCR North–South.

Babiker, M. (2005) 'Sudan: Country case study', paper presented to the UNDP workshop on 'Equitable Access to Land and Water Resources: Promoting Sustainable Livelihoods in the Arab States Region', 28–30 November 2005, Beirut, Lebanon, http://arabstates. undp.org/contents/file/Sudan.doc, accessed 16 November 2011.

Babiker, M. (2007) 'Resource conflict in Gedaref State, eastern Sudan: A time-bomb in the absence of effective land-use planning', in P. Goldsmith (ed.) *Fighting for Inclusion: Conflicts Among Pastoralists in Eastern Africa and the Horn*, Development Policy Management Forum, Addis Ababa, pp92–114.

Babiker, M. and Abdel-Gadir, M. Al-Amin (1999) 'Area development scheme, central Butana: Environmental capacity building', UNDP, Khartoum.

Barker, P. (1981) 'Tent schools of the Qashqa'i: A paradox of local initiative and state control', in M.E. Bonine, and N. Keddie (eds) *Modern Iran, The Dialectics of Continuity and Change*, State University of York Press, Albany.

Barnes, C. and Hassan, H. (2007) *The Rise and Fall of Mogadishu's Islamic Courts*, Africa Programme Briefing Paper no 07/02, Chatham House, London.

Barth, F. (1961) *Nomads of South Persia: The Basseri Tribe of the Khamseh Confederacy*, Little, Brown and Company, Boston.

Barth, F. (2000) 'Boundaries and connections', in A. Cohen (ed.) *Signifying Identities: Anthropological Perspectives on Boundaries and Contested Values*, Routledge, London, pp17–36.

Bassett, T.J. and Turner, M.D. (2007) 'Sudden shift or migratory drift? FulBe herd movements to the Sudano-guinea region of West Africa', *Human Ecology*, vol 35, no 1, pp33–49.

Bassi, M. (1997) 'Returnees in Moyale District, Southern Ethiopia: New means for an old interethnic game', in R. Hogg (ed.) *Pastoralists, Ethnicity and the State in Ethiopia*, Haan, London, pp23–5.

Bassi, M. (2005) *Decisions in the Shade: Political and Juridical Processes among the Oromo-Borana*, The Red Sea Press Inc., Trenton.

Bassi, M. and Tache, B. (2011) 'The community conserved landscape of the Borana Oromo, Ethiopia: Opportunities and problems', *Management of Environment Quality*, vol 22, no 2, pp174–186.

Baud, M. and Van Schendel, W. (1997) 'Toward a comparative history of borderlands', *Journal of World History*, vol 8, no 2, pp211–242.

Bauer, K. (2009) 'On the politics and the possibilities of participatory mapping and GIS: Using spatial technologies to study common property and land use change among pastoralists in central Tibet', *Cultural Geographies*, vol 16, no 2, pp229–252.

Baxter, P. (ed) (1991) *When the Grass is Gone: Development Interventions in African Arid Lands*, Scandinavian Institute for African Studies, Uppsala.

Bayart, J.-F. (1993) *The State in Africa: The Politics of the Belly*, Longman, New York.

Bayart, J.-F., Ellis, R. and Hibou, B. (1999) *The Criminalization of the State in Africa*, James Currey, Oxford.

Behnke, R.H. (1985a) 'Measuring the benefits of subsistence versus commercial livestock production in Africa', *Agricultural Systems*, vol 16, no 2, pp109–135.

Behnke, R.H. (1985b) 'Open range management and property rights in pastoral Africa: A case study of spontaneous range enclosures in South Darfur, Sudan', Pastoral Development Network Paper, 20f, Overseas Development Institute, London.

Behnke, R.H. (1987) 'Cattle accumulation and the commercialization of the traditional livestock industry in Botswana', *Agricultural Systems*, vol 24, pp1–29.

Behnke, R.H. (1988) 'Range enclosures in central Somalia', Pastoral Development Network Paper 25b, Overseas Development Institute, London.

Behnke, R.H. (2008) 'The drivers of fragmentation in arid and semi-arid landscapes', in K.A. Galvin, R.S. Reid, R.H. Behnke and N.T. Hobbs (eds) *Fragmentation in Semi-Arid and Arid Landscapes: Consequences for Human and Natural Systems*, Springer, Dordrecht, The Netherlands, pp305–340.

Behnke, R. and Kerven, C. (2011) 'Replacing pastoralism with irrigated agriculture in the Awash Valley, north-eastern Ethiopia: Counting the costs', paper presented at the International Conference on the Future of Pastoralism, 21–23 March 2011, organized by the Future Agricultures Consortium at the Institute of Development Studies, University of Sussex and the Feinstein International Center of Tufts University.

Behnke, R. and Muthami, D. (2011) *The Contribution of Livestock to the Kenyan Economy*, IGAD LPI Working Paper no 03–11, IGAD Livestock Policy Initiative, Intergovernmental Authority for Development, Djibouti.

Behnke, R.H. and Scoones, I. (1992) *Rethinking Range Ecology: Implications for Rangeland Management in Africa*, Environment Working Paper 53, World Bank, Washington DC.

Behnke, R.H., Scoones, I. and Kerven, C. (eds) (1993) *Range Ecology at Disequilibrium: New Models of Natural Variability and Pastoral Adaptation in African Savannas*, Overseas Development Institute, London.

Behnke, R.H., Devereux, S., Teshome, A., Wekesa, M. and White, R. (2007a) 'Extending the productive safety net programme into pastoral areas: Pilot activities', Programme Proposal, Food Security Coordination Bureau and the Pastoralist Task Force, Addis Ababa.

Behnke, R., Mogaka, M. and Barrow, E. (2007b) *Kenya's Drylands – Wastelands or an Undervalued National Economic Resource*, IUCN, Nairobi.

Behnke, R.H., Fernandez-Gimenez, M.E., Turner, M.D. and Stammler, F. (2011) 'Pastoral migration: Mobile systems of livestock husbandry', in E.J. Milner-Gulland, J.M. Fryxell, and A.R.E. Sinclair (eds) *Animal Migration: A Synthesis*, Oxford University Press, Oxford.

Bekele, G. and Abera, T. (2008) *Livelihoods-based Drought Response in Pastoralist Areas of Ethiopia*, impact assessment of Livestock Feed Supplementation, Feinstein International Center, Tufts University with Save the Children USA and United States Agency for International Development, Addis Ababa.

Berhanu, W. and Colman, D. (2007) 'Farming in the Borana rangelands of southern Ethiopia: The prospects for viable transition to agro-pastoralism' *Eastern African Social Science Review*, vol XXIII, no 3, pp79–101.

Bernal, V. (1997) 'Colonial moral economy and the discipline of development: The Gezira scheme and "modern" Sudan', *Cultural Anthropology*, vol 12, no 4, pp447–479.

Berry, S. (1993) *No Condition is Permanent: The Social Dynamics of Agrarian Change in Sub-Saharan Africa*, University of Wisconsin Press, Madison, WI.

Berry, S. (2009) 'Property, authority and citizenship: Land claims, politics and the dynamics of social division in West Africa', *Development and Change*, vol 40, no 1, pp23–45.

Beshir, M., El-Hillo, M. and El-Tayeb, W. (2005) *Resource-Based Conflicts and Mechanisms of Conflict Resolution in North Kordofan, Gedaref and Blue Nile States*, Sudanese Environmental Conservation Society, Khartoum.

Beyene, F. (2010) 'Interclan cooperation in a risky pastoral ecology: Some lessons from eastern Ethiopia', *Human Ecology*, vol 38, no 4, pp555–565.

Birch, I., Cavanna, S., Abkula, D. and Hujale, D. (2010) *Towards Education for Nomads: Community Perspectives in Kenya*, International Institute for Environment and Development, London.

Blench, R. (2001) *'You Can't Go Home Again': Pastoralism in the New Millennium*, Overseas Development Institute, London.

Blowfield, M. (2005) 'Corporate Social Responsibility: Reinventing the meaning of development?' *International Affairs*, vol 81, no 3, pp515–524.

Blowfield, M. and Frynas, J. (2005) 'Setting new agendas: Critical perspectives on Corporate Social Responsibility in the developing world' *International Affairs*, vol 81, no 3, pp499–513.

Bogale, A. and Korf, B. (2009) 'Resource entitlement and mobility of pastoralists in the Yerer and Daketa valleys, Eastern Ethiopia', *Human Ecology*, vol 37, no 4, pp453–462.

Bollig, M. (1992) 'East Pokot camel husbandry,' *Nomadic Peoples*, vol 31, pp34–50.

Borras Jr., S.M., McMichael, P. and Scoones, I. (2010) 'The politics of biofuels, land and agrarian change: Editors' introduction', *Journal of Peasant Studies*, vol 37, no 4, pp575–92.

Borras, J., Hall, R., Scoones, I., White, B. and Wolford, W. (2012) 'The new enclosures: Critical perspectives on corporate land deals', *Journal of Peasant Studies* (forthcoming, May).

Bradbury, M. (2008) *Becoming Somaliland*, Progressio, London.

Bradbury, M. and Kleinman, M. (2010) *Winning Hearts and Minds? Examining the Relationship between Aid and Security in Kenya*, Feinstein International Center, Tufts University, Medford, MA.

Breman, H. and de Wit, C. (1983) 'Rangeland productivity and exploitation in the Sahel', *Science*, vol 221, pp1341–1347.

Broch-Due, V. (1990) 'Livestock speak louder than sweet words: Changing property and gender relations among the Turkana', in P.T.W. Baxter and R. Hogg (eds) *Property, Poverty and People: Changing Rights in Property and Problems of Pastoral Development*, Department of Social Anthropology and the International Development Centre, Manchester.

Brockington, D. (2001) 'Women's income and the livelihood strategies of dispossessed pastoralists near the Mkomazi game reserve, Tanzania', *Human Ecology*, vol 29, no 3, pp307–338.

Brocklesby, M.A., Hobley, M. and Scott-Villiers, P. (2010) *Raising Voice – Securing a Livelihood: The Role of Diverse Voices in Developing Secure Livelihoods in Pastoralist Areas in Ethiopia*, IDS Working Paper, no 340, Institute of Development Studies, Brighton.

Brouwer, C., Goffeau, A. and Heibloem, M. (1985) *Irrigation Water Management: Training Manual No. 1 – Introduction to Irrigation*, FAO, www.fao.org/docrep/R4082E/R40 82E00.htm, accessed 30 October 2011.

Brückner G.K. (2011) 'Managing the risks of disease transmission through trade: A commodities-based approach?', *Scientific and Technical Review of the Office International des Epizooties*, vol 30, no 1, pp289–296.

Bryceson, D., Kay, C. and Mooij, J. (2000) *Disappearing Peasantries? Rural Labour in Africa, Asia and Latin America*, Intermediate Technology Publications, London.

Buchanan-Smith, M. and Lind, J. (2005) 'Armed violence and poverty in northern Kenya: A case study for the armed violence and poverty initiative', Centre for International Cooperation and Security, Department of Peace Studies, University of Bradford.

Bujra, A. (2005) 'Liberal democracy and the emergence of a constitutionally failed state', in A. Bujra (ed.) *Democratic Transition in Kenya: The Struggle from Liberal to Social Democracy*, African Centre for Economic Growth and the Development Management Policy Forum, Nairobi.

Calkins, S. (2009) 'Transformed livelihoods in the lower Atbara area: Pastoral Rashâyda response to crisis', *Nomadic Peoples*, vol 13, no 1, pp45–68.

Campbell, D., Luckert, M., Doré, D., Mukamuri, B. and Gambiza, J. (2000) 'Economic comparisons of livestock production in communal grazing lands in Zimbabwe', *Ecological Economics*, vol 33, pp413–438.

Carr-Hill, R. and Peart, E. (2005) *The Education of Nomadic Peoples in East Africa: Djibouti, Eritrea, Ethiopia, Kenya, Tanzania and Uganda*, review of the relevant literature, UNESCO-IIEP, Paris and Tunis.

Carrier, N. (2011) 'Reviving Yaaku: Identity and indigeneity in northern Kenya', *African Studies*, vol 70, no 2, pp246–263.

Casciarri, B. and Ahmed, A.G.M. (2009) 'Pastoralists under pressure in present-day Sudan: An introduction', *Nomadic Peoples*, vol 13, no 1, pp10–22.

Catley, A. and Iyasu, A. (2010) 'Moving up or moving out? A rapid livelihoods and conflict analysis in Mieso-Mulu woreda, Shinile Zone, Somali Region, Ethiopia', Feinstein International Centre, Tufts University Addis Ababa and Mercy Corps, Addis Ababa, https://wikis.uit.tufts.edu/confluence/pages/viewpage.action?pageId=38963623, accessed 18 November 2011.

Catley, A. and Leyland, T. (2001) 'Community participation and the delivery of veterinary services in Africa', *Preventive Veterinary Medicine*, vol 49, pp95–113.

Catley, A. and Mohammed, A.A. (1995) 'Ethnoveterinary knowledge in Sanaag Region, Somaliland: Notes on local descriptions of livestock diseases and parasites,' *Nomadic Peoples*, vol 36/37, pp3–16.

Catley, A. and Napier, A. (2010) *Rapid Review of the Cash-for-Work and Natural Resource Management Components of the RAIN Project*, Feinstein International Center, Tufts University, Addis Ababa.

Catley, A., Burns, J., Abebe, D. and Suji, O. (2008) *Participatory Impact Assessment: A Guide for Practitioners*, Feinstein International Center, Medford.

Chabal, P. and Daloz, J.-P. (1999) *Africa Works: Disorder as Political Instrument*, James Currey, Oxford.

Chambers, R. and Conway, G.R. (1992) *Sustainable Rural Livelihoods: Practical Consequences for the 21st Century*, Discussion Paper 296, Institute of Development Studies, Brighton, UK.

Cheung, W., Senay, G. and Singh, A. (2008) 'Trends and spatial distribution of annual and seasonal rainfall in Ethiopia', *International Journal of Climatology*, vol 28, pp1723–1724.

Chirchir, R. and Kidd, S. (2011) 'Scoping study for a "single registry" MIS for Kenya's social protection programmes', Development Pathways, Nairobi.

Christy, J.R., Norris, W.B. and McNider, R. (2009) 'Surface temperature variations in East Africa and possible causes', *Journal of Climate*, vol 22, no12, pp3342–3356.

Chronic Poverty Research Centre (2008) *Understanding Chronic Poverty and Vulnerability Issues in Karamoja Region: A Desk Study*, Manchester University CPRC Report.

Clapham, C. (1996) 'Boundary and territory in the Horn of Africa', in P. Nugent and A.I. Asiwaju (eds) *African Boundaries: Barriers, Conduits and Opportunities*, Pinter, London, pp237–250.

Clapham, C. (1999) 'Boundaries and states in the new African order', in D. Bach (ed.) *Regionalisation in Africa: Integration and Disintegration*, James Currey, Oxford.

Coalition for International Justice (2006) *Soil and Oil: Dirty Business in Sudan*, Coalition for International Justice, Washington DC.

Coppock, D.L. (1994) *The Borana Plateau of Southern Ethiopia: Synthesis of Pastoral Research, Development and Change, 1980–91*, International Livestock Center for Africa (ILCA), Addis Ababa, Ethiopia.

Coppolillo, P. (2000) 'The landscape ecology of pastoral herding: Spatial analysis of land use and livestock production in East Africa', *Human Ecology*, vol 28, no 4, pp527–560.

Cossins, N.J. (1983) 'Where the grass is greener: Bringing the answer closer to home', Tcheffa Valley Study Summary Paper, Joint Ethiopian Pastoral Systems Study: Research Report no 1, International Livestock Centre for Africa (ILCA) Study for Rangelands Development Project, Addis Ababa.

Cossins, N.J. and Upton, M. (1988) 'Options for improvement of the Borana Pastoral System', *Agricultural Systems*, vol 27, no 4, pp251–278.

Cotula, L. (2010) *Why it Makes More Sense to Invest in Farmers Than in Farmland*, IIED Opinion, International Institute for Environment and Development, London.

Cotula, L. and Leonard, R. (eds) (2010) *Alternatives to Land Acquisitions: Agricultural Investment and Collaborative Business Models*, IIED/SDC/IFAD/CTV, London/Bern/Rome/Maputo.

Cotula, L. and Vermeulen S. (2009) '"Land grabs" in Africa: Can the deals work for development?', IIED Policy Briefings, International Institute for Environment and Development, London.

Cronk, L. (2004) *From Mukogodo to Maasai: Ethnicity and Cultural Change in Kenya*, Westview Press, Boulder, CO.

Crosskey, A. and Ahmed Ismail, A.-F. (2009) 'Cross-border pilot livelihoods profiles. pastoral areas coordination, analysis and policy support project', Feinstein International Center, Tufts University, Addis Ababa.

Dahl, G. and Hjort, A. (1976) *Having Herds: Pastoral Herd Growth and Household Economy*, Stockholm Studies in Social Anthropology, Stockholm University Press, Stockholm.

Davies, J. (2004) 'The role of livestock in Afar pastoral livelihoods: Capitalisation, commoditisation and obligation', Ph.D. thesis, Department of Agricultural and Food Economics, University of Reading, UK.

Davies, J. and Nori, M. (2008) 'Managing and mitigating climate change through pastoralism', *Policy Matters*, no 16, pp127–162.

De Haan, C. (1994) *An Overview of the World Bank's Involvement in Pastoral Development*, ODI Pastoral Development Network Paper, no 36b, www.odi.org.uk/pdn/papers/36b.pdf, accessed 7 December 2011.

De Haan, C., Steinfeld, H. and Blackburn, H.W. (1997) *Livestock Environment Interactions: Finding a Balance*, report of a study coordinated by FAO, USAID and the World Bank, Food and Agriculture Organization, Rome.

De Haan, C., Schillhorn van Veen, T., Brandenburg, B., Gauthier, J., Le Gall, F., Mearns, R. and Siméon, M. (2001) *Livestock Development: Implications for Rural Poverty, the Environment, and Global Food Security*, World Bank, Washington DC.

De Jode, H. (ed.) (2010) *Modern and Mobile: The Future of Livestock Production in Africa's Drylands*, IIED and SOS Sahel, London.

De Matteis, A. (2006) *Market Functioning in Turkana District, Kenya*, Oxfam Kenya, Nairobi.

De Waal A. (1989) *Famines that Kill: Darfur 1984–85*, Clarendon Press, Oxford.

Dean, M. and Hindess, B. (eds) (1998) *Governing Australia: Studies in Rationalities of Government*, Cambridge University Press, Melbourne.

Delgado, C., Rosegrant, M., Steinfeld, H., Ehui, S. and Courbois, C. (1999) *Livestock to 2020: The Next Food Revolution*, Food, Agriculture, and the Environment Discussion Paper, no 28, IFPRI/FAO/ILRI (International Food Policy Research Institute/Food and Agriculture Organization/International Livestock Research Institute), Washington DC.

Delmet, C. (2005) 'The native Administration system in eastern Sudan: From its liquidation to its revival', in C. Miller (ed) *Land, Ethnicity and Political Legitimacy in Eastern Sudan*, CEDEJ/DSRC, Cairo/Khartoum, pp144–171.

Demberel and Penn, H. (2006) 'Education and pastoralism in Mongolia', in C. Dyer (ed.) *The Education of Nomadic Peoples: Issues, Provision and Prospects*, Berghahn Books, New York and Oxford.

Deng, L.B. (2002) '*Confronting Civil War: A Comparative Study of Household Assets Management in Southern Sudan*', IDS Discussion Paper, no 381, Institute of Development Studies, Brighton.

Deng, L. (2007) 'Increased rural vulnerability in the era of globalisation: Conflict and famine in Sudan during the 1990s', in S. Devereux (ed.) *The New Famines*, Routledge, London.

Desanker, P. and Magadza, C. (2001) '*Africa*', in IPCC Climate Change 2001. *Working Group II: Impacts, Adaptation and Vulnerability*, UNEP and WMO, New York.

Deshmukh, I. (1984) 'A common relationship between precipitation and grassland peak biomass for East and Southern Africa', *African Journal of Ecology*, no 22, pp181–186.

Dessalegn, R. (1984) *Agrarian Reform in Ethiopia*, Nordiska Afrikainstitutet, Stockholm.

Desta, A. (1996) 'Large-scale agricultural development and survival issues among pastoralists in the Awash valley', paper presented at *Conference on Pastoralism in Ethiopia*, 4–6 Feb 1993, Ministry of Agriculture, and IIED, Addis Ababa.

Desta, S. (1999) 'Diversification of livestock assets for risk management in the Borana pastoral system of southern Ethiopian rangelands', Utah State University, Logan.

Desta, S. and Coppock, D.L. (2002) 'Cattle population dynamics in the southern Ethiopian rangelands, 1980–97', *Journal of Range Management*, vol 55, no 5, pp439–451.

Desta, S. and Coppock, D.L. (2004) 'Pastoralism under pressure: Tracking system change in southern Ethiopia', *Human Ecology*, vol 32, no 4, pp465–486.

Desta, S., Berhanu, W., Gebru, G. and Amosha, D. (2008) *Pastoral Dropout Study in Selected Woredas of Borana Zone, Oromia Regional State*, CARE/USAID, Addis Ababa.

Desta, S., Gebru, G., Tezera, S. and Coppock, D.L. (2006) 'Linking pastoralists and exporters in a livestock marketing chain: Recent experiences from Ethiopia', in P. Little and J. McPeak (eds) *Pastoral Livestock Marketing in Eastern Africa: Research and Policy Challenges*, ITDG Publications, Bourton on Dunsmore, pp109–128.

Desta, Z.H. and Oba, G. (2004) 'Feed scarcity and livestock mortality in *Enset*-mixed farming systems in the Bale highlands southern Ethiopia', *Outlook on Agriculture*, vol 33, no 4, pp277–280.

Devereux, S. (2006) *Vulnerable Livelihoods in Somali Region, Ethiopia*, IDS Research Report, no 57, Institute of Development Studies, Brighton.

Devereux, S. (2010) 'Better marginalised than incorporated? Pastoralist livelihoods in Somali Region, Ethiopia', *European Journal of Development Research*, vol 22, no 5, pp678–695.

Devereux, S. and Sabates-Wheeler, R. (2004) *Transformative Social Protection*, IDS Working Paper 232, Institute of Development Studies, Brighton.

Devereux, S. and Vincent, K. (2010) 'Using technology to deliver social protection: Exploring opportunities and risks', *Development in Practice*, vol 20, no 3, pp367–379.

DFID (Department for International Development) (2004) *Disaster Risk Reduction: A Development Concern: A Scoping Study on Links between Disaster Risk Reduction, Poverty and Development*, DFID, London.

Diener, A.C. and Hagen, J. (2009) *Borderlines and Borderlands: Political Oddities at the Edge of the Nation-State*, Rowman and Littlefield Publishers, Plymouth.

Dietz, T. (1993) 'The state, the market and the decline of pastoralism: Challenging some myths, with evidence from West Pokot in Kenya and Uganda', in J. Markakis (ed.) *Conflict and the Decline of Pastoralism in the Horn of Africa*, MacMillan in association with the Institute of Social Studies, Basingstoke.

Dietz, T., Nunow, A.A., Roba, A.W. and Zaal, F. (2001) 'Pastoral commercialization: On caloric terms of trade and related issues', in M. Salih, T. Dietz and A.G. Mohamed, *African Pastoralism, Conflict, Institutions and Government*, Pluto Press, London, pp194–234.

Dirie, M.F. and Abdurahman, O. (2003) 'Observations on little known diseases of camels (*Camelus dromedarius*) in the Horn of Africa', *Scientific and Technical Review of the Office International des Epizooties*, vol 22, no 3, pp1043–1049.

Doherty, R.M., Sitch, S., Smith, B., Lewis, S.L. and Thornton, P.K. (2010) 'Implications of future climate and atmospheric CO_2 content for regional biogeochemistry, biogeography and ecosystem services across East Africa', *Global Change Biology*, no 16, pp617–640.

Donham, D. (1986) 'Old Abyssinia and the new Ethiopian empire: Themes in social history', in D. Donham and W. James (eds) *The Southern Marches of Imperial Ethiopia: Essays in History and Social Anthropology*, Cambridge University Press, Cambridge.

Donham, D.L. and James, W. (1986) *The Southern Marches of Imperial Ethiopia: Essays in History and Social Anthropology*, Cambridge University Press, Cambridge.

Doornbos, M., Cliffe, L., Ahmed, A.G.M. and Markakis, J. (eds) (1992) *Beyond Conflict in the Horn: Prospects for Peace, Recovery and Development in Ethiopia, Somalia and the Sudan*, James Currey, London.

Doti, T. (2005) 'Rural ties and urban migration opportunities among Borana labour migrants to Nairobi, Kenya', Masters Thesis, Department of International Environment and Development Studies (Noragric), Norwegian University of Life Sciences, Ås.

Duflo, E. (2005) *Gender Equality and Development*, MIT, http://econ-www.mit.edu/files/799, accessed on 30 November 2011.

Durali, S. (2008) 'The Middle East invests in Sudanese agriculture', *Americans for Informed Democracy*, 10 July, www.aidemocracy.org/students/the-middle-east-invests-in-sudan/, accessed 17 _May _2010.

Dyer, C. (ed) (2006) *The Education of Nomadic Peoples: Current Issues, Future Prospects*, Berghahn Books, Oxford.

East Sudan Conference (2009) Gedaref State Profile. Source: http://www.kuwait-fund. org/eastsudanconference/index.php?option=com_content&task=view&id=127&Itemid =293&lang=English, accessed on 9 March 2011.

Ebei, P.A., Oba, G. and Akuja, T. (2008) 'Long-term impacts of droughts on pastoral production and trends in poverty in north-western Kenya: An evaluation of 14-year drought early warning data series', in J. M. Sánchez (ed.) *Droughts: Causes, Effects and Predictions*, NOVA Science Publishers, Inc., New York.

Economist Intelligence Unit (2006) 'Somali country report, November 2006', The Economist Intelligence Unit, London.

Edward, P. and Tallontire, A. (2009) 'Business and development – towards re-politicisation?', *Journal of International Development*, vol 21, pp819–833.

Ekuam, D. (2009) *Livestock Identification, Traceability and Tracking: Its Role in Enhancing Human Security, Disease Control and Livestock Marketing in IGAD Region*, CEWARN and the Institute for Security Studies, Nairobi.

El Shakry, O. (2011) 'Egypt's three revolutions: The force of history behind this popular uprising', *Jadilliya*, February 6, www.jadaliyya.com/pages/index/569/egypts-three-revolutions_the-force-of-history-behi, accessed 23 November 2011.

El-Faki, A.-R. (2005) *The Problem of Land Use: The Issue and the Vision*, Ministry of Agriculture, Animal Resources and Irrigation in collaboration with Dinder National Park Project, HCENR, Gedaref [in Arabic].

Elhadary, Y.A.E. (2010) 'Challenges facing land tenure system in relation to pastoral livelihood security in Gedaref State, Eastern Sudan', *Journal of Geography and Regional Planning*, vol 3, no 9, pp208–218.

El-Hassan, A.M. (1981) 'The environmental consequences of open grazing in the central Butana, Sudan', *Monograph No. 1*. Institute of Environmental Studies, Khartoum.

Ellis, J. and Galvin, K. (1994) 'Climate patterns and land-use practices in the dry zones of Africa', *BioScience*, vol 44, no 5, pp340–349.

Ellis, J.E. and Swift, D.M. (1988) 'Stability of African pastoral ecosystems: Alternate paradigms and implications for development', *Journal of Range Management*, vol 41, pp450–459.

El-Tayeb, Galal El-Din (ed.) (1985) *Gedaref District Study Final Report*, Institute of Environmental Study, Khartoum.

El-Tayeb, Galal El-Din and Lewandowski, A. (1983) 'Environmental degradation in Gedaref District', *Sudan Environment*, vol 3, no 1, pp3–6.

Ensminger, J. (1992) *Making a Market: The Institutional Transformation of an African Society*, Cambridge University Press, Cambridge.

Ensminger, J. and Rutten, A. (1991) 'The political economy of changing property rights: Dismantling a pastoral commons', *American Ethnologist*, vol 18, no 4, pp683–688.

Ericksen, P., Thornton, P., Notenbaert, A., Cramer, L. and Herrero, M. (2011) 'Mapping hotspots of vulnerability to climate change', International Livestock Research Institute (ILRI) and Challenge Programme on Climate Change, Agriculture and Food Security (CCAFS).

Eriksen, S. and Lind, J. (2009) 'Adaptation as a political process: Adjusting to drought and conflict in Kenya's drylands', *Environmental Management*, vol 43, no 5, pp817–835.

European Civil Society (2009) *Foreign Land Grabbing in Africa*, Monitoring report, FIAN International: Heidelberg, http://www.europarl.europa.eu/document/activities/cont/201006/20100609ATT75756/20100609ATT75756EN.pdf, accessed on 1 March 2012.

Evans-Pritchard, E.E. (1940) *The Nuer: A Description of the Modes of Livelihood and Political Institutions of a Nilotic People*, Clarendon Press, Oxford.

Evans-Pritchard, E.E. (1949) *The Sanusi of Cyrenaica*, Clarendon Press, Oxford.

Fabusoro, E. (2009) 'Use of collective action for land accessibility among settled Fulani agro-pastoralists in southwest Nigeria', *Sustainable Science*, vol 4, no 2, pp199–213.

Facius, J.L. (2008) 'Water scarcity in Tanzania – conflict or cooperation? An analysis of the relationship between institutions and local water conflict and cooperation', Masters thesis at International Development Studies, Roskilde University, http://rudar.ruc.dk/bitstream/1800/3293/1/Thesis%20final.pdf, accessed 10 August 2011.

FAO (1997) *Irrigation in the Near East Region in Figures*, FAO, Rome.

FAO Aquastat (Eritrea) (2005) *Eritrea country database*, www.fao.org/nr/water/aquastat/countries/eritrea/index.stm, accessed on 1 December 2011.

FAO Aquastat (Somalia) (2005) *Somalia country database*, www.fao.org/nr/water/aquastat/countries/somalia/index.stm, accessed on 1 December 2011.

FAO Aquastat (Kenya) (2006) *Kenya country database*, www.fao.org/nr/water/aquastat/countries/kenya/index.stm, accessed on 1 December 2011.

Farah, K.O., Nyariki, D.M., Noor, A.A., Ngugi, R.K. and Musimba, N.K. (2001) 'The socio-economic and ecological impacts of small-scale irrigation schemes on pastoralists and drylands in Northern Kenya', *Journal of Social Sciences*, vol 7, no 4, pp267–274.

FDRE (Federal Democratic Republic of Ethiopia) (2003) *Poverty Reduction Strategy Papers (PRSP)*, Ministry of Finance and Economic Development, Addis Ababa.

FDRE (2005a) *Federal Rural Land Administration and Use Proclamation No. 456/2005*, Ministry of Finance and Economic Development, Addis Ababa.

FDRE (2005b) *Plan for Accelerated and Sustained Development to End Poverty*, Ministry of Finance and Economic Development, Addis Ababa.

FDRE (2010) *Growth and Transformation Plan (GTP) 2011–2015: Strategic Plans of the Federal Government*, Ministry of Finance and Economic Development, Addis Ababa.

Ferguson, J. (2006) *Global Shadows: Africa in the Neoliberal World Order*, Duke University Press, Durham and London.

Feyissa, D. and Hoehne, M. (2008) 'Resourcing state borders and borderlands in the Horn of Africa', Max Planck Institute for Social Anthropology Working Papers, no 107.

Feyissa, D. and Hoehne, M.V. (2010) *Borders and Borderlands as Resources in the Horn of Africa*, James Currey, Rochester, NY.

Fleisher, M.L. (2000) *Kuria Cattle Raiders: Violence and Vigilantism on the Tanzania/Kenya Frontier*, University of Michigan Press, Ann Arbor, MI.

Flintan, F. (2007) 'Sharing of past experiences', in A. Ridgewell and F. Flintan (eds) *Gender and Pastoralism: Volume II: Income Generation Development, Savings and Credit in Ethiopia*, SOS Sahel, Addis Ababa.

Flintan, F. (2008) *Women's Empowerment in Pastoral Societies*, September, IUCN/WISP, Nairobi.

Flintan, F. (2010) 'Sitting at the table: How can pastoral women most benefit from land tenure reforms in Ethiopia?', *Journal of East Africa Studies*, vol 4, no 1, pp153–178.

Flintan, F. (2011) *'Broken Lands: Broken Lives?' Causes, processes and impacts of land fragmentation in the rangelands of Ethiopia, Kenya and Uganda*, Report for the Regional Learning and Advocacy Project (REGLAP), Oxfam GB.

Fratkin, E. (1991) *Surviving Drought and Development: Ariaal Pastoralists of Northern Kenya*, Westview Press, Boulder.

Fratkin, E. (1992) 'Drought and development in Marsabit District', *Disasters*, vol 16, no 2, pp119–130.

Fratkin, E. (1998) *Ariaal Pastoralists of Kenya: Surviving Drought and Development in Africa's Arid Lands*, Allyn and Bacon, Boston.

Fratkin, E. (2004) *Ariaal Pastoralists of Northern Kenya*, second edition, Allyn and Bacon, Needham Heights, MA.

Fratkin, E. and Roth, E.A. (1990) 'Drought and economic differentiation among Ariaal pastoralists of Kenya', *Human Ecology*, vol 18, no 4, pp385–402.

Fratkin, E. and Roth, E.A. (eds) (2005) *As Pastoralists Settle: Social, Health, and Economic Consequences of Pastoral Sedentarization in Marsabit District, Kenya*, Springer Publishing Co., New York.

Fratkin, E. and Smith, K. (1995) 'Women's changing economic roles with pastoral sedentarization: Varying strategies in alternative Rendille communities', *Human Ecology*, vol 23, no 4, pp433–454.

Fratkin, E., Roth, E.A. and Nathan, M.A. (2004) 'Pastoral sedentarization and its effects on children's diet, health, and growth among Rendille of northern Kenya', *Human Ecology*, vol 32, no 5, pp531–559.

Friis, C. and Reenberg, A. (2010) *Land Grab in Africa: Emerging Land System Drivers in a Teleconnected World*, GLP Report, no 1, GLP–IPO, Copenhagen.

Frynas, J. (2006) 'Corporate Social Responsibility in emerging economies: Introduction', *Journal of Corporate Citizenship*, vol 24, pp16–19.

Fujita, M., Roth, E.A., Nathan, M.A., and Fratkin, E. (2004) 'Sedentism, seasonality and economic status: A multivariate analysis of maternal dietary and health statuses between pastoral and agricultural Ariaal and Rendille communities in northern Kenya', *American Journal of Physical Anthropology*, vol 123, no 3, pp277–291.

Fukui, K. and Markakis, J. (1994) *Ethnicity and Conflict in the Horn of Africa*, James Currey, Oxford.

Funk, C., Dettinger, M.D., Michaelsen, J.C., Verdin, J.P., Brown, M.E., Barlow M. and Hoell, A. (2008) 'Warming of the Indian Ocean threatens eastern and southern African food security but could be mitigated by agricultural development', *Proceedings of the National Academy of Sciences of America*, vol 105, no 32, pp11081–11086.

Galaty, J. (1992) '"This land is yours": Social and economic factors in the privatization, subdivision and sale of Maasai ranches', *Nomadic Peoples*, no 30, pp26–40.

Galaty, J. (1993) 'Maasai expansion and the new East African pastoralism', in T. Spear and R. Waller (eds) *Being Maasai: Ethnicity and Identity in East Africa*, James Currey, London, pp61–86.

Galaty, J. (2002) 'How visual figures speak: Narrative inventions of "The Pastoralist"' in R. Gordon and C. Kratz (eds) Special Issue, *East Africa, Persistent Popular Images of Pastoralists, Visual Anthropology*, vol 15, no 3–4, pp299–319.

Galaty, J. (in press) 'Modern mobility: Transformations in pastoralist tenure and territoriality in East Africa', in G. Schlee and A. Khazanov (eds) *Conditions of Pastoralist Mobility*, Berghahn Publishers, Oxford.

Galaty, J., D. Aronson, P. Salzman and A. Chouinard (eds) (1981) *The Future of Pastoral Peoples,* International Development Research Centre, Ottawa.

Galaty, J. and Johnson, D. (1990) *The World of Pastoralism*, Guildford Press, New York.

Galvin, K., Coppock, D.L., and Leslie, P.W. (1994) 'Diet, nutrition, and the pastoral strategy', in E. Fratkin, K. Galvin, and E.A. Roth (eds) *African Pastoralist Systems*, Lynne Rienner Publishers, Boulder.

Galvin, K., Reid, R., Behnke, R., and Thompson Hobbs, N. (eds) (2008) *Fragmentation in Semi-Arid and Arid Landscapes: Consequences for Human and Natural Systems*, Springer, New York.

Gamaledin, M. (1993) 'The decline of Afar pastoralism', in J. Markakis (ed.) *Conflict and the Decline of Pastoralism in the Horn of Africa*, Institute of Social Studies, Macmillan Press, UK, pp45–62.

Gebre, A. and Kassa, G. (2009) 'The effects of development projects on the mid-Awash Valley', in A. Pankhurst and F. Pignet (eds) *Moving People in Ethiopia: Development, Displacement and the State*, James Currey, London, pp66–80.

Gebre-Egziabher, Tegegne and Mulat Demeke (2004) *Small Businesses in Small Towns of the Eastern Amhara Region: Nature and Economic Performance*. Madison, WI: BASIS CRSP.

Gedi, A.A. (2005) 'Herder-farmer conflicts in the Dawa-Ganale River Basin area: The case of intra-clan conflict among the Degodia Somali of Dollo Ado District in the Somali Regional State of Ethiopia: Governance and Conflict Transformation', Working Paper 1, NCCR North–South, Bern.

Gedi, A., Salah, O., Ndambo, C., Mohamed, A.M., Ali, A.M., Kabaka, W and Farah, A.M. (2008) 'Garissa livestock market: A treasure for meeting the Millenium Development Goals in a pastoral based millenium municipality', presentation to the Regional Pastoralism and Livestock Policy Training, Nomads Palace Hotel, Garissa, Kenya 22–26 September 2008, Common Market for Eastern and Southern Africa, Lusaka.

Geshekter, C.L. (1993) 'Somali maritime history and regional sub-cultures: A neglected theme of the Somali crisis', paper presented at the First Conference of the European Association of Somali Studies, School of Oriental and African Studies, University of London.

Getachew, A. (2004) 'Determinants of wage labor participation among the Afar pastoralists: the case of Amibara district', M.A. thesis, Addis Ababa University.

Getachew, K.N. (2001) *Among the Pastoral Afar in Ethiopia: Tradition, Continuity and Socio-Economic Change*, International Books in association with OSSREA, Utrecht, The Netherlands.

Getahun, T. and Belay, K. (2002) 'Camel husbandry practices in eastern Ethiopia: The case of Jijiga and Shinile Zones,' *Nomadic Peoples*, vol 6, no 1, pp158–179.

Ghebremariam, B.H. (2006) *Community Spate Irrigation in Bada (Eritrea)*, www.spate-irrigation.org/pdf/badacasestudyspateirrigation.pdf, accessed 22 February 2011.

Ghebremariam, B.H. and van Steenbergen, F. (2007) 'Agricultural water management in ephemeral rivers: Community management in spate irrigation in Eritrea', *Africa Water Journal*, vol 1, no 1, pp51–68.

Giannini, A., Biasutti, M., Held, I. and Sobel, A. (2008) 'A global perspective on African climate', *Climatic Change*, vol 90, no 4, pp359–383.

Girma, M.M. and Awulachew, S.B. (2007) *Irrigation Practices in Ethiopia: Characteristics of Selected Irrigation Schemes*, Working Paper 124, International Water Management Institute, Colombo, Sri Lanka.

Goldsmith, P. (2008) 'Bigger brains or larger herds? Beyond the narrow focus on livestock markets in the North', *Policy: The Journal of the Institute of Economic Affairs*, November: 42–48.

Goldsmith, P. (2010) 'Kenyan real estate and the "mystery" of Somali capital', *The East African*, 23–29 April.

Goldsmith, P. (2011) *The Mombasa Republican Council: A Conflict Assessment*, Pact Kenya, Nairobi.

Goldsmith, P. with Ahmed, H. and Babiker, M. (2009) *Fighting for Inclusion: Conflicts among Pastoralists in Eastern Africa and the Horn*, Development Management Policy Forum, Nairobi.

Gomes, N. (2006) *Access to Water, Pastoral Resource Management and Pastoralists' Livelihoods: Lessons Learned from Water Development in Selected Areas of Eastern Africa (Kenya, Ethiopia, Somalia)*, FAO, Rome.

Graham, A., Aubry, S., Kunnemann, R. and Suárez, S.M. (2009) *The Impact of Europe's Policies and Practices on African Agriculture and Food Security*, Land Grab study, FIAN, CSO Monitoring 2009–2010, 'Advancing African Agriculture'.

Gray, S.J. (2000) 'A memory of loss: Ecological politics, local history, and the evolution of Karimojong violence', *Human Organization*, vol 59, no 4, pp401–418.

Gray, S., Sundal, M., Wiebusc, B., Little, M.A., Leslie, P.W., and Pike, I.L. (2003) 'Cattle raiding, cultural survival, and adaptability of East African pastoralists', *Current Anthropology*, vol 44, supplement.

Greenhalgh, P. and Orchard, J. (2005) *Establishing Quality Control and Certification Systems of Agricultural Export Products in Ethiopia, Volume 2: Commodity Profiles*, NRI Consultancy report for JICA, Chatham.

Grono, N. (2011) 'What are some of the challenges for conflict prevention and resolution over the next two decades?', oral presentation, conference on 'Global Conflict – Future Trends and Challenges towards 2030', Wilton Park, UK.

GSM Association (2008) 'The GSMA Development Fund Top 20: Research on the Economic and Social Impact of Mobile Communications in Developing Countries', London.

Gundel, J. (2006) *The Predicament of the Oday: The Role of Traditional Structures in Security, Rights, Law and Development in Somalia*, Danish Refugee Council/Oxfam Novib, Nairobi.

Hagmann, T. and Mulugeta, A. (2008) 'Pastoral conflicts and state-building in the Ethiopian lowlands', *Afrika Spectrum*, vol 43, no 1, pp19–37.

Hagmann, T. and Peclard, D. (eds) (2011) *Negotiating Statehood: Dynamics of Power and Domination in Africa*, Wiley Blackwell, London.

Hagos, F., Makombe, G., Namara, R.E. and Awulachew, S.B. (2009) 'Importance of irrigated agriculture to the Ethiopian economy: Capturing the direct net benefits of irrigation', Research Report, no 128, International Water Management Institute, Colombo, Sri Lanka.

Hamann, R. (2007) 'Is corporate citizenship making a difference?' *Journal of Corporate Citizenship*, vol 28, pp15–29.

Hampshire, K. (2006) 'Flexibility in domestic organization and seasonal migration among the Fulani of northern Burkina Faso', *Africa*, vol 76, no 3, pp402–426.

Harbeson, J.W. (1978) 'Territorial and development politics in the Horn of Africa: The Afar of the Awash valley', *African Affairs*, vol 77, no 309, pp479–498.

Harvey, P. and Lind, J. (2005) *Dependency and Humanitarian Relief: A Critical Analysis*, HPG Report 19, Humanitarian Policy Group, Overseas Development Institute, London.

Hary, I., Schwartz, H.J., Pielert, V.H.C. and Mosler, C. (1996) 'Land degradation in African pastoral systems and the destocking controversy', *Ecological Modelling*, vol 86, no 2–3, pp227–233.

Healy, S., Cramer, C., Styan, D. and Leonard, D. (2009) *The Economics of Conflict and Integration in the Horn of Africa*, summary record of a half-day workshop, Chatham House, London.

Heath, B. (2001) 'The feasibility of establishing cow calf camps on private ranches as a drought mitigation measure', report for the Natural Resources Institute, StockWatch, Nairobi.

Heffernan, C. and Rushton, J. (1999) *Restocking: A Critical Evaluation*, http://typo3.fao.org/fileadmin/user_upload/drought/docs/restocking%20heffer-rushton.pdf, accessed 4 December 2011.

Hein, L. (2006) 'The impact of grazing and rainfall variability on the dynamics of a Sahelian rangeland', *Journal of Arid Environments*, vol 64, no 3, pp488–504.

Helland, J. (1982) 'Social organization and water control among the Borana', *Development and Change*, vol 13, pp329–258.

HelpAge International (2011) *Strengthening State-citizen Relations in Fragile Contexts: The Role of Cash Transfers*, Help Age International, London.

Hendershot, C. (1965) *Report on the Tribal Schools of Fars Province: White Tents in the Mountains*, United States Agency for International Development (USAID), Washington, DC.

Hendrickson, D., Armon, J. and Mearns, R. (1998) 'The changing nature of conflict and famine vulnerability: The case of livestock raising in Turkana, Kenya', *Disasters*, vol 22, no 3, pp185–199.

Henry, S., Piché, V., Ouedraago, D. and Lambin, E.F. (2004) 'Descriptive analysis of the individual migratory pathways according to environmental typologies', *Population and Environment*, vol 25, no 5, pp397–422.

Herbst, J. (2000) *States and Power in Africa: Comparative Lessons in Authority and Control*, Princeton University Press, Princeton.

Herren, U. (1990a) *The Commercial Sale of Milk from Pastoral Herds in the Mogadishu Hinterland of Somalia*, Pastoral Development Network Paper, no 30a, Overseas Development Institute, London.

Herren, U. (1990b) 'Socio-economic stratification and small-stock production in Mukogodo Division, Kenya', *Research in Economic Anthropology*, vol 12, pp114–148.

Herren, U. (1991) '"Droughts have different tails": Response to crises in Mukogodo Division, north central Kenya, 1950s–1980s', *Disasters*, vol 15, no 2, pp93–107.

Herren, U.J. (1993) 'Cash from camel milk: The impact of commercial camel milk sales on Garre and Galljacel camel pastoralism in southern Somalia', in A. Hjort af Ornäs (ed) *The Multi-Purpose Camel: Interdisciplinary Studies on Pastoral Production in Somalia*, Department of Social and Economic Geography, Uppsala University, Uppsala, pp57–74.

Herrero, M., Ringler, C., van de Steeg, J., Thornton, P., Zuo, T., Bryan, E., Omolo, A., Koo J., and Notenbaert, A. (2010) 'Kenya: Climate variability and climate change and their impacts on the agricultural sector', Report submitted to the World Bank, Washington, D.C.

Herskovits, M. (1926) 'The cattle complex in east Africa', *American Anthropologist*, vol 28, no 1, pp230–272.

Hesse, C. and MacGregor, J. (2006) *Pastoralism: Drylands' Invisible Asset*, Issue Paper, no 142, Drylands Programme, International Institute for Environment and Development, London.

Hill, A. G. (1985) *Population, Health, and Nutrition in the Sahel: Issues in the Welfare of Selected West African Communities*, KPI, London.

Hodgson, D. (2000) *Rethinking Pastoralism in Africa: Gender, Culture and the Myth of the Patriarchal Pastoralist*, James Curry Publishers, Oxford, Kampala, Nairobi, Athens, OH.

Hodgson, D. (2001) *Once Intrepid Warriors: Gender, Ethnicity, and the Cultural Politics of Maasai Development*, Indiana University Press, Bloomington.

Hodgson, D. (2011) *Being Maasai, Becoming Indigenous: Postcolonial Politics in a Neoliberal World*, Indiana University Press, Bloomington.

Hogg, R. (1983) 'Irrigation, agriculture and pastoral development: A lesson from Kenya', *Development and Change*, vol 14, pp577–591.

Hogg, R. (1985) *Re-Stocking Pastoralists in Kenya: A Strategy for Relief and Rehabilitation*, Pastoral Development Network Paper 19c, Overseas Development Institute, London.

Hogg, R. (1986) 'The new pastoralism: Poverty and dependency in Northern Kenya', *Africa*, vol 56, no 3 pp319–333.

Hogg, R. (1987) 'Settlement, pastoralism and the commons: The ideology and practice of irrigation development in Northern Kenya', in D. Anderson and R. Grove (eds) *Conservation in Africa*, Cambridge University Press, Cambridge.

Hogg, R. (1988) 'Changing perceptions of pastoral development: A case study from Turkana District, Kenya', in D.W. Brokensha and P.D. Little (eds) *Anthropology of Development and Change in East Africa*, Westview Press, Boulder, CO, pp183–199.

Hogg, R. (1992) 'Should pastoralism continue as a way of life?', *Disasters*, vol 16, no 2, pp131–137.

Homan, S., Rischkowsky, B., Steinback, J., Kirk, M. and Mathias, E. (2008) 'Towards endogenous livestock development: Borana pastoralists' responses to environmental and institutional changes', *Human Ecology*, vol 36, no 4, pp503–520.

Homewood, K. (2008) *Ecology of African Pastoralist Societies*, James Currey, Oxford.

Homewood, K. and Rodgers, W. (1991) *Maasailand Ecology*, Cambridge University Press, Cambridge.

Homewood, K., Kristjanson, P. and Trench, P. (eds) (2009) *Staying Maasai? Livelihoods, Conservation and Development in East African Rangelands*, Springer, New York.

Horst, C.M.A. (2004) 'Money and mobility: Transnational livelihood strategies of the Somali diaspora', *Global Migration Perspectives*, no 9, Global Commission on International Migration (GCIM), Geneva.

Howell, J. and Lind, J. (2009) *Counter-Terrorism, Aid and Civil Society: Before and After the War on Terror*, Palgrave MacMillan, London.

Hoyle, S. (1977) 'The Khashm el Girba Agricultural Scheme: An example of an attempt to settle nomads', in P. O'Keefe and P. Wisner (eds) *Land Use and Development*, International African Institute, London, pp116–31.

HPG (2009a) *Demographic Trends, Settlement Patterns and Service Provision in Pastoralism: Transformation and Opportunity*, HPG Synthesis Paper: Humanitarian Policy Group, Overseas Development Institute, London.

HPG (2009b) *Getting it Right: Understanding Livelihoods to Reduce the Vulnerability of Pastoral Communities*, HPG Synthesis Paper, Humanitarian Policy Group, Overseas Development Institute, London.

HPG (2009c) *Pastoralism and Climate Change: Enabling Adaptive Capacity*, HPG Synthesis Paper, Humanitarian Policy Group, Overseas Development Institute, London.

Hughes, L. (2006) *Moving the Maasai: A Colonial Misadventure*, Palgrave MacMillan, Basingstoke.

Huho, J.M., Ngaira, J.K.W. and Ogindo, H.O. (2011) 'Living with drought: The case of the Maasai pastoralists of northern Kenya', *Educational Research*, vol 2, no 1, pp779–789.

Hulme, M., Doherty, R., Ngara, T., New, M. and Lister, D. (2001) 'African climate change: 1900–2100', *Climate Research*, vol 17, no 2, pp145–168.

Hundie, B. and Padmanabhan, M. (2008) 'The transformation of the commons: Coercive and non-coercive ways', in E. Mwangi, H. Markelova and R. Meinzen-Dick (eds) *Collective and Property Rights for Poverty Reduction: Lessons from a Global Research Project*, IFPRI, Washington DC.

Hunt, J.A. (1951) *A General Survey of the Somaliland Protectorate 1944–1950*, Crown Agents, London.

ICRC (International Committee of the Red Cross) (2005) *Regional Livestock Study in the Greater Horn of Africa*, ICRC.

IK News (2006) 'Sleeping sickness in Uganda: Fighting the epidemic', *IK News*, no 17 www.ikinvest.com/upload/IKNEWS.pdf, accessed 10 December 2011.

Illius, A.W. and O'Connor, T.G. (1999) 'On the relevance of non-equilibrium concepts to arid and semi-arid grazing systems', *Ecological Applications*, vol 9, no 3, pp798–813.

ILRI (International Livestock Research Institute) (2010) 'An assessment of the response to the 2008–2009 drought in Kenya', a report to the European Union delegation to the Republic of Kenya, International Livestock Research Institute, Nairobi.

ILRI (2011a) 'Massive livestock deaths in drought-ravaged Horn of Africa increase conflicts and close schools', http://ilriclippings.wordpress.com/2011/07/05/massive-livestock-deaths-in-drought-ravaged-horn-of-africa-increase-conflicts-and-close-schools/, accessed on 4 December 2011.

ILRI (2011b) 'Pastoralists in Drought-Stricken Northern Kenya Receive Insurance Payouts for Massive Livestock Losses', www.ilri.org/ilrinews/index.php/archives/7310, accessed on 21 November 2011.

Imperial Ethiopian Government (1955) *Revised Constitution of Ethiopia*, Imperial Ethiopian Government, Addis Ababa.

Imperial Ethiopian Government (1960) *Civil Code of Ethiopia*, Imperial Ethiopian Government, Addis Ababa.

IUCN (International Union for Conservation of Nature) (2011) 'Missing the point in the Horn: Pastoralism is the answer, not the question', 30 August, www.iucn.org/fr/propos/union/secretariat/bureaux/paco/?uNewsID=8085, accessed 2 December 2011.

Jackson, E. (2011) *The Role of Education in Livelihoods in the Somali Region of Ethiopia*, Feinstein International Center, Addis Ababa https://wikis.uit.tufts.edu/confluence/display/FIC/The+Role+of+Education+in+Livelihoods+in+the+Somali+Region+of+Ethiopia, accessed 27 November 2011.

Jahnke, H. (1982) *Livestock Production Systems and Livestock Development in Tropical Africa*, Kieler Wissenschaftsverlag, Kiel.

James, W. (2007) *War and Survival in Sudan's Frontierlands: Voices from the Blue Nile*, Oxford University Press, Oxford.

James, W., Donham, D.L., Kurimoto, E. and Triulzi, A. (2002) *Remapping Ethiopia: Socialism and After*, James Currey, Oxford.

Jenkins, R. (2005) 'Globalization, Corporate Social Responsibility and poverty', *International Affairs*, vol 81, no 3, pp525–540.

Joekes, S. and Pointing, J. (1991) *Women in Pastoral Societies in East and West Africa,* Dryland Issues Paper no 28, International Institute for Environment and Development, London.

Johnson, C., Jones R., Paasi, A., Amoore, L., Mountz, A., Salter, M. and Rumford, C. (2011) 'Rethinking "the border" in border studies', *Political Geography*, vol 30, pp61–69.

Johnson, D. (1993) 'Nomadism and desertification in Africa and the Middle East', *GeoJournal*, vol 31, pp51–66.

Johnson, D. (2003) *Root Causes of Sudan's Civil Wars*, James Currey, New York.

Johnson, D. and Anderson, D. (eds) (1988) *The Ecology of Survival: Case Studies from Northeast African History*, Lester Crook Academic Publishing, London.

Jok, J.M. and Hutchinson, S. (1999) 'Sudan's prolonged second civil war and the militarization of Nuer and Dinka ethnic identities', *African Studies Review*, vol 42, no 2, pp124–45.

Jones, P. and Thornton, P. (2009) 'Croppers to livestock keepers: Livelihood transitions to 2050 in Africa due to climate change', *Environmental Science and Policy*, vol 12, no 4, pp427–437.

Jones, P., Thornton, P. and Heinke, J. (2009) 'Generating characteristic daily weather data using downscaled climate model data from the IPCC's Fourth Assessment', unpublished report, http://ccafsclimate.org/docs/Generating_Characteristic_Daily_Weather_Data_using_Downscaled_Climate_Model_Data_Jones_Thornton_Heinke_2009.pdf, accessed 16 November 2011.

Kamara, A.B., Swallow, B. and Kirk, M. (2004) 'Policies, interventions and institutional change in pastoral resource management in Borana, Southern Ethiopia', *Development Policy Review*, vol 22, no 4, pp381–403.

Kaplan, R. (2009) 'Pakistan's fatal shore', *The Atlantic Monthly*, May 2009.

Karwitha, C. (2009) 'A drought assessment in Il Ngwesi Group Ranch', Northern Rangelands Trust, Isiolo.

Kassahun, A., Snyman, H.A. and Smit, G.N. (2008) 'Impact of rangeland degradation on the pastoral production systems, livelihoods and perceptions of the Somali pastoralists in Eastern Ethiopia', *Journal of Arid Environments*, vol 72, pp1265–1281.

Keenan, J. (2007) 'The banana theory of terrorism: Alternative truths and the collapse of the "second" (Saharan) front on the war on terror', *Journal of Contemporary African Studies*, vol 25, no 1.

Kenya Institute of Education (2002) *Primary Education Syllabus*, 2 volumes, Ministry of Education.

Kenya, Republic of (1991) In the Resident Magistrate's Court at Narok, Civil Case No. 15 of 1991, Nguruman Ltd. Versus Shompole Group Ranch. Ruling by G.N. Omdongi, Resident Magistrate, 29 November 1991.

Kenya, Republic of (2006) Odupoi Ole Kawuet, First Petitioner, and five others (Suing on their own behalf and on behalf of all members of the Shompole and Ol Kiramatian Land Group Ranches) Versus the Attorney-General and 14 other Respondents (including Hermus Philipus Steyn), Petition No. 625, in the High Court at Nairobi.

Kenya, Republic of (2007) Republic Versus The Resident Magistrate Narok and Shompole Group Ranch, with Nguruman Ltd. In the High Court of Kenya at Nairobi, Misc. Civil Application No. 930 of 1991.

Kenya, Republic of (2009) Civil Application, no 930 of 1991, Judgment 2 December.

Kerven, C. (1992) *Customary Commerce: A Historical Reassessment of Pastoral Livestock Marketing in Africa*, Overseas Development Institute, London.

Khalif, Z.K. (2010) 'Pastoral transformation: Shifta-war, livelihood, and gender perspectives among the Waso Borana in Northern Kenya', Ph.D. thesis of Norwegian University of Life Sciences, Ås.

Khan, A.R. (2004) 'Agriculture, development and poverty reduction in Sudan: An analysis of performance, policy and possibilities', a paper prepared for the UNDP project on 'Macroeconomic policies for poverty reduction in Sudan', United Nations Development Programme, Khartoum.

Kipuri, N. and Ridgewell, A. (2008) *A Double Bind: The Exclusion of Pastoralist Women in the East and Horn of Africa,* Minority Rights Group International, London.

Kitalyi, A., Mtenga, L., Morton J., McLeod, A. Thornton, P., Dorward, A. and Saadullah, M. (2005) 'Why keep livestock if you are poor?' in E. Owen, A. Kitalyi, N. Jayasuriya and T. Smith (eds) *Livestock and Wealth Creation: Improving the Husbandry of Animals Kept by Resource-Poor People in Developing Countries*, Nottingham University Press, Nottingham, pp13–27.

Klepp, K.-I., Biswalo, P.M. and Talle, A. (1995) *Young People at Risk: Fighting Aids in Northern Tanzania*, Scandinavian University Press, Oslo.

Kloos, H. (1982) 'Development, drought, and famine in the Awash Valley of Ethiopia', *African Studies Review*, vol 25, no 4, pp21–48.

Kloos, H., DeSole, G. and Aklilu, L. (1981) 'Intestinal parasitism in semi nomadic pastoralists and subsistence farmers in and around irrigation schemes in the Awash Valley, Ethiopia, with special emphasis on ecological and cultural associations', *Social Science & Medicine. Part B: Medical Anthropology*, vol 15, no 4, pp457–469.

Kloos, H. and Legesse, W. (eds) (2010) *Water Resources Management in Ethiopia: Implications for the Nile Basin*, Cambria Press, Amherst, New York.

Kraaij, T. and Milton, S.J. (2006) 'Vegetation changes (1995–2004) in semi-arid karoo shrubland, South Africa: Effects of rainfall, wild herbivores and change in land use', *Journal of Arid Environments*, vol 64, no 1, pp174–192.

Krätli, S. (2001) *Education Provision to Nomadic Pastoralists*, IDS Working Paper 126, Institute of Development Studies, Brighton.

Krätli, S. (2009) *ABEK (Alternative Basic Education for Karamoja) Strategic Review. Final report to Save the Children in Uganda (October 2009)*, Save the Children in Uganda, Kampala.

Krätli, S. with Dyer, C. (2006) 'Education and development for nomads: The issues and the evidence' in C. Dyer (ed) *The Education of Nomadic Peoples. Current Issues, Future Prospects*, Berghahn Books, New York and Oxford.

Krätli, S. and Dyer, C. (2009) *Mobile Pastoralists and Education: Strategic Options*, Education for Nomads, Working Paper 1, International Institute for Environment and Development, London.

Krätli, S. and Schareika, N. (2010) 'Living *off* uncertainty: The intelligent animal production of dryland pastoralists', *European Journal of Development Research*, vol 22, pp605–622.

Krätli, S. and Swift, J. (1999) *Understanding and Managing Pastoral Conflict in Kenya: A Literature Review*, Institute of Development Studies, Brighton.

Kurimoto, E. and Simonse, S. (eds) (1998) *Conflict, Age and Power in North East Africa*, James Currey, Oxford.

LaFranchi, H. (2011) 'US to aid groups: Feed the starving, even if Al Qaeda gets collateral benefits', *Christian Science Monitor*, 2 August, www.csmonitor.com/USA/Foreign-Policy/2011/0802/US-to-aid-groups-Feed-the-starving-even-if-Al-Qaeda-gets-collateral-benefits?cmpid=ema:nws:Daily%20Custom%2008032011&cmpid=ema:nws:NzQ4MD UzNTk0MwS2, accessed 7 December 2011.

Lamprey, H. (1975) 'Report on the desert encroachment reconnaissance in Northern Sudan 21 October to 10 November', UNESCO/UNEP, *Desertification Bulletin*, no 17, pp1–7.

Lamprey, H. (1983) 'Pastoralism yesterday and today: The overgrazing problem', in F. Bourlière (ed) *Tropical Savannas. Ecosystems of the World*, vol 13, Elsevier Scientific Publishing Co., Amsterdam.

Large, D. (2008) 'Beyond "dragon in the bush": The study of China–Africa relations', *African Affairs*, vol 107, no 426, pp45–61.

Lavers, T. (2012) '"Land grab" as development strategy? The political economy of agricultural investment in Ethiopia', *Journal of Peasant Studies*, vol 39, pp105–132.

Le Houérou, H. (1989) 'The grazing land ecosystems of the African Sahel', *Ecological Studies*, vol 75, Springer Verlag, Berlin.

Legesse, A. (1973) *Gada: Three Approaches to the Study of African Society*, Free Press, New York.

LEGS (2009) *Livestock Emergency Guidelines and Standards*, LEGS and Practical Action Publishing, Rugby, www.livestock-emergency.net, accessed 7 December 2011.

Lengoiboni, M., Van der Malen, P. and Bregt, A.K. (2011) 'Pastoralism within cadastral system: Seasonal instructions and access agreements between pastoralists and non-pastoralists', *Journal Arid Environments*, doi:1016/j.jaridenv.2010.12.011.

Leonard, D. (2009) *Recreating Political Order: The Somali Systems Today*, IDS Working Paper, no 316, Institute of Development Studies, Brighton.

Leslie, P.W. and Fry, P.H. (1989) 'Extreme seasonality of births among nomadic Turkana pastoralists', *American Journal of Physical Anthropology*, vol 79, no 1, pp103–115.

Lesnoff, M. (2007) 'DynMod: A tool for demographic projections of ruminants under tropical conditions', *User's Manual*, 29 pages, International Livestock Research Institute, Nairobi, Kenya.

Lesorogol, C. (2008) *Contesting the Commons: Privatizing Pastoral Lands in Kenya*, University of Michigan Press, Ann Arbor.

Lewis, I.M. (1961) *A Pastoral Democracy: A Study of Pastoralism and Politics among the Northern Somali of the Horn of Africa*, Oxford University Press for the International African Institute, Oxford.

Lewis, I.M. (ed) (1983) *Nationalism and Self-determination in the Horn of Africa*, Ithaca Press, London.

Lewis, I.M. (1988) *A Modern History of Somalia*, Westview Press, Boulder.

Lewis, M.P. (ed) (2009) *Ethnologue: Languages of the World*, sixteenth edition, SIL International, Dallas, Texas.

Lind, J. (Forthcoming, 2012) 'Manufacturing peace in "no man's land": Livestock, conflict and access to resources in the Karimojong Cluster of Kenya and Uganda', in H. Young and L. Goldman (eds) *Strengthening Post-Conflict Peace-Building through Natural Resource Management, Volume 4: Livelihoods*, Earthscan, Routledge, Abingdon.

Lind, J. and Howell, J. (2010) 'Counter-terrorism, the politics of fear and civil society responses in Kenya', *Development and Change*, vol 41, no 2, pp335–353.

Lindley, A. (2005) 'Somalia country study', a part of the report on Informal Remittance Systems in Africa, Caribbean and Pacific (ACP) countries (Ref: RO2CS008) for the Department of International Development UK, European Community's Poverty Reduction Effectiveness Programme, and Deloitte & Touche, ESRC Centre on Migration, Policy and Society, University of Oxford.

Lindley, A. (2007) *Remittances in Fragile Settings: A Somali Case Study*, Working Paper. no 27, Households in Conflict Network, Sussex University, Brighton.

Lindley, A. (2009) 'Between dirty money and development capital: Somali money transfer infrastructure under global scrutiny', *African Affairs*, vol 108, no 433, pp519–539.

Lister, S. (2004) *The Processes and Dynamics of Pastoralist Representation in Ethiopia*, IDS Working Paper, no 220, Institute of Development Studies, Brighton.

Little, M. and Leslie, P. (1999) *Turkana Herders of the Dry Savanna: Ecology and Biobehavioral Response of Nomads to an Uncertain Environment*, Oxford University Press, New York.

Little, P.D. (1983) 'Livestock-grain connection in northern Kenya', *Rural Africana*, no 15–16, pp91–108.

Little, P.D. (1985a) 'Absentee herd owners and part-time pastoralists: The political economy of resource use in northern Kenya', *Human Ecology*, vol 13, pp131–151.

Little, P.D. (1985b) 'Social differentiation and pastoralist sedentarization in northern Kenya', *Africa*, vol 55, no 3, pp243–261.

Little, P.D. (1989) *The Dairy Commodity System of the Kismayo Region, Somalia: Rural and Urban Dimensions*, Institute for Development Anthropology, Binghamton, NY.

Little, P.D. (1992) *The Elusive Granary: Herder, Farmer, and State in Northern Kenya*, Cambridge University Press, Cambridge.

Little, P.D. (1994) 'Maidens and milk markets: The sociology of dairy marketing in southern Somalia', in E. Fratkin, K. Galvin, and E. Roth (eds) *African Pastoralist Systems*, Lynne Rienner, Boulder, pp165–184.

Little, P.D. (1996) 'Conflictive trade, contested identity: The effects of export markets on pastoralists of southern Somalia', *African Studies Review*, vol 39, no 1, pp25–54.

Little, P.D. (2002) 'The global dimensions of cross-border trade in the Somalia Borderlands' in A.G.M. Ahmed (ed) *Globalisation, Democracy, and Development in Africa: Future Prospects*, OSSREA, Addis Ababa, Ethiopia.

Little, P.D. (2003) *Somalia: Economy Without State*, James Currey, Oxford, UK, Indiana University Press, Bloomington, IN.

Little, P.D. (2005) 'Pastoralism in a stateless environment: The case of the southern Somali borderlands', *Geography Research Forum*, no 25 (December Issue), pp128–147.

Little, P.D. (2006) 'Working across borders: Methodological and policy challenges of cross-border livestock trade in the Horn of Africa', in J. McPeak and P.D. Little (eds) *Pastoral Livestock Marketing in Eastern Africa: Research and Policy Challenges*, ITDG Publications, Warwickshire, UK.

Little, P.D. (2007) 'Unofficial cross-border trade in East Africa', workshop on 'Staple Food Trade and Market Policy Options for Promoting Development in Eastern and Southern Africa', UN Food and Agriculture Organization, Rome, 1–2 March.

Little, P.D. (2009) 'Income diversification among pastoralists: Lessons for policy-makers', Policy Brief no. 3, COMESA (Common Market for Eastern and Southern Africa), CAADP, www.caadp.net/pdf/COMESA%20Economic%20Diversification%20Pastoralists%20Policy%20Brief%203%20(2).pdf, accessed on 1 December 2011.

Little, P.D. and Mahmoud, H.A. (2005) *Cross-Border Cattle Trade along the Somalia/Kenya and Ethiopia/Kenya Borderlands*, Research Brief 05–03–PARIMA, Global Livestock Collaborative Research Support Program, University of California-Davis.

Little, P.D., Smith, K., Cellarius, B.A., Coppock, D.L. and Barrett, C.B. (2001) 'Avoiding disaster: Diversification and risk management among East African herders', *Development and Change*, vol 32, no 3, pp401–433.

Little, P.D., McPeak, J., Barrett, C. and Kristjanson, P. (2008) 'Challenging orthodoxies: Understanding poverty in pastoral areas of East Africa', *Development and Change*, vol 39, no 4, pp589–611.

Little, P.D., Aboud, A. and Lenachuru, C. (2009) 'Can formal education reduce risks for drought-prone pastoralists? A case study from Baringo District, Kenya', *Human Organization* 68, no 2, pp154–165.

LIU (Livelihoods Information Unit) (2008) 'Livelihood profile Oromia Region, Ethiopia – Southern pastoral and agro-pastoral livelihood zones', Livelihoods Integration Unit, Addis Ababa.

Lochhead, D. and Musoke, R.A. (2010) 'Evaluation of the Building Sustainable Peace and Development in Karamoja Project', Final Report, Government of Uganda/UNDP.

Lockheed, M., Jamison, D. and Lau, L. (1980) 'Farmer education and farm efficiency: A survey', *Economic Development and Cultural Change*, vol 29, no 1, pp37–76.

Lotira Arasio, R. (2004) 'Rebuilding herds by reinforcing *Gargar/Irb* among the Somali pastoralists of Kenya', evaluation of experimental restocking in Wajir and Mandera Districts of Kenya, African Union Interafrican Bureau for Animal Resources, Nairobi and Feinstein International Center, Tufts University, Medford.

Luckham, R. and Bekele, D. (1984) 'Foreign powers and militarism in the Horn of Africa: Part II', *Review of African Political Economy*, vol 31, pp7–28.

Lugo, A. (1997) 'Reflections on border theory, culture, and the nation', in S. Michaelsen and D.E. Johnson (eds) *Border Theory: The Limits of Cultural Politics*, University of Minnesota Press, Minneapolis.

Lybbert, T.J., Barrett, C.B., Desta, S., Coppock, D.L. (2004) 'Stochastic wealth dynamics and risk management among a poor population', *The Economic Journal*, vol 114, no 498, pp750–777.

Lyons, T. (2008) 'Ethiopia's convergence of crises', *Current History*, vol 107, no 708, pp154–160.

MAADE (1997/2005) *Operational Budget for 1998 [2006]*, Middle Awash Agricultural Development Enterprise, Melka Sedi, Afar Region, Ethiopia.

Mace, R. (1993) 'Transitions between cultivation and pastoralism in sub-Saharan Africa', *Current Anthropology*, vol 34, no 4, pp363–382.

Mahmoud, H.A. (2006) 'Innovations in pastoral livestock marketing: The emergence and the role of "Somali cattle-traders-cum-ranchers" in Kenya', in J.G. McPeak and P.D. Little (eds) *Pastoral Livestock Marketing in Eastern Africa: Research and Policy Changes*, IT Publication, Warwickshire, UK, pp129–144.

Mahmoud, H.A. (2008) 'Risky trade, resilient traders: Trust and livestock marketing in northern Kenya', *Africa: The Journal of the International African Institute*, vol 78, no 4, pp561–581.

Mahmoud, H.A. (2009) 'Conflicts and pastoral livelihoods in the Kenya-Ethiopia-Somalia borderlands', in P. Goldsmith (ed.) *Fighting for Inclusion: Conflicts among Pastoralists in Eastern Africa and the Horn*, Development Management Policy Forum, Nairobi, pp53–78.

Mahmoud, H. A. (2010) *Livestock Trade in the Kenyan, Somalia and Ethiopian Borderlands*, Briefing Paper, 2010/02, Chatham House, London.

Maimbo, S.M. (2006) 'Remittances and economic development in Somalia: An overview', Social Development Papers, *Conflict Prevention and Reconstruction*, no 38, The World Bank, Washington DC.

Maina, K. and Maalim, A. (2011) 'Kenya: Suspected Al Shabaab terror squad named' *Nairobi Star*, 8 March.

Markakis, J. (1994) 'Ethnic conflict and the state in the Horn of Africa' in K. Fukui and J. Markakis (eds) *Ethnicity and Conflict in the Horn of Africa*, James Currey, London.

Markakis, J. (2003) 'Anatomy of a conflict: Afar and Ise Ethiopia', *Review of African Political Economy*, vol 96, pp445–453.

Markakis, J. (2004) *Pastoralism on the Margin*, Minority Rights Group, London.

Markakis, J. (2011) *Ethiopia: The Last Two Frontiers*, James Currey, Woodbridge.

MAS (1991) *Amibara Irrigation Project II: Pastoralist and Forestry Development Studies*, Report to WRDA Volumes I and II, Macdonald Agricultural Services Ltd, Cambridge.

Mattli, W. (1999) *The Logic of Regional Integration: Europe and Beyond*, Cambridge University Press, Cambridge.

May, A. and McCabe, J.T. (2004) 'City work in a time of AIDS: Maasai labor migration in Tanzania', *Africa Today*, vol 51, no 2, pp3–32.

Mayunga, A. (2009) 'Villagers want agreement with Grumeti game investor revoked', *The Citizen* (Dar es Salaam), Tanzania, 22 August.

McCabe, J.T. (2003) 'Sustainability and livelihood diversification among the Maasai of northern Tanzania', *Human Organization*, vol 62, no 1, pp100–111.

McCabe, J.T. (2004) *Cattle Bring Us to Our Enemies: Turkana Ecology, Politics, and Raiding in a Disequilibrium System*, University of Michigan Press, Ann Arbor.

McCabe, J.T., Leslie, P.W. and Deluca, L. (2010) 'Adopting cultivation to remain pastoralists: The diversification of Maasai livelihoods in Northern Tanzania', *Human Ecology*, vol 28, pp321–334.

McCord, A. (2005) 'Win–win or lose–lose? An examination of the use of public works as a social protection instrument in situations of chronic poverty', paper presented at the conference on Social Protection for Chronic Poverty, University of Manchester, 23–24 February.

McHugh, M.J. (2006) 'Impact of South Pacific circulation variability on east African rainfall', *International Journal of Climatology*, vol 26, no 4, pp505–521.

McPeak, J.G. (2005) 'Individual and collective rationality in pastoral production: Evidence from northern Kenya', *Human Ecology*, vol 33, no 2, pp171–197.

McPeak, J.G. (2006) 'Livestock marketing in Marsabit District, Kenya, over the past fifty years', in J.G. McPeak and P.D. Little (eds) *Pastoral Livestock Marketing in East Africa: Research and Policy Challenges*, Intermediate Technology Publications, Rugby.

McPeak, J.B. and Barrett, C.B. (2001) 'Differential risk exposure and stochastic poverty traps among East African pastoralists', *American Journal of Agricultural Economics*, vol 83, no 3, pp674–679.

McPeak, J. and Little, P.D. (2005) 'Cursed if you do, cursed if you don't: The contradictory processes of pastoral sedentarization in northern Kenya', in E. Fratkin, and E.A. Roth (eds) *As Pastoralists Settle*, Springer Publishing Company, New York.

McPeak, J. and Little, P.D. (eds) (2006) *Pastoral Livestock Marketing in Eastern Africa: Research and Policy Challenges*, ITDG Publications, London.

McPeak, J., Little, P.D. and Demment, M. (2006) 'Conclusion: The policy implications and future research needs', in P. Little and J. McPeak (eds) *Pastoral Livestock Marketing in Eastern Africa: Research and Policy Challenges*, ITDG Publications, Bourton on Dumsmore, pp247–256.

McPeak, J.G., Little, P.D. and Doss, C.R (2011) *Risk and Social Change in an African Rural Economy: Livelihoods in Pastoralist Communities*, Taylor and Francis, London.

McVeigh, T. (2011) 'Charity president says aid groups are misleading the public on Somalia.' *The Guardian*. 3 September 2011, www.guardian.co.uk/global-development/2011/sep/03/charity-aid-groups-misleading-somalia?INTCMP=SRCH, accessed 7 December 2011.

MDNKOAL (Ministry for Development of Northern Kenya and Other Arid Lands) (2010a) *Getting to the Hardest to Reach: A Strategy to Provide Education to Nomadic Communities in Kenya through Distance Learning*, Minister of State for Development of Northern Kenya and Other Arid Lands (Office of the Prime Minister) and Education for Nomads programme, Nairobi http://pubs.iied.org/G02742.html, accessed 22 November 2011.

MDNKOAL (2010b) *Education for Nomads PHASE 2, Manual. Nomadic Radio Education Trials*, written by Jeremy Swift and Saverio Krätli for the Ministry of State for the Development of Northern Kenya and other Arid Lands, International Institute for Environment and Development, London.

Meehl, G.A., Stocker T.F., Collins, W.D., Friedlingstein P., Gaye, A.T., Gregory, J.M., Kitoh, A., Knutti, R., Murphy, J.M., Noda, A., Raper, S.C.B., Watterson, I.G., Weaver, A.J. and Zhao, Z.-C. (2007) 'Global climate projections', in S. Solomon, D. Qin, M. Manning, Z. Chen, M. Marquis, K.B. Averyt, M. Tignor and H.L. Miller (eds) *Climate Change 2007: The Physical Science Basis. Contribution of Working Group I to the Fourth Assessment Report of the Intergovernmental Panel on Climate Change*, Cambridge University Press, Cambridge and New York.

Menkhaus, K. (2007) 'The crisis in Somalia: Tragedy in five acts', *African Affairs*, vol 106, no 204, pp357–390.

Menkhaus, K. (2008) 'The rise of a mediated state in northern Kenya: The Wajir story and its implications for state-building', *Afrika Focus*, vol 11, no 2, pp23–38.

Metahara Sugar Factory (2008) Financial Statement of 2007/08, Metahara.

Milanovic, B. (2008) 'Qat expenditures in Yemen and Djibouti: An empirical analysis', World Bank and Carnegie Endowment for International Peace, Washington DC, USA, *Journal of African Economies*, vol 17, no 5, pp661–687.

Minear, L. (2001) 'Pastoralist community harmonization in the Karamoja cluster: Taking it to the next level', Feinstein International Famine Center, Tufts University, Medford.

Mirzeler, M. and Young, C. (2000) 'Pastoral politics in the northeast periphery in Uganda: AK-47 as change agent', *Journal of Modern African Studies*, vol 38, no 3, pp407–429.

Mkutu, K. (2007) 'Small arms and light weapons among pastoral groups in the Kenya–Uganda border area', *African Affairs*, vol 106, no 422, pp47–70.

Mkutu, K. (2009) *Guns and Governance in the Rift Valley: Pastoralist Conflict and Small Arms*, James Currey, Oxford.

MOESTK (Ministry of Education, Science and Technology) (2005) *A Policy Framework for Education, Training and Research*, Sessional Paper, No. 1, Ministry of Education, Science and Technology, Republic of Kenya, Nairobi.

MOESTK (2007) *Kenya Vision 2030*, Ministry of Education, Science and Technology, Republic of Kenya, Nairobi.

MOESTK (2008a) *Education Statistics Booklet*, Ministry of Education, Science and Technology, Republic of Kenya, Nairobi.

MOESTK (2008b) *Policy Framework for Nomadic Education in Kenya*, draft of July 2008, Ministry of Education, Science and Technology and UNICEF, Republic of Kenya, Nairobi.

MOESTK (2008c) *Report on the Policy Framework for Nomadic Education in Kenya*, Ministry of Education, Science and Technology and UNICEF, Republic of Kenya, Nairobi.

MOESTK (2009) *Education Facts and Figures: Update 1st October 2009*, Ministry of Education, Nairobi.

MOESTK (2010) *Policy Framework for Nomadic Education in Kenya*, Ministry of Education, Republic of Kenya, Nairobi.

Mohammed, Y.A. (2008) *Islamic Relief Kenya Irrigation Projects in Mandera: Lessons Learned*, www.ochaonline.un.org/OchaLinkClick.aspx?link=ocha&docId, accessed 25 October 2011.

Monod, T. (ed) (1975) *Pastoralism in Tropical Africa*, Oxford University Press, Oxford.

Moritz, M. (2006) 'Changing contexts and dynamics of farmer-herder conflicts across West Africa', *Canadian Journal of African Studies*, vol 40, no 1, pp1–40.

Moritz, M. (2008) 'Competing paradigms in pastoral development from the far north of Cameroon', *World Development*, vol 36, no 11, pp2243–2254.

Moritz, M. (2010) 'Crop-livestock interactions in agricultural and pastoral systems in West Africa', *Agriculture and Human Values*, vol 27, no 2, pp119–128.

Morton, J. (2005) *Legislators and Livestock: A Comparative Analysis of Pastoralist Parliamentary Groups in Ethiopia, Kenya and Uganda*, Final Report for the NRI/PENHA Research Project on Pastoralist Parliamentary Groups.

Morton, J. (2006) 'Pastoralist coping strategies and emergency livestock market intervention' in P. Little and J. McPeak (eds) *Pastoral Livestock Marketing in Eastern Africa: Research and Policy Challenges*, ITDG Publications, Bourton on Dumsmore, pp227–246.

Morton, J. (2008) *DFID's Current and Potential Engagement with Pastoralism: A Scoping Study*, Natural Resources Institute, University of Greenwich.

Morton, J. (2010a) *The Innovation Trajectory of Sleeping Sickness Control in Uganda: Research Knowledge in its Context*, Research Into Use Discussion Paper No.8, East Malling.

Morton, J. (2010b) 'Why should governmentality matter for the study of pastoral development?', *Nomadic Peoples*, vol 14, no 1, pp6–30.

Morton, J. and Meadows, N. (2001) *Pastoralism and Sustainable Livelihoods: An Emerging Agenda*, NRI Policy Series 11, Chatham, UK.

Mutai, C.C. and Ward, M.N. (2000) 'East African rainfall and the tropical circulation/convection on intraseasonal to interannual timescales', *Journal of Climate*, vol 13, no 22, pp3915–3939.

Mwangi, E. (2007) *Socioeconomic Change and Land Use in Africa: The Transformation of Property Rights in Maasailand*, Palgrave MacMillan, New York.

Nathan, M.A., Roth, E.A., Fratkin, E., Wiseman, D. and Harris, J. (2005) 'Health and morbidity among Rendille pastoralist children: Effects of sedentarization', in E. Fratkin and E.A. Roth (eds) *As Pastoralists Settle*, Springer Publishing Company, New York.

National Assembly (2010) Official Report for 1 Thursday July 2010, Question No.057: Revival of Rapsu/Kinna/Malka-Daka/Gafarsa Irrigation Schemes.

NCSP (National Council for Strategic Planning) (2007) *The Five-Year Plan (2007–2011)*, National Council for Strategic Planning, Khartoum, http://planipolis.iiep.unesco.org/upload/Sudan/Sudan_five_year_plan.pdf, accessed 7 August 2011.

New Agriculturalist (2011) *Stamping out Sleeping Sickness in Uganda*, www.new-ag.info/en/focus/focusItem.php?a=2259, accessed 10 December 2011.

Newman, D. (2006) 'The lines that continue to separate us: Borders in our "borderless" world', *Progress in Human Geography*, vol 30, no 2, pp143–161.

Ngigi, S.N. (2002a) 'Preliminary evaluation of irrigation development in Kenya', in H.G. Blank, C.M. Mutero and H. Murray-Rust (eds) *The Changing Face of Irrigation in Kenya: Opportunities for Anticipating Change in Eastern and Southern Africa*, IWMI, Colombo, Sri Lanka, pp93–111.

Ngigi, S.N. (2002b) 'Review of irrigation development in Kenya', in H.G. Blank, C.M. Mutero and H. Murray-Rust (eds) *The Changing Face of Irrigation in Kenya: Opportunities for Anticipating Change in Eastern and Southern Africa*, IWMI, Colombo, Sri Lanka, pp35–54.

Niamir-Fuller, M. (1999) *Managing Mobility in African Rangelands: The Legitimisation of Transhumance*, Intermediate Technology Publications, London.

Nicholson, S.E. (2001) 'Climatic and environmental change in African during the last two centuries', *Climate Research,* vol 17, no 2, pp123–144.

Nicol, A. (2000) 'Contested margins: Water resources, decentralisation and the state in the Awash valley, Ethiopia, 1985–1998', Ph.D. thesis, School of Oriental and African Studies, University of London.

Njoroge to Attorney General (2003) legal correspondence.

Njoroge to Kamau (2003) legal correspondence.

Nkedianye, D., Ogutu, J.O., Said, M.Y., Herrero, M., Kifugo, S.C., Reid, R.S., de Leeuw, J., Dickson, K.S. and Van Gardingen, P. (2011) 'Pastoral mobility: A blessing or a curse? The impact of the 2005–06 drought on livestock mortality in Maasailand', *Pastoralism*, vol 1, pp1–17.

Nori, M., Switzer, J. and Crawford, A. (2005) *Herding on the Brink: Towards a Global Survey of Pastoral Communities and Conflict*, International Institute for Environment and Development, London.

Nugent, P. (2002) *Smugglers, Secessionists and Loyal Citizens on the Ghana-Togo Frontier*, Ohio University Press, Athens.

Nyangaga, J., Gebremedhin, B., Baker, D., Lukuyu, B., Ounga, T. and Randolph, T.F. (2009) 'Irrigated fodder supports peri-urban livestock and livelihoods in the Mandera Triangle', Regional symposium on livestock marketing in the Horn of Africa, conference paper, ILRI, Nairobi.

O'Connor, T.G. (1994) 'Composition and population responses of an African savanna grassland to rainfall and grazing', *Journal of Applied Ecology*, vol 31, pp155–171.

Oba, G. (2001) 'The effects of multiple droughts on cattle in Obbu, Northern Kenya', *Journal of Arid Environments*, vol 49, no 2, pp375–386.

Oba, G. and Kaitira, L.M. (2006) 'Herder knowledge of landscape assessments in arid rangelands in northern Tanzania', *Journal of Arid Environments*, vol 66, no 1, pp168–186.

Oba, G., Stenseth, N.C. and Lusigi, W. (2000a) 'New perspectives on sustainable grazing management in arid zones of sub-Saharan Africa', *BioScience*, vol 50, pp35–51.

Oba, G., Post, E., Stenseth, N.C. and Lusigi, W. (2000b) 'Role of small ruminants in arid zone environments: A review of research perspectives', *Annals of Arid Zone,* vol 39, pp305–332.

Oba, G., Vetaas, O.R. and Stenseth, N.C. (2001a) 'Relationships between biomass and plant species richness in arid zone grazing lands', *Journal of Applied Ecology*, vol 38, pp836–845.

Oba, G. Post, E. and Stenseth, N.C. (2001b) 'Sub-Saharan desertification and productivity are linked to hemispheric climate variability', *Global Change Biology*, vol 7, no 3, pp241–246.

Oba, G., Stenseth, N.C., and Weladji, R.B. (2002) 'Impact of shifting agriculture on a floodplain woodland regeneration in dryland Kenya', *Agriculture, Ecosystems & Environment*, vol 90, no 2, pp211–216.

Oba, G., Weladji, R.B., Lusigi, W.J., and Stenseth, N.C. (2003) 'Scale-dependent effects of grazing on rangeland degradation in Northern Kenya: A test of equilibrium and non-equilibrium hypothesis', *Land Degradation & Development*, vol 14, no 1, pp83–94.

Oba, G., Sjaastad, E. and Roba, H.G. (2008a) 'Framework for participatory assessments and implementation of global environmental conventions at the community level', *Land Degradation & Development*, vol 19, pp65–76.

Oba, G., Byakagaba, P., and Angassa, A. (2008b) 'Participatory monitoring of biodiversity in East African grazing lands', *Land Degradation & Development*, vol 19, pp636–648.

ODI (2010) 'Pastoralism demographics, settlement and service provision in the Horn and East Africa: Transformation and opportunities', Humanitarian Policy Group, Overseas Development Institute, London.

OECD–FAO (2011) *Agricultural Outlook* 2011–2020, FAO, Rome.

Orindi, V., Nyong, A. and Herrero, M. (2007) 'Pastoral livelihood adaptation to drought and institutional interventions in Kenya', Human Development Report Office, Occasional Paper, no 54, United Nations Development Programme (UNDP), New York, USA.

Osman, E.I. (2009) 'The Funj region pastoral FulBe: From "exit" to "voice"', *Nomadic Peoples*, vol 13, no 1, pp92–112.

Ottaway, M. (1982) *Soviet and American Influence in the Horn of Africa*, Praeger, New York.

Pankhurst, R. and Johnson, D.H. (1988) 'The great drought and famine of 1888–92 in northeast Africa', in D. Anderson, and D.L. Johnson (eds) *The Ecology of Survival: Case Studies from North-East Africa History*, Westview Press, Boulder, Colorado, pp47–70.

Pankhurst, A. and Piguet, F. (eds) (2004) *People, Space and the State: Migration, Resettlement and Displacement in Ethiopia*, proceedings of the workshop held by the Ethiopian Society of Sociologists, Social workers and Anthropologists and The United Nations Emergencies Unit for Ethiopia, 28–30 January 2003, Addis Ababa, Ethiopia.

Pantuliano, S. and Pavanello, S. (2009) 'Taking drought into account: Addressing chronic vulnerability among pastoralists in the Horn of Africa', HPG Policy Brief 35, Overseas Development Institute, London.

Pantuliano, S. and Wekesa, M. (2008) 'Improving drought response in pastoral areas of Ethiopia', Humanitarian Policy Group, Overseas Development Institute, London.

Pavanello, S. (2009) 'Pastoralists' vulnerability in the Horn of Africa: Exploring political marginalisation, donors' policies and cross-border issues – Literature review', Humanitarian Policy Group, Overseas Development Institute, London.

Pedersen, J. and Benjaminsen, T.A. (2008) 'One leg or two? Food security and pastoralism in the Northern Sahel', *Human Ecology*, vol 36, no 1, pp43–57.

Pickup, G. (1995) 'A simple model for predicting herbage production from rainfall in rangelands and its calibration using remotely-sensed-data', *Journal of Arid Environments*, vol 30, pp227–245.

Pike, I.L. (2004) 'The biosocial consequences of life on the run: A case study of Turkana of Kenya', *Human Organization*, vol 63, no 2, pp221–235.

PLI Policy Project (2010a) *Impact Assessment of the ACDI/VOCA Livestock Markets in Pastoralist Areas of Ethiopia*, Feinstein International Center, Tufts University, Addis Ababa.

PLI Policy Project (2010b) *Impact Assessment of Small-Scale Pump Irrigation in the Somali Region of Ethiopia*, Feinstein International Center, Tufts University, Addis Ababa.

PR Newswire (2011) 'Grumeti Reserves and Paul Tudor Jones partner with Singita to expand eco-tourism in Tanzania', 5 May, www.prnewswire.co.uk/cgi/news/release?id=170095, accessed 2 December 2011.

Prieto-Carrón, M., Lund-Thomsen, P., Chan, A., Muro, A. and Bhushan, C. (2006) 'Critical perspectives on CSR and development: What we know, what we don't know, and what we need to know', *International Affairs*, vol 82, no 5, pp977–987.

PMAC (Provisional Military Administrative Council) of Ethiopia (1975) *Proclamation to Provide Public Ownership of Rural Land, no 31/1975*.

Quan, J. (2000) 'Land tenure, economic growth and poverty in sub-Saharan Africa', in C. Toulmin and J. Quan (eds) *Evolving Land Rights, Policy and Tenure in Africa*, DIFC/IIED/NRI, London.

Randall, D.A., Wood, R.A., Bony, S., Colman, R., Fichefet, T., Fyfe, J., Kattsov, V., Pitman, A., Shukla, J., Srinivasan, J., Stouffer, R.J., Sumi, A. and Taylor, K.E. (2007) 'Climate Models and Their Evaluation', in S. Solomon, D. Qin, M. Manning, Z. Chen, M. Marquis, K.B. Averyt, M. Tignor and H.L. Miller (eds) *Climate Change 2007: The Physical Science Basis. Contribution of Working Group I to the Fourth Assessment Report of the Intergovernmental Panel on Climate Change*, Cambridge University Press, Cambridge and New York.

Randall, S. (1996) 'Whose reality? Local perceptions of fertility versus demographic analysis', *Population Studies*, vol 50, no 2, pp221–234.

Randall, S. (2005) 'The demographic consequences of conflict, exile and repatriation: A case study of Malian Tuareg', *European Journal of Population*, vol 21, no 2–3, pp291–320.

Randall, S. (2008) 'African pastoralist demography', in K. Homewood (ed.) *Ecology of African Pastoralist Societies*, James Currey Ltd, Oxford, pp199–226.

Rawls, J. (1971) *A Theory of Justice*, Harvard University Press, Cambridge.

Republic of Kenya (2005) 'Garissa district strategic plan 2005–2010 for implementation of the national population policy', Nairobi Government Printing Office.

Rettberg, S. (2010) 'Contested narratives of pastoral vulnerability and risk in Ethiopia's Afar Region', *Pastoralism*, vol 1, no 2, pp248–273.

Reusse, E. (1982) 'Somalia's nomadic livestock economy: Its response to profitable export opportunity', *World Animal Review*, vol 43, pp2–11.

Roba, H.G. (2010) 'Pastoralists' mobility in northern Kenya and southern Ethiopia: Adaptation to spatial and temporal resource variability and risk management strategies', consultancy report for Codaid and European Commission, Nairobi.

Roba, H.G. and Oba, G. (2008) 'Integration of herder knowledge and ecological methods for land degradation assessment around sedentary settlements in a sub-humid zone in Northern Kenya', *International Journal of Sustainable Development & World Ecology*, vol 15, no 3, pp251–264.

Roba, H.G. and Oba, G. (2009) 'Community participatory landscape classification and biodiversity assessment and monitoring grazing land in northern Kenya', *Journal of Environmental Management*, vol 90, no 2, pp673–682.

Robb, J. (2007) *Brave New World: the Next Stage of Terrorism and the End of Globalization*, John Wiley and Sons, New Jersey.

Robbins, P. (1998) 'Nomadization in Rajasthan, India: Migration, institution, and economy', *Human Ecology*, vol 26, no 1, pp87–112.

Robinson, L.W. and Berkes, F. (2010) 'Applying resilience thinking to questions of policy for pastoralist systems: Lessons from the Gabra of northern Kenya', *Human Ecology*, vol 38, no 3, pp335–350.

Roe, E. (1994) *Narrative Policy Analysis: Theory and Practice*, Duke University Press, Durham.

Roesler, M. and Wendl, T. (eds) (1999) *Frontiers and Borderlands: Anthropological Perspectives*, Peter Lang, Frankfurt and New York.

Ronfeldt, D. and Arquilla, J. (2001) *Networks and Netwars: The Future of Terror, Crime, and Militancy*, RAND, Washington DC.

Roth, E.A. (1994) 'Demographic systems: Two East African examples' in E. Fratkin, K. Galvin, and E.A. Roth (eds) *African Pastoralist Systems*, Lynne Rienner Publishers, Boulder.

Roth, E.A., Ngugi, E.N. and Fujita, M. (2009) 'HIV/AIDS risk and worry in northern Kenya', *Health, Risk & Society*, vol 11, no 1, pp231–239.

Rutherford, M.C. and Powrie, L.W. (2010) 'Severely degraded rangeland: implications for plant diversity from a case study in succulent karoo, South Africa', *Journal of Arid Environments*, vol 74, no 6, pp692–701.

Rutledge, D. and Roble, A. (2010) 'The infrastructure of migration and the migration regime: Human rights, race, and the Somali struggle to flee violence', *Race/Ethnicity: Multidisciplinary Global Contexts*, vol 3, no 2, pp153–178.

Ruttan, V. (1982) 'Cultural endowments and economic development: What can we learn from anthropology?', *Economic Development and Cultural Change*, vol 36, no 3, supplement.

Rutten, M. (1992) *Selling Wealth to Buy Poverty: The Process of the Individualization of Land Ownership among the Maasai Pastoralists of Kajiado District, Kenya, 1890–1990*, Verlag für Entwicklungspolitik, Saarbrücken.

Sabates-Wheeler, R. and Devereux, S. (2010) 'Cash transfers and high food prices: Explaining outcomes on Ethiopia's productive safety net programme', *Food Policy*, vol 35, no 4, pp274–285.

Said, A. (1992) 'Resource use conflicts between pastoralism and irrigation development in the Middle Awash Valley of Ethiopia', MSc thesis, Noragric, Agricultural University of Norway.

Salem-Murdock, M. (1989) *Arabs and Nubians in New Halfa: A Study of Settlement and Irrigation*, University of Utah Press, Salt Lake City, UT.

Salesa, H. (2011) 'Isiolo MPs accuse state of laxity over security', *Nairobi Star*, 25 October.

Salih, M.A.M. (1995) 'Pastoralist migration to small towns in Africa', in J. Baker and T.A. Aina (eds) *The Migration Experience in Africa*, Scandinavian Institute of African Studies, Uppsala, pp181–196.

Samatar, A.I. (2004) 'Ethiopian Federalism: Autonomy versus control in the Somali region', *Third World Quarterly*, vol 25, no 6, pp1131–1154.

Samatar, A.I. (2007) 'Somalia's post-conflict economy: A political economy approach', *Bildhaan: An International Journal of Somali Studies*, vol 7, pp126–168.

Samuels, M.I., Allsopp, N., and Hoffman, T. (2008) 'Mobility patterns of livestock keepers in semi-arid communal rangelands of Namaqualand, South Africa', *Nomadic Peoples*, vol 12, no 1, pp123–148.

Sandford, S. (1983) *Management of Pastoral Development in the Third World*, John Wiley and Sons, Chichester.

Sandford, S. (2006) *Too Many People, Too Few Livestock: The Crisis Affecting Pastoralists in the Greater Horn of Africa*, www.future-agricultures.org/pdf files/, accessed on 1 December 2011.

Sandford, S. and Scoones, I. (2006) 'Opportunistic and conservative pastoral strategies: Some economic arguments', *Ecological Economics*, vol 58, no 1, pp1–6.

Saperstein, A. and Farmer, E. (2006) *Livestock Value Chain Analysis Report for Afar and Northern Somali Regions of Ethiopia*, report by ACDI-VOCA for USAID Pastoralist Livelihoods Initiative, Addis Ababa.

Sato, S. (1997) 'How the East African pastoral nomads, especially the Rendille, respond to the encroaching market economy', *African Studies Monographs*, vol 18, no 3-4, pp121–135.

Schlee, G. (1989) *Identities on the Move: Clanship and Pastoralism in Northern Kenya*, Gideon S. Were Press, Nairobi.

Schlee, G. (2003) 'Redrawing the map of the Horn: The politics of difference', *Africa*, vol 73, no 3, pp343–368.

Schlee, G and Watson, E.E. (2009) *Changing Identifications and Alliances in North-East Africa: Sudan, Uganda and the Ethiopia-Sudan Borderlands*, Berghahn Books, Oxford.

Scholte, P. and Babiker, M. (2005) 'Terminal evaluation for the conservation, management of habitat, species and sustainable community use of biodiversity in Dinder National Park, SUD/98/G41', report to UNDP-GEF, Higher Council for Environment and Natural Resources, Khartoum.

Scholte, P., Kari, S., Moritz, M. and Prins, H. (2006) 'Pastoralist responses to floodplain rehabilitation in North Cameroon', *Human Ecology*, vol 34, no 1, pp27–51.

Schreck, C.J. and Semazzi, F.H.M. (2004) 'Variability of the recent climate of eastern Africa', *International Journal of Climatology*, vol 24, no 6, pp681–701.

Scoones, I. (1991) 'Wetlands in drylands: Key resources for agriculture and pastoral production in Africa', *Ambio*, vol 20, no 8, pp366–371.

Scoones, I. (ed) (1995a) *Living with Uncertainty: New Directions in Pastoral Development in Africa*, IT Publications, London.

Scoones, I. (1995b) 'Exploiting heterogeneity: Habitat use by cattle in dryland Zimbabwe', *Journal of Arid Environments*, vol 29, pp221–237.

Scoones, I. (1998) *Sustainable Rural Livelihoods: A Framework for Analysis*, IDS Working Paper 72, University of Sussex.

Scoones, I. (2004) 'Climate change and the challenge of non-equilibrium thinking', *IDS Bulletin*, vol 35, no 3, pp114–119.

Scoones, I. (2007) 'Sustainability', *Development in Practice*, vol 17, no 4–5, pp589–596.

Scoones, I. and Adwera, A. (2009) *Pastoral Innovation Systems: Perspectives from Ethiopia and Kenya*, Occasional Paper no 1, Future Agricultures Consortium, Brighton.

Scoones, I. and Graham, O. (1994) 'New directions for pastoral development in Africa', *Development in Practice*, vol 4, no 3, pp188–198.

Scoones, I. and Wolmer, W. (2006) *Livestock, Disease, Trade and Markets: Policy Choices for the Livestock Sector in Africa*, IDS Working Paper, no 269, Institute of Development Studies, Brighton.

Scoones, I., Bishi, A., Mapitse, N., Moerane, R., Penrith, M.-L., Sibanda, R., Thomson, G. and Wolmer, W. (2010) 'Foot-and-mouth disease and market access: Challenges for the beef industry in southern Africa', *Pastoralism*, vol 1, no 2, pp135–164.

Scott, J.C. (1976) *The Moral Economy of the Peasant: Rebellion and Subsistence in Southeast Asia*, Yale University Press, New Haven.

Scott, J.C. (1998) *Seeing like a State: How Certain Schemes to Improve the Human Condition have Failed*, Yale University Press, New Haven.

Scott, J.C. (2009) *The Art of Not Being Governed: An Anarchist History of Upland Southeast Asia*, Yale University Press, New Haven.

Scott-Villiers, P. (2005) 'A bitter-sweet crop in Kenya', in A. Scott-Villiers, *Rain, Prosperity and Peace: The Global Pastoralist Meeting, Turmi, Ethiopia 2005*, Institute of Development Studies, Brighton.

Scott-Villiers, P., Ungiti, H.B., Kiyana, D., Kullu, M., Orto, T., Reidy, E. and Sora, A. (2011) *The Long Conversation: Customary Approaches to Peace Management in Southern Ethiopia and Northern Kenya*, Working Paper 022, Future Agricultures Consortium, Institute of Development Studies, Brighton.

Scudder, T. (1991) 'The need and justification for maintaining transboundary flood regimes: The Africa case', *Natural Resources Journal*, vol 31, no 1, pp75–107.

Scudder, T. (2006) *The Future of Large Dams: Dealing with Social, Environmental, Institutional and Political Costs*, Earthscan, London.

SCUK (Save the Children UK) (2005) *Livelihoods Baselines, Somali Region*, Save the Children UK, Addis Ababa.

SCUK (2007) *Vulnerability and Dependency in 4 Livelihood Zones of North Eastern Province, Kenya*, Assessment using the Household Economy Approach (HEA), September 2007, www.feg-consulting.com/resource/reports/report-library-1/HEA%20North%20Eastern%20Kenya%202007.pdf, accessed 2 December 2011.

SCUK and DPPC (2008) *Livelihoods and Vulnerabilities: An Understanding of Livelihoods in Somali Regional State, Ethiopia* (updated version), Save the Children UK, Addis Ababa.

SCUK, DPPB and Partners (2002) *An HEA Baseline of the Dawa-Ganale Riverine Food Economy Zone in Liban Administrative Zone*, Somali Region, Ethiopia.

Sellen, D. (2000) 'Seasonal ecology and nutritional status of women and children in a Tanzanian pastoral community', *American Journal of Human Biology*, vol 12, no 6, pp758–781.

Shahshahani, S. (1995) 'Tribal schools of Iran: Sedentarization through education', *Nomadic Peoples*, no 36–37, pp145–156.

Shazali, S. (1988) *South Kassala Nomadic Survey*, CARE-Sudan, Khartoum.

Shazali, S. and Abdel, G.M.A. (1999) 'Pastoral land tenure and agricultural expansion: Sudan and the Horn of Africa', *Drylands Programme Issue Paper*, no 85, International Institute for Environment and Development, London.

Sheik-Mohamed, A. and Velema, J.P. (1999) 'Where health care has no access: The nomadic populations of sub-Saharan Africa', *Tropical Medicine and International Health*, vol 4, no 10, pp695–707.

Shepherd, A.W. (1983) 'Capitalist agriculture in the Sudan dura prairies', *Development and Change*, vol 14, no 2, pp297–321.

Shide, A. (2005) '"Conflict is everyday business": Changing nature of local conflict in federal Ethiopia: the case study of Ma'eso district', Master thesis, Institute of Development Studies, Brighton.

Shivji, I. (1998) *Not yet Democracy: Reforming Land Tenure in Tanzania*, International Institute for Environment and Development, London.

Sieff, D.F. (1997) 'Herding strategies of the Datoga pastoralists of Tanzania: Is household labor a limiting factor?', *Human Ecology*, vol 25, no 4, pp519–544.

Simpkin, S.P. (1996) 'The effects of breed and management on milk yields of camels in Kenya', Ph.D. dissertation, University of Newcastle.

Sinclair, A.R.E. and Fryxell, J.M. (1985) 'The Sahel of Africa: Ecology of a disaster', *Canadian Journal of Zoology*, vol 63, pp987–994.

Smith, A. (1992) *Pastoralism in Africa: Origins and Development Ecology*, Hurst, London.

Smith, K. (1998) 'Sedentarization and market integration: New opportunities for Rendille and Ariaal women of northern Kenya', *Human Organization*, vol 57, no 4, pp459–468.

Smith, K. (1999) 'The farming alternative: Changing age and gender roles among sedentarized Rendille and Ariaal', *Nomadic Peoples*, (New Series) vol 3, no 2, pp131–146.

Solomon, A., Workalemahu, A., Jabbar, M.A., Ahmed, M.M. and Hurrissa, B. (2003) *Livestock Marketing in Ethiopia: A Review of Structure, Performance and Development Initiatives*, Socio-Economics and Policy Research Working Paper 52, International Livestock Research Institute, Addis Ababa.

Somaliland Chamber of Commerce, Agriculture and Industry (2010) *Yearly Report 1st January 2010 to 31 December 2010*, Somaliland Chamber of Commerce, Agriculture and Industry, Hargeisa.

Sörbö, G. (1991) 'Systems of pastoral and agricultural production in eastern Sudan', in G.M. Craig (ed) *The Agriculture of the Sudan*, Oxford University Press, Oxford, pp214–229

Soussana J.-F., Graux, A.-I., Tubiello, F.N. (2010) 'Improving the use of modelling for projections of climate change impacts on crops and pastures', *Journal of Experimental Botany*, vol 61, no 8, pp2217–2228.

Spear, T. (1997) *Mountain Farmers: Moral Economies of Land and Agricultural Development in Arusha and Meru*, James Currey Publishers, London.

Spencer, P. (1973) *Nomads in Alliance*, Oxford University Press, Oxford.

Spencer, P. (1998) *The Pastoral Continuum: The Marginalization of Tradition in East Africa*, Oxford University Press, Oxford.

Stave, J., Oba, G. and Stenseth, N.C. (2001) 'Temporal changes in woody-plant use and the ekwar indigenous tree management system along the Turkwel River, Kenya', *Environmental Conservation*, vol 28, pp150–159.

Stave, J., Oba, G., Stenseth, N.C. and Nordal, I. (2005) 'Environmental gradients in the Turkwel River forest, Kenya: Hypotheses on dam-induced vegetation change', *Forest Ecology & Management*, vol 212, no 1–3, pp184–198.

Stave, J., Oba, G., Nordal, I. and Stenseth, N.C. (2007) 'The traditional ecological knowledge of a riverine forest in Turkana, Kenya: Implications for research and management', *Biodiversity Conservation*, vol 16, pp1471–1489.

Steiner-Khamsi, G. and Stolpe, I. (2005) 'Non-traveling "best practices" for a traveling population: The case of nomadic education in Mongolia', *European Educational Research Journal*, vol 4, no 1, pp22–35.

Steinfeld, H., Mooney, H.A. and Schneider, F. (eds) (2010) *Livestock in a Changing Landscape, Volume 1: Drivers, Consequences, and Responses*, Island Press with the Scientific Committee on Problems of the Environment, Washington, DC.

Stenning, D. (1959) *Savanna Nomads: A Study of the WoDaabe Pastoral Fulani of Western Bornu Province, Northern Region, Nigeria*, Oxford University Press, Oxford.

Stites, E., Akabwai, D., Mazurana, D. and Ateyo, P. (2007) *Angering Akuj: Survival and Suffering in Karamoja*, Feinstein International Center, Medford, Massachusetts.

Storas, F. (1991) 'Cattle complex or begging complex: Livestock transaction and the construction of Turkana society', in R. Gronhaug, G. Haaland and G. Henriksen (eds) *The Ecology of Choice and Symbol: Essays in Honour of Frederik Barth*, Alma Mater Forlang As, Bergen.

Sudan Tribune (2009) 'Minister of Agriculture sells components of Sudan's Gezira Scheme to members of the NCP ruling party', *Sudan Tribune*, 17 May, www.sudantribune.com/spip.php?article31424, accessed 13 June 2009.

Sugule, J. and Walker, R. (1998) 'Changing pastoralism in the Ethiopian Somali National Regional State (Region 5)', South East Rangelands Project (SERP), United Nations Development Programme Emergency Unit for Ethiopia, Addis Ababa.

Sullivan, S. and Rohde, R. (2002) 'On non-equilibrium in arid and semi-arid grazing systems', *Journal of Biogeography*, vol 29, no 12, pp1595–1618.

Swift, J. (1986) 'The economics of production and exchange in West African pastoral societies', in M.J. Adamu and A.H.M. Kirk-Greene (eds) *Pastoralists of the West African Savanna*, Manchester University Press, Manchester.

Swift, J. (1989) 'Planning against drought and famine in Turkana: A district famine contingency plan', in T. Downing, K. Gitu, and C. Kamau (eds) *Coping with Drought in Kenya: National and Local Strategies*, Lynne Rienner, Boulder.

Swift, J., Barton, D. and Morton, J. (2002) 'Drought management for pastoral livelihoods – Policy Guidelines for Kenya', www.nri.org/projects/pastoralism/kenyapolicy.pdf, accessed 12 December 2011 .

Tache, B. (2000) 'Individualising the commons: Changing resource tenure among the Boorana Oromo of southern Ethiopia', M.A. Thesis, School of Graduate Studies, Addis Ababa University.

Tache, B. (2008) 'Pastoralism under stress: Resources, institutions and poverty among the Borana Oromo of southern Ethiopia', Ph.D. thesis, Norwegian University of Life Sciences, Ås.

Tache, B. (2009) 'Pastoral land use planning and resource management in Southern Oromia: An integrated landscape approach', final report submitted to SOS Sahel Ethiopia, Addis Ababa.

Tache, B. (2010) 'Participatory impacts assessment of drought reserve areas in Guji and Borana Zones, Oromia region', report prepared for Save the Children USA, March 2010, Addis Ababa.

Tache, B. and Oba, G. (2009) 'Policy-driven inter-ethnic conflicts in Southern Ethiopia', *Review of African Political Economy*, vol 36, no 121, pp409–426.

Tache, B. and Oba, G. (2010) 'Is poverty driving Borana herders in southern Ethiopia to crop cultivation?', *Human Ecology*, vol 38, no 1, pp639–649.

Talle, A. (1988) 'Women at a loss: Changes in Maasai pastoralism and their effects on gender relations', *Stockholm Studies in Social Anthropology*, no 19, Department of Social Anthropology, University of Stockholm, Stockholm.

Talle, A. (1999) 'Pastoralists at the border: Maasai poverty and the development discourse in Tanzania', in D.M. Anderson and V. Broch-Due (eds) *The Poor Are Not Us: Poverty and Pastoralism in Eastern Africa*, James Currey Publishers, Oxford.

TNRF (Tanzania Natural Resource Forum) (2011) *Integrating Pastoralist Livelihoods and Wildlife Conservation: Options for Land Use and Conflict Resolution in Loliondo Division, Ngorongoro District*, Tanzania Natural Resource Forum.

Tefera, S., Dlamini, B.J. and Dlamini, A.M. (2010) 'Changes in soil characteristics and grass layer condition in relation to land management systems in semi-arid savannas of Swaziland', *Journal of Arid Environments*, vol 74, no 6, pp675–684.

Terer, T., Ndiritu, G.G., and Gichuki, N.N. (2004) 'Socio-economic values and traditional strategies of managing wetland resources in lower Tana River, Kenya', *Hydrobiologia*, vol 527, pp3–14.

The Economist (2009) 'Buying farmland abroad: Outsourcing's third wave', 21 May, www.economist.com/node/13692889, accessed 11 July 2009.

Thomson, G.R., Tambi, E.N., Hargreaves, S.K., Leyland, T.J., Catley, A.P., van 't Klooster, G.G. and Penrith, M.L. (2004) 'International trade in livestock and livestock products: The need for a commodity-based approach', *Veterinary Record*, vol 155, no 14, pp429–433.

Thomson, G.R., Leyland, T.J. and Donaldson, A.I. (2009) 'Deboned beef – an example of a commodity for which specific standards could be developed to ensure an appropriate level of protection for international trade', *Transboundary and Emerging Diseases*, vol 56, no 1–2, pp9–17.

Thornton, P.K. and Herrero, M. (2010) *The Inter-Linkages Between Rapid Growth in Livestock Production, Climate Change, and the Impacts on Water Resources, Land Use, and Deforestation*, background paper for the 2010 World Development Report, Policy Research Working Paper 5178, The World Bank, Washington, US.

Thornton, P., van de Steeg, J., Notenbaert, A. and Herrero, M. (2009) 'The impacts of climate change on livestock and livestock systems in developing countries: A review of what we know and what we need to know', *Agricultural Systems*, vol 101, no 3, pp113–127.

Thornton, P.K., Jones, P.G., Ericksen, P.J. and Challinor, A.J. (2010) 'Agriculture and food systems in sub-Saharan Africa in a four-plus degree world', *Philosophical Transactions of the Royal Society A*, vol 369, no 1934, pp117–136.

Thurston, A. (2011) 'Welcome to Azania/Jubaland: The world's newest pseudostate', http://blog.foreignpolicy.com/posts/2011/04/06/welcome_to_azania_somalias_newest _pseudostate, accessed 27 November 2011.

Tilly, C. (1992) *Coercion, Capital and European States, AD 990–1992*, Blackwell, Malden, MA.

Tolossa, F. (2011) 'Land grab in Africa: The case of Ethiopia', A speech delivered at the Commonwealth Club of California, http://nazret.com/blog/index.php/2011/03/03/ land-grab-in-africa-the-case-of-ethiopia?blog=15, accessed 2 December 2011.

Tooley, J., Dixon, P., Stanfield, J. (2008) 'Impact of free primary education in Kenya: A case study of private schools in Kibera', *Educational Management, Administration & Leadership*, vol 36, no 4, pp449–469.

Toulmin, C. (2009) *Climate Change in Africa*, Zed Books, London.

Toulmin, C. and Gue'ye, B. (2003) 'Transformations in West African agriculture and family farms IIED', Issue Paper 123, http://pubs.iied.org/pdfs/9309IIED.pdf accessed 22 November 2011.

Tsing, A.L. (1993) *In the Realm of the Diamond Queen: Marginality in an out-of-way Place*, Princeton University Press, Princeton.

Turner, M.D. (1999) 'Labor process and the environment: The effects of labor availability and compensation on the quality of herding in the Sahel', *Human Ecology*, vol 27, no 2, pp267–296.

Turner, M. D. (2011) 'The new pastoral development paradigm: Engaging the realities of property institutions and livestock mobility in dry land Africa', *Society and Natural Resources*, vol 24, no 5, pp469–484.

Turton, D. (2006) *Ethnic Federalism: The Ethiopian Experience in Comparative Perspective*, James Currey, Oxford.

UCRT (Ujamaa Community Resource Team) (2010) *Participatory Land Use Planning as a Tool for Community Empowerment in Northern Tanzania*, IIED (with Fred Nelson, Malisaili Initiatives), *Gatekeeper*, no 147.

Umar, A. (1997) 'Resource Utilisation, Conflict and Insecurity in Pastoral Areas of Kenya', a paper for the USAID Organised Seminar on Conflict Resolution in the Horn of Africa, Kenya Pastoral Forum, Nairobi.

Umar, A., with Baluch, B. (2007) *Risk Taking for a Living: Trade and Marketing in the Somali Region, Ethiopia*, UN-OCHA/Pastoral Communication Initiative Project, Addis Ababa, Ethiopia.

UNDP (2006) *Share the Land or Part the Nation: The Pastoral Land Tenure System in Sudan*. United Nations Development Programme, Khartoum [Authors: Salahel Din El Shazli, Team Leader; Farah Hassan Adam; Imadel Din Bashier Adam].

UNEP (2007) *Sudan: Post-Conflict Environmental Assessment*, United Nations Environment Programme, Nairobi.

UNESCO (2009) *EFA Global Monitoring Report 2009: Overcoming Inequality: Why Governance Matters*, Oxford University Press, Oxford.

UNESCO (2010) *EFA Global Monitoring Report 2010: Reaching the Marginalized*, Oxford University Press, Oxford.

UNFPA (2011) 'Dadaab population swells as hungry and weary families arrive from Somalia', 5 August 2011, www.unfpa.org/public/home/news/pid/8123, accessed 17 November 2011.

UNICEF (2007) *Nomadic Education in the Islamic Republic of Iran*, Eastern and Southern Africa Regional Office (ESARO).

UNOCHA-PCI (2007) *The Future of Pastoralism in Ethiopia*, UNOCHA - Pastoralists Communications Initiative, Addis Ababa.

Unruh, J.D. (1990) 'Integration of transhumant pastoralism and irrigated agriculture in semi-arid East Africa', *Human Ecology*, 18, pp223–246.

Unruh, J.D. (2005) 'Changing conflict resolution institutions in the Ethiopian pastoral commons: The role of armed confrontation in rule-making', *GeoJournal*, vol 64, no 3, pp225–237.

USAID (2008) *Enhanced Livelihoods in Pastoral Areas*, CAADP Pillar 3 Early Action (powerpoint presentation) http://eastafrica.usaid.gov/en/Page/161/Regional_Enhanced_Livelihoods_in_Pastoral_Areas_RELPA_RFA_Support_Documents, accessed 4 December 2011.

USAID (2010) *Impact Assessment of Small Scale Pump Irrigation in the Somali Region of Ethiopia*, USAID, Feinstein International Centre, Tufts University.

Van den Boogaard, R. (2006) *Experiences of Targeting Resource Transfers and Interventions to Pastoral and Agro-pastoral Communities: Horn of Africa and Ethiopia*, Save the Children UK and Save the Children USA, Addis Ababa.

Van Steenbergen, F., Lawrence, P., Haile, A.M., Salman M. and Faurès, J.-M. (2010) 'Guidelines on spate irrigation', FAO Irrigation and Drainage Paper 65, FAO, Rome.

Varlet, H. and Massoumian, J. (1975) 'Education for tribal populations in Iran', *Prospects* vol 5, no 2, pp275–281.

Vatin, F. (1996) *Le Lait et la Raison Marchande*, Presses Universitaires de Rennes, Rennes.

Verdin, J., Funk, C., Senay, G. and Choularton, R. (2005) 'Climate science and famine early warning', *Philosophical Transactions of the Royal Society B*, vol 360, no1463, pp2155–2168.

Vetter, S. (2005) 'Rangelands at equilibrium and non-equilibrium: Recent developments in the debate', *Journal of Arid Environments*, vol 62, pp321–41.

Vidal, J. (2010) 'Billionaires and mega-corporations behind immense land grab in Africa', *Mail & Guardian*, 11 March.

Von Benda-Beckmann, F., von Benda-Beckmann, K. and Wiber, M. (eds) (2006) *Changing Properties of Property*, Oxford, Berghahn Books.

Waller, R. (1988) 'Emutai: Crisis and response in Maasailand 1883–1902', in D. Johnson and D. Anderson (eds) *The Ecology of Survival*, Lester Crook Academic Publishing, London.

Waller, R.D. (1999) 'Pastoral poverty in historical perspective', in D.M. Anderson and V. Broch-Due (eds) *The Poor Are Not Us: Poverty and Pastoralism in Eastern Africa*, James Currey, Oxford.

Washington, R., New, M., Rahiz, M. and Karmacharya, J. (2011) 'Climate change in CCAFS Regions: recent trends, current projections, crop-climate suitability and prospects for improved climate model information. Part 2, East Africa', Working Paper, CGIAR Research Program on Climate Change, Agriculture and Food Security (CCAFS), ccafs.cgiar.org .

Waters-Bayer, A. (1988) *Dairying by Settled Fulani Women in Central Nigeria: The Role of Women and Implications for Dairy Development*, Wissenschaftsverlag Van Kiel, Kiel.

Waters-Bayer, A. and Bayer, W. (1994) 'Coming to terms: Interactions between immigrant Fulani cattle keepers and indigenous farmers in Nigeria's subhumid zone', *Cahiers d'Études africaines*, vol 34, no 133–135, pp213–229.

Watson, D.J. and van Binsbergen, J. (2008) 'Livelihood diversification opportunities for pastoralists in Turkana, Kenya', ILRI Research Report no 5, International Livestock Research Institute, Nairobi, Kenya.

WCED (1987) *Our Common Future: Report of the World Commission on Environment and Development*, Oxford University Press, Oxford.

Wekessa, M. (2005) *Terminal Evaluation of the Restocking/Rehabilitation Programme for the Internally-Displaced Persons in Fik Zone, Somali Region of Ethiopia*, Save the Children UK, Addis Ababa.

Western, D. (1982) 'The environment and ecology of pastoralists in arid savannas', *Development and Change*, vol 13, pp183–211.

Westoby, M, Walker, B.H. and Noy-Meir, I. (1989) 'Opportunistic management for rangelands not at equilibrium', *Journal of Range Management*, vol 42, no 4, pp266–274.

WFP (2009a) *Evaluation of Kenya Emergency Operation 10374.0 and Country Programme 10264.0 (2004–2008)*, www.alnap.org/pool/files/erd-3616-full.pdf, accessed 4 December 2011.

WFP (2009b) 'Protracted relief and recovery operations approved by correspondence between the First Regular Session and the Annual Session 2009 – Kenya 10666.0', http://one.wfp.org/operations/current_operations/project_docs/200174.pdf, accessed 12 December 2011.

Wilby, R.L., Troni, J., Biot, Y., Tedd, L., Hewitson, B.C., Smith, D.M. and Sutton, R.T. (2009) 'A review of climate risk information for adaptation and development planning', *International Journal of Climatology*, vol 29, pp1193–1215.

William, J. and Tavneet, S. (2011) 'Mobile Money: The Economics of M-PESA', Working Paper 16721, www.nber.org/papers/w16721, accessed on 30 November 2011.

Williams, A.P. and Funk, C. (2010) 'A westward extension of the warm pool leads to a westward extension of the Walker circulation, drying eastern Africa', *Climate Dynamics*, www.springerlink.com/content/u0352236x6n868n2/, accessed 16 November 2011.

World Bank (2001) *Engendering Development: Through Gender Equality in Rights, Resources, and Voice*, World Bank Policy Research Report, no 21776.

World Bank (2006) *Gender Equality as Smart Economics: A World Bank Group Action Plan*. World Bank, Washington, DC.

World Bank (2010) *Rising Global Interest in Farmland: Can it Yield Sustainable and Equitable Benefits?* Report of the Agriculture and Rural Development Department, Washington DC.

World Bank Development Indicators (2011) http://databank.worldbank.org/ddp/, accessed 17 November 2011.

You, L., Ringler, C., Nelson, G., Wood-Sichra, U., Robertson, R., Wood, S., Guo, Z., Zhu, T. and Sun, Y. (2010) *What is the Irrigation Potential for Africa? A Combined Biophysical and Socioeconomic Approach*, IFPRI Discussion Paper 00993, International Food Policy Research Institute, Washington, DC.

Young, C. (1994) *The African Colonial State in Comparative Perspective*, Yale University Press, New Haven.

Young, Y. (1999) 'Along Ethiopia's western frontier: Gambella and Benishangul in transition', *The Journal of Modern African Studies*, vol 37, no 2, pp321–346.

Young, H., Osman, A.M., Aklilu, Y., Dale, R., Badri, B. and Fuddle, A.J.A. (2005) *Darfur: Livelihoods under Siege*, Feinstein International Famine Center, Tufts University, Medford, MA.

Young, H., Osman, A.M., Abusin, A.M., Asher, M. and Egemi, O. (2009) *Livelihoods, Power and Choice: The Vulnerability of the Northern Rizaygat, Darfur, Sudan*, Feinstein International Center, Tufts University, Medford, MA.

Zaal, F. (1998) *Pastoralism in a Global Age*, Thela Press, Amsterdam.

Zaal, F. and Dietz, T. (1999) 'Of markets meat, maize and milk: Pastoral commoditization in Kenya', in D. Anderson and V. Broch-Due (eds) (1999) *The Poor Are Not Us: Poverty and Pastoralism in Eastern Africa,* James Currey Press, Oxford, pp163–198.

Zoomers, A. (2010) 'Globalisation and the foreignisation of space: Seven processes driving the current global land grab', *Journal of Peasant Studies*, vol 37, no 2, pp429–47.

Zwaagstra, L., Sharif, Z., Wambile, A., de Leeuw, J., Johnson, N., Njuki, J., Said, M., Ericksen, P. and Herrero, M. (2010) *An Assessment of the Response to the 2008–2009 Drought in Kenya*, ILRI, Nairobi, Kenya, http://cgspace.cgiar.org/bitstream/handle/10568/2057/assessment_drought_2010.pdf?sequence=3, accessed 16 November 2011little.

INDEX

Note: Page numbers in **bold** are for figures, those in *italics* are for tables.